Comprehensive School Health Education

Totally Awesome Strategies for Teaching Health

Linda B. Meeks, M.S.
Chairperson and
Associate Professor
Health Education
College of Education
Associate Professor
Allied Medicine
College of Medicine
The Ohio State University

Philip Heit, Ed.D.
Professor
Health Education
College of Education
Professor
Allied Medicine
College of Medicine
The Ohio State University

MeeksHeit
Publishing Company

Editorial, Sales, and Customer Service Offices
P.O. Box 121
Blacklick, OH 43004

Project Editor: Ann Turpie
Design: J.D. Studios
Production: Jim Dildine, Tim Schenk, Eileen London
Art: John Uhrich
Medical Illustrations: Jim Brower Studio

Printed in the United States of America
        6 7 8 9 10   95 94

Library of Congress Catalog Card Number: 91-090488

ISBN 0-9630009-0-X

Reviewers

We are committed to quality health education in our schools. We selected colleagues to review this manuscript who share this commitment and who teach health education courses at colleges and universities, provide inservice programs for school districts, and work with school districts and state departments of education in curriculum development. We are grateful for their diligent efforts and suggestions.

Consultant

Wanda Jubb, Ed.D.
Coordinator
Comprehensive School Health Education
Centers for Disease Control

Reviewers

Sally E. Dellinger, M.A.
Program Manager
School of Health, Physical Education,
and Recreation
The Ohio State University

Peggy Holstedt, M.S.
Health Promotion Specialist
Oregon Department of Education

Dianne L Kerr, M.A.
Assistant Professor
Health Education
Department of Adult, Counseling,
Health and Vocational Education
Kent State University

Judith K. Kisselle, M.S.
Assistant Professor
Health Education Division
School of Health, Physical Education,
and Recreation
Bowling Green State University

Becky Kennedy Koch, M.Ed., A.T.C.
Instructor
Health Education
School of Health, Physical Education,
and Recreation
The Ohio State University

Loretta M. Liptak, Ph.D.
Professor
Health Education
Youngstown State University

J. Leslie Oganowski, Ph.D.
Associate Professor
Health Education
University of Wisconsin at LaCrosse

Ralph W. Perrin, DHSc., MPH
Professor
Health Sciences
Walla Walla College

Dennis W. Smith, Ph.D.
Assistant Professor
Health Education
The University of Houston

Mary Sutherland, Ed.D., MPH, C.H.E.S.
Associate Professor
Health Education
Department of Human Services and Studies
The Florida State Unviersity

Preface

We are committed to the quality of life of children and adolescents. They are our future and they help us to transcend our lives long after we have left this life. As evidence of our commitment, we have chosen the profession of education. Through teaching health, providing inservice for teachers, writing health education curriculum, and developing materials for teachers, children, adolescents, and parents, we believe that we can influence the quality of life.

At The Ohio State University, we teach a course for elementary teachers as well as a course for middle and secondary students. We wanted to develop a textbook that included everything teachers and future teachers needed to implement the comprehensive school health program and to meet the objectives identified in *America 2000* and *Healthy People 2000*. We worked with a team of comprehensive school health education experts including Wanda Jubb, Ed.D., Comprehensive School Health Education Coordinator, Centers for Disease Control. *Comprehensive School Health Education: Totally Awesome Strategies for Teaching Health* is the result of our efforts and commitment to provide teachers with a textbook that provides everything needed to implement creative, dynamic, and effective health education in the school. This textbook is designed to be used in colleges and universities in the professional preparation of elementary school teachers. It is also designed for use in professional preparation programs with an emphasis on middle school, junior high, and high school. And, of course, it is designed as a classroom resource for those already teaching. Our experience in training teachers at all levels has given us the expertise to write this textbook. For many years, we have been involved in providing teacher training workshops focusing on **"totally awesome"** strategies for teaching health. We have trained thousands of teachers in using creative strategies and adapting them to the grade level they teach. Flexibility is the key. Suggestions are made for using the strategies in this textbook at the different grade levels.

What are the key components in this textbook that make it the most appealing health education methods book to date?

Section 1. A Framework for Comprehensive School Health Education includes four chapters that provide background information needed for the development of a comprehensive school health program. Chapter 1 focuses on the healthful and risk behaviors in which today's youth participate and a rationale for implementing comprehensive school health education. Chapter 2 provides information on school health services and the health needs of youth with information on topics such as abuse, the dysfunctional family, AIDS, suicide, sexually transmitted diseases, screening, drug use, dying and death, emergency care, etc. Chapter 3 examines school health education and curriculum development. This chapter provides a philosophy of health and information about writing curriculum, scope and sequence, objectives, life skills, responsible decision making, resistance skills, teaching strategies, and tests. Chapter 4 describes different instructional strategies providing the strengths, weaknesses, and helpful hints for using each. There is a special feature on gaining classroom control.

Section 2. Background Information and Totally Awesome Strategies for Teaching Health is divided into ten content areas: Mental and Emotional Well-Being, Family and Relationship Skills, Growth and Development, Nutrition, Personal Fitness, Substance Use and Abuse, Diseases and Disorders, Consumer Health, Safety and Injury Prevention, and Community and Environment. These are the ten content areas which can be adapted to most state curriculums. Background information or content to prepare the teacher is provided for each of the ten areas. Then there are twenty teaching strategies for each area that can be adapted to different grade levels. Each strategy has been field tested in schools. All of the materials needed to implement the strategies are readily available to teachers. The strategies focus on outcomes. Each is designed to help students practice a life skill or healthful action.

Section 3. **Totally Awesome Teaching Masters and Student Masters** provides short lesson plans and teaching masters and student masters for each of the ten content areas. The perforated pages in this textbook make it easy to make overhead transparencies or handouts from teaching masters and worksheets from student masters.

Section 4. **Resources That Enhance The Teaching of Health** contains a Health Resource Guide that provides the names, addresses, and telephone numbers of agencies and organizations involved in promoting each of the ten content areas. Within each major heading of the content areas are sub-headings of specialized areas. Whenever possible, toll-free telephone numbers are listed to reduce costs.

We are enthusiastic about *Comprehensive School Health Education: Totally Awesome Strategies for Teaching Health*. We are committed to the "hands on" approach to training teachers. In our experience, teachers want something they can use. They want to know it works. And, they want to know that students will respond and be enthusiastic about what they are doing. There is a saying in education, "Students do not care how much you know until they know how much you care." We "care" and we have written this textbook because we want you to have a textbook that will make a difference in your teaching.

Linda Meeks
Philip Heit

Comprehensive
School Health Education

TABLE OF CONTENTS

8 *NUTRITION*   234

9 *PERSONAL FITNESS*   280

Background Information   280

Totally Awesome Strategies for Teaching   284

13   SAFETY AND INJURY PREVENTION

14   *COMMUNITY AND ENVIRONMENT*   488

Background Information   488

Totally Awesome Strategies for Teaching   491

Section 4
Resources That Enhance The Teaching of Health

16 *HEALTH RESOURCE GUIDE*

Section 1

A Framework for Comprehensive School Health Education

This Section contains four chapters that provide background information needed for the development of a Comprehensive School Health Program. Chapter 1 summarizes current statistics to show the risk behaviors in which today's children and adolescents participate and a discussion of the reasons they are placing their health and safety and that of others at risk. The role of comprehensive school health education in promoting healthful behaviors and responsible decisions is discussed focusing on a plan to reach the objectives of *Healthy People 2000*. Chapter 2 describes School Health Services and ways that health is promoted through this aspect of the Comprehensive School Health Program. There is a detailed discussion of the special health concerns of students in grades kindergarten through grade 12 as well as a discussion of ways to handle common emergencies. Chapter 3 focuses on School Health Education and includes a description of the components of the comprehensive school health education curriculum. There is a discussion of the philosophy, content, behavioral objectives, life skills, scope and sequence chart, and techniques of evaluation for the curriculum. Chapter 4 examines instructional strategies that make the health education classroom exciting with a discussion of the strengths, weaknesses, and helpful hints for using each. There is a discussion of ways to use instructional aids and a special feature on gaining classroom control by using effective discipline strategies.

O ver 90 percent of babies born in the United States are healthy. Shortly after birth, these babies are exposed to conditions which may pose risks to their health status . As these babies grow and develop into children and adolescents, they begin to make choices about their health status. Some children and adolescents in the United States make choices that place their health status at risk. What choices do these children and adolescents make? Why do they make these choices? How do these choices affect their health status? How might the quantity and quality of life for children and adolescents be improved?

THE STATISTICS:
HEALTH STATUS OF CHILDREN AND ADOLESCENTS

A careful examination of the statistics that have been gathered about childhood and adolescent health status helps to answer these questions.

Health Status of Children

In the past forty years, the health profile of American children has changed significantly. Forty years ago, our children's health was threatened by the major infectious diseases. Polio, diphtheria, scarlet fever, pneumonia, measles, and whooping cough were leading causes of death in children. Widespread immunization eliminated many of these diseases and caused a steep decline in others. Infectious diseases are no longer the leading cause of death in children.

Today, unintentional injuries pose the greatest risk of death in children (Figure 1-1). The leading cause of injury-related deaths is motor vehicle deaths. Motor vehicle crashes are responsible for about half of all childhood deaths. There has been a decline in deaths from motor vehicle accidents due to increasing use of safety seats as well as the safer design of automobiles.[15] All 50 states require safety restraints for young children. Yet some states do not mandate restraints after a child reaches the age of 5. When children are not in safety restraints, there is a greater risk that they will be injured or die in an accident. Rates of injury and death are also much higher when children are in child safety seats that are not attached to the car seat or are attached incorrectly.[16]

Most other injury-related deaths in children are the result of drownings and fires. Many children drown in swimming pools and home spas because covers and childproof enclosures have not been used. Household fires are especially dangerous because it is difficult for children to escape as easily as adults. Children who live in homes that do not have smoke detectors and who live in below-standard housing are especially vulnerable for fire-related injuries, burns, and death.[7]

The environment in which children live may affect health status. The crime rate in certain parts of the country is higher than that in others. Violence in the United States has been of growing concern. Homicide is a leading cause of death while abuse (physical, sexual,

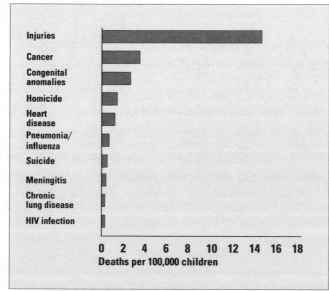

Figure 1-1
Leading causes of death for Children Aged 1 through 14
Source: National Center for Health Statistics (CDC), 1987.

A NATION AT RISK: THE NEED FOR COMPREHENSIVE SCHOOL HEALTH EDUCATION

and emotional) is a leading cause of injury. Neglect also contributes to a decline in the health status of children. Recent data indicate that children are attempting and committing suicide in increasing numbers. Many childhood suicides are linked to abuse and to the use of alcohol and other drugs.

The air children breathe is believed to affect their health status. The chief illness-related reasons that children miss school are respiratory infections and influenza. The incidence of asthma in children living in large cities has increased in recent years.[14]

Children from lower socioeconomic status have a greater risk than children of higher socioeconomic status for having developmental problems. A major risk factor for developmental problems is lead poisoning. In substandard housing, there may be old flaking lead-based paint, dust, and soil. In houses built with higher standards, the old lead-based paint has been replaced. Severe lead poisoning can contribute to profound mental retardation, coma, seizures, and death. Children who are exposed to low levels of lead may have delayed cognitive development, hearing problems, and retarded growth.[1]

Children may develop habits during their childhood which later affect their health status. The use of alcohol and other drugs in adolescence and adulthood has been linked to early use and experimentation with these drugs.[4] Although the incidence of cigarette smoking has declined in all age groups, those who smoke were more likely to have begun smoking during childhood. When high school seniors were surveyed, about one-quarter who had ever smoked reported that they smoked their first cigarette by grade 6. Over half of those who had smoked, reported that they smoked their first cigarette by grades 7 or 8, and three-quarters by grade 9. Children who experiment with smoking may do so because they are pressured by peers, watch their parents smoke, lack knowledge about the health consequences, are influenced by television, or have easy access to cigarettes in vending machines.

Children are in situations in which they are pressured to begin early use of drugs other than tobacco. The average first use of alcohol and marijuana is 13, but pressure to use both of these drugs began in childhood for many. One study reported that 26 percent of 4th graders and 40 percent of 6th graders said many of their peers had tried beer, wine, distilled spirits, or wine coolers.[17]

There is evidence that children who fail to develop healthful nutrition and exercise habits during childhood are unlikely to develop these habits as adults. The average American diet consists of more than 36 percent of calories derived from fat. Recent recommendations for good health are to derive no more than 30 percent of calories from fat with no more than 10 percent being from saturated fats. The eating habits of children are not believed to follow these recommendations. Unfortunately, poor eating habits in childhood are usually carried into adolescence and adulthood.

Establishing the habit of regular exercise in childhood is believed to promote fitness and control weight throughout childhood and to have carry-over value into adolescence and adulthood. Yet, a comparison of skinfold thickness, a measure of body fat, shows a steady increase in children over the last several years. In 1984, slightly more than two-thirds of children aged 10 through 17 reported regularly engaging in vigorous physical activity.[21]

Health Status of Adolescents and Young Adults

The leading causes of death for adolescents and young adults aged 15 to 24 (Figure 1-2) are revealing in understanding the choices this group makes which place them at risk. Also revealing were the results of a national survey sponsored by the American School Health Association, Association for the Advancement of Health Education, and The Society for Public Health Education funded by the Office of Disease Prevention and Health Promotion, Centers for Disease Control, and National Institute on Drug Abuse. The *National Adolescent Student Health Survey (NASHS)*, which questioned more than 11,000 eighth and tenth graders nationwide, revealed data on 1) adolescent knowledge about AIDS and other sexually transmitted diseases, 2) adolescent behavior related to violence, suicide, and injury prevention, and 3) adolescent use of alcohol, tobacco, and other drugs. In all, the survey addressed eight health topic areas: AIDS, injury prevention, violence, suicide, alcohol, drug and tobacco use, sexually transmitted disease, consumer health, and nutrition.[2]

Unintentional Injury

One-half of all deaths for the 15 to 24 age group can be attributed to unintentional injuries. Motor vehicle crashes account for three-quarters of these deaths.

Figure 1-2
Leading Causes of Death for Youth Aged 15 through 24

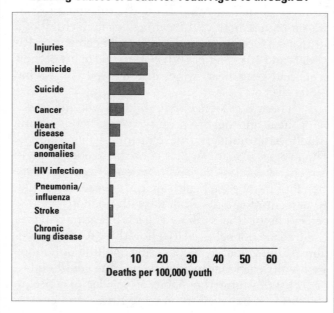

Source: *Monthly Vital Statistics Report,* **Supplement, September 26, 1989.**

Alcohol is involved in one-half of these motor vehicle crashes. It was believed that raising the drinking age reduced the number of deaths from motor vehicle crashes for a short time. But, this seemed to be offset shortly by the raising of the speed limit on rural interstate highways. Findings from NASHS suggest that adolescents place themselves at risk for unintentional injuries in several ways.[2]

- More than half of the students (56%) reported that they did not wear a seat belt the last time they rode in a car, truck, or van.
- About four of 19 10th grade students (44%) and approximately one-third of the 8th grade students reported that during the past months they rode with a driver who was under the influence of alcohol or other drugs.

- Nearly 9 out of every 10 students (87%) ride a bicycle, but 92% of those report never having worn a helmet and 72% report never having used a light at night.
- Six out of every 10 students (60%) ride a motorcycle or minibike, but 42% of those report that they rarely or never wear a helmet.
- Approximately one out of every six 10th grade students (17%) report having been under the influence of alcohol or other drugs while swimming or boating during the past year.
- About six out of every 10 boys (64%) and two out of every 10 girls (19%) report having used a gun in the past year.

Homicide and Other Acts of Violence

The second leading cause of death for all adolescents and young adults is homicide. Homicide is the leading cause of death for black males in this age group. Several factors tend to increase the likelihood of adolescents and young adults placing themselves at risk of being victims of homicide. Among these factors are sex, race, socioeconomic status, and drug use. Males are much more likely to be victims than females. Black males have the highest incidence of homicide although socioeconomic status is linked more closely than race. About half of homicides are associated with alcohol use. Nationally, an additional 10 percent are related to illicit drug use. However, in large cities the percentage of drug-related homicides is much higher. More than 50 percent of the victims of this age group have been murdered by family members or acquaintances. Firearms are the weapons most likely to be used.[4] Findings from NASHS suggest reasons for the increase in homicides and other acts of violence.[2]

- Almost half of the boys (49%) and about one-fourth of the girls (28%) report having been in at least one fight (defined as when two people hit each other or attack each other with weapons) during the past year.
- More than one-third of the students (34%) report that someone threatened to hurt them, 14% report having been robbed, and 13% report having been attacked while at school or on a school bus during the past year.
- One-third of the students (33%) report that someone threatened to hurt them, 15% report having been robbed, and 16% report having been attacked while outside of school during the past year.
- Nearly one in five girls (18%) report that during the past year while outside of school, someone tried to force them to have sex against their wishes.
- Four out of every 10 boys (41%) and nearly one-fourth of the girls (24%) report that they

could obtain a handgun if they wanted one.

- About one-fourth of the boys (23%) report having carried a knife to school at least once during the past year. Seven percent of the boys report carrying a knife to school on a daily basis.
- Three percent of the boys report having carried a handgun to school at least once during the past year. One percent of the boys report carrying a handgun on a daily basis.
- Nearly three-fourths of the students (73%) report walking alone late at night.
- More than six out of every 10 students (63%) report going to places known to be dangerous.
- Approximately two-thirds of the students (67%) do not know that alcohol is involved in half of all murders.
- Fewer than half of the students (46%) are aware that most murder victims know their assailants.

Suicide

Suicide is the third leading cause of death among all adolescents and young adults. It is the second leading cause of death among white males in this age group. The rate of suicide among black adolescents and young adults is half of that of whites. The suicide rate for young white and black females is much lower than that of young white and black males. However, young females attempt suicide unsuccessfully approximately three times more often than males.[12] Approximately 60 percent of suicides among this age group are committed with firearms. Findings from NASHS give statistics for suicide attempts and depression and suggest the difficulty adolescents have when a friend talks about suicide.[2]

- About four out of every 10 girls (42%) and one-fourth of the boys (25%) report that they have "seriously thought" about committing suicide at some time in their lives.
- Nearly one out of every five girls (18%) and one out of every 10 boys (11%) report that they have "actually tried" to commit suicide.
- More than half of the girls (56%) and about one-third of the boys (35%) report that it is hard for them to deal with stressful situations at home and at school.
- More than twice as many girls (34%) as boys (15%) report that they often feel sad and hopeless.
- About one out of every six girls (18%) and one out of every 10 boys (9%) report that they often feel they have nothing to which they can look forward.
- More than half of the students (56%) report that they would find it hard to tell a teacher

or school counselor about a potentially suicidal friend; nearly two-thirds (63%) would find it hard to tell a member of their friend's family.

Tobacco, Drug, and Alcohol Use

The habits of adolescents and young adults are clearly related to the likelihood they will develop chronic diseases such as coronary heart disease and cancer and will experience death or injury due to unintentional injuries, homicide, or suicide. The United States Surgeon General has advised that cigarette smoking is the single most preventable cause of death. Almost one-third of cancer-related deaths are directly attributable to cigarette smoking. Evidence links cigarette smoking with coronary heart disease as well. And new evidence shows that persons who live with a cigarette smoker have an increased incidence of coronary heart disease. The earlier a person begins to smoke cigarettes, the less likely the person is to quit. Fortunately, there has been a decline in cigarette smoking in males. However, there has not been a decline in females. Adolescent females are beginning to smoke at a younger age.

The use of alcohol and other drugs increases the likelihood of unintentional injury, homicide and suicide. Although drug use has declined since the 70s, experts warn that use of alcohol and other drugs poses a serious threat to society. Findings from NASHS suggest that adolescents are experimenting with the use of a number of drugs as well as alcohol.[2]

- One out of every five adolescents smoked cigarettes during the past month.
- More than half of the 8th grade students (51%) and nearly two-thirds of the 10th grade students (63%) reported having tried cigarettes.
- About one out of every six 8th grade students (16%) and one out of every four 10th grade students (26%) report having smoked a cigarette during the past month.
- More than one-fourth of adolescents report one occassion of heavy drinking during the past two weeks.
- Nearly eight out of every 10 8th grade students (77%) and 9 out of every 10 10th grade students (89%) report having tried an alcoholic beverage.
- About one-third of the 8th grade students (34%) and more than half of the 10th grade students (53%) report having had an alcoholic beverage during the past month.
- About one-fourth of the 8th grade students (26%) and more than one-third of the 10th grade students (38%) report having had five or more drinks on one occasion during the past two weeks.
- About one out of every 10 adolescents smoked

marijuana in the past month.

- Nearly one out of every six 8th grade students (15%) and about one-third of the 10th grade students (35%) report having tried marijuana.
- Six percent of the 8th grade students and 15% of the 10th grade students report having used marijuana during the past month.
- About one out of every 15 adolescents have tried cocaine.
- About one out of every 20 8th grade students (5%) and nearly one out of every 10 10th grade students (9%) report having tried cocaine.
- Two percent of the 8th grade students and three percent of the 10th grade students report having used cocaine during the past month.
- About one out of every five adolescents have tried glue sniffing.
- About one out of every five 8th and 10th grade students (21%) report having tried glue sniffing.
- Seven percent of the 8th grade students and five percent of the 10th grade students report having sniffed glue during the past month.

Sexual Activity

The majority of adolescent males and females and young adults are engaging in behaviors that may result in unwanted pregnancy, unwanted parenthood, and infection with HIV (the virus which causes AIDS) and other sexually transmitted diseases. An estimated 78 percent of adolescent females and 86% of adolescent males have engaged in sexual intercourse by age twenty.[18] Of the 1.1 million females aged 15 through 19 who become pregnant each year, 84 percent say they did not intend to become pregnant. Data indicate that teenage mothers are more likely to drop out of school, be unemployed, live at poverty level, and have low birthweight babies with health problems.[6] Teenage fathers are also more likely to drop out of school, be unemployed, and live at poverty level. Teenage fathers also lack parental and coping skills putting babies born to them and to teenage mothers at risk for being abused.

Approximately 25% of those with AIDS in the United States were infected with HIV during the teenage years. Currently, one fifth of persons who have AIDS are in their twenties. Findings from NASHS suggest that adolescents place themselves at risk for becoming pregnant and being infected with HIV and sexually transmitted diseases when they have limited information, many misconceptions, and engage in risky behavior.[2]

- More than 9 out of every 10 students (94%) know that there is an increased risk of HIV infection from having intercourse with some one infected with HIV.
- About 9 out of every 10 students (91%) know that there is an increased risk of HIV infection by sharing drug needles.
- Approximately eight out of every 10 students (82%) know that there is an increased risk of HIV infection by having more than one sex partner.
- More than eight out of every 10 students (86%) know that condoms are an effective way to reduce the risk of becoming infected with HIV.
- About 9 out of every 10 students (91%) agree that people their age should use condoms if they have sex.
- Seven out of every 10 students (71%) mistakenly believe that blood transfusions are a common way to become infected with HIV today.
- Almost half of the students (47%) mistakenly believe that there is an increased risk of becoming infected with HIV when donating blood.
- About half of the students (51%) are either unsure or mistakenly believe that washing after sex reduces one's chances of being infected with HIV.
- More than 9 out of every 10 girls (94%) and three-fourths of the boys (76%) believe it is acceptable to "say no" to having sex.
- More boys (62%) than girls (43%) believe it is acceptable for people their age to have sex with someone they have dated for a long time.
- More boys (18%) than girls (4%) believe it is acceptable for people their age to have sex with several different people.
- More than four out of every 10 students (44%) do not know or are unsure that a discharge of pus from the sex organs is an early sign of having an STD or that experiencing pain when going to the bathroom is an early sign of STD infection (41%).
- More than half of the students (55%) do not know that taking birth control pills is ineffective in avoiding STDs.
- Two-thirds of the students (67%) do not know that washing after sex is ineffective in avoiding STDs.
- About three-fourths of the students (76%) are either unsure or mistakenly believe that the Public Health Department must inform parents about STD in patients under age 18.
- Nearly eight out of every 10 students (79%) are either unsure or mistakenly believe that most clinics must have parental permission to treat patients under age 18 for STD.
- More than one-third of the students (38%) report that they would not know where to go for medical care.
- Nearly half of the students (49%) report that it would be hard for them to pay for treatment.

- More than four out of every 10 students (39%) report that they would be embarrassed to ask a doctor what was wrong with them.
- Nearly four out of every 10 students (39%) report that they do not know an adult to whom they could talk if they thought they had an STD.

Nutritional and Diet Choices

Seven out of ten of the leading causes of death in the United States are related to nutritional and diet choices. The nutritional and diet choices of adolescents and young adults contribute to patterns of growth and development as well as the incidence of chronic diseases and obesity in the later years. NASHS reported the following findings with regard to nutritional and diet choices of adolescents. [2]

- More than twice as many adolescent girls (61%) report having dieted during the past year as boys (28%). Some adolescents tried to control their weight using unsafe methods.
- Of the students who diet, about half (51%) report that they fast to control their weight.
- Of the students who diet, 12% report that they vomit after eating and eight percent report that they use laxatives to control their weight.
- Nearly four out of every 10 students (39%) eat fried foods four or more times a week.
- On average, students report eating three snacks a day. More than half of these snacks (59%) are foods high in fat and/or sugar.
- Approximately three-fourths of the students (73%) know that eating foods high in saturated fats may be related to heart problems.
- About eight out of every 10 students (79%) know that eating too much salt may be related to high blood pressure.
- Only 16% of the students know that eating too little fiber may be related to colon cancer.
- About half of the girls (48%) and one-third of the boys (32%) report having eaten breakfast two or fewer days during the past week.
- More than three-quarters of the boys (76%) and about two-thirds of the girls (64%) report having eaten lunch at least five days during the past week.
- About eight out of every 10 students (83%) report having eaten dinner at least five days during the past week.

Consumer Choices

Consumer health involves the ability to take responsibility for health by making informed choices about health products and services. Without adequate knowledge and skills, choices may be made which influence health adversely. Findings from NASHS suggest that adolescents' consumer knowledge and skills are lacking. [2]

- Given a cereal box label, more than half of the students (57%) were unable to determine which cereal ingredient was present in the largest amount.
- Given two cereal box labels, nearly half of the students (47%) were unable to select the cereal containing less sugar.
- Approximately six out of every 10 students (58%) do not know the meaning of the date stamped on dairy products.

THE ROOTS: FAMILIES, COMMUNITIES, AND SCHOOLS

The statistics are convincing—children, adolescents, and young adults in the United States are making choices that place their health status in jeopardy. The next questions become: "What are the roots of the problem?" "Why are children, adolescents, and young adults choosing behaviors that place their health status at risk?" The following tale can be used to illustrate why this question must be asked.

Imagine a person walking alongside a river who sees someone drowning. This person jumps in, pulls the victim out, and begins artificial resuscitation. While this is going on, another drowning person calls for help; the rescuer jumps into the water again and pulls the new victim out. The process repeats itself several times until the rescuer gets up and begins to run upriver. A bystander, surprised to see the rescuer moving away from the victims, calls out, "Where are you going?" The rescuer replies, "I'm going upstream to find out who's pushing all these people in and to see if I can can stop it or teach them how to swim." [11,19]

A careful examination of the American way of life including a study of the family, the community and its services, and the school will explain "what's pushing" children, adolescents, and young adults into choosing behaviors and situations that threaten health status. This explanation also provides insight into reasons why many children, adolescents, and adults choose health enhancing behaviors and situations and avoid those that threaten health status.

The Role of The Family

Persons often comment, "he is a chip off the old block" or "she is the spitting image of her mother." The subtle and not so subtle influences of the family have a profound impact on behavior and experiences. The parents, stepparents, guardians, and other adults who assume the parenting role within the family might be viewed as coaches who help children and adolescents develop a wide range of skills for living. Just as coaches have different ranges of ability in helping the members of their teams to develop skills, so do the adults responsible for parenting within the family unit.

Referring to the original analogy, some adults responsible for parenting teach youth to excel at swimming, others promote very good swimmers, others average or below average swimmers, and some provide such little skill that those under their influence are likely to drown. A careful look at the family will help to explain why many children and adolescents make choices which place their health status at risk. It is necessary to examine those who become excellent swimmers when pushed into the water.

Fortunately, many children and adolescents have positive family experiences. These youngsters learn skills that will assist them for a lifetime. The skills that they learn help them to steer toward behaviors, situations, decisions, and relationships that promote optimal health and well-being.

A key skill these youngsters develop is the capacity for intimacy. John Burt, Professor and Dean of The College of Health and Human Performance at The University of Maryland, says that intimacy is the capacity for connecting closely with others.[13] "Intimacy," says Burt, "can be philosophical, psychological, creative, and physical." Intimacy is a state that everyone desires- all people long for closeness and connectedness to others.

Philosophical intimacy is the sharing of one's beliefs with others. Those responsible for parenting who teach their children and adolescents philosophical intimacy provide them with an important tool for living. They teach them to examine beliefs and values and to match their behaviors and decisons with these beliefs and values. In families where there is philosophical intimacy, children and adolescents "get practice" for situations in which their beliefs and values are challenged. This practice helps them solidify clear thinking and to become prepared for pressures from others.

Psychological intimacy is the sharing of needs, drives, weaknesses, strengths, intentions, emotional feelings, and deepest problems. Psychological intimacy allows a person to feel understood and to feel safe. When a family unit has psychological intimacy, children and adolescents feel that there is somewhere to go to share what is happening in their personal world. They feel this safety. Psychological intimacy is necessary for developing strong feelings of self-worth. And feelings of self-worth again help children and youth say NO to pressures that might threaten their health status.

Creative intimacy is the sharing in the work or development of a project, task, or creation of something new. Creative intimacy is different than philosphical and psychological intimacy in that the medium of sharing goes beyond discussion and emo-

tional response. In creative intimacy, family members learn cooperation. They learn to blend their talents for the good of the family. The joys of jobs well done are experienced. Those responsible for parenting who pass this gift to family members help them learn the value of cooperation in meeting goals. They also learn how their behaviors and decisions affect the ability of the family to reach its goals. They learn to balance what they believe is appropriate for them with what is best for the family and society as a whole.

Physical intimacy is the appropriate sharing of physical expressions of caring and affection. Those responsible for parenting within families provide the first information that children and adolescents have about physical affection. If there is sufficient physical expressions of caring and affection within the family, children and adolescents feel loved. They are not needy nor do they engage in sexual behaviors that threaten their health status as a way to make up for affection that is lacking in the home.

Those responsible for parenting who give their children and adolescents the gifts of philosphical, psychological, creative, and physical intimacy have given them a foundation for health and well-being. There is another skill that is provided by the healthy family. This skill is related to coping with life crises.

Elisabeth Kubler Ross identified five stages of dying and death: denial, bargaining, anger, depression, and acceptance.[10] Her five stages have been widely accepted as important stages in handling dying and death. Interestingly, these five stages also are stages that each person experiences when dealing with life crises and stressful situations.

For example, suppose a child has just been told that the family will move to a new city. At first, the child may deny that this is really happening. When the "for sale" sign is placed in front of the house, the child may bargain. (S)he thinks of ways the family can stay in its present location. When bargaining does not work, the child is angry. A period of sadness and depression follows. Eventually, the child adjusts to this life crisis, accepts it, works through the pain, and accepts the move.

Those responsible for parenting help their children and adolescents move through the phases of dealing with a crisis no matter how big or small. Being able to handle different crises in life is important. Learning to struggle and having the support of others for the struggle helps children and youth learn ways to deal with difficult situations. There are seldom instant solutions to difficult problems and situations in life. This is an important lesson to learn. And the patience developed from learning to struggle through situations is a gift which enhances self-esteem and future coping skills.

The **dysfunctional family** is a family in which the needs for intimacy -philosophical, psychological, creative, and physical -are not met and children and adolescents do not learn to delay gratification and struggle successfuly to solve problems. The term dysfunctional family was first used to describe families in which there was alcoholism. The person with alcoholism was viewed as not functioning in a healthful way and the family members who lived with this person began to show symptoms of functioning in harmful ways as well.

The term dysfunctional family is now applied to all families in which there is a lack of intimacy, inability to delay gratification, and inability to struggle to solve problems. Alcoholism and other drug related problems contribute to dysfunctional families but so do other conditions. Families in which children and adolescents are abandoned by one parent may become dysfunctional. Families in which there is emotional, physical, or sexual abuse are dysfunctional. Families in which one or both parents are emotionally unavailable because of workaholism or character disorders are viewed as dysfunctional.

Why are children and adolescents from dysfunctional families so vulnerable to engaging in behaviors that place their health status at risk? Intimacy is essential to mental health and well-being. Without philosophical intimacy, children and adolescents are confused. They do not learn a sense of values and have clear ideas of what is right and wrong. Without psychological intimacy, children and adolescents have no place to feel safe and to develop good feelings about themselves. Without positive self-esteem, it is difficult to withstand the pressures of others when asked to engage in harmful behaviors and situations. When children or adolescents' needs and feelings are not respected at home, it is difficult for them to expect others to show them respect.

Without physical intimacy, children and adolescents are especially vulnerable. The need for affection exists in everyone. When this need is not met in healthful ways, children and adolescents may turn to sexual involvement when what they really need is the affection from a loving family.

Without creative intimacy, children and adolescents may not learn cooperation. They may not learn to use their talents for the good of themselves as well as others. Children and adolescents from dysfunctional families are more likely to be self-centered and selfish. They have not been exposed to role models who carefully weigh the consequences of their behaviors on the family and on society.

Finally, children and adolescents from dysfunctional families have not been a part of a family that struggles in healthful ways to deal with life crises. When life gets tough, they have not developed the self-discipline and the coping strategies to struggle to solve problems. They prefer instant gratification to delayed gratification. They become vulnerable and may participate in harmful behaviors, decisions, and relationships to have quick relief from the pain they feel.

When children and adolescents from loving, functional families are contrasted with those from dysfunctional families, it is easy to see why the latter are more likely to choose behaviors that put their health status at risk. Of course, these are two extremes. Many of the children and adolescents in the United States are raised in families that are somewhere in the middle of the continuum between having loving families and dysfunctional families. As a result, they have many skills which help them protect their health and safety while they lack other skills which may make them vulnerable to making destructive choices.

The Role of The Community

In his classic book, *We The Lonely*, David Reissman examined the significance of having and belonging to community in order to have a sense of well-being. According to Reissman, people even shop at the same grocery store at the same time each week to see familiar faces and have a sense of belonging.

The need to have a sense of belonging in one's community is important to everyone, but the impact is perhaps no where more apparent than in adolescence. How can children and adolescents who feel they belong to a community be contrasted from those who don't? Why do children and adolescents who lack the attachment to community place their health status at risk when other children and adolescents do not?

A sense of community helps children and adolescents feel rooted and gives them a sense of belonging. Children and adolescents who regularly worship with those adults responsible for their parenting are much less likely to use drugs and to become sexually active than those who do not. Children and adolescents who participate in school activities and belong to clubs and athletic teams are much less likely to use drugs and to become sexually active than those who do not. The connectedness to community and feeling of belonging that results from this connectedness helps young people feel good about themselves. They are much less self-centered. They are less needy and less likely to be looking for the feeling of belonging.

There is another important aspect of community that helps children and adolescents have a sense of well-being. This involves helping in their communities. Robert Bellah in his national bestseller, *Habits of the Heart*, discusses the habits which contribute to well-being. In his book, Bellah emphasizes that persons need to develop "habits of the heart" that result in actions that show caring and concern for others.[3] Children and adolescents who are given the opportunity to do good deeds for others appreciate their individualism, but learn the good feelings that come from contributing to society. They learn that they are part of the "bigger picture" and that their behavior and the decisions they make do, in fact, make a difference.

In contrast, some children and adolescents do not feel this sense of belonging and significance. They are not involved in school activities which connect them in positive ways with their peers. They begin to look for this connection to fill their needs. They become vulnerable to the pressure of peers who want them to be part of gangs or other destructive groups. Rather than being lured by violence into joining the gang, they are really lured by the need to belong and to feel significant. Looking to fill the void in their lives, they become involved in destructive behaviors and relationships. Not having an opportunity to do good deeds for others in a community intensifies the risk that they will choose destructive behaviors. They do not feel a part of a society that is working to better itself.

The Role of The School

The quality of school life contributes to the lives of children and adolescents. Referring back to the use of McKinley's tale, the rescuer at first pulled the persons from the river who were drowning. But, finally the rescuer wanted to learn why the victims could not swim.

Schools can and should be in the business of teaching young people to swim, that is, teaching them skills they need for a quality life. The learning environment becomes especially important when this approach to education is utilized. When schools do not teach young people skills for living in a positive learning environment, young people are turned off when they go to school. They spend much of their day bored and uninvolved. They may turn to behaviors which threaten the health and safety of themselves and others. Consider the kind of school described in the following poem. The poem was given to a teacher by a high school senior shortly before the student committed suicide.

About School

He always wanted to say things. But
    no one understood.
He always wanted to explain things.
    But no one cared.
So he drew.

Sometimes he would just draw and it
    wasn't anything. He wanted to carve
    it in stone or write it in the sky.
He would lie out on the grass and look
    up in the sky and it would be only
    him and the sky and the things
    inside that needed saying.

And it was after that, that he drew the
    picture. It was a beautiful picture.
    He kept it under the pillow and
    would let no one see it.

And he would look at it every night
    and think about it. And when it was
    dark, and his eyes were closed, he
    could still see it.
And it was all of him. And he loved it.

When he started school he brought it
    with him. Not to show anyone, but
    just to have with him like a friend.

It was funny about school.
He sat in a square, brown desk like all
    the other square, brown desks and
    he thought it should be red.
And his room was a square, brown
    room. Like all the other rooms. And
    it was tight and closed. And stiff.

He hated to hold the pencil and the
    chalk with his arm stiff and his feet
    flat on the floor, stiff, with the
    teacher watching and watching.

And then he had to write numbers.
    And they weren't anything. They
    were worse than the letters that
    could be something if you put them
    together.
And the numbers were tight and
    square and he hated the whole
    thing.

The teacher came and spoke to him.
    She told him to wear a tie like all
    the other boys. He said he didn't
    like them and she said it didn't
    matter.

After that they drew. And he drew all
    yellow and it was the way he felt
    about morning. And it was
    beautiful.
The teacher came and smiled at him.
    "What's this?" she said. "Why don't
    you draw something like Ken's
    drawing? Isn't that beautiful?"
It was all questions.

After that his mother bought him a tie
    and he always drew airplanes and
    rocket ships like everyone else. And
    he threw the old picture away.
And when he lay out alone looking at
    the sky, it was big and blue and all
    of everything, but he wasn't
    anymore.

He was square inside and brown, and
      his hands were stiff and he was like
      anyone else. And the thing inside
      him that needed saying didn't need
      saying anymore.

It had stopped pushing. It was
      crushed. Stiff.
Like everything else.

There is an important saying that demands the attention of educators, "Students do not care how much you know, until they know how much you care." Just as adults responsible for parenting within families may provide the roots which nurture or inhibit the growth and development of children and adolescents, so do teachers and specific school settings.

THE SOLUTION: COMPREHENSIVE SCHOOL HEALTH EDUCATION

There is no single solution to improving the health status of children and adolescents in America. Families, communities, schools, governments, and health care professionals and agencies each can play a significant role. The focus of this textbook centers upon the role that the school can play. The role that you, the teacher, play is of vital importance.

Comprehensive School Health Program

The school's commitment to health is demonstrated through efforts to have a comprehensive school health program. A **comprehensive school health program** is an organized set of policies, procedures, and activities designed to protect and promote the health and well-being of students and staff which has traditionally included health services, healthful school environment, and health education. It should also include, but not be limited to, guidance and counseling, physical education, food service, social work, psychological services, and employee health promotion.[17]

Figure 1-3 depicts A Model for The Comprehensive School Health Program. Examining the Model, you will notice that the school health advisory committee plays a central role in the comprehensive school health program. This committee consists of representatives from the community, family, and student body, as well as teachers and administrators. Community representatives include persons from voluntary health organizations, official health agencies, medical and dental professional associations, health care professions, business and industry, religious organizations, and adult service clubs. A **voluntary health organization** is a non-profit association supported by contributions dedicated to conducting research and providing education and/or services related to particular health problems or concerns.[17] An **official health agency** is a publicly supported governmental organization mandated by law and/or regulation for the protection and improvement of the health of the public.[17]

Student representatives are selected from the student body at large and from various youth groups. Family representatives include persons from the school board, concerned parent groups, and parent teacher associations and organizations.

Teachers and administrators are important representatives on the school health advisory committee. Schools and/or school districts may have a health education coordinator and/or a health education administrator responsible for the school health advisory committee. A **health education coordinator** is a professional health educator who is responsible for the management and coordination of all health education policies, activities, and resources within a particular setting or circumstance.[17] A **health education administrator** is a professional health educator who has the authority and responsibility for the management and coordination of all health education policies, activities, and resources within a particular setting or circumstance.[17]

The school health advisory committee coordinates efforts for the comprehensive school health program. From the Model in Figure 1-3, you can see that the primary focus is upon school health services, school health environment, and school health education. Also, included as key components in an expanded concept of the comprehensive school health program are guidance and counseling, physical education, food service, social work, psychological services, and employee health promotion.

As a teacher, you may be asked to serve on the school health advisory committee. This is a challenging and rewarding task. But, even if you are not a member of the school health advisory committee, you play a vital role in the implementation of the comprehensive school health program. Let's examine the role you have in school health services, school health environment, and school health education.

School Health Services

School health services is that part of the comprehensive school health program provided by physicians, nurses, dentists, health educators, and other allied health personnel, social workers, teachers, and others to appraise, protect, and promote the health of students and school personnel. These services are designed to ensure access to and appropriate use of primary health care services, prevent and control communicable disease, provide emergency care for injury or sudden illness, promote and provide concurrent learning opportunities which are conducive to the maintenance and promotion of individual and community health.[17]

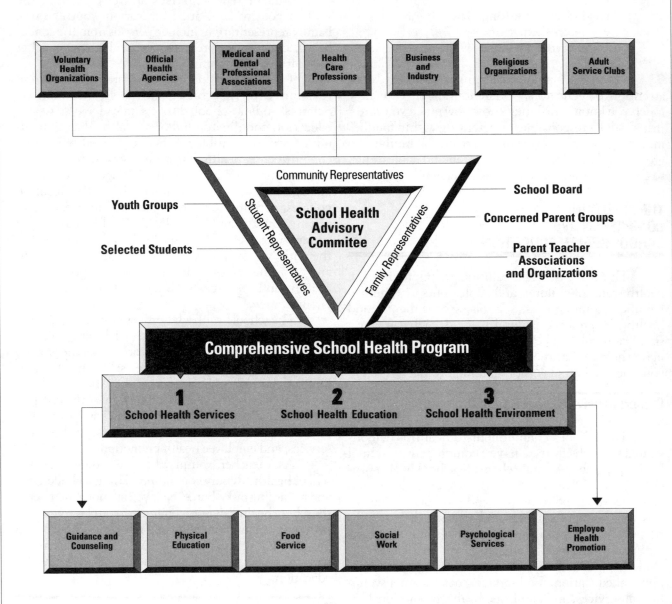

Figure 1-3
A Model for The Comprehensive School Health Program

As a teacher, you are a part of the school health services team. The school health services "team" works to: 1) develop school readiness programs including preschool health screening and assessment of emotional and social readiness, 2) appraise and evaluate the health status of students and personnel through periodic observation and examination, 3) counsel students, parents, and school personnel when necessary, 4) refer students and school personnel to appropriate health care services when a health status problem exists, 5) follow up on appraisal, counseling, and referring of students and school personnel.

School health services provide a foundation for lifelong attitudes and behaviors. Through school health services, students learn to value professional health services and to have their health evaluated regularly. As a teacher, your attention to school health services helps promote student health and fosters positive attitudes. School health services will be explored further in Chapter 2.

School Health Environment

Healthful school environment is the part of the comprehensive school health program that focuses on the school day, school building and surrounding area, and specific school activities, procedures, and policies that protect the health and safety of faculty, staff, and students. As a teacher, the mental health in your classroom is perhaps your most significant contribution to healthful school environment. But, you also have other important responsibilities.

The "team" responsible for healthful school environment works together to: 1) promote positive, affirming faculty, staff, and student relationships, 2) schedule the school day in such a way as to be conducive to learning and to optimal well-being, 3) plan a school site with adequate size and suitable location, 4) assure school construction meets standards for sanitation, safety features, lighting, heating, cooling, ventilation, acoustics, and furnishings, 5) provide for proper school maintenance and school inspections, 6) develop procedures to follow for fire and disaster and conduct regular practice drills, 7) provide adequate and safe physical education and recreational activities, 8) implement safe school transportation policies, 9) train youth in ways to stay safe at school and while coming to and from school, and 10) meet nutritional standards for school lunches, milk programs, and parties at school.

Healthful school environments also provide a foundation for lifelong attitudes and behaviors. Students learn that the quality of their different environments affects their health status. They learn that their environments can be manipulated in ways that promote optimal well-being. They learn by watching you, their teacher, take control of the environment and facilitate positive changes.

School Health Education

School health education is the component of the comprehensive school health program which includes the development, delivery, and evaluation of a planned instructional program and other activities for students in pre-school through grade 12, for parents and for school staff, and is designed to influence positively the health knowledge, attitudes, and skills of individuals.[17] Teachers who are responsible for school health education are referred to as school health educators. A **school health educator** is a practitioner who is professionally prepared in the field of school health education, meets state teaching requirements, and demonstrates competence in the development, delivery, and evaluation of curricula for students in the school health setting that enhances health knowledge, attitudes, and problem solving skills.[17]

How does school health education play a significant role in alleviating the problems of, "A Nation At Risk?" Although there are many solutions to promoting the health status of youth in America, three have been discussed in this chapter: 1) emphasizing family life and family values and promoting healthful family behavior, 2) promoting community involvement, and 3) having school programs that promote life skills within a caring environment.

The remainder of this book focuses on the latter solution. Young people can learn life skills that enable them to choose behaviors that promote optimal health status when a school district takes the comprehensive school health program seriously. The classroom becomes a laboratory through which comprehensive school health education gives students an opportunity to learn and practice life skills that promote health status. **Comprehensive school health education** refers to the development, delivery, and evaluation of a planned curriculum, pre-school through 12, with goals, objectives, content sequence, and specific classroom lessons.[17] As a teacher, YOUR efforts and YOUR role in comprehensive school health education can and will make the difference.

THE PLAN: HEALTHY PEOPLE 2000

You may ask, "What is it that I am specifically committed to accomplishing?" It is important to ask this question and to have goals and objectives to answer it. **Goals** are specific outcomes toward which a person directs effort. **Objectives** are statements that describe what children and adolescents in your classes will do after they have completed comprehensive school health education. The following saying is relevant:

There are three kinds of teachers.
There are those teachers who make things happen.
There are those teachers who watch things happen.
And there are those teachers who wonder what happened.

As a committed and caring teacher, your task is "to make things happen." Goals and objectives are essential so that you are clear as to WHAT you want to make happen.

Healthy People 2000

In 1987, a consortium that has grown to 300 national membership organizations and all the state health departments, facilitated by the Institute of Medicine of the National Academy of Sciences, in cooperation with the United States Public Health Service developed goals and objectives to help improve the health and well-being of people in the United States. The efforts of the organizations involved in this undertaking were culminated in the development of a document titled *Healthy People 2000: The National Health Promotion and Disease Prevention Objectives*.[8] This document offered insight for the coming century by identifying ways the quality and quantity of life could be enhanced.

Healthy People 2000 sets broad public health goals to be attained by the year 2000. The three principal goals are to: 1) increase the span of healthy life of Americans, 2) reduce health disparities among Americans, and 3) achieve access to preventive services for all Americans. To help meet these goals, 298 specific objectives were identified in 22 separate priority areas such as physical fitness, alcohol and other drugs, unintentional injuries, mental health and mental disorders, and educational and community based programs.

To promote the achievement of the objectives that focus on age and population groups at special risk, the U.S. Public Health Service's Office of Disease Prevention and Health Promotion funded different organizations to work with particular high risk populations in specific settings. The American Medical Association received funding to focus on the adolescent population through its "Healthier Youth by the Year 2000 Project." The AMA assembled a special volume called *Healthy Youth 2000* that includes the objectives from *Healthy People 2000* that pertain to all or part of the 10 to 24 age group.[9] The objectives are identified as belonging to one of the following three categories: 1) Health Status- objectives to reduce death, disease, and disability, 2) Risk Reduction- objectives to reduce the prevalence of risks to health or to increase behaviors known to reduce such risks, and 3) Services and Protection- objectives to increase comprehensiveness, accessibility, and/or quality of preventive services and preventive interventions.

The goal is to make a plan to reach each of these objectives by the year 2000. But, before, beginning to work on the plan, it is imperative to know the objectives toward which you and others will be working. Table 1-1 identifies Year 2000 Objectives for Youth for the following areas: physical activity and fitness, nutrition, tobacco, alcohol and other drugs, family planning, mental health and mental disorders, violent and abusive behavior, educational and community-based programs, unintentional injuries, environmental health, oral health, maternal and child health, HIV infection, sexually transmitted diseases, immunization and infectious diseases, and clinical preventive services. Table 1-2 identifies Year 2000 Objectives for Schools. Being familiar with these objectives prepares you for the task ahead. You will know what you are expected to help MAKE HAPPEN. In the remaining chapters of this book, you will gain the knowledge and skills that you need.

Table 1-1
Year 2000 Objectives for Youth

Physical Activity and Fitness

Risk Reduction

Increase to at least 20 percent the proportion of aged 18 and older and to at least 75 percent the proportion of children and adolescents aged 6 through 17 who engage in vigorous physical activity that promotes the development and maintenance of cardiorespiratory fitness 3 or more days per week for 20 or more minutes per occasion.

(Baseline: 12 percent for people aged 18 and older in 1985; 66 percent for youth aged 10 through 17 in 1984)

Objective #1.4

Services and Protection

Increase to at least 50 percent the proportion of children and adolescents in 1st through 12th grade who participate in daily school physical education.

(Baseline: 36 percent in 1984-6)

Objective #1.8

Services and Protection

Increase to at least 50 percent the proportion of school physical education class time that students are being physically active, preferably engaged in lifetime physical activities.

(Baseline: Students spent an estimated 27 percent of class time being physically active in 1984)

Objective #1.9

Related Objectives

Risk Reduction

Increase to at least 30 percent the proportion of people aged 6 and older who engage regularly, preferably daily, in light to moderate physical activity for at least 30 minutes per day.

(Baseline: 22 percent of people aged 18 and older were active for at least 30 minutes 5 or more times per week and 12 percent were active 7 or more times per week in 1985)

Objective #1.3, 15.11, 17.3

Risk Reduction

Reduce to no more than 15 percent the proportion of people aged 6 and older who engage in no leisure-time physical activity.

(Baseline: 24 percent for people aged 18 and older in 1985)

Objective #1.5

Risk Reduction

Increase to at least 40 percent the proportion of people aged 6 and older who regularly perform physical activities that enhance and maintain muscular strength, muscular endurance, and flexibility.

(Baseline data available in 1991)

Objective #1.6

Risk Reduction

Increase to at least 50 percent the proportion of overweight people aged 12 and older who have adopted sound dietary practices combined with regular physical activity to attain an appropriate body weight.

(Baseline: 30 percent of overweight women and 25 percent of overweight men for people aged 18 and older in 1985)

Objective #1.7, 2.7

Nutrition

Health Status

Reduce overweight to a prevalence of no more than 20 percent among people aged 20 and older and no more than 15 percent among adolescents aged 12 through 19.

(Baseline: 26 percent for people aged 20 through 74 in 1976-80, 24 percent for men and 27 percent for women; 15 percent for adolescents aged 12 through 19 in 1976-80)

Objective #1.2, 2.3, 15.10, 17.11

Risk Reduction

Increase calcium intake so at least 50 percent of youth aged 12 through 24 consume three or more servings daily of foods rich in calcium.

(Baseline: 7 percent of women and 14 percent of men aged 19 through 24 consumed three or more servings in 1985-6)

Objective #2.8

Related Objectives

Risk Reduction

Reduce iron deficiency to less than 3 percent among children aged 1 through 4 and among women of childbearing age.

(Baseline: 5 percent for women aged 20 through 44 in 1976-80)

Objective #2.10

Risk Reduction

Increase to at least 85 percent the proportion of people aged 18 and older who use food labels to make nutritious food selections.

(Baseline: 74 percent used labels to make food selections in1988)

Objective #2.13

Tobacco

Risk Reduction

Reduce the initiation of cigarette smoking by children and youth so that no more than 15 percent have become regular cigarette smokers by age 20.

(Baseline: 30 percent of youth had become regular cigarette smokers by ages 20 through 24 in 1987)

Objective #3.5

Risk Reduction

Reduce smokeless tobacco use by males aged 12 through 24 to a prevalence of no more than 4 percent.

(Baseline: 6.6 percent among males aged 12 through 17 in 1988; 8.9 percent among males aged 18 through 24 in 1987)

Objective #3.9

Related Objectives

Risk Reduction

Increase to at least 50 percent the proportion of cigarette smokers aged 18 and older who stopped smoking cigarettes for at least one day during the preceding year.

(Baseline: In 1986, 34 percent of people who smoked in the preceding year stopped for at least one day during that year)

Objective #3.6

Risk Reduction

Increase smoking cessation during pregnancy so that at least 60 percent of women who are cigarette smokers at the time they become pregnant quit smoking early in pregnancy and maintain abstinence for the remainder of their pregnancy.

(Baseline: 39 percent of white women aged 20 through 44 quit at any time during pregnancy in 1985)

Objective #3.7

Alcohol and Other Drugs

Health Status

Reduce deaths among people aged 15 through 24 caused by alcohol-related motor vehicle crashes to no more than 18 per 100,000..

(Baseline: 21.5 per 100,000 in 1987)

Objective #4.1b

Risk Reduction

Increase by at least 1 year the average age of first use of cigarettes, alcohol, and marijuana by adolescents aged 12 through 17.

(Baseline: Age 11.6 for cigarettes, age 13.1 for alcohol, and age 13.4 for marijuana in 1988

Objective #4.5

**Risk
Reduction**

Reduce the proportion of young people who have used alcohol, marijuana, and cocaine in the past month, as follows:

Substance/age		Baseline 1988	Target 2000
Alcohol/aged	12-17	25.2%	12.6%
Alcohol/aged	18-20	57.9%	29.0%
Marijuana/aged	12-17	6.4%	3.2%
Marijuana/aged	18-25	15.5%	7.8%
Cocaine/aged	12-17	1.1%	.6%
Cocaine/aged	18-25	4.5%	2.3%

Objective #4.6

**Risk
Reduction**

Reduce the proportion of high school seniors and college students engaging in recent occasions of heavy drinking of alcoholic beverages to no more than 28 percent of high school seniors and 32 percent of college students.

(Baseline: 33 percent of high school seniors and 41.7 percent of college students in 1989).

Objective #4.7

**Risk
Reduction**

Reduce alcohol consumption by people aged 14 and older to an annual average of no more than 2 gallons of ethanol per person.

(Baseline: 2.54 gallons of ethanol in 1987)

Objective #4.8

**Risk
Reduction**

Increase the proportion of high school seniors who perceive SOCIAL DISAP-PROVAL associated with the heavy use of alcohol, occasional use of marijuana, and experimentation with cocaine, as follows:

Behavior	Baseline 1989	Target 2000
Heavy use of alcohol	56.4%	70%
Occasional use of marijuana	71.1%	85%
Trying cocaine once or twice	88.9%	95%

Objective #4.9

Increase the proportion of high school seniors who associate RISK OF PHYSICAL OR PSYCHOLOGICAL HARM with the heavy use of alcohol, regular use of marijuana, and experimentation with cocaine, as follows:

Behavior	Baseline 1989	Target 2000
Heavy use of alcohol	44%	70%
Regular use of marijuana	77.5%	90%
Trying cocaine once or twice	54.9%	80%

Objective #4.9

Reduce to no more than 3 percent the proportion of male high school seniors who use anabolic steriods.

Objective #4.11

Related Objectives

Reduce drug-related deaths to no more than 3 per 100,000 people..

Objective #4.3

Family Planning

Reduce pregnancies among girls aged 17 and younger to no more than 50 per 1,000 adolescents. (Baseline: 71.1 pregnancies per 1,000 girls aged 15 through 17 in 1985)

Special Population Targets

Pregnancies per 1,000	1985 Baseline	2000 Target
Black adolescents 15-19	186	120
Hispanic adolescents 15-19	158	105

Objective #5.1

Reduce the proportion of adolescents who have engaged in sexual intercourse to no more than 15 percent by age 15 and no more than 40 percent by age 17

(Baseline: 27 percent of girls and 33 percent of boys by age 15, 50 percent of girls and 66 percent of boys by age 17; reported in 1988)

Objective #5.4, 18.3, 19.9

**Risk
Reduction**

Increase to at least 90 percent the proportion of sexually active, unmarried people aged 19 and younger who use contraception, especially combined method contraception that both effectively prevents pregnancy and provides barrier protection against disease.

Objective #5.6

(Baseline: 78 percent at most recent intercoure and 63 percent at first intercourse; 2 percent used oral contraceptives and the condom at most recent intercourse; among young women aged 15 through 19 reporting in 1988)

**Services and
Protection**

Increase to at least 85 percent the proportion of and people aged 10 through 18 who have discussed human sexuality, including values surrounding sexuality, with their parents and/or have received information through another parentally-endorsed source, such as youth, school, or religious programs.

Objective #5.8

(Baseline: 66 percent of people aged 13 through 18 have discussed sexuality with their parents; reported in 1986)

**Services and
Protection**

Increase to at least 60 percent the proportion of primary care providers who provide age-appropriate preconception care and counseling.

Objective #5.10, 14.12

(Baseline data available in 1992)

Related Objectives

**Health
Status**

Reduce to no more than 30 percent the proportion of pregnancies that are unintended.

Special Population Target

Unintended pregnancies	1988 Baseline	2000 Target
Black women	78%	40%

Objective #5.2

(Baseline: In 1988, 56% of pregnancies in the previous five years were unintended, either unwanted or earlier than desired)

Mental Health and Mental Disorders

Reduce suicides among youth aged 15 through 19 to no more than 8.2 per 100,000 people.

Objective #6.1a and 7.2a

(Age adjusted baseline: 10.3 per 100,000 in 1987)

Health Status

Reduce suicides among men aged 20-34 to no more than 21.4 per 100,000 people.

(Age adjusted basline: 25.2 per 100,000 people in 1986)

Objective #6.1b and 7.2b

Health Status

Reduce by 15 percent the incidence of injurious suicide attempts among adolescents aged 14 through 17.

(Baseline data available in 1991)

Objective #6.2 and 7.8

Health Status

Reduce to less than 10 percent the prevalence of mental disorders among children and adolescents.

(Baseline: An estimated 12 percent among youth younger than age 18 in 1989)

Objective #6.3

Related Objectives

Health Status

Reduce to less than 35 percent the proportion of people aged 18 and older who experienced adverse health effects from stress within the past year.

Special Population

	Target 1985 Baseline	2000 Target
People with disabilities	53.5%	40%

(Baseline: 42.6 percent in 1985)

Objective #6.5

Risk Reduction

Increase to at least 20 percent the proportion of people aged 18 and older who seek help in coping with personal and emotional problems.

Special Population Target

	1985 Baseline	2000 Target
People with disabilities	14.7%	30%

(Baseline: 11.1 percent in 1985)

Objective #6.8

Risk Reduction

Decrease to no more than 5 percent the proportion of people aged 18 and older who report experiencing significant levels of stress who do not take steps to reduce or control their stress.

(Baseline: 21 percent in 1985)

Violent and Abusive Behavior

Health Status

Reduce homicides to no more than 7.2 per 100,000 people.

Special Population Targets

Homicide Rate per 100,000	1987 Baseline	2000 Target
Black men aged 15-34	90.5	72.4
Hispanic men aged 15-34	53.1	42.5
Black women aged 15-34	20.0	16.0

(Age adjusted baseline: 8.5 per 100,000 in 1987)

Objective #7.1

Health Status

Reduce weapon-related deaths to no more than 12.6 per 100,000 people from major causes.

(Age adjusted baseline: 12.9 per 100,000 firearms; 1.9 per 100,000 by knives in 1987)

Objective #7.3

Health Status

Reverse to less than 25.2 per 1,000 children the rising incidence of maltreatment of children younger than age 18.

Type Specific Targets

Type of per 1,000	1986 Baseline	2000 Target
Physical abuse	5.7	<5.7
Sexual abuse	2.5	<2.5
Emotional abuse	3.4	<3.4
Neglect	15.9	<15.9

(Baseline: 25.2 per 1,000 in 1986)

Objective 7.4

Health Status

Reduce rape and attempted rape of women aged 12 through 34 to no more than 225 per 100,000.

(Baseline: 250 per 100,00 in 1986)

Objective #7.7a

Risk Reduction

Reduce by 20 percent the incidence of physical fighting among adolescents aged 14 through 17.

(Baseline data available in 1991)

Objective #7.9

Risk Reduction

Reduce by 20 percent the incidence of weapon-carrying by adolescents aged 14 through 17.

(Baseline: data available in 1991)

Objective #7.10

Related Objectives

Health Status

Reduce assault injuries among people aged 12 and older to no more than 10 per 1,000 people.

(Baseline: 11.1 per 1,000 in 1986)

Objective #7.6

Educational and Community- Based Programs

Risk Reduction

Increase the high school graduation rate to at least 90 percent, thereby reducing risks for multiple problem behaviors and poor mental and physical health.

(Baseline: 79 percent of people aged 20 through 21 had graduated from high school with a regular diploma in 1989)

Objective #8.2

Service and Protection

Establish community health promotion programs that separately or together address at least three of the Healthy People 2000 priorities and reach at least 40 percent of each state's population.

(Baseline data available in 1992)

Objective #8.10

Related Objectives

Services and Protection

Increase to at least 75 percent the proportion of people aged 10 and older who have discussed issues related to nutrition, physical activity, sexual behavior, tobacco, alcohol, other drugs, or safety with family members on at least one occasion during the preceding month.

(Baseline data available in 1991)

Objective #8.9

Unintentional Injuries

Health Status

Reduce deaths among youth aged 15 through 24 caused by motor vehicle crashes to no more than 33 per 100,000 people

(Baseline: 36.9 per 100,000 people in 1987)

Objective #9.3b

Health Status

Reduce drowning deaths to no more than 1.3 per 100,000 people.

Special Population Targets

Drowning deaths per 100,000	1987 Baseline	2000 Target
Men aged 15-34	4.5	2.5
Black males	6.6	3.6

(Age-adjusted baseline: 2.1 per 100,000 in1987)

Objective #9.5

Health Status

Reduce nonfatal spinal cord injuries so that hospitalizations for this condition are no more than 5.0 per 100,000 people.

(Baseline: 5.9 per 100,000 in 1988)

Objective #9.10

Risk Reduction

Increase use of helmets to at least 80 percent of motorcyclists and at least 50 percent of bicyclists.

(Baseline: 60 percent of motorcyclists in 1988 and an estimated 8 percent of bicyclists in 1984)

Objective #9.13

Environmental Health

Health Status

Reduce asthma morbidity, as measured by a reduction in asthma hospitalizations, to no more than 160 per100,000 people.

Special Population Targets

Hospitalizations per 100,000	1987Baseline	2000 Target
Blacks and other nonwhites	334	265
Children (aged 14 and younger)	284	225

(Baseline: 188 per 100,000 in 1987)

Objective #11.1

Oral Health

Reduce dental caries (cavities) so that the proportion of children with one or more caries... is no more than 60 percent among adolescents aged 15.

Special Population Target

Prevalence of caries 1983-4	Baseline	2000 Target
American Indian/Alaskan Native aged 15	93%	70%

(Baseline: 75 percent of adolescents aged 15 in 1986-7)

Objective #13.1

Reduce untreated dental caries so that the proportion of children with untreated caries is no more than... 15 percent among adolescents aged 15.

Special Population Targets

Untreated dental caries	1986-7 Baseline	2000 Target
Adolescents aged 15 whose parents have less than a high school education	41%	25%
American Indian/Alaskan Native adolescents aged 15	84%*	40%
Black adolescents aged 15	38%	20%
Hispanic adolescents aged 15	31-47%**	25%

  *1983-84 baseline
**1982-84 baseline

(Baseline: 23 percent of adolescents aged 15 in 1986-7)

Objective #13.2

Increase to at least 50 percent the proportion of children who have received protective sealants on the occlusal (chewing) surfaces of permanent molar teeth.

(Baseline: 11 percent of children aged 8 and 8 percent of adolescents aged 14 in 1986-7)

Objective #13.8

Maternal and Infant Health

Related Objectives

**Health
Status**

Reduce the maternal morality rate to no more than 3.3 per 100,000 live births.

Special Population Target

Maternal Mortality	1987 Baseline	2000 Target
Blacks	14.2*	5*

*per 100,000 live births

(Baseline: 6.6 per 100,000 in 1987

Objective #14.3

**Health
Status**

Reduce the incidence of fetal alcohol syndrome to no more than 0.12 per 1,000 live births.

Special Population Target

Incidence per 1,000 births	1987 Baseline	2000 Target
American Indians and Alaskan Natives	4	2
Blacks	0.8	0.4

(Baseline: 0.22 per 1,000 live births in 1987)

Objective #14.4

**Risk
Reduction**

Reduce low birth weight to an incidence of no more than 5 percent of live births and very low birth weight to no more than 1 percent of live births.

Special Population Target

Incidence	1987 Baseline	2000 Target
Low Birth Weight-Blacks	12.7%	9%
Very Low Birth Weight-Blacks	2.7%	2%

(Baseline: 6.9 and 1.2 percent, respectively, in 1987)

Objective #14.5

**Risk
Reduction**

Increase to at least 85 percent the proportion of women who achieve the minimum recommended weight gain during their pregnancies.

(Baseline: 67 percent of married women in 1980)

Objective #14.6

Risk Reduction

Reduce severe complications of pregnancy to no more than 15 per 100 deliveries.

(Baseline: 22 hospitalizations prior to delivery per 100 deliveries in 1987)

Objective #14.7

Risk Reduction

Increase abstinence from tobacco use by pregnant women to at least 90 percent and increase abstinence from alcohol, cocaine, and marijuana by pregnant women by at least 20 percent.

(Baseline: 75 percent of pregnant women abstained from tobacco use in 1985)

Objective #14.10

Services and Protection

Increase to at least 90 percent the proportion of all pregnant women who receive prenatal care in the first trimester of pregnancy.

(Baseline: 76 percent of live births in 1987)

Special Population Targets

Proportion of Pregnant Women Receiving Early Prenatal Care	1987 Baseline	2000 Target
Black Women	61.1*	90*
American Indian/Alaska Native	60.2*	90*
Hispanic Women	61.0*	90*

*Percent of live births

Objective #14.11

Services and Protection

Increase to at least 90 percent the proportion of pregnant women and infants who receive risk-appropriate care.

(Baseline data available in 1991)

Objective #14.14

HIV Infection

Risk Reduction

Increase to at least 60 percent the proportion of sexually active, unmarried young women aged 15 through 19 whose partners have used a condom at last sexual intercourse .

(Baseline: 26 percent of sexually active, unmarried, young women reported that their partners used a condom at last sexual intercourse in 1988)

Objective #18.4a and 19.10a

Increase to at least 75 percent the proportion of sexually active, unmarried young men aged 15 through 19 who used a condom at last intercourse.

(Baseline: 57 percent of sexually active, unmarried young men reported that they used a condom at last sexual intercourse in 1988)

Objective #18.4b amd 19.10b

Related Objectives

Increase to at least 50 percent the estimated proportion of all intravenous drug abusers who are in drug abuse treatment programs.

(Baseline: An estimated 11 percent of opiate abusers were in treatment in 1989)

Objective #18,5

Increase to at least 50 percent the estimated proportion of intravenous drug abusers not in treatment who use only uncontaminated drug paraphernalia ("works").

(Baseline: 25 to 35 percent of opiate abusers in 1989)

Objective #18.6

Sexually Transmitted Diseases

Reduce gonorrhea among adolescents 15-19 to no more than 750 cases per 100,000.

(Baseline: 1,123 per 100,000 in 1989)

Objective #19.1b

Immunization and Infectious Diseases

Reduce indigenous cases of vaccine-preventable diseases as follows:

Disease:	1988 Baseline per 100,000	2000 Target per 100,000
Diptheria among those 25 and younger	1	0
Tetanus among those 25 and younger	3	0
Polio (wild type virus) Measles	3,058	0
Rubella	225	0
Congenital Rubella Syndrome	6	0
Mumps	4,866	500
Pertussis	3,450	1,000

Objective #20.1

Clinical Preventive Services

Risk Reduction

Increase to at least 50 percent the proportion of adolescents aged 13 through 18 who have received, as a minimum within the appropriate interval, all of the screening and immunization services and at least one of the counseling services appropriate for their age and gender as recommended by the U.S. Preventive Services Task Force.

(Baseline data available in 1991)

Objective #21.2c

Table 1-2 Year 2000 Objectives for Schools

Services and Protection

Increase to at least 90 percent the proportion of school lunch and breakfast services and child care food services with menus that are consistent with the nutrition principles in the Dietary Guidelines for Americans.

(Baseline data available in 1993)

Objective #2.17

Services and Protection

Increase to at least 75 percent the proportion of the nation's schools that provide nutrition education from preschool through 12th grade, preferably as part of quality school health education.

(Baseline data available in 1991)

Objective #2.19

Services and Protection

Establish tobacco-free environments and include tobacco use prevention in the curricula of all elementary, middle, and secondary schools, preferably as part of quality school health education.

(Baseline: 17 percent of school districts totally banned smoking on school premises or at school functions in 1988; anti-smoking education was provided by 78 percent of school districts at the high school level, 81 percent at the middle school level, and 75 percent at the elementary school level in 1988)

Objective #3.10

Services and Protection

Provide to children in all school districts and private and secondary school educational programs on alcohol and other drugs, preferably as a part of quality school health education.

(Baseline: 63 percent provided some instruction, 39 percent provided counseling, and 23 percent referred students for clinical assessments in 1987)

Objective #4.13

Services and Protection

Increase to at least 50 percent the proportion of elementary and secondary schools that teach nonviolent Protection conflict resolution skills, preferably as a part of quality school health education.

(Baseline data available in 1991)

Objective #7.16

Services and Protection

Increase to at least 75 percent the proportion of the nation's elementary and secondary schools that provide planned and sequential kindergarten through 12th grade quality school health education.

(Baseline data available in 1991)

Objective #8.4

Services and Protection

Increase to at least 50 percent the proportion of post-secondary institutions with institution wide health promotion programs for students, faculty, and staff.

(Baseline: At least 20 percent of higher education institutions offered health promotion activities for students in 1989-90)

Objective #8.5

Services and Protection

Provide academic instruction on injury prevention and control, preferably as part of quality school health education, in at least 50 percent of public school systems (grades K through 12).

(Baseline data available in I992)

Objective #9.18

Services and Protection

Extend requirement of the use of effective head, face, eye, and mouth protection to all organizations, agencies, and institutions sponsoring sporting and recreation events that pose risks of injury.

(Baseline: Only National Collegiate Athletic Association football,hockey, and lacrosse; high school football; amateur boxing; and amateur ice hockey in 1988)

Objective #9.19, 13.16

Services and Protection

Increase to at least 95 percent the proportion of schools that have age-appropriate HIV education curricula for students in 4th through 12th grade, preferably as part of quality school health education.

Objective #18.10

(Baseline: 66 percent of school districts required HIV education but only 5 percent required HIV education in each year for 7th through 12th grade in 1989)

Note: Strategies to achieve this objective must be undertaken sensitively to avoid indirectly encouraging or condoning sexual activity among teens who are not yet sexually active.

Services and Protection

Provide HIV education for students and staff in at least 90 percent of colleges and universities.

(Baseline data available in 1995)

Objective #18.11

Services and Protection

Include instruction in sexually transmitted disease transmission prevention in the curricula of all middle and secondary schools, perferably as part of quality school health education

Objective #19.12

(Baseline: 95 percent of schools reported offering at least one class on sexually transmitted diseases as part of their standard curricula in 1988)

Note: Strategies to achieve this objective must be undertaken sensitively to avoid indirectly encouraging or condoning sexual activity among teens who are not yet sexually active.

References

1. Agency for Toxic Substances and Disease Registry.(1988) *The Nature and Extent of Lead Poisoning in Children in the United States: A Report to Congress*. Washington, DC: U.S. Department of Health and Human Services.

2. American School Health Association, Association for the Advancement of Health Education, Society for Public Health Education. (1988) "National Adolescent Student Health Survey," *Journal of Health Education*. August/September, 4-8. Statistics from this article reprinted with permission from the *Journal of Health Education*, a publication of the American Alliance for Health, Physical Education, Recreation, and Dance, 1900 Association Drive, Reston, Virginia, 22091.

3. Bellah, R., et.al. (1985) *Habits of the Heart*. New York: Perennial Library.

4. Centers for Disease Control. (1986) *Homicide Surveillance: High Risk Racial and Ethnic Groups, Black and Hispanics, 1970 to 1983*. Atlanta, GA: U.S. Department of Health and Human Services.

5. Clarfield, A.M. (1988) "The reversible dementias: Do they reverse?" *Annuals of Internal Medicine*. (109) 476-86.

6. Furstenberg, F.F. Jr. (1976) *Unplanned Parenthood: The Social Consequences of Teenage Childbearing*. New York: Free Press.

7. Hall, J.R. (1985) " A decade of detectors: Measuring the effect." *Fire Journal*. (79), 37-43.

8. *Healthy People 2000: National Health Promotion and Disease Prevention Objectives*. (1991) U.S. Department of Health and Human Services, U.S. Government Office.

9. *Healthy Youth 2000: National Health Promotion and Disease Prevention Objectives for Adolescents*. (1991) American Medical Association Healthier Youth by the Year 2000 Project. Chicago, Illinois: American Medical Association.

10. Kubler-Ross, E. (1975) *Death: The Final Stage of Growth*. Englewood Cliffs, NJ.

11. McKinley,JB. (1979)"A case for refocusing up stream: the political economy of illness." In e.g. Jaco (ed.), *Patients, physicians, and illness: a sourcebook in behavioral sciences and health*. New York: Free Press, 9-25.

12. Mecham, P.J. et al.(1990) "Suicide attempts among adults." Paper presented at the 39th Annual Epidemic Intelligence Service Conference, Atlanta, GA.

13. Meeks, L., Heit, P., and Burt, J. (1992) *Education for Sexuality and HIV/ AIDS: Curriculum and Teaching Strategies*. Columbus: Meeks Heit Publishing Company.

14. National Center for Health Statistics. (1990) *Health, United States, 1989 and Prevention Profile*. DHHS Pub. No. (PHS) 90-1232. Hyattsville, MD: U.S. Department of Health and Human Services.

15. National Highway Traffic Safety Administration. (1988) *Fatal Accident Reporting System, 1987*. Washington, D.C.: U.S. Department of Transportation.

16. National Highway Traffic Safety Administration's 19 Cities Survey, U.S. Department of Transportation, Washington, D.C.

17. National Institute on Drug Abuse. (1989) *National Survey Results from High School, College, and Young Adult Populations 1975-1988*. DHHS Pub. No. (ADM) 89-1638. Washington, DC: U.S. Department of Health and Human Services.

18. National Research Council. (1987) *Risking the Future: Adolescent Sexuality, Pregnancy, and Childbearing*. Washington, DC: National Academy Press.

19. O'Rourke, T. (1989) "AAHE Scholar Presentation-Reflections On Directions in Health Education: Implications for Policy and Practice," *Health Education*. 20(6): 4-14.

20. "Report of the 1990 Joint Committee on Health Education Terminology," (1991) *Health Education*. 22(2): 97-108.

21. U.S. Department of Health and Human Services. (1987) "National children and youth fitness study II," *Journal of Physical Education, Recreation, and Dance*. 58: 50-96.

Along with the school nurse, you, the teacher will play an integral role in school health services. Through school health services, you will be in a position to appraise, protect, and promote the health of your students. Through school health services, you will have access to health care services that prevent and control communicable diseases, provide emergency care for injury or sudden illness, and provide learning opportunities conducive to the maintenance and promotion of individual and community health. The school nurse can serve as a major link between you and the students for whom you are responsible.

THE SCHOOL NURSE AND HEALTH SERVICES

There are many different roles played by the school nurse. Some of these roles have been managed in the traditional sense. Among these roles are:

1. Maintain individual health records and histories.
2. Interpret the results of health appraisals.
3. Provide information to school personnel about community health resources.
4. Perform health screening in such areas as scoliosis, head lice, vision, and hearing.
5. Help students seek help for personal health problems.
6. Provide emergency care for injuries and illnesses.
7. Counsel parents, students, and teachers about special health concerns.
8. Assist in the identification of students who need special health-related attention.

Recently, the role of the school nurse has expanded to include involvement in the health education program. Many college preparation programs provide nurses with the skills they need to teach health education. In many school districts, the school nurse is also a health educator. The school nurse serves on curriculum and textbook committees, implements faculty wellness programs, and offers health education inservice programs for faculty.

Unfortunately, the standards for school nurses in the United States are not uniform. In many school systems, school nurses are the first people in a school terminated when there are budget cuts. In many school districts, there are too few school nurses. Ideally, there should be a school nurse in every school. But often, there may be one nurse assigned for an entire school district if that school district is small. Some school districts will employ health aides to assist the school nurse. Health aides may perform tasks such as handling clerical responsibilities, answering telephones, and arranging screening examinations. Health aides can be extremely helpful to the school nurse.

THE TEACHER AND HEALTH SERVICES

As a teacher, you are in a position to observe when students deviate from the norm physically, mentally, emotionally, and socially. You will be able to suspect and detect abnormalities, thus placing you in the position to refer students to the appropriate person or agency. Your role does not involve diagnosing diseases, illnesses, or injuries. It involves recording observations and getting prompt help in emergency situations.

As a teacher, you are in a position to observe when a student's appearance, behavior, and/or emotional expression seems unusual. You are responsible for intervening on behalf of the student. (See Table 2-1, Conditions Requiring Special Attention.) The principal, guidance counselor, or school nurse needs to be notified of your observations. But referring a student for help does not mean that your responsibility has been fulfilled. Once a student has been referred, it is important for you to follow through on what interventions are being implemented. For the majority of the student health problems that arise in school, perhaps no two people play a more significant role than that of the teacher and school nurse.

SCHOOL HEALTH SERVICES: PROMOTING STUDENT HEALTH

2

Table 2-1
CONDITIONS REQUIRING SPECIAL ATTENTION

General Conditions

Fever, very thin or overweight, extreme changes in weight, tired expressions such as yawning and rubbing eyes, pale or flushed skin, rashes, nausea, lethargic, irritable toward peers, prone to accidents, uncoordinated, wants to be excused from activities, stomachaches, headaches, dizziness.

Eyes

Crossed or turned out, watery, repeated styes, red, crusted eyelids, holding materials too close to eyes, squinting or frowning, favors one eye, rubs eyes, desires to sit near front of room, cannot see clearly.

Ears

Discharge from ear, excess wax, picking ear, tilts or turns head to one side, monotone or poor voice pitch, speech problems, leans forward when someone speaks, asks for things to be repeated, ringing in ears, asks teacher to talk louder.

Skin and Scalp

Rashes or sores, acne and blackheads, nits on hair, bald spots, hives, scratching, keeping certain areas covered, pain on touch, rough areas on skin.

Nose, Throat, and Mouth

Irregular teeth, excess tartar on teeth, cracks in corner of mouth, halitosis, persistent mouth breathing, bleeding gums, nasal discharge, stuffy nose, coughing, wheezing, shortness of breath, picks teeth, toothaches, sore throat, difficulty breathing.

SPECIAL HEALTH CONCERNS

You will be faced with many responsibilities that were nonexistent a number of years ago. With the number of students who come to school with health-related complaints and problems, you will be asked to expand your responsibilities. The kinds of problems with which students come to school are varied and many. In this part of the chapter, the major health issues and concerns will be addressed.

Abuse

As a teacher, you will be in a position to recognize cases of child abuse. **Child abuse** is maltreatment of a child under the age of 18. There are four kinds of child abuse - physical abuse, emotional abuse, neglect, and sexual abuse. By law, any teacher or health professional must report suspected cases of abuse. For the most part, school districts have specific policies about the reporting of abuse. A teacher who reports a case of suspected abuse has immunity from civil and criminal liability. When an abuse case is filed, the identity of the person doing the reporting remains confidential. Reports of child abuse are often made to child welfare agencies or the police. Most reported cases of child abuse will be investigated rapidly. If an investigation indicates that a child is in danger, that child will be placed in protective custody or in a foster home.

Child abuse occurs in all sectors of society. It occurs to children whose families are living in poverty, wealth, urban areas, suburban areas, and rural counties. Abusers can be men, women, other children, and community workers. In 85-90 percent of cases, the abuser is a family member.

How would you, as a teacher, know if a student in your class was being or has been abused? The student might tell you (s)he is being abused. If this were to happen, it would be extremely important that you report the abuse to your principal and/or follow procedures established in your school district. While this information may be shared with you in strictest confidence by the student, you have an obligation to report it promptly to protect the student and to abide by the law.

In most cases of abuse, the abused student tells no one. Help is provided only when a responsible, caring adult recognizes the signs and symptoms and obtains help for the student. You can be aware of these signs and symptoms and of other characteristics that will help you assist students who are abused.

Physical Abuse

Physical abuse is maltreatment that harms the body. A student who is unusually bruised may be suffering from physical abuse. Bruises may appear on the back, genitals, face, eyes, and buttocks. Sometimes the outline of a hand or implement used to cause the bruise is evident. For example, a student may have an imprint of a stick or electrical cord where the contact was made. There may be strap marks around the buttocks or back. Some bruises may be red or reddish-blue in color. Other bruises may be yellow or pale green indicating that the healing process has begun.

Sometimes heavy implements are used to inflict pain. A student may have been hit with a baseball bat or a heavy rubber tube. In these cases, bruises may not be evident, yet internal injury to the muscles and internal organs may be evident on an x-ray.

The presence of burn marks is another indication of physical abuse. Burns may result from being forcibly held in hot water. This is usually evident by burns around the buttocks and genitals since the student is usually held in a jackknife position in a bath tub. Cigarette burns are common indicators of physical abuse. They are often found on the palms of the hand, the soles of the feet, and the back.

Biting is another form of inflicting physical abuse on a child. Any part of the body can be bitten. Usually, bite marks are evident. In many cases, tooth impressions are used as evidence in abuse cases.

Other signs that a student has been physically abused include internal injuries, fractures, especially of the long bones, and abrasions on different body parts.

Neglect

Neglect is maltreatment that involves lack of proper care and guidance. A parent may not follow practices that protect a child from injury. A parent may not provide adequate food, shelter, clothing, or medical care for his or her child. Neglect may involve not arranging for adequate supervision when parents are not home. Parents who do not arrange for adequate supervision in their absence leave their children vulnerable to suffer from injury and violence.

The following may indicate neglect:

- A student is always hungry and appears sleepy.
- A student wears dirty, smelly, and tattered clothing.
- A student does not receive medical attention when it appears needed.

If the home in which a neglected student lives is visited, one may find that the conditions in the home are unsanitary, there is no food in the refrigerator, water and electricity are not present, and the living areas are untidy. Some of these conditions may exist in many homes, but extreme cases indicate neglect.

Emotional Abuse

Emotional abuse is maltreatment that involves assault in a nonphysical way. For example, excessive verbal assaults may take the form of threatening, yelling, belittling, and blaming. Ignoring a child and not communicating in any way is also a form of emotional abuse.

You may have students in your class who are suffering from emotional abuse. There are signs that may be indicative of emotional abuse:

- The student is depressed and/or apathetic.
- The student exhibits behavioral difficulties.
- The student withdraws from peers.
- The student verbally indicates that (s)he is being emotionally abused. The student might say, "My father always tells me he doesn't care about me."

Just as physical abuse is dangerous, so is emotional abuse. The student may have low self-esteem. This student may believe that he or she cannot succeed at anything. Students who are emotionally abused are more likely to attempt suicide.

Unfortunately, determining emotional abuse may be difficult. Unlike other kinds of abuse, determining emotional abuse is more subjective. If a teacher suspects emotional abuse, the school psychologist or another responsible individual in the school should be notified. Most likely, counseling can be recommended for the family to handle this condition.

Sexual Abuse

Sexual abuse is maltreatment that involves inappropriate sexual behavior between an adult and a child. Sexual abuse can take many different forms. It can consist of a single incident of sexual contact or prolonged sexual contact between an adult and a child. Kinds of sexual abuse include rape, incest, lewd acts upon a child, oral or genital intercourse, penetration of any object into the genitalia or anus, or any form of sexual molestation. Exploitation can consist of promoting minors to engage in sex acts, being used to produce pornography, or encouraging and promoting prostitution.

Admitting to another person that one has been sexually abused can be very difficult. A person may feel unjustly ashamed and guilty. However, television programs, articles in newspapers and magazines, and school-based educational programs on sexual assault have prompted students to tell someone they have been sexually abused.

You can be aware of behaviors that indicate a

student may have been abused. If a student has only one of the behaviors or signs, sexual abuse may have occurred. If a student has more than one behavior or sign, the likelihood of sexual abuse is increased. The behaviors and signs include:

- Indirect questions about sexual abuse. For example, during a classroom discussion, a student says, "What could I do if I think a friend of mine is being abused sexually?" Often, students make statements in the third person when in effect, they are telling you about personal abuse.
- The presence of a sexually transmitted disease.
- Pregnancy.
- Itching or scratching in the genital or anal area.
- A strong knowledge of sexual terms and behavior.
- Inappropriate sexual acting out with friends and younger children.
- A strong curiosity about sexual matters.
- Problems with schoolwork.
- Poor relationships with peers.
- Crying and depression in school.
- Attempted suicide.
- Fear of using public showers or restrooms.
- Difficulty walking or sitting due to pain in the genital area or anus.
- Discharge or infection in the genital area.

Incest is the most common forms of sexual abuse. Most often, heterosexual contact takes place between a father, stepfather, or mother's boyfriend and a young girl. The second most common type of incest is homosexual contact involving male family members and a boy. Incest involving a female adult and a girl or boy is less common.

A student who is sexually abused may have difficulty sharing information about this abuse. The student may fear that his or her parent will be penalized by law enforcement authorities. The student may worry that the family will break up. As a result, the student is reluctant to report the abuse.

AIDS

One of the most pressing issues in recent times is that of AIDS, acquired immune deficiency syndrome. Many issues about AIDS are school-related. Should teachers in schools teach about AIDS? Should students who are HIV infected or have AIDS be permitted to attend school? Can other students in school become infected from the student who has tested positive for HIV or has AIDS? To best understand about AIDS, the teacher needs basic information about this condition.

By definition, **AIDS** is a condition in which the immune system cannot defend the body, leaving the body vulnerable to opportunistic infections. Many people often use the word AIDS when they mean infected with HIV. When HIV enters the body, a person is said to be infected with HIV. Being infected with HIV does not mean a person has AIDS. Only after the presence of certain signs and symptoms is a person diagnosed as having AIDS. It may take ten or more years from the time a person is infected with HIV until the time that AIDS will develop. According to former Surgeon General Koop, any combination of the following signs and symptoms indicate potential HIV infection:

- Rapid weight loss for no apparent reason.
- Recurring fever or night sweats.
- Swollen lymph glands.
- Diarrhea that lasts for more than one week.
- White spots or unusual blemishes on the tongue, in the mouth, or in the throat.
- Memory loss, depression, and other neurological disorders.
- Persistent dry cough or shortness of breath.
- Recent appearance of pink or purple blotches under the skin or inside the mouth, nose or eyelids.
- Recurring infections.[3]

HIV is transmitted in different ways. The major modes of transmission in adults include sexual contact with an infected partner and sharing an infected needle to inject IV drugs. The most common way HIV is transmitted sexually is by male-to-male sexual contact. However, heterosexual transmission is rapidly increasing. IV drug use is the next most common mode of transmission. A third mode of transmission involves an HIV positive woman infecting her offspring during pregnancy. Her baby is born HIV positive and develops AIDS during childhood.

A fourth mode of transmission involves a person receiving HIV-infected blood through a blood transfusion. This is no longer a major method of transmission because all blood is screened before it is used.

There are many implications of HIV/AIDS for schools. The federal government as well as most states have developed guidelines for school districts to follow regarding HIV/AIDS. Children who are infected with HIV should be allowed to attend school. Children who are infected with HIV and who bite, vomit, or cannot control their bowels or bladder should not attend school. School personnel should follow guidelines to protect against infection. Body fluids that are spilled should be wiped immediately with a one to ten dilution of chlorox while wearing rubber gloves. Students with HIV should not attend school if there is an outbreak of communicable diseases such as flu since these students have a weakened immune system. Becoming infected with a communicable disease can be serious. If a student must be excluded from school, that student should have the right to receive an alternative education.

To date, education is considered the best way to prevent HIV infection as there is no vaccine currently available.[2] According to the U.S. Department of Health and Human Services, there are guidelines school personnel can follow for implementing effective AIDS education programs.[3] There are a variety of materials that meet these guidelines. Table 2-2 identifies the important objectives covered in a responsible and effective AIDS education program.

Table 2-2
A Responsible and Effective AIDS Education Program

Grades One and Two
Students will:
- define what germs are.
- explain what a virus is.
- recognize that there are different kinds of viruses.
- identify ways viruses can be spread.
- recognize that the body has cells that fight germs.
- describe how vaccines are used to fight germs.
- explain that AIDS is caused by a virus.
- discuss why a person with AIDS may get many illnesses.
- explain that the AIDS virus can be spread through blood.
- identify grown-ups with whom they could talk about AIDS.
- list ways people cannot get the AIDS virus.
- realize that there is no medicine or vaccine for AIDS.

Source: Meeks, L. and P. Heit. (1991) *About You*. Columbus: Merrill Publishing Company.

Grades Three and Four
Students will:
- describe ways in which germs are spread.
- describe how T-cells and antibodies help protect a person from illness.
- explain why the AIDS virus is dangerous.
- describe ways the AIDS virus is spread.
- describe ways the AIDS virus is not spread.
- describe what it is like to have AIDS.

Source: Meeks, L. and P. Heit. (1991) *Your Family*. Columbus: Merrill Publishing Company.

Grades Five and Six
Students will:
- discuss the role of the immune system in protecting against disease.
- define AIDS and explain how infection with HIV breaks down the immune system.

- explain how HIV is transmitted through sexual contact.
- explain how HIV is transmitted through IV drug use.
- explain how a pregnant female may infect her unborn child with HIV if she is infected.
- identify ways HIV infection has not occurred to this date.
- discuss the signs and symptoms and the progression of AIDS.
- describe how a diagnosis of AIDS is made.
- identify ways to never become infected with HIV.

Source: Meeks, L. and P. Heit (1991) *Your Relationships*. Columbus: Merrill Publishing Company.

Junior and Senior High School
Students will:
- define immunity and describe the role of body defenses in protecting the body against disease.
- explain how HIV infection results in a breakdown of the immune system.
- explain why opportunistic infections develop in persons with AIDS.
- identify body fluids in which HIV is present in high concentrations.
- discuss ways in which HIV can be transmitted during sexual contact and intravenous drug use.
- explain why it is risky to be sexually active, have multiple sex partners, and/ or have sex with a prostitute.
- discuss reasons why use of drugs such as alcohol, marijuana, and cocaine may increase the chances of engaging in risk behaviors.
- identify ways that HIV is not transmitted.
- discuss why abstinence is a responsible choice for teens.
- identify refusal skills for saying NO to sex and drugs.
- discuss reasons why sexually active teens should change their behavior.
- explain that a latex condom with nonoxynol-9 reduces the likelihood of infections with HIV, but is not 100% effective.
- discuss testing procedures for HIV and the importance of early treatment.
- conclude that a person who has HIV will always have it.
- identify signs and symptoms of AIDS including characteristics of Kaposi's sarcoma, pneumocystis carinii pneumonia, and AIDS dementia complex.
- discuss drugs such as AZT and research into vaccines.
- identify school policies for HIV/AIDS.
- discuss the loss of loved ones with AIDS.
- identify changes in health care due to AIDS.

Source: L. Meeks and P. Heit. (1991) *AIDS: Understanding and Prevention*. Columbus: Glencoe.

Asthma

Asthma is an allergic disease of the lungs manifest by constrictions of the small air passages called bronchioles. An asthma attack causes a person to have difficulty breathing. Most cases of asthma are moderate although a number of young children have severe asthma. Children may be treated with shots or medications taken orally. If treatment is needed during the school day, the parent can make arrangements with the school nurse. The school nurse has directions to follow if a child has an attack. Many children use an inhaler to get medicine that helps them breathe easier. If a child is using an inhaler, it is important that it be used correctly. It should be held about three inches from the mouth. The child should exhale as strongly as possible and then inhale the mist from the inhaler as deeply as possible.

Death

At some time, you will be faced with a student in your class who has experienced the death of a loved one. Perhaps a student's grandparent died. Maybe a parent died from a sudden or prolonged illness. A student's pet might have died.

A student who suffers a loss will experience any number of reactions. Death of a parent is the most stressful life event for a school-age child. The kind of reaction that a student has will often depend on the situation. For example, when a family member had a prolonged illness prior to death, a student may have already begun the grieving process. The family influences how a student adjusts to the death. A student whose family discusses death in an open and honest manner will be able to grieve openly and share feelings more easily than a student whose family does not share feelings and information about death. The age of a student also determines how he or she reacts to death. For the first five years of life, a child does not comprehend the meaning of death. The child believes that death is temporary and sleeplike. Between ages five and nine, children understand the finality of death and that death can be caused by an environmental force. Once a child is past the age of nine, death will be seen as a part of the life cycle. Death is viewed as being able to happen to anyone.

Elisabeth Kubler Ross identified five stages that accompany dying and death. These are denial, anger, bargaining, depression, and acceptance. At first, children experience denial. They do not believe that someone they know or to whom they have been close has died. When they realize the person will not return, they are angry. Then they bargain believing the person can come back. They focus on it not being fair to have this loss. This is followed by depression and sadnesses.

Guilt may accompany depression. Much support is needed. Young people can be vulnerable to thoughts of their own death. Finally, acceptance is reached. But, remember in young people the grieving process is not short.

There are ways that you can help a student who has experienced the death of someone to whom he or she was close.

1. Do not shield students from or mislead them about death. Students need to know that death is not temporary and it is not like sleeping.
2. When questions are raised, give simple, direct answers. For example, a student asks, "Why did my grandma die?" An appropriate answer is, "Grandma was very ill for a long time and her heart finally stopped beating." If the student is given a discourse that is extremely complex and long, confusion may result.
3. Answer questions as they arise. If you do not have an answer to a question, indicate so. But you can tell the child you will try to find an answer.
4. Recognize that students need to grieve. Remember the five stages. Help the students understand the grieving process. For example, if a student acts out in angry ways, you might say, "You are very angry that your father died. I can understand you feel it is unfair." This helps the student understand feelings.
5. Watch for signs of severe depression. Remember students are especially vulnerable if a parent dies. Extra support is needed.

Diabetes

Diabetes is a condition in which the pancreas produces too little or no insulin. Insulin regulates the sugar in the blood. There are two types of diabetes. Type I is called juvenile-onset diabetes. Type II is called adult-onset diabetes. The age at which a child develops type I diabetes is usually between eleven and thirteen years of age. However, type I can occur at any age during childhood. It is very rare that a child will develop type II diabetes. Type I diabetes will be discussed because it is the type you will see in the school setting.

The symptoms of type I diabetes include frequent urination, thirst, weight and appetite loss. There may also be blurred vision, itching, and infections of the skin. These symptoms can progress rapidly. If diabetes is suspected, a school nurse may be able to have a student take a urine test. School nurses have urine test paper strips that can be used to detect diabetes.

As a teacher, it is important to understand that a student who has diabetes can suffer from fluctuations in blood sugar levels. Therefore, any unusual behavior of a student who has diabetes can be indicative of an imbalance of blood sugar.

Students who have type I diabetes always need to take insulin. In most cases, they will receive doses of insulin at home - in the morning before school and in the early evening after coming home from school. It is important that a student who has diabetes follow a strict diet. Meals are to be eaten at specific times during the day.

The teacher needs to be aware of complications that may occur. The most common complication is **hypoglycemia** or low blood sugar. Hypoglycemia is caused by too much insulin in the body. The signs and symptoms of hypoglycemia include pale skin, blurred vision, trembling, sweating, and rapid pulse. If this happens, the student should be given a glass of milk or orange juice. If not treated, confusion, disorientation, and possible unconsciousness can result. This will cause the sugar in the blood to rise.

Another complication of diabetes is **diabetic acidosis** which is elevated sugar in the blood. Symptoms include thirst, loss of appetite, increased urination, nausea and vomiting. Diabetic acidosis is treated with insulin.

Drug Abuse

One of the most pressing health problems among school-age youth is the abuse of drugs. When discussing drug-related problems, one must be aware of the many different types of drugs that are used and abused. Drugs that are most often abused include stimulants, depressants, hallucinogens, marijuana. alcohol, tobacco, and anabolic steroids. A question that often arises is, "How would I know if a student in my class is using drugs?" Signs and symptoms that indicate a student might be abusing drugs are:

1. Neglect of personal hygiene and appearance.
2. Depression, irritability, and mood swings.
3. A decline in academic performance.
4. A change in friendships to those who are suspected of using drugs.
5. Inability to remain alert.
6. A fascination with drug-related music and drawings.
7. Stealing.
8. Possessing drug paraphernalia.

Alcohol

Alcohol is a depressant drug found in beverages such as beer, wine, and whiskey. Alcohol is one of the most commonly abused drugs of school-age youth. According to the Department of Health and Human Services, nine out of ten high school seniors drank alcohol at least once in the previous month.[4] One-in-

four families are affected by a family member who drinks. Young people who have alcohol-related problems may exhibit one or more of the following signs and symptoms:

- Drinking secretively.
- Lying about drinking.
- Drinking during times of stress or worry.
- Gulping drinks.
- Trying to find parties where alcoholic beverages will be served.
- Preoccupation with drinking.
- Declining grades.
- Decrease in muscular coordination.
- Not following through on class projects.
- Becoming irritable too easily.

Many students are affected by the drinking behavior of family members. Students may come to school tense and inappropriately fed. They may withdraw so that they do not call attention to drinking problems at home. Students who come from families in which drinking is a problem often have low self-esteem and do not want to invite friends back to their home for fear of being embarrassed by a parent who is drunk. Because of the behavior they experience at home, these students are more likely to begin drinking themselves. With recent research concerning a genetic link to alcoholism, students from families where there is alcoholism have an especially high risk. Table 2-3 identifies additional high risk factors for alcohol in adolescence.

Marijuana

Marijuana is a drug derived from the hemp plant that is often abused by students. Students who use marijuana, especially those who use marijuana regularly develop amotivational syndrome. Students with **amotivational syndrome** report being apathetic, having a lack of concern toward friends and schoolwork, and lacking motivation. They often will not show any enthusiasm about anything. When marijuana use is discontinued, these symptoms may disappear. But when marijuana use continues, they lapse back to the same signs and symptoms they exhibited during initial use.

You can recognize marijuana use by amotivational syndrome and body odor that will appear on the clothes of students using marijuana.

Designer Drugs

Designer drugs are synthetic forms of illegal drugs that differ in chemical structure from known illegal drugs. These drugs are supposed to simulate the effects of the more common types of illegal drugs. For example, MDMA, also known as ecstasy, is a designer drug that is made in the home by amateur chemists. Designer drugs are particularly harmful because they contain unknown quantities and combinations of

Table 2-3
High-Risk Factors for Alcohol and Other Drug Problems in Adolescence

The following risk factors are important at different development periods, but the more of them present in a student's life, the greater the threat of adolescent drug use.

Community Risk Factors:
• Economic and social deprivation;
• Low neighborhood attachment and community disorganization;
• Community laws and norms favorable toward use; and
• Availability of drugs, including alcohol and tobacco.

Family Risk Factors:
• Family management problems;
• Family history of alcoholism;
• Parental drug use and positive attitudes toward use; and
• Low expectations for children's success.

School Risk Factors:
• Academic failure;
• Transitions from elementary to middle to high school to college;
• Little commitment to school; and
• Lack of enforcement of school policies.

Individual and Peer Risk Factors:
• Early antisocial behavior and peer rejection;
• Alienation, rebelliousness, and lack of social bonding;
• Antisocial behavior in late childhood and early adolescence;
• Friends who use drugs or sanction use;
• Favorable attitudes toward drug use;
• Early first use (before age 15); and
• Physiological factors.

Protective Factors for Alcohol and Other Drug Problems in Adolescence

A home-school-community partnership can protect students, reduce risk, and increase resistance to drugs by employing the following measures.

Protective Factors:
• Clear norms and standards of behavior in the home, school, and community;
• Skills to resist social influences, solve problems, and make decisions; and
• Bonding to family, school, and community, which can be promoted by:

1. Active participation in group activities;
2. Learning skills for working with others; and
3. Recognition for skillful individual and group performance.

General Principles of Prevention:
• Focus on reducing risk factors.
• Intervene early-before behavior stabilizes.
• Target high-risk persons and high-risk communities, but avoid "labeling" students and setting up negative expectations for behavior.
• Employ a variety of initiatives in a comprehensive, multicomponent prevention effort.

Source: Hawkins, D. and Catalano, R. in *National Commission on Drug-Free Schools. (Toward A Drug-Free Generation: A Nations Responsibility.)* U.S. Department of Education, Washington, D.C., September, 1990

harmful chemicals. As a result, people who use these drugs are at great risk of harming themselves.

Heroin

Heroin is a depressant drug that is is derived from the opium poppy. Since heroin has depressing effects, its use can result in cardiac and respiratory failure. One of the major problems associated with heroin use is its ability to cause physical dependence easily. **Physical dependence** is a bodily need for a drug.

Most people who use heroin will usually inject the drug or "mainline" it. Once a person is physically dependent on heroin, he or she will need another dose every four to six hours.

Another major problem associated with the use of heroin is HIV infection. Since many heroin users share needles to inject this drug, HIV can be transmitted. In many of the major cities in the United States, using infected needles is the most common way HIV is spread from person-to-person. Signals that a student may be using heroin include track marks on the arm, a dream-like euphoria, and a drop in academic performance.

Cocaine

Cocaine is a stimulant that is derived from the coca plant. A student who uses cocaine will often "snort" it. A small quantity of the cocaine powder is placed on a hard surface or mirror and inhaled through the nose through straw-like implements.

Some users freebase cocaine. **Freebasing** refers to the use of a purified form of cocaine that is processed from hydrochloride salt and smoked through a water pipe.

Crack cocaine is processed cocaine to a base state in which baking soda and water are used. It is hardened and smoked through a pipe.

Regardless of the form in which cocaine is used, it is dangerous. It narrows the blood vessels and increases heartbeat rate and blood pressure. It can interfere with the electrical messages that are conducted for proper heart function. The result is heart failure and death. Signals that a student is using cocaine include a runny nose, constantly wiping the nose, and acting unusually "up."

Tobacco

The use of tobacco products is accountable for numerous preventable deaths. Tobacco products in the form of smoking tobacco and smokeless tobacco are extremely harmful. There is new evidence that links cigarette smoking in childhood to leukemia and to other cancers such as breast, bladder, prostate, and liver. Cigarette smoking is the single most preventable cause of death. Half of cancer deaths are related to smoking.

A significant number of young people have begun to use smokeless tobacco because they believe they will not harm their bodies since no smoke is inhaled. These young people fail to realize that smokeless tobacco contains sand and grit that can wear the enamel from the teeth. Smokeless tobacco also causes the gums to recede from the teeth causing the roots of the teeth to be exposed, thereby causing tooth destruction. Smokeless tobacco causes leukoplakia, a whitish patch inside the mouth that is precancerous.

Inhalants

Inhalants are drugs that are inhaled through solvents, volatile substances, aerosols, and anesthetics. Solvents that may become inhalants include paint thinners, model cement, and nailpolish removers. Aerosols include products such as nitrous oxide that are gases released by propellants. Anaesthetics that may become inhalants include ether and chloroform. Children are most apt to abuse inhalants that are in the form of aerosols or volatile substances. The abused inhalants are most likely to be emptied or sprayed into an empty bag which is placed over the nose or head and inhaled.

Inhalants produce loss of coordination and light-headedness. Their use can result in brain damage and death. As a teacher, explain the importance of using glue, paint, nailpolish, and aerosols with proper ventilation.

Anabolic Steroids

Anabolic steroids are powerful derivatives from the male hormone testosterone. Steroids have been used by athletes, both male and female, to build muscles. However, they are now illegal and have been banned from use in sporting events.

The effects of steroids are not pleasant. Males may develop breasts and experience testicle shrinkage and ceased sperm production. Females may experience breast reduction and sterility. Males and females may experience liver tumors, kidney damage, and heart disease. Behavioral changes including aggression and violence accompany steroid use. Upon discontinuing the use of steroids, persons often become severely depressed and suicidal. Unfortunately, the damage caused by the use of steroids often cannot be reversed.

Signs of steroid use include quick weight gain, development of muscle mass, and overly aggressive behavior.

Preventing Drug Abuse

One of the six goals for education issued by the United States government in 1991 emphasized that schools become drug free by the year 2000. It is a conclusion in *Healthy Youth 2000* (1990) that comprehensive school health education, K-12, be implemented to prevent drug use and abuse by the year 2000. Table 2-4 identifies elements of a comprehensive drug education and prevention program.

Yet schools cannot take all the responsibility for drug abuse prevention. Responsibility must begin at home. A loving and supportive family helps reduce the vulnerability to drug use. Parents need to provide their children with skills that will enable them to grow up drug-free. Community agencies need to work with parents and schools to offer prevention, intervention, and treatment options. Teachers need to be able to refer students who may have drug-related problems to the proper personnel. In school, teachers can refer students to the school nurse or guidance services. Drug misuse and abuse is on the decline.

Eating Disorders

Eating disorders are food-related dysfunctions in which a person changes eating habits in a way which is harmful to the mind body. One type of food-related disorder is anorexia nervosa. **Anorexia nervosa** is an eating disorder in which a person is preoccupied with being excessively thin. Anorexia nervosa affects mostly females. About one in one hundred families has a member who has anorexia nervosa. A large number of people who have anorexia nervosa fall between the ages of 12 and 18.

Table 2-4
Elements of a Comprehensive Drug Education and Prevention Program

A comprehensive drug education and prevention program should include the following eight elements:

- Student survey, school needs assessment, and resource identification.
- Leadership training of key school officials and staff with authority to develop policies and programs.
- School policies that are clear, consistent, and fair, with responses to violations that include alternatives to suspension.
- Training for the entire staff on the following:
  - the school's alcohol and drug policies and policy implementation;
  - drug use, abuse, and dependency;
  - effects on family members and others; and
  - intervention and referral of students.
- Assistance programs/ support for students from preschool through grade 12, including the following:
  - tutoring, mentoring, and other academic activities;
  - support groups (e.g., Alcoholics Anonymous and Children of Alcoholics);
  - peer counseling;
  - extracurricular activities (e.g., sports, drama, journalism);
  - vocational programs (e.g., work-study and apprenticeship);
  - social activities (including drug-free proms and graduation activities);
  - alternative programs (e.g., Upward Bound and Outward Bound); and
  - community service projects.
- Training for parents, including the following information:
  - the effects of drug use, abuse, and dependency on users, their families, and other people;
  - ways to identify drug problems and refer people for treatment;
  - available resources to diagnose and treat people with drug problems
  - laws and school policies on drugs, including alcohol and tobacco;
  - the influence of parents' attitudes and behaviors toward drugs including alcohol and tobacco, and of parents' expectations of graduation and academic performance of their children;
  - the importance of establishing appropriate family rules, monitoring behavior of children, imposing appropriate punishments, and reinforcing positive behavior;
  - ways to improve skills in communication and family and conflict management; and
  - the importance of networking with other parents and knowing their children's friends and their families.
- Curriculum for preschool through grade 12, including the following subjects:*

- information about all types of drugs, including medicines;
- the relationship of drugs to suicide, AIDS, drug-affected babies, pregnancy, violence, and other health and safety issues;
- the social consequences of drug abuse;

- Curriculum must be developmentally oriented, age-appropriate, up-to-date, and accurate. Individual components work best as part of a comprehensive curriculum program. Individually, components such as information about drugs can exacerbate the problem.

  - respect for the laws and values of society, including discussions of right and wrong.
  - the importance of honesty, hard work, achievement, citizenship, compassion, patriotism, and other civic and personal values;
  - promotion of healthful, safe, and responsible attitudes and behavior;
  - ways to build resistance to influences that encourage drug use, such as peer pressure, advertising, and other media appeals (refusal skills);
  - ways to develop critical thinking, problem-solving, decision-making, persuasion, and interpersonal skills;
  - ways to increase self-control and self-esteem based on achievement and to cope with stress, anger, and anxiety;
  - strategies to get parents, family members, and the community involved in preventing drug use;
  - information on contacting responsible adults when young people need help and on intervention and referral services;
  - sensitivity to cultural differences in the school and community and to local drug problems; and
  - information about how advertising works.
- Collaboration with community services to provide the following services:
  - student assistance programs;
  - employee assistance programs for school staff;
  - latch-key child care;
  - social wellfare services;
  - probation services;
  - continuing education for dropouts and pushouts;
  - in-service training for teachers and counselors in intervention techniques and procedures; and
  - programs for students at high-risk of drug use.

Source: *National Commision on Drug-Free Schools (Toward A Drug-Free Generation: A Nation's Responsibility).* U.S. Department of Education, Washington, D.C., September, 1990.

A person is considered as having anorexia when (s)he has a weight loss that exceeds 15% below the expected weight, has a fear of gaining weight even when underweight, or feels fat even when not. A female may miss three consecutive menstrual cycles.

School-age girls who have anorexia are usually perfectionists. They have a neat appearance and are well-groomed, have good grades, but show little enjoyment from success. These girls are usually very obedient, intelligent, and thoughtful. They are sad and lonely and preoccupied with weight loss. They have an unrealistic body image. Girls with anorexia nervosa will not want to dress for physical education classes. If you notice these signs and symptoms, report them to the school nurse who can keep a record of weight.

Students who have anorexia nervosa need to receive medical treatment. Treatment may require a hospital stay or may be done on an outpatient basis. Psychological treatment is emphasized and goals such as gaining specific amounts of weight are set.

Bulimia is an eating disorder in which a person will have uncontrollable urges to eat excessively and then either go to sleep or most likely, engage in self-induced vomiting. The gorging on food is called binging or binge eating. Binge eating usually occurs in solitude. The person will stop if observed by someone else. Unlike the person who has anorexia nervosa, the person who has bulimia often is near normal weight. Yet, a person who has bulimia may eat up to 10,000 calories or more per binge.

A person who has bulimia may develop feelings of depression and hopelessness. In some cases, suicide is seen as an option. Psychological and medical interventions are prescribed for a person who has bulimia.

Epilepsy

Almost every teacher will have a student in his or her class who has epilepsy. **Epilepsy** is a condition in which there is a disturbance of impulses in the brain leading to seizures. Witnessing a seizure can be frightening if a person does not know what to do.

In the typical grand mal seizure, a student will experience a major convulsion, drop to the ground, exhibit jerking motions, and stop breathing temporarily. A student usually knows when a seizure is about to occur because an aura precedes the seizure. An **aura** is a dreamlike state in which there are unusual bodily sensations.

A student who has petit mal seizures, also called absence spells, experiences a brief loss of consciousness. The student may drop whatever he or she is holding. More common however, is a very small change such as staring into space, rolling the eyes, or losing the place in a sentence when reading. A teacher may view this lapse as inattention rather than epilepsy.

In psychomotor epilepsy, a child may experience a jerking of the mouth or face. Consciousness is rarely lost. This type of seizure can last from one to ten minutes.

During a seizure, a student should be protected from injury. Nothing should be placed in the mouth between the teeth. The American Red Cross states that a person rarely bites the tongue.

Sexually Transmitted Diseases

Sexually transmitted diseases (STDs) are communicable infections spread through sexual contact. The majority of adolescents are engaging in behaviors that promote the spread of sexually transmitted diseases (STDs). This has implications for teachers and health care professionals. In their book **Adolescent Medicine** (1991), Strasburger and Brown have identified certain principles applicable to adolescents and STDs.

1. Sexually active adolescents should be screened for STDs annually.
2. Sexual partners of adolescents who have STDs should be evaluated and treated.
3. Sexually active teenagers should be counseled about barrier types of contraceptives to prevent the spread of microorganisms that cause STDs.
4. Adolescents should be aware that by law, confidentiality between them and medical professionals regarding STDs is required.
5. After treatment, adolescents should be re-evaluated to be certain they are cured from STDs.

There are a number of different kinds of STDs that are known to infect adolescents. Following are the major kinds of STDs, their signs and symptoms, diagnoses, and treatment.

Trichomoniasis

Trichomoniasis is an STD that is caused by a protozoan. It is believed that as many as half of all females may have this organism present in the vaginal area but remain free of all symptoms until the defense system is weakened. In females, the signs and symptoms of trichomoniasis include a vaginal discharge that is yellowish-green and frothy. There may also be burning and itching in the vaginal area as well as painful urination. Trichomoniasis is diagnosed by a Pap smear and a culture. Treatment of trichomoniasis includes oral medication. Both sexual partners must be treated because partners can pass the disease back and forth.

Herpes Simplex Infections

Herpes simplex infections is a general term for diseases that involve herpes simplex virus type 1 (HSV

1) and herpes simplex virus type 2 (HSV 2). About 90 percent of HSV infections are HSV 2. As many as 12 percent of sexually active female adolescents have positive cultures for HSV 2. Once HSV gets into the body, usually through the mucous membranes of the genital area, there will be a sensation of burning or redness at the site of the infection. Then a small blister filled with clear fluid will develop. The blisters may be present for three to fifteen days after which time they will heal. The virus will remain dormant. Recurrences of the blisters occur but the reasons are not entirely known. It appears that stress can play a role. HSV is diagnosed through lab tests using cultures. HSV is not curable, but it is treatable. Acyclovir is the medicine of treatment for HSV. Topical medications can be used on the blisters, but HSV can be spread to other body parts when one part of the body is infected from the virus that appears on another part.

Human Papillomavirus Infection

Human papillomavirus (HPV) infection causes a condition called genital warts. HPV is the most common viral STD in the United States today with adolescents being at great risk. A person becomes infected when HPV penetrates the skin and mucous membrane of the genital area. If the virus enters inside the reproductive tract, a person may experience no signs. In others, small, itchy bumps on the genitals may appear. These bumps appear as warts, ranging in size from a small pinhead to having a large, cauliflower-like appearance. Detection of HPV is made via a Pap smear or a special procedure called a colposcopy. Treatment for HPV warts can be several. Warts can be painted with a medication called podophyllin which causes them to dry up and fall off. Warts may also be removed by treatment with liquid nitrogen or by excision. Large warts can be removed by laser surgery.

Chlamydia

Chlamydia is the most prevalent bacterial STD in the United States. Chlamydia is the most common STD seen in the adolescent population. In fact, 10-20 percent of sexually active female teenagers have chlamydial infections and of these, 70 percent may have no symptoms. In males, the symptoms include painful and frequent urination and a watery, pus-like discharge from the urethra. Symptoms in the female include a yellowish discharge, spotting between periods, and spotting after intercourse. Diagnosis is made by examination of cells removed from the cervix using a cotton swab. Antibiotics such as tetracycline are used to treat chlamydia.

Gonorrhea

Gonorrhea is one of the most common STDs in the United States and is caused by a bacterium. While the number of cases of gonorrhea has dropped over the past five years, it has increased in the adolescent population, specifically increasing in the ten to fourteen year age group. In males, the signs include a white, milky discharge from the urethra along with painful, burning urination about two to nine days after infection. Most males will have signs of gonorrheal infection while most females who are infected will show no signs. About 20 percent of females will experience a discharge and burning sensation during urination. Diagnosis of gonorrhea is made by analyzing a cervical culture. Antibiotics such as spectinomycin given intramuscularly will cure gonorrhea.

Syphilis

Syphilis is an STD caused by a bacterium called a spirochete. There has been an increase in the number of cases of syphilis since 1987, especially among teenagers. In the first stage of syphilis, or primary syphilis, a person will develop a sore called a chancre. A chancre is an ulcer that is painless. The chancre will appear about three to four weeks after contact with an infected person. It will completely disappear after three to eight weeks. Secondary symptoms may appear from one month to one year later. This is known as secondary syphilis. Symptoms may include a rash or white patches on the skin or mucous membrane of the mouth, throat, or genitals. Fever and headache may also be present. The symptoms may disappear again only to reappear in the stage called tertiary syphilis. During this stage, damage to the heart and central nervous system can occur. Fortunately, most people will seek medical treatment before reaching the tertiary stage. A test called dark-field will detect the presence of spirochetes. Treatment with antibiotics is effective in curing a person of syphilis. It is significant that the presence of a chancre poses an increased risk of HIV infection. The chancre can serve as a portal for receiving HIV from an infected person. A person who has chancres as well as being HIV infected can infect others easily because HIV from the chancre can enter the body of another person.

Pelvic Inflammatory Disease

Pelvic inflammatory disease also known as PID is an inflammation of the lining of the abdominopelvic cavity. PID is one of the most significant diseases among female adolescents. One in eight 15-19 year olds who are sexually active have PID. Having multiple sex partners is a risk factor for PID. Any number of different bacteria can be responsible for causing PID. Lower abdominal pain is the most common symptom of PID in adolescents. Other signs include fever, vaginal discharge and irregular vaginal bleeding. Cervical cultures can help detect PID as well as analyzing the presence of other symptoms. Oral or intravenous antibiotics is the treatment choice for PID.

Suicide

Suicide is the intentional taking of one's life. It is a leading cause of death among children and adolescents. Suicide attempts have been reported in children as young as 5 or 6 years old. Suicide attempts among preteens are increasing.

There are a number of reasons why children and preteens attempt suicide. They may be abused, have difficulty at school, lack love from families, experience separation or divorce of parents or death of a parent, or have poor peer relationships. Teenagers' reasons for attempting suicide include: fighting with parents, not living up to parents' expectations, feelings of inferiority, difficulty making positive social adjustments, friction with peers, difficulty at school, breakup of an opposite sex relationship, and depression.

Changes in the family may precipitate a student's suicide attempt. Death of a parent or a family breakup may be linked to suicide attempts. Academic failure and depression are also related to suicide attempts. Students who have no hope and cannot forsee this as changing are prime suspects for suicide attempts.

Teens and preteens who are thinking about a suicide attempt will usually give indications. Some of these indications may be through conversations. They may mention they are thinking about attempting suicide. They may make statements such as, "I sometimes wish I were dead." or "I'm not important to anyone so why not take my life. No one will miss me."

Some students indicate they are considering a suicide attempt by exhibiting certain behaviors. A student who has made a previous attempt is at risk for making another attempt. Students who are contemplating a suicide attempt may plan for their death. They may do things such as give away their valuable possessions to peers or siblings. Other behavioral indicators include extreme changes in mood, feelings of guilt, truancy, involvement with drugs, promiscuity, quitting teams and after school clubs and activities, and aggressive behavior.

A student may share with you his or her intention of making a suicide attempt. If a student confides in you, there are school procedures to follow. Usually, this involves notifying the school counselor who notifies the family. When a crisis is imminent, do not leave the student alone. Most of the time, a student is seeking help and telling a teacher is one way of asking for help. If a student indicates he or she is thinking of suicide, do not panic. Tell the student you are really concerned about him or her and that you would like to offer your help. In addition to school personnel, there are many different community health agencies such as community mental health agencies that have trained personnel to help the student. The family, school personnel, and mental health professionals work together to support the student. The student learns additional coping strategies.

Teenage Pregnancy

Each year, one million teenage students become pregnant in the United States. The United States has one of the highest rates of teenage pregnancy in the developed world. The results of teenage pregnancy are startling and depressing. Many teens do not seek early prenatal care. As a result, they have more problem pregnancies than those women who are older, married, and seek prenatal care. Teenagers are at increased risk to give birth to premature and low birth weight infants. Their babies are at risk of being physically and intellectually behind, and born with health-related problems that can have lifelong consequences. Teens who have babies have higher dropout rates from school, poorer academic performances, greater problems meeting economic and financial needs, and increased risk of having repeated pregnancies. In addition, teenage parents are more likely to abuse their children.

Pregnant girls and their partners have unique needs. Pregnant girls need to know what is happening to their bodies and what to expect during their pregnancy. They need information about ways to prevent additional unwanted pregnancies. Their partners also need this information. They may also need support. Teenage fathers and mothers need counseling to help them handle the needs of the baby as well as their relationship. They need to make financial plans for supporting the baby. Most states now require the male to make child-support payments when no marriage occurs.

As is with other health matters, schools can play a significant role in the prevention of pregnancy through education. Whether or not to teach about pregnancy prevention is something that is determined by each school district. The United States government promotes the teaching of abstinence in schools. The teaching of contraception is accepted in some school districts but not in others. Students need to be taught how to use refusal skills to say "no" to being sexually active.

In some cities in the United States, contraceptives are now being offered through school-based clinics. The services offered in school-based clinics vary from city-to-city. School-based clinics offer physical examinations and screenings, treatment of minor injury and illness, counseling, and referral services. Some clinics will offer gynecological examinations, weight control counseling, and mental health counseling. Others distribute contraceptives to teenage students.

Many school districts have teen pregnancy programs in which education about prenatal care is provided. In health education classes, students are given the opportunity to learn about the consequences of teenage pregnancy and why choosing to practice abstinence is a responsible choice during the teen years. The best way to prevent teenage pregnancy is to provide students with information, responsible decision making skills, and reasons why abstinence is the best choice.

HANDLING COMMON EMERGENCIES

As a teacher, you will be faced with numerous situations in which students will need attention for a myriad of injuries and illnesses faced in school. The information that follows in this section will provide you with the skills you will need to handle common emergencies of school-age boys and girls.

Emergencies Related to Breathing, Bleeding, and Shock

There are several emergency situations that can be life-threatening if not handled promptly and appropriately. These emergency situations are related to stoppage of breathing, bleeding, and shock.

Airway Obstruction

Almost everyone has choked on an object he or she was chewing. You will have students in your class who will choke on a piece of food. In almost all cases, the food will become dislodged by itself. But on occasion, a student may choke on a piece of food and not be able to dislodge it by himself/herself.

A student may have a partial airway obstruction or a complete airway obstruction. A student who has a partial airway obstruction may be able to inhale and exhale but will gasp for air. The student may cough or attempt to cough. (S)he may clutch at the throat with one or two hands. This is known as the universal distress signal for choking. The student may also have cyanosis (bluishness) around the lips and mouth. If the airway is completely obstructed, the person will not be able to speak, breathe, or cough.

The first aid for a conscious person who is choking is to give abdominal thrusts, also called the Heimlich maneuver. Ask the student if he or she is choking. If the student can speak or cough easily, do not do anything. If the student cannot speak, breathe, or cough, stand behind him or her and wrap your hands around his or her waist. Make a fist with one hand and place the thumb side of the fist into the victim's abdomen above the navel and below the rib cage. Grab your fist with the other hand and give quick, upward thrusts into the abdominal area. Repeat these thrusts until the object is dislodged. Each thrust should be separate and distinct.

If you are not successful dislodging the object, the student may become unconscious. Call emergency medical service immediately. Open the student's airway by grasping the lower jaw and tongue. Lift the jaw. Using what is called finger sweep, attempt to dislodge and remove the object by sweeping it out with your finger. Use a hooking action with your finger. If nothing happens, give the student two full breaths, tilting the head and lifting the chin. If air does not get into the lungs, the airway is still blocked. Give 6-10 abdominal thrusts. To give abdominal thrusts, straddle the student's thighs. Place the heal of one hand on the victim's abdomen just above the navel but below the tip of the breastbone. Place your other hand on top of the first. Make sure the fingers of your hands point toward the student's head. Give quick, upward thrusts. If nothing happens after about 6-10 thrusts, do another finger sweep. Then give two full breaths. If you cannot get breaths into the student, repeat the same procedures - thrusts, finger sweeps, and two breaths. Do this sequence until emergency medical personnel arrive.

Cardiopulmonary Resuscitation

Cardiopulmonary resuscitation or CPR is an emergency procedure that is used to revive a person whose heart has stopped beating. CPR should be used by a person trained to administer this procedure.

The American Red Cross suggests the following procedure be administered. If a person is not breathing, pinch the nose shut, seal your lips tightly around the person's mouth, and give two full breaths that last about one to one-and-a-half seconds. Watch to see that the chest rises indicating the breaths have entered the lungs. Feel the pulse for 5-10 seconds. If a pulse is present, check for severe bleeding and recheck breathing. CPR begins if a person does not have a pulse. At this time, it is also important to send someone to call for emergency medical care.

To perform CPR, do the following:

1. Locate the notch of the lower end of the sternum with the index and middle fingers. Place the heel of the other hand on the sternum next to the fingers. Remove the hand from the notch and put it on top of the other hand. Keep the fingers off the chest.
2. Positions your shoulders over your hands and compress the sternum one-and-a-half to two inches. Do 15 compressions in about 10 seconds. Compress up and down smoothly.
3. Open the airway with a head-tilt/chin lift, pinch the nose shut, and seal your lips tightly around the person's mouth. Give two full breaths that last one to one-and-a-half seconds. Watch the chest to see if it rises.
4. Repeat the compression/breathing cycles three times.
5. Recheck the pulse for five seconds. If the person has a pulse and is breathing, keep the airway open, monitor breathing, and await the arrival of emergency medical personnel. If a person has a pulse but is still not breathing, do rescue breathing until emergency medical personnel arrive. If no pulse or breathing is

present, continue CPR.

6. Give two full breaths, each lasting one to one-and-a-half seconds making sure the chest rises.
7. Continue the compression/breathing cycles. Locate the correct hand position, continue cycles of 15 compressions and two breaths, and recheck the pulse every few minutes.

Bleeding

Many students sustain injuries that result in bleeding. External bleeding occurs when there is a break in the skin. Generally, bleeding is easy to control. The simplest way to control bleeding is by applying direct pressure. Direct pressure is pressure placed over the wound with the purpose of restricting blood flow and allowing normal clotting. Suppose a student suffers a wound in which there is bleeding. Do the following:

1. Place direct pressure over the wound using a sterile gauze or a clean washcloth or towel. This will help keep germs from entering the wound.
2. Place firm pressure over the wound.
3. Elevate the injured area above the level of the heart.
3. If blood soaks through the gauze or whatever other bandage you are using, do not remove that bandage. Add more bandages on top of the one already used.

You should be sure to get emergency medical care. Meanwhile, you may need to compress the artery supplying blood to the area if bleeding does not stop. The site where this pressure is applied is called a pressure point. The two main pressure points are the brachial artery in the arm and the femoral artery in the groin area. You should be skilled in first aid before using pressure points.

Most wounds you will see in the school setting are minor. You need to keep all wounds clean. Use a sterile gauze or a clean cloth that is saturated with soap and water to clean a wound. Gently wash away dirt from the edges of the wound. Any foreign matter such as dirt or gravel that is in the wound should be removed to reduce the risk of infection. Cover the wound with sterile gauze. Do not keep the dressing airtight. An airtight bandage traps moisture from the skin and this encourages bacterial growth.

Shock

Any person who suffers an injury should be treated for shock. **Shock** is a condition in which blood cannot be circulated to all parts of the body. Shock can be caused by any kind of sudden illness or injury. Signals of shock are rapid and weak pulse, rapid breathing, pale or bluish color skin, cool moist skin, nausea,

vomiting, drowsiness or loss of consciousness.

Should you come across a student who has gone into shock, you should help that person retain normal body temperature. Place blankets around the victim. Assuming no other injury exists, elevate the legs and feet keeping them locked. The legs and feet should be elevated 8-12 inches while the student lies on his/her back. Do not lie a student on the back if there is head injury or if breathing difficulties or chest injuries exist.

Emergencies Related to Injuries

The leading cause of death and disability to students is injury. Injury is the primary reason why people see physicians. Many injuries are both predictable and preventable.

Injuries To Tissues

The most common types of injuries you will find among your students are injuries to the soft tissues. Soft tissues include the layers of the skin, fat, and muscles. The most common wound you will see among your students are scrapes, also known as abrasions. **Abrasions** usually occur when a student falls and the skin rubs away, most often at the knees and elbows. The most important concern for this type of injury is infection as bleeding will usually be minimal. Abrasions should be cleansed with soap and water. Most kinds of soaps will be effective in removing harmful bacteria. Other wounds such as lacerations, avulsions (the skin and other soft tissue is torn away), and punctures, may need medical attention. Of particular concern with punctures is the possibility of tetanus. **Tetanus** is bacteria that grow in the body and produce a strong poison that affects the nervous system and muscles. A person who sustains a puncture wound should receive a tetanus shot from a physician to prevent tetanus.

Be aware of signs of infection in any kind of wound. The early signs of infection are redness and swelling around the the wound. The area around the wound may feel warm and there may be a throbbing sensation present. If the infection is not treated, other signs may be present such as fever and a feeling of illness. Any initial signs of infection should be treated. Keep the wound clean and apply an antibiotic ointment such as Neosporin. The coverings over the wound should be changed daily. Of course, treatment should be left to the parent of the student or to medical personnel.

Injuries To Bones

Many students sustain fractures. A **fracture** is a break in a bone. A bone that is fractured may be chipped or broken partially or completely broken.

If a bone is broken, there will be any number of signs

and symptoms. Pain and tenderness will be present. In some cases, there will be deformity in the area of the break. Swelling and discoloration in the area may be present and the victim may not be able to use the injured body part. If you suspect a student has suffered a fracture, treat the student for shock. Be sure not to move the injured area as a broken bone might move and cause further injury to the underlying tissue in the surrounding area. Be sure to call for emergency medical personnel immediately.

Another common bone injury is a dislocation. A **dislocation** is the separation of a bone from its joint. Dislocations will often result in the same kinds of signs and symptoms as a broken bone. There may be deformity, discoloration, severe pain, swelling, and an inability to move the area. First aid includes not moving the joint and applying ice.

Another common injury is a sprain. Although not technically an injury to the bone, a **sprain** is a partial or complete tearing of ligaments at a joint. Many sprains occur to twisted ankles and knees. The most common symptom of a sprain is pain. Treatment consists of the RICE method. The "R" means rest. Do not move the injured area. The "I" stands for ice. Apply ice to the injured area to help reduce swelling. The "C" stands for compression. Press the ice over the wound. "E" indicates elevation. The injured body part should be elevated above the level of the heart.

Some people become confused between a sprain and a strain. A **strain** is a stretching or tearing of muscles, usually due to overexertion. A strain should be treated the same way as a sprain.

Injuries to The Head Area

Most injuries to the head area will not be serious. But on occasion, a student will suffer a blow to the skull. The student may fall to the ground and hit his or her head. If the student is conscious, keep him or her still. If there is blood flowing from the ear, do not block its flow. Blocking the flow will cause undue pressure to build up on the brain. Keep the student in a semisitting position. Do not elevate the legs as this will cause increased blood flow to the brain. Do not give the student anything to eat or drink and get medical help. If the student is unconscious, check the airway for breathing and get emergency medical help.

Many students suffer from nosebleeds. Most nosebleeds are caused by a blow to the nose. Females may have nosebleeds during the first few years of the menstrual periods. Most of the time, it is easy to control nosebleeds. Have the student sit with the head slightly forward and pinch the nostrils together. Sitting slightly forward enables the blood to flow from the nose instead of back down the back of the throat. The nostrils should be pinched for about five minutes before releasing. The student should breathe through the mouth. You may also choose to apply an ice pack to the bridge of the nose. If the bleeding does not stop, seek medical care.

Eye injuries present another problem for the teacher. Foreign bodies such as dirt and sand can get on the eyeball. This will be irritating but it can also cause significant damage to the eyeball. The first thing to do if a piece of dirt or sand gets on the eyeball is to have the victim blink several times. If the foreign body is not removed, have the student flush the eye with water. If the object remains, the student needs to receive medical attention.

Another common injury is that of a tooth being knocked out of its socket in the mouth. There are various thoughts on how to respond to this situation. The following recommendation is that of the American Red Cross and is to be used for children. Place the tooth in a cup of milk or in water if milk is not available. The student should see a dentist immediately as the sooner the tooth is placed back inside the socket, the better the chance it can be saved. With proper treatment, the overwhelming majority of knocked-out teeth can be saved.

Medical Emergencies

Any kind of an illness or injury can occur suddenly. It is important to react quickly and correctly in all situations.

Fainting

Fainting is one of the most common sudden emergencies that occurs. **Fainting** is the partial or complete loss of consciousness that occurs when there has been reduced blood flow to the brain.

First aid for a student who has fainted begins with laying the student on the ground. Elevate the legs 8-12 inches. Loosen any clothing that is restrictive such as a collar or a belt. Do not give the student anything to eat or drink and do not splash water on the face. Usually the student will recover rather quickly and there will be no lasting effects. However, the student should seek medical care if there are any suspicions about underlying health problems.

Plant Poisoning

One of the more common types of poisoning that affects school-age boys and girls is that from poisonous plants that may be growing on or near school grounds. The most common types of plant poisoning results from contact with poison ivy, poison oak, and poison sumac. Suppose a student has contact with a poison plant. Immediately wash the affected area thoroughly with soap and water. If a rash begins to develop apply wet compresses. Calamine lotion, zinc oxide, or Caladryl may help soothe the affected area. If the condition worsens, medical care by a physician will be needed.

Insect Poisoning

Most of the time, insect stings are painful, but this is the extent of the problem. If you come across a student who is stung by an insect, you need to remove the stinger from the skin. Scrape the stinger away from the skin with your fingernail or something thin and sturdy such as a plastic credit card. Do not remove the stinger with a tweezer since there is usually a sac with venom attached to the stinger. The squeeze of the tweezer against the sac will force venom into the body.

After the stinger is removed, wash the affected area with soap and water. Cover it and keep it clean. You can apply an ice pack to the area to reduce pain and swelling.

Some students will suffer from allergic reactions when stung by an insect. Every student who is stung by an insect should be observed for about a half-hour for reactions. Many students who are allergic to stings carry special medication or the school nurse would have made arrangements with a student's family for treatment procedures. Immediate treatment is needed if there is an allergic reaction.

In most parts of the country, there are spiders that are extremely dangerous. Two kinds of spiders whose bites can be fatal are the black widow spider and the brown recluse spider. The black widow spider is black with a red dish hourglass shape underneath its body. The brown recluse spider is light brown and has a darker brown violin-shaped mark on top of its body. If a student thinks he or she has been bitten by either of these insects immediate medical care is needed.

Recently, there has been a great concern about ticks. Ticks can cause a number of diseases. Two such diseases are Rocky Mountain Spotted Fever, and of increasingly greater concern, Lyme disease. **Lyme disease** is a specific set of symptoms caused by a tick that feeds on field mice and deer. Lyme disease is prevalent in many different parts of the country. It is now found in the Midwest and west, in addition to having originated on the east coast.

The ticks that carry Lyme disease commonly attach themselves to field mice and deer. The ticks appear very small when attached to the skin. They can be as small as a poppy seed. Once an infected tick bites, Lyme disease can be transmitted. Usually a rash starts and spreads to be about seven inches across. The center of the rash is light red and the outer ridges are darker red and raised. A student may have fever, headaches, and weakness. When these symptoms appear, a student needs to seek medical help. The sooner medical help is gotten, the better the chances for an easier recovery.

If a tick is found on the body, it should be removed. Grasp the tick with tweezers. Pull it slowly away from the skin. Once the tick is removed, wash the area with soap and water. Observe the site for the development of the bulls-eye type rash. If symptoms of Lyme disease follow, a physician should be seen. Antibiotics taken early will be effective.

Exposure to Heat and Cold

Younger students are at risk for illnesses that result from exposure to heat and cold. They need to be protected from overexposure to elements in the environment to protect their health.

Heat Emergencies

Heat cramps, heat exhaustion, and heat stroke are the most common heat-related illnesses. **Heat cramps** are painful muscle spasms that most often occur in the legs and arms due to excessive fluid loss through sweating. A student with heat cramps should rest comfortably in a cool place and be given cool water to drink. The affected muscle should be stretched lightly and massaged. The student can resume activity when the spasms, or cramps, go away.

Heat exhaustion is extreme tiredness due to the inability of the body temperature to be regulated. Signals of heat exhaustion include body temperature that is below normal, cool, moist, pale, or red skin, nausea, headache, dizziness, and weakness. As soon as a student feels these signals during activities, he or she should rest in a cool place and drink cool water. If heat exhaustion is not treated, it can progress to heat stroke.

Heat stroke is a beginning of stoppage of the body functions due to cessation of functioning of normal body temperature. Sweating ceases so that the body cannot regulate its temperature. Body temperature raises. Pulse and breathing rates increase and the skin becomes hot, wet, and dry. The student may feel weak, dizzy, and have a headache. A student who suffers from heat stroke should be placed in a cool environment. Preferably, the student should be wrapped in cool, wet towels. A student who suffers heat stroke should receive immediate medical care.

Cold Emergencies

The most common types of cold-related emergencies are frostbite and hypothermia. **Frostbite** is the freezing of body tissues, most likely those tissues of the extremities. Most cases of frostbite occur to the fingers, toes, ears, and nose. A student who is exposed to sub-freezing temperatures or snow is at risk for developing frostbite. Signs of frostbite include numbness in the affected area, waxy appearance of skin, skin that is cold to touch, and discolored skin.

Treatment for frostbite includes handling the affected area gently. The area should be warmed by soaking the affected part in water that has a temperature between 100 degrees to 105 degrees Fahrenheit. To know if the water is too warm, you should soak your hand in it. If the water feels too warm to you, than it is too warm for the person who needs treatment. Keep the affected body part in water until it appears red and feels warm. Do not rub the affected part.

As a teacher, you will be called on to handle at least some of the medical emergencies identified in this chapter. Being a responsible provider of emergency care also means that you will need to know your limitations. When you are not sure what your responsibilities are, get help from someone who does. The safety and well-being of your students is a priority. Hypothermia is a reduction in the body temperature so that it is lower than normal. **Hypothermia** results from exposure to a cool environment. The temperature can be as high as 50 degrees F. and yet a person can suffer from hypothermia. A combination of cool temperatures, and exposure to moisture and wind can cause a person to go into hypothermia. Most of the time, hypothermia will be mild. A person will shiver and feel cold. As body temperature drops, the pulse rate may slow down and become irregular. Eventually a person can become unconscious and if not treated, death can result.

The best treatment for hypothermia is to place the person in a warm environment and remove any wet clothing and replace it with dry clothing. The best approach to cold-related illnesses is prevention. Wearing the proper clothing and avoiding exposure to harmful conditions will reduce the risks of cold-related illnesses.

References

1. American Red Cross. (1991). *First Aid: Responding to Emergencies*. St. Louis: Mosby Year Book.

2. Healy, R. and Colemen, T., (1988). *A Primer on AIDS for Health Professionals*, 19(6), 4-10.

3. Koop, E.C. (1986). *Surgeon general's report on acquired immune defeciency syndrome*. Washington, D.C: U. S. Department of Health and Human Services.

4. U. S. Department of Health and Human Services. (1987). *Drug use among American high school students, college students, and other young adults*. (Publication No. DHHS, ADM 86-145D). Washington, D.C.: U.S. Government Printing Office.

5. U.S. Department of Health and Human Services. (1988). *Guidelines for Effective School Health Education To Prevent the Spread of AIDS*. MMWR, Atlanta: Centers for Disease Control, Vol. 37.

Your role in the school health education component of comprehensive school health education is challenging. Because health is related to the quality of life, you have the opportunity to enhance the quality of life for your students. Ultimately, students must take responsibility for their own health. The teacher of health is a facilitator and motivator in this internalization process. Kahlil Gibran has aptly described this approach to teaching in his book, **The Prophet**:

> No man can reveal to you ought but that which already lies half asleep in the dawning of your knowledge.
> The teacher who works in the shadow of the temple of his own followers, gives not of his wisdom but rather of his faith and lovingness.
> If he is indeed wise, he does not bid you enter the house of his wisdom; but rather leads you to the threshold of your own mind.[2]

Your challenge as a school health educator is to foster a desire in students to be healthy and to teach them a process to attain and maintain optimal well-being throughout their lives.

THE COMPREHENSIVE SCHOOL HEALTH EDUCATION CURRICULUM

The **comprehensive school health education curriculum** is an organized plan to accomplish school health education. A well-developed comprehensive school health education curriculum includes: 1) A carefully formulated philosophy with identified content areas, 2) A model for character development that assists students with making responsible decisions and saying NO to decisions that result in harm to their health, 3) A list of behavioral objectives and life skills to be achieved, 4) A scope and sequence chart, 5) A creative approach to the classroom as a laboratory for practicing skills for healthful living, and 6) A checklist of special curriculum concerns that is examined frequently.

Philosophy and Content

The first step in writing a curriculum is to formulate a philosophy of health. The philosophy should explain what health is and should define all relevant terminology. It should be personalized and show the interrelationships among the content areas that will serve as the framework of the curriculum. A discussion of philosophy and content in a model curriculum follows.

Health is the quality of life that includes physical, mental-emotional, family-social, and spiritual health. **Physical health** is the condition of a person's body. Eating healthful meals and getting exercise and sleep are examples of ways to keep the body in good condition. **Mental-emotional health** is the condition of a person's mind and the ways that a person expresses feelings. The mind requires as much, if not more, conditioning than the body. Reading, having challenging conversations, and learning new vocabulary words are examples of ways that the mind is kept in top condition. Taking the time to understand feelings, express them in healthful ways, and meet needs without interfering with the rights of others are ways to keep emotional health in condition. **Family-social health** is the condition of a person's relationships with others. Focusing on expressing oneself clearly and listening intently when others are speaking are examples of ways to keep family-social health in good condition. Learning to give affection in appropriate ways and to receive the affection of others is also an aspect of family-social health.

Spiritual health is the way in which one's purpose and meaning in life contributes to a sense of well-being. When a person has a strong faith that promotes a positive attitude and caring and concern for others, spiritual health is in good condition. Ways to keep spiritual health in good condition might be to study one's religious beliefs, discuss these beliefs with family members, and use these beliefs when making decisions.

SCHOOL HEALTH EDUCATION: PROMOTING SELF-RESPONSIBILITY

3

Wellness Scale

Wellness is another way to describe the quality of life. **Wellness** is the quality of life that includes physical, mental-emotional, family-social, and spiritual health. The **Wellness Scale** (Figure 3-1) depicts the ranges in the quality of life from optimal well-being to high level wellness, average wellness, minor illness or injury, major illness or injury, and premature death. There are at least five factors that influence health and wellness:

1. The behaviors a person chooses.
2. The situations in which a person participates.
3. The relationships in which a person engages.
4. The decisions that a person makes.
5. The resistance skills that a person uses.

Health status is the sum total of the positive and negative influence of these behaviors, situations, relationships, decisions, and use of resistance skills on a person's health and wellness. Each influence which is positive is viewed as a plus (+) while each influence which is negative is viewed as a minus (-). A person's health status fluctuates on The Health and Wellness Scale depending on these influences.

Factors that influence Health and Well-Being

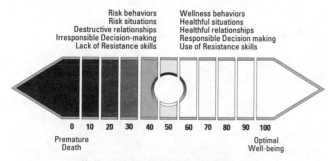

Health status is the sum total of the positive and negative influences of behaviors, situations, relationships, decisions and use of resistance skills.

Figure 3-1
Wellness Scale

Health Knowledge

Health knowledge consists of facts that are needed to evaluate behaviors, situations, and relationships, to make responsible decisions, and to use resistance skills. There are ten areas in which health knowledge is needed: 1. Mental and Emotional Well-Being, 2. Family and Relationship Skills, 3. Growth and Development, 4. Nutrition, 5. Personal Fitness, 6. Substance Use and Abuse, 7. Diseases and Disorders, 8. Consumer Health, 9. Safety and Injury Prevention, and 10. Community and Environment. These ten areas provide a framework for the content areas in the health education curricula.

Healthful Behaviors and Risk Behaviors

Knowledge is essential to evaluate behavior to determine whether or not it promotes health status. **Healthful behaviors** or **wellness behaviors** are actions that promote health, prevent illness, injury, and premature death, and improve the quality of the environment. Examples of healthful behaviors include eating a balanced breakfast, reducing the amount of saturated fat in the diet, wearing a safetybelt, and recycling products. **Risk behaviors** or **harmful behaviors** are voluntary actions that threaten health, increase the likelihood of illness, injury, and premature death, and destroy the quality of the environment. Examples of risk behaviors include smoking cigarettes, sunbathing without a sunscreen having an adequate sun protective factor (SPF), walking into the street between parked cars, and burning trash.

Healthful Situations and Risk Situations

Most persons recognize that health knowledge assists in evaluating behaviors, but it also is essential in evaluating the situations in which one chooses to be. **Healthful situations** or **wellness situations** are circumstances that promote health, prevent illness, injury, and premature death, and improve the quality of the environment. Examples of healthful situations are attending drug-free parties, sitting in non-smoking sections of restaurants, being a passenger in a car driven by someone who obeys safety rules, and living in a home with a safe radon level. **Risk situations** or **harmful situations** are involuntary circumstances that threaten health, increase the likelihood of illness, injury, and premature death, and destroy the quality of the environment. Examples of risk situations include travelling to a third world country without knowingly having proper immunizations, being in a family in which people in the same home smoke, and living near a nuclear power plant.

Healthful Relationships
and Destructive Relationships

A current area of emphasis in examining the factors which influence health status focuses upon relationships. **Healthful relationships** are relationships that promote self-esteem and productivity, encourage health-enhancing behavior, and are energizing. Examples of healthful relationships might be those in which persons identify strengths in each other, encourage each other to complete projects, support each other's exercise or diet plans, and motivate each other to be energetic. Sidney Jourard, psychologist and author of **Transparent Self**, says healthful relationships "inspirit" persons.[4] A person feels

lifted up and energized as a result of being in healthful relationships.

Destructive or **unhealthful relationships** destroy self-esteem, interfere with productivity and health, and are energy depleting. Examples of destructive relationships are those in which one or both persons unjustly criticize each other, interrupt each other's work, encourage each other to engage in risk behaviors, and drain each other of energy. Sidney Jourard says destructive relationships "dispirit" persons. New research focuses on the association between relationships which "dis-spirit" persons and the likelihood that these persons will suffer from "dis-ease."

Responsible Decision Making Skills

Health knowledge also is needed to make responsible decisions, a fourth factor which is a determinant of health status. The **Responsible Decision Making Model** is a series of steps to follow to assure that the decisions a person makes lead to actions which 1) promote health, 2) promote safety, 3) protect laws, 4) show respect for self and others, 5) follow guidelines set by responsible adults such as parents and guardians, and 6) demonstrate good character and moral values. Table 3-1 shows the steps in The Responsible Decision Making Model.

Table 3-1
Responsible Decision Making Model

1.**Clearly describe the situation you face.** If no immediate decision is necessary, describe the situation in writing. If an immediate decision must be made, describe the situation out loud or to yourself in a few short sentences. Being able to describe a situation in your own words is the first step in developing clarity.

2.**List possible actions that can be taken.** Again, if no immediate decision is necessary, make a list of possible actions. If an immediate decision must be made, state possible actions out loud or to yourself.

3.**Share your list of possible actions with a responsible adult who protects community laws and demonstrates character.** When no immediate decision is necessary, sharing possible actions with a responsible adult is helpful. This person can examine your list to see if it is inclusive. Responsible adults have a wide range of experiences that allow them to see situations maturely. They may add possibilities to the list of actions. In some situations, it is possible to delay decision making until there is the opportunity to seek counsel with a responsible adult. If an immediate decision must be made, explore possibilities. Perhaps a telephone call can be made. When ever possible, avoid skipping this step.

4.**Carefully evaluate each possible action using six criteria.** Ask each of the six questions to learn which decision is best.
- Will this decision result in an action that will promote my health and the health of others?
- Will this decision result in an action that will protect my safety and the safety of others?
- Will this decision result in an action that will protect the laws of the community?
- Will this decision result in an action that shows respect for self and others?
- Will this decision result in an action that follows guidelines set by responsible adults such as my parents or guardian?
- Will this decision result in an action that will demonstrate that I have good character and moral values?

5.**Decide which action is responsible and most appropriate.** After applying the six criteria, compare the results. Which decision best meets the six criteria?

6.**Act in a responsible way and evaluate the results.** Follow through with this decision with confidence. The confidence comes from paying attention to the six criteria.

Table 3-2
Model for Using Resistance Skills

1. **Use assertive behavior.** There is a saying, "You get treated the way you 'train' others to treat you." Assertive behavior is the honest expression of thoughts and feelings without experiencing anxiety or threatening others. When you use assertive behavior, you show that you are in control of yourself and the situation. You say NO clearly and firmly. You look directly at the person(s) pressuring you. Aggressive behavior is the use of words and/or actions that tend to communicate disrespect. This behavior only antagonizes others. Passive behavior is the holding back of ideas, opinions, and feelings. Holding back may result in harm to you, others, or the environment.

2. **Avoid saying "NO thank you."** There is never a need to thank a person who pressures you into doing something that might be harmful, unsafe, illegal, or disrespectful or which may result in disobeying parents or displaying a lack of character and moral values.

3. **Use nonverbal behavior that matches verbal behavior.** Nonverbal behavior is the use of body language rather than words to express feelings, ideas, and opinions. Your verbal NO should not be confused by misleading actions. For example, if you say No to cigarette smoking, do not pretend to take a puff.

4. **Influence others to choose responsible behavior.** When a situation poses immediate danger, remove yourself. If no immediate danger is present, try to turn the situation into a positive one. Suggest to others alternative ways to behave that are responsible. Being a positive role model helps you feel good about yourself and helps gain the respect of others.

5. **Avoid being in situations in which there will be pressure to make harmful decisions.** There is no reason to put yourself into situations in which you will be pressured or tempted to make unwise decisions. Think ahead.

6. **Avoid being with persons who choose harmful actions.** Your reputation is the impression that others have of you, your decisions, and your actions. Associate with persons known for their good qualities and character so you will not be misjudged.

7. **Report pressure to engage in illegal behavior to appropriate authorities.** You have a responsibility to protect others and to protect the laws of your community. Demonstrate good character and moral values. Table 3-1 shows the steps in The Responsible Decision Making Model.

Using Resistance Skills

Health knowledge also is needed to ascertain when to resist pressure from others to engage in a risk behavior. **Resistance skills** or **refusal skills** are skills that are used when a person wants to say No to an action and/or leave a situation. The **Model for Using Resistance Skills** contains a list of suggested ways for effectively resisting pressure to engage in actions which 1) threaten health, 2) threaten safety, 3) break laws, 4) result in lack of respect for self and others, 5) disobey guidelines set by responsible adults, and 6) detract from character and moral values. Table 3-2 identifies The Model for Using Resistance Skills.

Model of Health and Well-Being

The **Model of Health and Well-being** (Figure 3-2) shows the relationship between the four dimensions of health, the ten areas of health knowledge, and the five factors that influence health status. Three of the dimensions of health— physical health, mental-emotional health, and family-social health—provide the framework for the outside of the model. The fourth dimension of health, spiritual health, is at the core of the Model.

Surrounding the core of the Model, there is a Well-Being Wheel. The Well-Being Wheel is composed of the ten content areas for which knowledge is needed to: 1) choose healthful behaviors, 2) participate in healthful situations, 3) develop healthful relationships, 4) make responsible decisions, and 5) use resistance skills. The ten content areas are connected. In turn, they influence the four dimensions of health. The connectedness that the five factors that influence health status have with the ten content areas and the four dimensions of health is referred to as **holistic health.** The **holistic effect** means that a behavior, situation, relationship, or decision in any one of the ten content areas will affect other areas and the four dimensions of health.

To visualize holistic health and the holistic effect, visualize the Well-Being Wheel as a large jar of water. All ten content areas and the four dimensions of health are contained within the jar. Now take a drop of red ink. Drop it into the jar. The red ink represents positive influences on health status: wellness behaviors, wellness situations, healthful relationships, responsible decisions, and resistance skills. Red is used

Figure 3-2
Model of Health and Well-Being

Physical Health

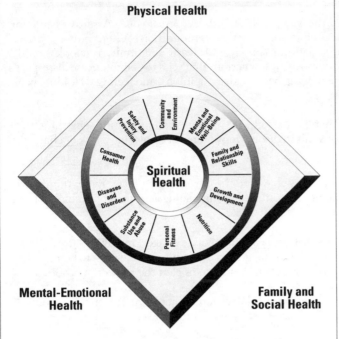

Mental-Emotional Health

Family and Social Health

Health and Well-Being is dependent upon:

1 choosing healthful behaviors.
2 participating in healthful situations.
3 developing healthful relationships.
4 making responsible decisions.
5 using resistance skills.

because it is the color of blood and represents "life-giving" behavior. Soon, the entire jar of water becomes red. There has been an holistic effect.

Now take another her jar of water. This time use blue ink. The blue ink represents negative influences on health status: risk behaviors, risk situations, destructive relationships, irresponsible decisions, and harmful pressure from others. Blue is used to denote "illness, injury, and premature death." Soon, the entire jar of water becomes blue. There has been an holistic effect.

The philosophy of the comprehensive school health education curriculum focuses upon this Model: In order to promote health status, personal responsibility must be assumed for behaviors, situations, relationships, decisions, and pressures within each of the ten content areas that influence the four dimensions of health.

Behavioral Objectives and Life Skills

After a philosophy with identified content areas is formulated and a model for character development including responsible decision making skills and resistance skills is developed, objectives and life skills must be identified. Clearly stated objectives and life skills increase the teacher's ability to focus on what needs to

be accomplished. They provide the basis for selecting the topics to be taught for the ten content areas, the most appropriate learning strategies, and the techniques to be used for evaluation. Objectives and life skills provide accountability for administrators, parents, and students.

Developing Behavioral Objectives

A **behavioral objective** is a statement of what a learner is to be like when (s)he completes a learning experience. There are five rules for writing behavioral objectives.

Rule #1. A behavioral objective should be expressed in terms of student behavior. It would be correct to say, "The *student* will.." It would be incorrect to say, "The *lesson* describes.." or "The *teacher* will.." The first part of a behavioral objective is referred to as the WHO.

Rule #2. A behavioral objective must specify the kind of behavior that will be accepted as evidence. Some words that specify evidence of student behavior are *to list, to compare, to identify, to differentiate, to solve, to write*, and *to recite*. Words which are incorrect because there is no evidence of behavior are to know, to understand, to have faith in, to believe, to really understand, and to appreciate. Part two of a behavioral objective is referred to as the BEHAVIOR.

Rule #3. A behavioral objective must include content about the specific learning experience. The student will identify *the effects of alcohol on the body*. Part three of the behavioral objective is referred to as the CONTENT.

Rule #4. A behavioral objective describes the important conditions under which the behavior will be expected to occur. Some examples of conditions are: *with textbook open, after seeing a film, using a model of a heart, and given a fifty-minute time period*. Part four of the behavioral objective is referred to as the CONDITION.

Rule #5. A behavioral objective must specify the criteria for acceptable performance by describing how well the learner must perform to be acceptable. Thus, the objective, "The student will write an essay on the danger signals of heart disease," would not be an example of an objective with acceptable criteria. Correctly stated, the objective with criteria would read, "The student will write an essay about heart disease *that includes at least two danger signals*.

Table 3-3 provides examples of two behavioral objectives. Each of the behavioral objectives is broken down into the 1) who, 2) behavior, 3) content, 4) condition, and 5) criteria.

Table 3-3
Constructing A Behavioral Objective

With an open textbook, the student will write a balanced menu for one day that includes the correct number of servings from the healthful food groups.

WHO:	the student
BEHAVIOR:	will write
CONTENT:	a balanced menu for one day
CONDITION:	With an open textbook
CRITERIA:	that includes the correct number of servings from the four healthful food groups

After viewing the film on self-protection, the student will write a pamphlet on child abuse that identifies at least five signs and symptoms of physical abuse.

WHO:	the student
BEHAVIOR:	will write
CONTENT:	a pamphlet on child abuse
CONDITION:	After viewing the film,
CRITERIA:	that identifies at least five signs and symptoms of physical abuse

Classifying Behavioral Objectives

In addition to constructing behavioral objectives correctly, the teacher needs to differentiate between desirable student behaviors. Student behaviors can generally be described as thinking behaviors, feeling or attitudinal behaviors, or action behaviors. These three different categories of behavior make it necessary to classify objectives into three domains: the cognitive domain, the affective domain, and the psychomotor or action domain.

The **cognitive domain** is a category of objectives dealing with thinking behavior. Objectives in the cognitive domain emphasize learning and problem solving tasks. Cognitive objectives are divided into six classifications.[5]

Low Level

1. *Knowledge* objectives that require students to reproduce or recall something that they have experienced previously in the same or similar form. Words used in writing knowledge objectives: define, recall describe, identify, list, match, name, and recite.

2. *Comprehension* objectives require students to reproduce or recall something previously experienced in a new form. Words used in writing comprehension objectives: explain, summarize, interpret, rewrite, estimate, convert, infer, translate, rearrange, and paraphrase.

Higher Level

3. *Application* objectives require students to use previously experienced procedures or knowledge in new situations. Words used in writing application objectives: change, compute, demonstrate, operate, show, use, and solve.

4. *Analysis* objectives require students to break down into its component elements something which they have not broken down previously. Words used in writing analysis objectives: outline, break down, subdivide, deduce, discriminate, diagram, order, categorize, and distinguish.

5. *Synthesis* objectives require students to put something together which they have not put together previously. Words used in writing synthesis objectives: combine, compile, compose, create, design, rearrange, plan, and produce.

6. *Evaluation* objectives require students to render judgements regarding something for which they have not rendered judgement previously. Words used in writing evaluation objectives: justify, appraise, criticize, compare, support, conclude, and contrast.

The **affective domain** is a category of objectives dealing with feelings and attitudes. The objectives in the affective domain contain the behaviors that have emotional overtones and encompass likes and dislikes, attitudes, values, and beliefs. Affective objectives are divided into five classifications.[1]

Low level

1. *Receiving* objectives require students to recognize and receive certain phenomenon and stimuli.

2. *Responding* objectives require students to demonstrate a wide variety of reactions to stimuli.

Higher level

3. *Valuing* objectives require students to display a behavior with sufficient consistency.

4. *Organizing* objectives require students to or-

body during puberty and adolescence and discuss these changes with parents.

13. I will learn the different products used for menstrual health.
14. I will practice breast self-examination or testicular self-examination.
15. I will have regular medical checkups.
16. I will recognize the risks of teenage parenthood to the mother, father, and baby and choose abstinence to avoid placing myself and others at risk.
17. I will learn the behaviors that promote healthful pregnancy and if I am female I will practice these behaviors now recognizing they may affect me having a healthful pregnancy later in life.
18. I will make a plan to begin aging in a healthful way.
19. I will recognize the stages in dying and death and ask questions I have about death to my parents or other adult family member.
20. I will express sympathy to others who are grieving over the loss of a loved one.

Nutrition

1. I will eat the correct number of servings from the healthful food groups each day.
2. I will reduce my intake of foods that are high in sugar, salt, and fat.
3. I will increase my intake of fiber.
4. I will get an adequate amount of calcium in my diet.
5. I will have at least one source of vitamin C each day.
6. I will eat healthful snacks.
7. I will eat a healthful breakfast each day.
8. I will consume the equivalent of six to eight glasses of water each day.
9. I will follow the dietary guidelines.
10. I will read food labels for nutritional information.
11. I will follow the dietary suggestions of the American Heart Association and the American Cancer Society.
12. I will make and follow a plan to maintain my desirable weight.
13. I will exercise regularly to maintain a healthful percentage of body fat.
14. I will avoid drinking alcohol.
15. I will make a grocery list before shopping and follow guidelines for getting the best nutritional value for the dollar.
16. I will limit the amount of saturated fat and cholesterol in my diet.
17. I will consider nutritional needs when participating in activities.
18. I will avoid food products with additives that have a warning.
19. I will seek professional advice if an eating disorder is suspected.
20. I will check restaurant menus for American Heart Association approved foods.

Personal Fitness

1. I will participate in a variety of exercises.
2. I will participate in exercises to promote cardiovascular health.
3. I will get adequate amounts of sleep and rest.
4. I will warm up before and cool down after exercise.
5. I will exercise to develop muscular strength and endurance.
6. I will wear correct clothing for exercise and sport.
7. I will follow safety rules for sports and games.
8. I will participate in aerobic and anaerobic activities.
9. I will take part in individual and lifetime physical fitness activities.
10. I will be cooperative when playing sports and games.
11. I will follow a plan that promotes all areas of fitness.
12. I will wear proper protective equipment for activities.
13. I will follow safety rules when exercising.
14. I will exercise three times per week for at least twenty minutes at my target heart rate.
15. I will avoid the use of anabolic steroids.
16. I will sit, stand, and walk with correct posture.
17. I will exercise when I experience stress.
18. I will plan for weather conditions when I exercise.
19. I will use stretching exercises to remain flexible.
20. I will consult with a weight training consultant before using weight training machines.
21. I will follow principles of specificity, overload, progression, and frequency for all exercise activity.
22. I will work to improve my fitness skills.
23. I will avoid overtraining.
24. I will use the RICE treatment for musculoskeletal injuries.
25. I will seek medical treatment for fitness-related injuries.
26. I will follow responsible guidelines related to sports and diet.

Substance Use and Abuse

1. I will use medicine only with adult supervision.
2. I will not take any substances unless recommended or prescribed by a physician or adult.
3. I will follow directions for taking medicines.
4. I wil read labels to learn the harmful effects of substances.
5. I will place medicines back in their appropriate packages.
6. I will never take another person's medications.
7. I will carefully read all labels on medications.

8. I will tell parents if a medication I have taken produces a side effect.
9. I will tell my parents or another trusted adult if an illegal drug is offered to me.
10. I will keep informed of the harmful effects of drugs such as alcohol, nicotine, crack, cocaine, marijuana, LSD, PCP, etc.
11. I will not use illegal drugs and I will report persons who do.
12. I will not use an over-the-counter drug if the seal is broken.
13. I will use resistance skills if offered an illegal drug.
14. I will recognize that there is no such thing as "responsible" drinking for those under the legal age for drinking.
15. I will be aware of the health agencies and facilities in my community where persons can get help for abuse of drugs and chemical dependency.
16. I will choose friends who do not use illegal or harmful drugs.
17. I will avoid being in situations and attending parties where others use illegal or harmful drugs.
18. I will not smoke cigarettes.
19. I will avoid being around others who smoke cigarettes.
20. I will encourage my family to have a no smoking policy in our home.
21. I will not ride in an automobile with a driver who has been drinking alcohol or using other harmful drugs.
22. I will develop social poise and confidence with out the use of alcohol.
23. I will leave parties if alcohol or other drugs are being used.
24. I will keep a list of medications I have used for my family health record.

Diseases and Disorders

1. I will rest when I have a cold or other illness.
2. I will use precautions around others who have a cold or other communicable disease.
3. I will wash my hands before eating or handling food.
4. I will engage in behaviors to avoid infecting others when I have a communicable disease.
5. I will not share personal health products such as a toothbrush, comb, or brush with others.
6. I will tell an adult if I have symptoms of illness.
7. I will wash my hands often using soap.
8. I will respond to persons with disabilities in respectful and caring ways.
9. I will learn the signs and symptoms, diagnosis, and treatment for sexually transmitted diseases and learn where these diseases can be treated in my community.

10. I will practice sexual abstinence to avoid sexually transmitted diseases.
11. I will use precautions when taking aspirins or other medications.
12. I will not consume food that looks or smells spoiled.
13. I will store food properly.
14. I will have regular physical checkups.
15. I will demonstrate sensitivity to persons with chronic diseases.
16. I will seek medical care for injuries and illnesses when needed.
17. I will avoid IV drug use and sexual contact to prevent infection with HIV/AIDS.
18. I will not smoke cigarettes and I will avoid exposure to other known carcinogens.
19. I will avoid overexposure to the sun and will wear sunblock or sunscreen when exposed to the sun.
20. I will seek medical help for the warning signals of cancer.
21. I will be aware of my blood cholesterol level and will practice behaviors to keep it within a healthful range.
22. I will seek help from the school nurse when necessary.
23. I will avoid substances that trigger allergies.
24. I will avoid foods that increase the risks of developing heart disease.
25. I will keep a record of genetic diseases in my family and share this record with medical persons.

Consumer Health

1. I will have regular dental examinations.
2. I will have regular medical examinations.
3. I will practice behaviors to keep the skin, hair, and nails clean.
4. I will brush and floss my teeth regularly.
5. I will read ads for health products carefully.
6. I will take time to be well-groomed.
7. I will wear safety equipment for exercising.
8. I will wear a safety belt when riding in a car.
9. I will make price comparisons when shopping for health products.
10. I will select entertainment that promotes mental and physical health.
11. I will evaluate ads before making decisions about buying products.
12. I will apply guidelines for recognizing quackery.
13. I will select products for grooming carefully.
14. I will follow guidelines for choosing health facilities and personnel.
15. I will prepare and follow a budget.
16. I will follow directions for using cosmetics wisely.
17. I will read labels on all products before purchasing them.

18. I will follow family values when purchasing products.
19. I will be able to perform bodily monitoring procedures such as taking my temperature and respiration rate.
20. I will read the directions for using health care products such as deodorants.
21. I will follow guidelines for choosing health care providers.
22. I will learn the benefits of different kinds of health insurance.

Safety and Injury Prevention

1. I will avoid situations in the home that increase the risk of having an accident such as placing objects on stairs.
2. I will practice safety procedures on school buses and in cars.
3. I will follow rules for pedestrian safety.
4. I will participate in fire drills and other drills related to environmental hazards such as earthquakes.
5. I will avoid contact with poisons.
6. I will follow safety rules around heat and electricity.
7. I will follow guidelines to prevent falls.
8. I will practice bicycle safety rules.
9. I will follow safety rules around pools, rivers, and lakes.
10. I will follow safety precautions for being around firearms.
11. I will have a plan to follow for each possible natural disaster such as a hurricane, tornado, earthquake, etc.
12. I will use and check smoke and heat detectors in my home.
13. I will practice making an emergency phone call.
14. I will follow first aid procedures for injuries and illnesses.
15. I will follow first aid procedures for poisoning.
16. I will demonstrate how to use the abdominal thrust.
17. I will be able to use CPR when appropriate.
18. I will have a first aid kit available.
19. I will avoid talking to strangers who approach me.
20. I will not allow someone to touch me in an unsafe way.
21. I will not allow someone to abuse me physically, mentally, sexually, or emotionally or by neglect.
22. I will report any cases of abuse to a trusted adult.
23. I will remove myself from situations in which I am being abused or harmed.
24. I will follow guidelines for being safe when I am at home alone.
25. I will not engage in violent behaviors or crimes.
26. I will follow guidelines to prevent violent crimes.
27. I will report violent crimes to trusted adults and authorities.
28. I will follow guidelines for handling obscene telephone calls.

Community and Environment

1. I will keep my personal possessions neat and well maintained.
2. I will not litter.
3. I will conserve energy in the home by not wasting water and electricity.
4. I will save objects for recycling.
5. I will practice ways to improve the environment by engaging in behaviors such as riding bikes instead of travelling in motor vehicles.
6. I will avoid using products that pollute the environment including products such as certain kinds of propellents in spray cans.
7. I will check the radon level in my home with an adult.
8. I will follow directions for the safe use of pesticides.
9. I will be able to contact persons who can offer emergency medical care.
10. I will follow laws for the disposal of products.
11. I will try to use products that can be recycled.
12. I will use the services of professional organizations when appropriate.
13. I will participate in health screening programs.
14. I will follow recommendations from health professionals about safety and the environment.
15. I will use voluntary and public health agencies when appropriate.
16. I will follow public health laws.
17. I will volunteer to help at home and/or in my community.
18. I will support legislation to promote a healthful environment.

Table 3-5

The Scope and Sequence Chart

The following Scope and Sequence Chart is an example of topical areas that are covered in the document, *A Framework for Comprehensive School Health Education* developed by Meeks Heit for use by the Ohio Department of Education. The Scope and Sequence Chart includes the ten areas identified for health instruction: Mental and Emotional Well-Being, Family and Relationship Skills, Substance Use and Abuse, Diseases and Disorders, Consumer Health, Safety and Injury Prevention, and Community and Environment.

Mental Well-Being and Positive Adjustments

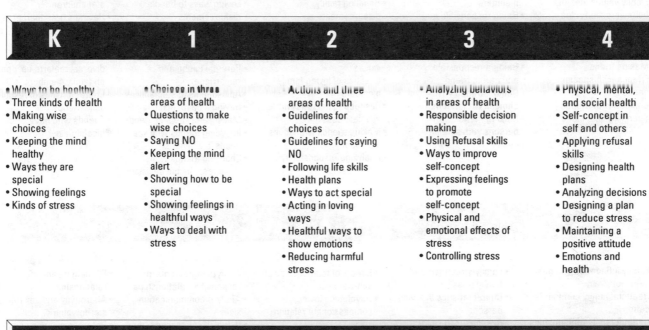

K	1	2	3	4
• Ways to be healthy • Three kinds of health • Making wise choices • Keeping the mind healthy • Ways they are special • Showing feelings • Kinds of stress	• Choices in three areas of health • Questions to make wise choices • Saying NO • Keeping the mind alert • Showing how to be special • Showing feelings in healthful ways • Ways to deal with stress	• Actions and three areas of health • Guidelines for choices • Guidelines for saying NO • Following life skills • Health plans • Ways to act special • Acting in loving ways • Healthful ways to show emotions • Reducing harmful stress	• Analyzing behaviors in areas of health • Responsible decision making • Using Refusal skills • Ways to improve self-concept • Expressing feelings to promote self-concept • Physical and emotional effects of stress • Controlling stress	• Physical, mental, and social health • Self-concept in self and others • Applying refusal skills • Designing health plans • Analyzing decisions • Designing a plan to reduce stress • Maintaining a positive attitude • Emotions and health

5	6	7	8	9-12
• Dimensions of health • Healthful behaviors, risk behaviors, and risk situations • Ten areas of health • Health knowledge and responsible decision making • Refusal skills and health behavior • Self-concept and responsible decision making • Sex roles and stereotyping • Emotions and decision making • Stress, eustress, and distress	• Achieving wellness • Avoiding risk behavior and risk situations • Demonstrating refusal skills • Constructing health behavior contracts • Strengthening self-concept • Improving weaknesses • Personality strengths • Philosophy of life and goals • Emotions, stress, eustress, and distress • Depression and suicide prevention	• Optimal physical, mental, and social health • Wellness and behavior • Life skills and health behavior contracts • Peer pressure and decision making • Refusal skills and peer pressure • Stages of general adaptation syndrome during stress • Coping with depression • Suicide prevention strategies	• Effects of behavior on physical, mental, social, and family health • Evaluating guidelines for responsible decision making • Evaluating refusal skills used for peer pressure • Maintaining and improving health status • Sample health behavior contracts • Characteristics of mental health • Causes, symptoms, and treatment for depression • Eustress, distress, and stress management skills • General adaptation syndrome and body changes • Recognizing signs of suicide	• Health appraisals • Healthful behaviors and risk behaviors • Responsible decision making • Nation's health goals and objectives • Influences on personality • Private self, public self, and ideal self • Causes of mental illness • Anxiety and depression • Suicide prevention • Community resources in mental health • Causes and effects of stress • Stress management strategies

Character and Relationship Skills

K	1	2	3	4

K
- Family and family members
- Similarities and differences in families
- Ways families change
- Love and families
- Sharing feelings in families
- Family values, health behaviors, and rules
- Family chores
- Ways to be a good friend
- Making friends
- Friends with special needs
- Choices with friends
- Spending time alone

1
- Belonging to a family
- Ways families are special
- Ways to show love in families
- Feelings when there are family changes
- Having new family members
- Being responsible and doing chores
- Family rules for health and safety
- Being a responsible and caring friend
- Demonstrating wise choices with friends
- Making friends with persons with special needs

2
- Special names of family members
- Two parent, single parent, and stepfamilies
- Ways families are different and alike
- Adjustments to family changes
- Handling family disagreements
- Developing positive family memories
- Following healthful family values
- Qualities of loving family members
- Respecting persons with special needs
- Making friends with adults at school
- Analyzing responsibility in friendships

3
- Ways persons are related
- Structures of families
- Role of parents in families
- Importance of love in marriage
- Parental love and expression
- Family members, birth, adoption, and foster children
- Loving ways to handle disagreements
- Marital disagreements, resolutions, separation, divorce
- Parental dating and remarriage
- Adjustments to stepfamilies
- Having a death in the family
- Making and keeping friends
- Including friends with special needs in activities
- Choosing friends who make responsible decisions

4
- Family heredity, environment, and lifestyle
- Family cooperation
- Loving families and difficult families
- Respect for family values
- Newborn babies, adopted children, foster children stepchildren
- Having a grandparent or older person live with the family
- Effects of separation, divorce, remarriage, death on family members
- Characteristics of responsible friends
- Friends who have disabilities

5	6	7	8	9-12

5
- Family influences on health behavior
- Healthful family communication
- Difficult family relationships
- Community resources for difficult family relationships
- Adjustments to serious illness and death in family
- Impact of separation and divorce on family members' health
- Single parent families, parental dating, and remarriage
- Bonding in stepfamilies
- Communication skills for friendship
- Bragging versus sharing feelings
- Physical, mental, and emotional attraction to others
- Sexual feelings and body changes
- Reasons for sexual abstinence
- Parental guidelines and behavior
- Factors in successful marriage
- Responsibilities and rewards of parenting
- Needs of newborns
- Characteristics of responsible friendship
- Friendship needs of the disabled

6
- Family structures and family roles
- Characteristics of loving persons
- Responses to separation, divorce, remarriage, stepfamilies
- Grieving, illness, and death
- Self-loving and self-centered behavior
- Showing gratitude, taking responsibility, using manners
- Benefits of being assertive
- Effects of name calling and labelling
- Responsibilities in relationships
- Characteristics of intimacy
- Progression of sexual feelings and physical affection
- Establishing limits and choosing sexual abstinence
- Resisting peer pressure to be sexually active
- Resisting teen marriage and parenthood
- Respecting the institution of marriage and the importance of parenthood
- Choosing friends with family values

7
- Effects of relationships on self-concept
- Developing loving, compassionate relationships
- Using "I" messages and active listening
- Differentiating between assertive, passive, and aggressive behavior
- Skills for opposite sex relationships
- Understanding sexual feelings and body changes
- Establishing behavior guidelines to promote abstinence
- Developing positive family communication
- Developing values and good character
- Characteristics of successful marriages and parenthood
- Examining adjustments to family changes
- Evaluating difficulties of teen marriage and parenthood

8
- Analyze ingredients in responsible relationships
- Analyze communication skills
- Using "I" messages rather than "you" messages
- Giving feedback in conversations
- Development of healthful sex roles
- Personality and sexuality
- Sexual orientation and sexual behavior
- Dating and limits on sexual behavior
- Advantages of sexual abstinence
- Qualities in a good date
- Factors that influence successful marriage
- Factors that influence successful parenting
- Effect of marital conflict and breakup on family members
- Adjustments to difficulties in families
- Disadvantages of teenage marriage and parenthood

9-12
- Forming meaningful relationships
- Androgyny and sex role stereotyping
- Heterosexual and homosexual sexual orientation
- Becoming a loving person
- Healthful relationships within families
- Family values and character
- Dysfunctional families
- Characteristics of friendships
- Communication skills
- Analyzing effects of friends' behavior
- Responsibilities when dating
- Advantages of sexual abstinence
- Using refusal skills to resist pressure to be sexually active
- Characteristics of relationships that may lead to successful marriage
- Benefits of engagement
- Difficulties of teenage marriages lasting
- Readiness for parenting
- Difficulties facing teenage parents
- Spousal abuse
- Family conflict, separation, divorce, remarriage and stepfamilies

Growth and Development

K	1	2	3	4

- Babies and parents
- Characteristics of babies
- Differences in boys' and girls' bodies
- Body parts and growth
- Changes and growth
- Changes in older people
- Questions about birth, growth, and death

- Cells
- Body organs develop
- Body parts change as they grow
- Functions of heart, brain, lungs
- How the senses protect people
- Body systems have different organs
- Keeping body systems healthy
- How a baby is born

- Cells, organs, and body systems
- Protecting five senses
- Caring for organs in body systems
- How a baby is made
- Caring for a newborn

- Cells, tissues, organs, body systems
- Keeping the skeletal system healthy
- Keeping the nervous system healthy
- Keeping the digestive system healthy
- Keeping the circulatory system healthy
- Keeping the reproductive system healthy
- Fertilization and birth
- Preparing for a new baby

- Characteristics of cells, tissues, organs, and systems
- Voluntary and involuntary muscles
- Functions of skin
- Process of digestion
- Blood flow through the circulatory system
- Process of respiration
- Effects of heredity
- Changes during puberty
- Fertilization and the birth process
- Structure and function of the reproductive system
- Development of the embryo and fetus
- Birth process

5	6	7	8	9-12

- Structure, function, and care of body systems
- Characteristics of different stages of the life cycle
- Pituitary and thyroid gland
- Function of hormones
- Reproductive system and menstruation
- Menstrual health products
- Fertilization and pregnancy
- Risk behaviors and pregnancy
- Parents' role in pregnancy and birth

- Health behaviors that influence body systems
- Structure and function of the male reproductive system
- Structure and function of the female reproductive system
- Hormonal influence on male reproductive system
- Hormonal influence on female reproductive system
- Puberty and physical and emotional health
- Factors that influence spermatogenesis
- Fertilization, pregnancy, labor, and delivery
- Stresses of teenage pregnancy and teenage parenthood
- Growth during infancy, childhood, adolescence, adulthood, old age
* Aging process

- Care of the skeletal, muscular, integumentary, nervous, endocrine, reproductive, digestive, respiratory, circulatory, and urinary systems
- Secretions of the endocrine system
- Stages of the menstrual cycle
- Menstrual health and menstrual health products
- Process of conception
- Development of the embryo and fetus from conception to birth
- Puberty and adolescence
- Growth and development from infancy through old age
- Life skills and aging
- Stages of dying and death

- Health behaviors that influence the skeletal, nervous, integumentary, muscular, endocrine, digestive, urinary, respiratory, circulatory, and reproductive systems
- Physiology of menstrual cycle
- Toxic shock syndrome
- Premenstrual syndrome, amenorrhea, and dysmenorrhea
- Spermatogenesis and ejaculation
- Fertilization and conception
- Avoiding Pregnancy
- Pregnancy, prenatal care, and embryonic development
- Labor, delivery, and newborn care
- Breastfeeding
- Characteristics of newborns, infants, children, adolescents, young adults, and old age
- Skills needed for parenthood
- Aging process
- Process of death and dying

- Wellness and the skeletal, muscular, integumentary, nervous, digestive, circulatory, respiratory, urinary, endocrine, and reproductive systems
- Changes of the body during puberty
- Physiological changes in female during stages of menstrual cycle
- Menstrual health products
- Premenstrual syndrome, toxic shock syndrome, dysmenorrhea, an amenorrhea
- Physiological explanation of spermatogenesis, ejaculation
- Fertilization and in-vitro fertilization
- Ectopic pregnancy, identical and fraternal twins
- Growth and development during each trimester of pregnancy
- Prenatal care, healthful habits, and risk factors
- Childbirth options
- Stages of labor and delivery
- Postpartum period
- Responsibilities of parenthood
- Natural family planning
- Pregnancy prevention
- Use, advantages, disadvantages, and effectiveness of birth control methods

Growth and Development

5	6	7	8	9-12

9-12
- Sterilization procedures
- Family values and abortion
- Unique characteristics of different stages of the life cycle
- Harvard Medical School criteria for death
- Kubler-Ross stages of death and dying
- Issues regarding euthanasia and family values
- Customs regarding funerals and burial options
- Purposes of living wills
- Grieving

Nutrition

K	1	2	3	4

K
- The healthful food groups
- The others group
- Foods high in sugar, salt, and fat
- Choosing snacks
- Eating breakfast
- Eating at restaurants
- Importance of water

1
- Need for variety of foods
- Balanced diet
- Ways food helps the body
- Eating less sugar and salt
- Planning breakfast
- Planning snacks
- Healthy drinks
- Healthy fast foods

2
- Foods and drinks in the milk group
- Foods in the meat group
- Foods and drinks in the fruit and vegetable group
- Foods in the grain group
- Foods in the others group
- Why too much sugar, salt, and fat is harmful
- Snacks in food groups
- Breakfast and food groups
- Eating out and food groups

3
- Choices to follow diet guidelines
- Foods with calcium
- Foods with vitamin C
- Foods with too much sugar, salt, and fat
- Choosing snacks to follow diet guidelines
- Breakfasts that follow diet guidelines
- Healthful daily menus
- Menus at restaurants

4
- Nutrients
- Foods as sources of nutrients
- Importance of water
- Planning a balanced diet
- Health benefits of the dietary guidelines
- Information on food labels
- Choosing healthful fast foods
- Planning a healthful breakfast

5	6	7	8	9-12

5
- Foods as sources of nutrients
- Using dietary guidelines when choosing food
- Reducing fat and saturated fat
- Increasing calcium and vitamin C
- Increasing fiber
- Factors that influence food choices
- Methods of gaining and losing weight
- Nutrition guidelines for sports
- Food preparation and storage
- Ethnic variations in food choices

6
- Nutrient functions, sources, and deficiencies
- Analyzing dietary guidelines
- Information on food labels
- Healthful ways to gain and lose weight
- Advantages and disadvantages of popular diets
- Causes, effects, and treatments for eating disorders
- Importance of breakfast
- Nutrient values of common snacks and fast foods
- Use of food additives

7
- Dietary guidelines and wellness
- Six classes of nutrients
- Eating foods with sources of fiber, vitamin C, and calcium
- Limiting salt, sugar, saturated fat, and cholesterol
- Effects of drinking alcohol on obtaining nutrients
- Guidelines of the American Cancer Society
- Guidelines of the American Heart Association
- Food selection, storage, and preparation
- Nutrient values of beverages
- Analyzing nutrient values of breakfast foods
- Food labels, comparison

8
- Planning meals to follow dietary guidelines
- Analyzing food labels for fat, saturated fat, cholesterol, fiber, calcium, vitamin C, and salt
- Megadosing
- Planning meals to meet American Heart Assocation and American Cancer Society guidelines
- Vitamin and mineral sources and deficiencies
- Snacks, beverages, and fast food values
- Energy equation and weight management
- Body composition and weight control

9-12
- United States Recommended Dietary Allowances
- Simple and complex carbohydrates
- Saturated and unsaturated fats
- Cholesterol, LDLs, and HDLs
- Functions of water
- Vitamins, minerals, and deficiencies
- Importance of a healthful breakfast
- Nutritional value of snacks and convenience foods
- Relationship between diet and cancer
- Relationship between diet and heart disease

Nutrition

5	6	7	8	9-12

| | | shopping, and unit pricing
• Weight management strategies
• Eating disorders, anorexia nervosa, bulimia
• Exercise, sport, and diet | • Consequences of eating disorders, anorexia nervosa and bulimia
• Fad diets
• Dietary guidelines for athletes
• Carbohydrate loading | • Relationship between diet and weight
• Weight management strategies
• Fad dieting
• Consumer information and food labelling
• Causes, symptoms, and treatment of eating disorders
• American Heart Association guidelines for eating out
• Nutrition and athletics |

Personal Fitness

K	1	2	3	4
• Different ways to exercise • Exercise and the heart • Rest and sleep • Fitness	• Kinds of exercise • How exercise helps the heart and lungs • Exercises that help the heart and lungs • Exercises to make muscles strong • Warm up and cool down • Rest and sleep • Being fit	• Health and physical fitness • Exercises that help fitness • Exercises that make heart and lungs fit • Exercises that make muscles fit • Fitness and injury prevention • Rest and sleep and fitness • Warming up and cooling down when exercising	• Benefits of physical fitness • Muscular strength, endurance, and flexibility • Cardiovascular fitness • Principles of warming up and cooling down • Safety when playing games and sports • Cooperation in sports and games • Physical activities with families • Physical fitness tests	• Physical, mental, and social benefits of fitness • Tests to measure fitness • Exercise for different body areas • Aerobic and anaerobic exercise • Developing exercise plans • Advantages of lifetime sports • Cooperation in team and group activities • Warm up and cool down and vigorous exercise

5	6	7	8	9-12
• Five areas of total fitness • Kinds of anaerobic, aerobic, isokinetic, and isotonic exercises • Cardiovascular fitness and the heart and blood vessels • Planning warm up and cool down for aerobic exercise • Guidelines for prevention of exercise related injuries • Physical fitness testing	• Exercises to develop muscular strength, muscular endurance, cardiovascular endurance, flexibility, and low fat body composition • Five fitness areas • Advantages of participating in lifetime sports • Physical activity levels • Individual physical fitness plans • Injuries in team sports • Safety rules for running, walking, swimming, biking • Prevention and care for muscle injuries • Passing physical fitness tests	• Role of exercise in preventing atherosclerosis, reducing cholesterol, and reducing cancer • Participating in exercise to strengthen muscles • Dangers of anabolic steroid use • Posture and muscular development • Role of exercise in promoting sleep, rest, and weight management • Exercises to reduce body fat composition • Benefits of isotonic, isometric, isokinetic, aerobic, and anaerobic exercise • Benefits of lifetime sports • Developing agility, balance,	• Benefits of muscular strength, muscular endurance, cardiovascular endurance, flexibility, and low percentage of body fat • Testing for the five areas of fitness • Exercise plans that include aerobic, anaerobic, isokinetic, and isotonic exercises • Warming up and cooling down • Rest and sleep for total fitness • Effects of weight management • Beta-endorphins and aerobic exercise	• Physical fitness and mental, social, physical, and family health • Achieving muscular strength, endurance, flexibility, cardiovascular endurance, low body fat composition • Guidelines for isometric, isotonic, isokinetic, aerobic, and anaerobic exercise • Importance of nutrition, rest, and sleep to fitness • Research on exercise, premature heart disease, cancer, and aging • Training principles to reduce injuries • Physical fitness plans and lifetime sports • Harmful effects of anabolic steroids • Sample physical fitness plans

Personal Fitness

5	6	7	8	9-12

| | | coordination, reaction time, power, and speed • Principles of exercise and training • Physical fitness planning • Standards for physical fitness | • Exercising and the family • Participating in lifetime sports • Exercise related injuries and weather conditions, safety rules, biome chanics, and physical profiling • Body type and exercise selection • Total physical fitness plans | |

Substance Use and Abuse

K	1	2	3	4
• Drugs to help health • Medicines as drugs • Safe places for medicines • Drugs which harm bodies • How alcohol effects health • How cigarettes effect health	• Drugs, medicine, and safety • Drugs that are harmful • Dangers of cigarette smoking and being near smoke • Dangers of marijuana • Dangers of alcohol • Saying NO to harmful drugs	• Rules for safe use of drugs and medicines • Healthful and harmful drugs • Alcohol and the body • Tobacco, cigarette smoke, and the body • Marijuana and the body • Effects of cocaine, heroin, and LSD • Telling adults about illegal drug use • Knowing when and how to say NO	• Medicine, prescription, and over-the-counter drugs • Side effects and actions • Drug use, misuse, and abuse • Effects of cigarette smoking, breathing the smoke from others, and using smokeless tobacco • Harmful effects of drinking alcohol • Effects of stimulants, depressants, inhalants • Harmful effects of marijuana • Skills used to resist peer pressure	• Differentiating drug use, misuse, and abuse • Prescription and over-the-counter drugs • Health risks of smoking and smokeless tobacco • Health risks of drinking alcohol • Health risks of stimulants, depressants, and inhalent • Health risks of using marijuana, crack, and cocaine • Substance abuse, the individual and family • Characteristics of chemical dependency • Refusal skills and illegal drugs

5	6	7	8	9-12
• Legal and illegal drugs • Categorizing depressants, stimulants, hallucinogens, inhalants • Effects and risks of alcohol • Alcoholism and family treatment • Blood alchol level • Health and marijuana, crack, and cocaine • Drug dependence and addiction • Treatment facilities • Establishing smoke free environments	• Characteristics of drug use, misuse, abuse, and dependence • Pressures to experiment with harmful drugs • Refusal skills used to stop drug use • Choosing friends who are drug free • Use of drugs to promote health • Dangers of opiates and stimulants • Combining drugs • Ethyl and methyl alcohol	• Drugs and society • Illegal drug use • Drug free lifestyles • Resisting pressures to use illegal drugs • Drug terminology • Withdrawal from opiates, barbiturates, and tranquilizers • Effects of crack, cocaine, and amphetamines • Effects of marijuana, LSD, PCP, and inhalant • Combing dangerous drugs • Prevention and treatment of alcoholism and chemical	• Promoting a drug free society • Outlining ways to stay drug free • Pressures to use drugs • Refusal skills and resistance strategies • Healthful use of drugs • Examining drug use, drug abuse, drug misuse, chemical dependence, tolerance, and withdrawal • Opiates and the nervous system • Dangers of opiates,	• Drug use, misuse, and abuse • Ways drugs enter the body • Factors which influence drug action • Characteristics of chemical dependence • Using and storing prescription and over-the-counter drugs • Effects of stimulants, depressants, and

Substance Use and Abuse

5	6	7	8	9-12

- Methods of quitting smoking
- Preventing drug use
- Benefits of drug free lifestyle
- Peer pressure and drug use
- Resisting peer pressure and saying no

- Stages of alcohol dependency and alcoholism
- Treatment for alcoholism and the family
- Effects of marijuana, crack, cocaine, and tobacco on the body, mind, and spirit
- Dangers of sidestream smoke
- Tobacco free lifestyles
- Resisting pressure to use tobacco

dependency
- Effects of chemical dependency on the family and society
- Harmful ingredients in tobacco
- Diseases related to tobacco use
- Sidestream smoke and laws
- Health protection for nonsmokers

barbiturates, tranquilizers, crack, cocaine, amphetamines, marijuana, LSD, PCP, and inhalant
- Dangers of combining drugs
- Alcohol as a family disease
- Alcohol free lifestyle
- Treatment modalities for alcoholism and chemical dependence
- Cigarette smoking and smokeless tobacco use and risk
- Diseases that result from drug use
- Drug laws
- Consumer influence on drug laws

hallucinogens on the body
- Why combining drugs is dangerous
- Emergency care procedures for drug overdose
- Ways of classifying drugs
- Resisting pressure to drink alcohol
- Effects of alcohol
- Signs of alcoholism
- Impact of alcoholism on family members
- Treatment programs and support for familes with alcoholism
- Cigarette smoking, tobacco use, and health
- Sidestream smoke and mainstream smoke
- Smoking or drinking during pregnancy
- Tobacco cessation programs
- Actions to protect the rights of nonsmokers
- Analyzing peer pressure to use drugs
- Using strategies to prevent drug use

Diseases and Disorders

K	1	2	3	4

- Habits and illness
- How germs are spread
- Common cold
- Keeping hands clean
- How the body fights germs
- Shots and vaccines
- AIDS is a sickness
- Ways you cannot get AIDS
- Knowing someone with AIDS
- Asking questions about AIDS

- Characteristics of a healthy person
- Body cells that fight germs
- Immunizations
- Kinds of viruses
- How viruses are spread
- Ways to avoid germs
- Symptoms of cold, sore throat
- HIV and AIDS
- Ways HIV gets into the body
- Ways people cannot get HIV
- Finding a cure for AIDS
- Having a classmate with AIDS

- Transmission of germs
- Preventing transmission of germs
- Body protection from germs
- Vaccines and medicines
- Cause of AIDS
- How HIV breaks down body protection
- Diseases and infections that result
- How HIV is spread
- How HIV is not spread
- No cure or treatment for AIDS
- Lives of persons with AIDS
- Understanding disabilities

- How germs multiply
- Diseases caused by viruses
- Body's defense system
- How HIV destroys T-cells
- Development of AIDS
- HIV remains a lifetime
- Ways HIV is spread
- How a baby can get HIV
- Noncommunicable diseases
- Ways to prevent heart disease
- Ways to prevent cancer
- Kinds of disabilities

- Difference between communicable and noncommunicable disease
- Kinds of pathogens
- How the body protects itself from pathogens
- Risk factors for noncommunicable diseases
- Heart disease and hypertension
- Cancer
- Arthritis
- Diabetes
- Health and disabilities
- Sexually transmitted diseases
- Guidelines to prevent STDs
- HIV and AIDS
- Dangers of being infected with HIV
- Ways HIV is and is not spread
- What it is like to have AIDS
- Being around a person with AIDS
- Preventing HIV infection

Diseases and Disorders

5	6	7	8	9-12

5
- Understanding communicable, noncommunicable, and chronic disease
- Risk behaviors and noncommunicable diseases
- Risk factors, prevention, and treatment for heart disease
- Emergency care for heart attack
- Risk factors, prevention, and treatment for cancer
- Kinds of chronic diseases
- Understanding congenital heart disease and rheumatic heart disease
- Characteristics of diabetes, epilepsy, multiple sclerosis, and cystic fibrosis
- Disabilities and health status
- Pathogens which cause communicable disease
- Preventing the spread of pathogens
- Sore throat and strep throat
- Reye syndrome
- Food poisoning prevention and treatment
- Prevention and treatment for sexually transmitted diseases
- HIV/AIDS and the immune system
- HIV infection through intravenous drug use, sexual contact and during pregnancy
- Ways HIV infection has not occurred
- Risk behavior and HIV infection
- Signs, symptoms, and progression of HIV/AIDS
- Preventing HIV infection

6
- Classifications of diseases
- Risk factors, prevention, and treatment for atherosclerosis
- Risk factors, prevention, and treatment for cancer
- Characteristics and treatment for multiple sclerosis, epilepsy, cerebral palsy, hemophilia, and muscular dystrophy
- Kinds of diabetes
- Asthma, allergies, and health status
- Sickle cell anemia
- Pathogens that cause communicable diseases
- Stages of disease progression
- Common communicable diseases
- HIV destruction of the immune system
- Transmission of HIV
- Ways HIV is not transmitted
- Signs, symptoms, and progression of AIDS
- Opportunistic infections
- Guidelines to prevent HIV infection

7
- Kinds of diseases
- Risk factors, signs and symptoms, treatment and prevention for heart disease
- Risk factors, signs and symptoms, treatment, and prevention for cancer
- Research about tanning beds, malignant melanoma
- Treatment and prognosis for headaches, epilepsy, multiple sclerosis, cerebral palsy, peptic ulcers
- Risk factors, signs and symptoms, treatment, and prevention for diabetes
- Hay fever and allergies effect on health status
- Transmission of pathogens causing communicable diseases
- Characteristics of mononucleosis, strep throat, pneumonia, and flu
- Cause, transmission, signs and symptoms, consequences, prevention, and treatment of chlamydia, gonorrhea, syphilis, genital herpes, genital warts
- Cause, transmission, signs and symptoms, prevention, and treatment of HIV/AIDS
- Importance of sexual abstinence and drug free lifestyle in prevention of HIV infection

8
- Similarities and differences between communicable and noncommunicable diseases
- Administration of medicines and over-the-counter drugs
- Antibodies and vaccines
- Kinds of heart disease, prevention, and treatment
- Kinds of cancers, prevention, and treatment
- Health behavior contracts for heart disease and cancer risk factors
- Malignant melanoma
- Sex-linked and recessive inherited diseases
- Down syndrome
- Epilepsy and guidelines to follow if seizures occur
- Alzheimers disease
- Diabetes, arthritis, allergies, and asthma
- Ways pathogens are transmitted and cause disease
- Pathogens, body defenses, and the immune system
- Signs, symptoms, complications, treatment, transmission and prevention of genital herpes, genital warts, chlamydia, gonorrhea, and syphilis
- CDC definitions of HIV and AIDS
- Transmission of HIV/AIDS
- HIV immune system breakdown and opportunistic diseases
- Development of AIDS
- Research into HIV/AIDS treatment modalities and vaccines
- Prevention of AIDS with abstinence and drug free style
- Health care workers and AIDS
- Social, economic, and legal implications of HIV/AIDS

9-12
- Spread of pathogens via direct and indirect contact
- Stages of communicable diseases
- Ways that immunity can be acquired
- Common respiratory infections
- Cause, transmission, treatment, and prevention of gonorrhea, syphilis, genital herpes, genital warts, trichomoniasis, moniliasis, scabies, pediculosis
- HIV/AIDS definitions
- Transmission, risk factors, progression, diagnosis, treatment and prevention for HIV/AIDS
- Cardiovascular health, atherosclerosis, angina pectoris, hypertension, coronary thrombosis, rheumatic heart disease, and stroke
- Kinds of cancer, signs and symptoms, risk factors, treatment, and prevention
- Diseases linked to heredity
- Diseases linked to absence of a chromosome or additional chromosome
- Recessive inherited diseases and sex linked diseases
- Genetic mutations and inherited disorders
- Epilepsy, multiple sclerosis, diabetes, arthritis, cerebral palsy
- Disabilities and handicaps

Consumer Health

K	1	2	3	4
• Keeping the body clean • Health habits for grooming • Correct posture • Using health products • Kinds of health care workers • Medical and dental checkups • Dental health care	• Ways to be well-groomed • Care of hair, skin, nails • Correct handwashing • Having correct posture • Sleep and rest • Doctors and checkups • Dentists, dental hygienists, and checkups • Taking care of teeth	• Health products for grooming • Health products for skin, hair, and nails • Having regular medical checkups • Having regular dental checkups • Reasons for sleep and rest • Brushing, flossing, and foods for teeth	• Consumer choices • Products and services • Ads for health products • Choices for products for hair, skin, nails • Procedures during medical checkups • Procedures during dental checkups • Making a dental health plan	• Roles of health care workers • Guidelines for care of hair, skin, nails • Personal health care • Product labelling • Care of eyes, sty, black eye, pink eye • Care of ears, hearing losses • Screening examinations • Kinds of medical care • Kinds of dental care • Purchasing dental products • Guidelines for protecting teeth from injury • Ads for health products and services

5	6	7	8	9-12
• Examples of consumer choices • Kinds of health products and services • Kinds of health care professionals • Good grooming plans • Scoliosis screening, prevention, and treatment • Nearsightedness, farsightedness, and eye checkups • Hearing tests and hearing loss • Thorough medical examinations • Thorough dental examinations • Making a time management plan • Spending money wisely • Characteristics of health quackery • Consumer protection agencies • Making a consumer complaint	• Consumer health products and services • Guidelines for purchasing products • Products that promote healthful thoughts • Necessary and unnecessary grooming products • Standards for health services • Community resources that provide health. • Strategies used to advertise products • Consumer protection • Planning for dental health care and services • Gingivitis and periodontal disease • Complete physical examinations	• Following a time management plan • Making a budget • Health products and services for families • Analyzing ads and commercials for appeals • Selecting clothes, entertainment, and grooming • Evaluating kinds of quackery • Governmental agencies that protect consumers • Responsibility for health care • Regular medical checkups • Preventive dental health planning • Health care services and facilities in the community • Health care insurance • Advantages and disadvantages of health care maintainence organizations	• Decisions about health care products and services • Time managment plans and health status • Guidelines for spending money on consumer products • Budgeting for consumer services • Persuasion in advertisements and commercials • Recognizing quackery • Governmental agencies to protect consumers • Signs and symptoms which warrant medical care • Procedures for physical examinations • Signs and symptoms warranting dental care • Procedures for dental care • Health care facilities in the community • Volunteer opportunities for youth • Selection of health care providers • Insurance policies and payment for health care	• Creating a personal budget • Creating a time management plan • Analyzing consumer behavior • Evaluating advertise ments and commercials • Recognizing quackery • Identifying health agencies in the community • Making a personal health management plan • Using over-the-counter drugs • Planning to be well-groomed • Purchasing products for grooming • Evaluating posture • Evaluating guidelines for selecting health care providers • Having regular medical and dental examinations • Health services available in individual and group practices, hospitals,

Consumer Health

5	6	7	8	9-12

urgent care centers, and extended care centers
• Forms of health payment including preferred provider organizations, health maintenance organizations, and private and public health insurance plans

Safety and Injury Prevention

K	1	2	3	4

K
• Causes of accidents
• Safe places to play
• Ways to cross the road safely
• Making an emergency phone call
• Preventing fires and burns
• Stop, drop, and roll
• Preventing falls
• Keeping safe from poisonous products
• Caring for minor wounds
• Grownups who help with injuries
• Going to and from school
• safely
• Wearing safetybelts
• Use of safety helmets
• Being safe at home alone
• Safe and unsafe touch
• Safety from strangers

1
• Injuries and accidents
• Using electrical appliances safely
• Using the stop, drop, and roll technique
• Following bicycle safety rules
• Wearing safetybelts and safety helmets
• Understanding first aid
• Scrapes, cuts, nosebleeds, burns, and stings
• Staying away from poisons
• Understanding kinds of abuse
• Private body parts
• Recognizing safe and unsafe touch
• Getting help for abuse
• Protection from persons who may harm others

2
• Kinds of injuries and accidents
• Safety rules for riding in cars and buses
• Safety rules for riding a bicycle
• Safety rules for water sports
• Safety rules to prevent poisoning
• Safety rules to prevent injuries with guns and weapons
• Safety rules for winter activities
• Safety rules for escaping from fires
• Safety rules to follow around strangers
• Understanding first aid basics
• Making an emergency telephone call
• First aid for cuts, nosebleeds, fractures, burns, stings, animal bites
• Difference between child abuse and discipline
• Understanding bodily harm
• Understanding safe and unsafe touch
• Telling grownups about abuse

3
• Importance of safety rules
• Protecting against injuries from falls
• Protecting against injuries from fires
• Protecting against injuries while playing
• Remaining safe as a pedestrian
• Remaining safe on a bicycle
• Hazards of ATVs
• Safety while swimming
• Persons who can give first aid
• Making emergency telephone calls
• Methods to control bleeding
• Having a sprain
• Having a blocked airway
• Having contact with poison
• Being responsible for personal safety
• Hiding a house key
• Having rules for safety when home alone
• Safe use of the telephone
• Safety from strangers
• Reasons why some adults abuse children
• Physical abuse, emotional abuse, and neglect
• Safe and unsafe touch
• Reporting and getting help for abuse

4
• Importance of safety rules
• Preventing falls
• Protection from fires
• Safety outside the home
• Guidelines for pedestrian safety
• Bicycle and ATV safety
• Safety while swimming
• Knowing who can give first aid
• Making an emergency telephone call
• How to control bleeding
• First aid for sprains
• First aid for blocked airway
• First aid for poisonous plants
• Self-protection strategies
• Entering the home safely
• Safety on the telephone
• Safety around strangers
• Kinds of abuse
• Safe and unsafe touch
• Reporting abuse

Safety and Injury Prevention

5	6	7	8	9-12

5
- Importance of following safety rules
- Safety hazards at home and school
- Pedestrian and motor vehicle safety
- Bicycle and ATV safety
- Safety for water sports
- Fire escape plans for home and school
- Getting help for an emergency
- First aid for sunburn, insect stings, scrapes, cuts puncture wounds, fractures, objects in the eye
- Heimlich maneuver
- Self-protection strategies
- Being safe at home
- Actions to take for physical abuse, emotional abuse, neglect, and sexual abuse
- Community resources that help the abused and abuser

6
- Rules for giving first aid
- Performing the Heimlich maneuver
- Controlling bleeding
- Helping poison victims
- First aid for shock, dislocation, fractures, burns
- First aid for heat cramps, heat exhaustion, heat stroke
- Prevention and treatment of sunburn
- First aid for frostbite and hypothermia
- Stress and drugs increase accidents
- Safety belts, airbags, and safety helmets
- Safety around pools, oceans, lakes, rivers
- Fires and falls in the home
- Safety procedures during tornadoes, earthquakes, and electrical storms
- Good Samaritan Law
- Recognizing violence and violent behavior
- Protection from physical abuse, emotional abuse, neglect, and sexual abuse
- Getting help for the abused and abuser

7
- Accidents and stress, drugs, and alcohol
- Safety guidelines and first ` aid procedures
- Smoke detectors and heat detectors
- Guidelines for swimming, camping, hiking, cycling, and boating
- Safety features of automobiles and farm machinery
- Handling pesticides
- First aid for shock, fainting, bleeding, and wounds
- CPR and the Heimlich maneuver
- First aid for insect stings, burns, poisoning
- First aid for fractures
- Characteristics, prevention, and reporting procedures for physical abuse, emotional abuse, sexual abuse, and neglect
- Sexual assault, sexual harassment, date or acquaintance rape, and homicide
- Staying safe from violence
- Reporting abuse and other violent actions
- Getting help for victims of crimes

8
- Leading causes of injuries and accidents
- Safety guidelines for fires in buildings
- Safety guidelines for equipment
- Safety guidelines for bikes and ATVs
- Drownproofing and safety while swimming
- Pedestrian safety rules
- Safety during natural disasters
- Safety while hunting
- Benefits of understanding first aid
- Procedures for helping persons with a
- Using artificial respiration and CPR
- Procedures for controlling bleeding
- First aid for fractures
- First aid for injuries to the eye
- Strategies for dealing with physical abuse, emotional abuse, sexual abuse, and neglect
- Strategies for dealing with sexual harrassment, rape, date or acquaintance rape, homicide, and assault
- Strategies for dealing with voyeurism, exhibitionism, and obscene telephone calling

9-12
- Types of crime
- Strategies for preventing and reporting sexual harassment, sexual assault, rape
- Strategies for preventing and reporting physical abuse, emotional abuse, sexual abuse, and rape
- Myths about acquaintance rape
- Strategies for dealing with voyeurism, exhibitionism, and obscene telephone calling
- Ways fatigue, drugs, alcohol and stress increase injury
- Guidelines to prevent motor vehicle accidents
- Guidelines to prevent accidents around water
- Guidelines to prevent accidents at home
- Guidelines to prevent accidents in the workplace
- Guidelines for safety during tornadoes, hurricanes, and earthquakes
- Benefits of being trained to give first aid
- Procedures for clearing an obstructed airway
- Procedures for giving CPR
- Procedures for controlling bleeding
- First aid procedures for shock, heart attack, and stroke
- First aid procedures for fractures, dislocations, sprains, and strains
- First aid procedures for snakebites, insect bites, and objects in the eye
- First aid procedures for heat stroke, heat exhaustion, heat cramps
- First aid procedures for hypothermia and over exposure to the cold

Table 3-7
Sample Teaching Strategy
The Message in Music

Objective

Students will explain the importance of choosing entertainment that promotes healthful living and positive moral values.

Life Skill

I will listen to music whose words promote healthful living and positive moral values.

Materials

Compact disc player, popular compact discs to which students listen, construction paper, aluminum foil, scissors, markers, tape

Motivation

1 Ask students to bring in compact discs to which they enjoy listening. Make a list of their favorite songs that appear on these discs. Play some of the songs. Ask students to summarize the message in each of the songs in one sentence.

2 Discuss the importance of choosing healthful entertainment. Healthful entertainment promotes physical, mental-emotional, and family-social health. It encourages the development of positive moral values.

3 Have students examine their list of favorite songs and the messages conveyed in each. Which of these songs promote health and positive moral values? Which songs encourage risk behaviors and immorality?

4 Make a bulletin board of "Healthful Messages in Music." Have students cut cardboard in the shape of a compact disc. Then have them cover their discs with aluminum foil. Now have them cut a strip of construction paper upon which they are to write a current song title and one sentence which summarizes the message conveyed in this song. The message must be healthful and moral. Place all the discs on the bulletin board.

Evaluation

Have students identify five current songs which promote health and positive moral values and five which do not. Have them discuss why it is better to listen to music which has a healthful and moral message.

a student 1) understand a particular concept, and/or 2) practice a specific life skill. Table 3-7 shows a sample illustration of a teaching strategy. A teaching strategy should include: 1) the life skill to be practiced, 2) the objective to be achieved, 3) the materials needed, 4) the motivation or technique for getting the student involved in understanding the concept and/or practicing the life skill, and 5) the evaluation that measures student performance of the objective and/or life skill.

The effectiveness of comprehensive school health education is very much dependent upon the quality and creativity of the teaching strategies that are utilized in the classroom. You will want your lessons to be motivating and challenging. Therefore, you will need to have your students involved. Part II of this book contains "Totally Awesome Strategies for Teaching Health."

Health Behavior Contracts

Often as a result of being exposed to health education and the "totally awesome" strategies that you will use in your classroom, students will take responsibility for changing previous habits. They will be motivated to practice life skills which enable them to work toward optimal health. You can assist your students in this commitment by making health behavior contracts a part of your lessons. A **health behavior contract** is a plan that is written to develop the habit of following a specific life skill. A health behavior contract includes: 1) the life skill for which a habit needs to be formed, 2) a few statements describing the importance of this life skill to optimal well-being, 3) a plan for practicing this life skill, 4) an evaluation including a method of reporting progress, and 5) a statement of the results experienced from practicing this life skill. Table 3-8 shows a sample Health Behavior Contract.

Teaching about health behavior contracts is especially important in helping students learn the process of committing themselves to a healthful lifestyle. Explain to students that they can make health behavior contracts for the rest of their lives. Whenever a new life skill is desired, or to put it another way, whenever a healthful habit needs to be formed, a health behavior contract is helpful. Making a contract is helpful for several reasons. First, the life skill that is desired is written on paper. Most of the research completed on goal setting emphasizes that persons who write down what they

Table 3-8
Health Behavior Contract

Life Skill:	I will engage in aerobic exercise for at least 30 minutes three times a week.
Effect on My Well-being:	Aerobic exercise will strengthen my heart muscle and result in a lower resting heart beat rate. Beta-endorphins are released after several weeks of regular aerobic exercise. They will help me to have a feeling of well-being. Aerobic exercise will reduce my percentage of body fat and help me to maintain my desirable weight.
My Plan:	I will select one of the following aerobic exercises: walking, running, roller skating, swimming, bicycling, snow skiing.
Evaluating My Progress:	I will complete the following chart to indicate the aerobic exercise selected and the amount of time in which I participated in the exercise.

Monday	Tuesday	Wednesday	Thursday

Friday	Saturday	Sunday

Results:

Life Skill:	I will do exercises for my heart for thirty minutes three times a week.
How This Life Skill Helps Me:	Exercise for my heart makes my heart muscle very strong. My heart will work better. I will not get out of breath when I work and play. These exercises help me look and feel good.
My Plan:	I will draw a picture of an exercise I can do for my heart.
How I Follow My Plan:	I will color one piece of the heart each day I do my heart exercise.
How I Feel:	I will circle the way I feel when I do exercise for my heart.

want to accomplish are more likely to accomplish it. Writing down the life skill helps a person focus on what is desired. In Table 3-8, the life skill for the health behavior contract is, "I will engage in aerobic exercise for at least thirty minutes three times a week."

Second, the health behavior contract allows for an individualized plan to be made. The life skill in Table 3-8 is important throughout a person's life, yet the plan to accomplish the life skill might change. For example, during elementary school a student might ride his/her bicycle as a means of getting aerobic exercise. During high school, the student might be on the track team and switch to running. Later in life, this same person might engage in walking. This individualization is particularly important for the classes that you teach because it allows for multicultural sensitivity. For example, students might make a health behavior contract for the life skill, "I will eat a healthful balanced breakfast each day." Their plans might include different breakfast choices yet each could fulfill the life skill.

Third, health behavior contracts allow for monitoring progress. Part of taking self-responsibility for health is being aware of one's behavior and making constant choices for positive behavior. By completing a chart or journalling to monitor progress, awareness of health behavior is brought into focus. For example, if a student is listing the breakfast foods (s)he eats, the student becomes more aware of his/her patterns of eating. Perhaps the student eats a lot of foods containing sugar for breakfast and does not eat foods rich in fiber. This becomes apparent to the student and becomes the basis for change.

Fourth, health behavior contracts enable students to analyze the results of following life skills. They are asked to record ways in which following a specific life skill improves their physical, mental-emotional, family-social, and spiritual well-being.

The practice of making and following health behavior contracts is so important that you will want to involve the families of your students. You may want to duplicate a sample health behavior contract and send it home with directions for its completion. Often, families and individual family members of students begin to use health behavior contracts as they become aware of the value of this tool in changing behavior or adopting new behaviors.

Staying Motivated Incentives

There is a saying, "Your success is measured by your ability to complete the things you say you will do." Another way to say this is, "A winner is a finisher." What are some strategies that you can use in your classroom to help students stay motivated to practice life skills and to follow health behavior contracts to make new life skills a habit?

• *Use reminders.* Have students write the life skill they want to develop on a few index cards. Have them place the cards in locations where they will be reminded of the life skill and the health behavior contracts they have made.

• *Share progress made on plans.* Set aside time for students to share their progress on their plans with their classmates. This will allow students to opportunity to receive feedback on what they are doing. Of course, you will want to respect confidentiality and not ask students who would rather keep their contracts in confidence to share with classmates.

• *Develop support systems.* Suggest that students working on similar life skills form support networks. For example, students desiring to lose weight might have a meeting time to share their obstacles and feelings and to encourage one another. Students who are desiring to ride bicycles to engage in aerobic exercise might plan some bicycling trips together. Usually, it is easier to stay motivated when there are others upon whom you can count for support and encouragement.

• *Use role models as encouragers.* You might use resource persons who practice specific life skills to share their stories with your class. These persons can be those who have been committed to a life skill such as distance walking and want to share their joys with students. They might also be persons who used to have other habits that have been changed. For example, a person who used to eat poorly who became serious about eating healthfully and maintaining ideal weight.

• *Reward progress.* Examine ways students can be rewarded for their progress in making a life skill a habit. For example, students who are trying to reduce their weight might indulge in buying a new pair of shorts for exercise after sticking to their diets for two weeks. Another way of rewarding students is to make progress part of the health education grade. You can individually contract with students for bonus points to be rewarded for progress toward making a life skill a habit.

TECHNIQUES FOR EVALUATING COMPREHENSIVE SCHOOL HEALTH EDUCATION

Evaluation is the procedure used to measure the results of efforts toward a desired goal. The emphasis on accountability in education has made evaluation increasingly important in recent years. With regard to comprehensive school health education, there are at least three foci for evaluation: 1) evaluation of the curriculum, 2) evaluation of student performance, and 3) evaluation of teacher performance.

Evaluating the Curriculum

You have already learned that the comprehensive school health education curriculum needs philosophy and content, behavioral objectives and life skills, a scope and sequence chart, and lessons in responsibility. But, there are other considerations to examine in making the curriculum as effective as possible. These considerations can be stated in the form of a checklist that can be used as an evaluation tool.

A responsible comprehensive school health education curriculum:

1. *Adheres to a plan in which an adequate amount of time is spent on health education.* The Society of State Directors of Health, Physical Education, and Recreation recommends at least two hours per week of health instruction for the elementary grades. The Society recommends a daily period of health instruction for at least two semesters in the middle and junior high school. For high school, the Society recommends a daily period of health instruction for at least two semesters. These are the minimal recommendations of the Society.

2. *Achieves stated objectives as well as life skills for the ten content areas.* Those responsible for health education focus on student attainment of the stated objectives and life skills. In addition to the attainment of the objectives, there is an emphasis on measuring student behavior. For example, in mathematics teachers are concerned as to whether students can understand how to make a budget and how to take 20% off the purchase price for an item on sale. The end result is on skills that can be used for living. The same is true of health. Emphasis must be placed on desired behaviors. There needs to be concern at every grade level for skill mastery. Are students brushing and flossing teeth? Do they have flexibility, endurance, and muscular strength? Are they eating a healthful breakfast that is high in fiber?

3. *Provides a foundation of health knowledge.* The objectives and life skills will dictate what content needs to be taught. As a teacher, you have a responsibility for being well-informed and helping your students to learn ways they can continue to be well-informed beyond your classroom. Health is a process that includes life-long learning.

4. *Focuses upon character development.* An end result of education is the development of responsible citizenship. Students need to experience their connectedness to their community, nation, and world. This global perspective helps them to see that what they do does affect the quality of life for others. Protecting the quality of life for others is an essential ingredient in building character. This foundation is set during many of the lessons in the classroom. For example, all lessons on drugs should include information about drug laws. All lessons on violence should help students see their role in preventing violence and the importance of their behavior being respectful of others. During lessons using strategies that focus on responsible decision making, students must be taught to demonstrate behaviors that are healthful, safe, legal, respectful of self and others, and in compliance with the standards set by responsible adults. Students must be taught to report the behaviors of peers that are not responsible or that are illegal.

5. *Uses "totally awesome" teaching strategies.* The classroom must be set up as a laboratory in which students are involved in learning concepts and practicing life skills. "Seeing is believing" and "doing is believing" are cliches to remember in teaching. Learning is much more impactful when students are involved in the process. This is why Section II of this book contains "totally awesome" strategies for you to use. These are "hands on" activities for you to use.

6. *Provides for different learning styles.* Research indicates that students learn in different ways. Students who learn best from right brain activities learn more easily with visual lessons including art and music projects. Students who learn best from left brain activities are more suited to traditional styles of teaching. However, all students respond to variety and involvement. By varying teaching style, the classroom remains stimulating.

7. *Makes provisions for students with special needs.* As lessons are planned to meet stated objectives and life skills, there should be provisions made for students with special needs. For example, a student who has diabetes might complete a health behavior contract in which a daily menu is planned differently than a student who does not have special diet considerations. A student who has a physical disability might be given assistance in learning ways to achieve the benefits from aerobic exercise from sports and games in which (s)he can participate given his/her limitations. In addition, there can be provisions for students with different learning abilities. Students who are able to achieve easily may be given challenging tasks labelled as "challenge" or "enrichment" in the curriculum. When there are students who have difficulty learning, the teacher can focus upon "reteaching." **Reteaching** occurs when the teacher uses an alternate strategy for a concept or life skill after the first strategy used was not clearly understood by students.

8. *Provides opportunities for critical thinking.* Madeline Hunter popularized higher order thinking skills (HOTS) with the idea that schools should develop the process of critical thinking in students. In every lesson and every topic, students need to be challenged to think critically about the issues that affect themselves, their peers, their community, their country, and their world.

9. *Uses a positive approach.* The attitude of those responsible for health education permeates what happens in the curriculum and then in the classroom. Approaching health and well-being with the attitude that it is rewarding, exciting, and fun to be well is more desirable than emphasizing illness and injury. Research indicates that students are more likely to be motivated by a positive approach than by a scare tactic approach. Positive wording is important. For example,

it is better to say, "Most young people do not smoke" than "Many young people smoke." It is better to show audiovisuals depicting young people engaging in wellness behaviors than showing them engaging in risk behaviors. A picture is worth a thousand words and you want students identifying with wellness behaviors and healthful situations not risk behaviors and risk situations.

10. *Uses a multicultural approach.* The curriculum must be multiculturally sensitive. Family health practices vary depending on cultural backgrounds. An earlier example was provided when discussing health behavior contracts. In that example, it was mentioned that students from different backgrounds might choose different foods for breakfast. Thus, when the nutrition area of the curriculum is developed it would be important to include examples of diets that are typical of your students' families. A multicultural approach to curriculum makes health education more relevant.

11. *Provides opportunities for integrating skills.* When planning the health education curriculum, strategies can be developed in which students integrate skills needed for other academic disciplines into health. Examples of integrating skills are numerous. Students use writing skills when they develop essays which entail critical thinking about health issues. They use reading skills when they review newspaper articles and magazines articles that relate to current health issues. They use mathematics skills when they compute their target heart rates for aerobic exercise. When developing posters and collages, they use their creative art skills. When doing an experiment to show the fat content in specific foods, they are introduced to the laboratory skills typical of science courses.

12. *Includes the family.* For health education to be most effective, the family must be involved. Parents and guardians must be kept current on the health issues studied in the classroom. You might develop a family health newsletter for your students' families or ask your students' families to purchase one that you have selected. When your students design and follow health behavior contracts, you might have them share these contracts with family members. Some of the health behavior contracts might be developed for the family rather than for the individual students. For example, a health behavior contract might be designed for the family to plan at least two healthful activities per week. In addition to the newsletters and health behavior contracts, you might contact local health agencies for materials that might be sent to parents. The American Heart Association has prepared guidelines for dining out. This type of pamphlet provides helpful information for the family.

13. *Uses community resources.* There are many materials from community resources that can be integrated into the curriculum. The National Dairy Council, The American Cancer Society, The Ameri-

can Heart Association, and The National Society to Prevent Blindness are just a few national agencies that have local and state agencies that provide materials for the curriculum. You can call the educational director at these agencies and ask for samples of the materials available. There are also many persons who might serve as resources by donating time, supplies and materials, and/or speaking to your students.

Evaluating the Students

The shift in emphasis in health education from what students know to what students believe, feel, and do has changed the nature of evaluation of students. What are some techniques for evaluating what students believe, think, and do as well as some techniques for measuring what students know?

Techniques for Measuring Beliefs, Feelings, and Behaviors

There are a variety of techniques that might be used to gather feedback about student beliefs, feelings, and behaviors as a result of comprehensive school health education.

Observation. Perhaps the most obvious method involves direct observation. You can observe students to see what they are doing. What choices are they making for school lunches? Are they following school guidelines for safety? Are students being reported for breaking guidelines involving the use of alcohol and other drugs? Although this technique of evaluation is subjective, you will want to be a keen observer to learn what students are doing.

Health Behavior Contracts. Health behavior contracts require the students to report data about their health behavior and changes or improvements in their health behavior. There has been increasing emphasis on using health behavior contracts as part of the grade for the health education course. Students contract individually with the teacher to obtain a certain number of points toward their total number of points that determine their grade by showing progress or completion of the life skill they have identified. Some teachers are skeptical about using health behavior contracts as part of a grade because it requires good faith on the part of the student in honest self-reporting. Yet, a trusting relationship between teacher and student is necessary for effective education to take place anyway.

Likert Scales. A **Likert scale** is a technique used to measure beliefs and attitudes in which students react to statements with a response of strongly agree, agree, neutral, disagree, and strongly disagree. The following is an example of a Likert scale designed to measure attitudes students have about cigarette smoking.

Example of A Likert Scale

Directions: Please give your reactions to the following statements regarding cigarette smoking. Record your first reaction.

Draw a circle around SA if you strongly agree with the item.
Draw a circle around A if you are in partial agreement.
Draw a cirlce around N if you are neutral.
Draw a circle around D if you are in partial disagreement.
Draw a circle around SD if you strongly disagree with the item.

SA A N D SD 1. Smoking in restaurants should be banned.

SA A N D SD 2. The cigarette manufacturers have too much influence on the U.S. government.

SA A N D SD 3. People who smoke cigarettes do not care about the health of those around them.

Semantic Differential. A **semantic differential** is a technique used to measure beliefs and attitudes in which students are asked to circle a letter from A-B-C-D-E to indicate their preference on a continuum. The following example of a semantic differential is used to describe students' attitudes and beliefs about smoking.

Example of a Semantic Differential

Directions: In this study, I would like to find out how you describe different things. The rest of this page has pairs of words that you will use to describe your image of the heading at the top of the page. Place a circle around the letter that best indicates the image you have about the heading.

Cigarette Smoking

Healthful	A B C D E	Unhealthful
Legal	A B C D E	Illegal
Enjoyable	A B C D E	Unenjoyable
Responsible	A B C D E	Irresponsible
Adultlike	A B C D E	Childish

Techniques for Measuring Knowledge

While the current emphasis in comprehensive school health education is upon student mastery of life skills, there is still a need for students to master health knowledge. Health knowledge is essential for creating informed behavior change. Assessment of student knowledge can take place through the use of teacher constructed tests- either in the form of short answers (objective) or essay. In developing essay or short answer tests, the teacher needs to examine course objectives to identify the kinds of behavior that need to be assessed.

The teacher should keep the following principles in mind when constructing an examination:

1. Test construction must take into account the use to be served by the test.

2. The types of test items used should be determined by the specific outcomes to be measured.

3. Test items should be based on a representative sample of the course content and the specific learning outcomes to be measured.

4. Test items should be of the proper level of difficulty.

5. Test items should be so constructed that extraneous factors do not prevent the pupil from responding.

6. Test items should be so constructed that the pupil obtains the correct answer only if he has attained the desired learning outcome.

7. The test should be so constructed that it contributes to improved teacher-learning practices.

Keeping these principles in mind, Table 3-9 provides information on the Construction of Examinations to Measure Knowledge. Most educators believe that it is helpful to use a variety of examinations. Student performances vary depending on the type of examination administered.

Unfortunately, some students may try to cheat on examinations to improve their scores. Cheating is often prevented when students feel that the teacher is their advocate and that trying their best will be rewarded and supported. However, this is not always the case. If you suspect a student is cheating on an examination, be certain that you have proof before making an accusation. If you suspect a student is looking at another student's paper, you might try one of the following:

- Make an announcement to the class that you have noticed some people looking at other's papers and the next time action will be taken.
- Stare at the student to indicate your caution. Students will frequently watch a teacher to determine when they might have an opportunity to get answers. Knowing that the teacher is

aware helps to stop this action.
- Stand beside suspected students to give them a nonverbal warning that you are aware of attempts at cheating.
- Move the suspected students to other seats in the classroom.

Table 3-9
Construction of Examinations to Measure Knowledge

Essay Examinations

Advantages of essay examinations:
1. They are easy to construct since few questions need be asked.
2. They allow students the opportunity to be creative and show organizational skills.
3. They can be used for any topic in the health education curriculum.
4. They allow students to apply knowledge.

Disadvantages of essay examinations:
1. They are difficult to grade.
2. It is sometimes difficult to word them.
3. There is low reliability in scoring them.
4. Students with better writing ability and less knowledge may score well.
5. It is time consuming to grade them.

Hints for the construction of essay examinations:
1. In writing an essay examination, be specific. For example, a nonspecific item would be: Do you feel that smoking in public places should be banned? A student might write a simple "yes" or "no" and provide an accurate response. A better item would be: Select a position, pro or con, on whether smoking should be banned in public places and provide at least five reasons for your position.
2. Always make the criteria for acceptable performance clear. In the previous essay item, students were asked to provide "at least five reasons for your position." If this criterion were not identified, those students who provided one reason and those who provided five would have fulfilled what the teacher had asked. It would be unfair to grade them differently.
3. If you plan to count spelling, grammar, creativity, convincing evidence, etc., be certain to state this on the exam. State how many points each is worth.
4. Assign a point value to each essay item. This will enable students to set priorities in allocating their time when writing answers to more than one question.

5. Take the exam or have a student take the exam before it is given to the class to determine a reasonable amount of time in which it should be completed.

Hints for grading essay examinations:
1. Prior to grading essay examinations, make a checklist of the items for which you plan to look and the number of points each is worth. In the previous example given, your checklist might include: 1) provides at least five reasons (5 points), 2) provides convincing evidence (3 points), 3) is grammatically correct (2 points), etc. As you read the essay answers, use your checklist for grading. If possible, duplicate this checklist for student feedback.
2. Read only several papers during a time period. During the reading of essay examinations, especially those requiring many pages of writing, you may begin by grading objectively and then tire of reading the same kinds of answers. After a while, all grades may become similar. Short breaks between sets of papers such as every five will minimize this effect.

True-False Examinations

Advantages of true-false examinations:
1. They are easy to construct since each question consists of only one statement.
2. They can be graded objectively.
3. They are easy to score.
4. There is no confusion over correct and incorrect responses.

Disadvantages of true-false examinations:
1. Students have a 50-50 chance of a correct guess.
2. Questions are often ambiguous or tricky.
3. It is difficult to measure a higher thought process.

Hints for the construction of true-false examinations:
1. Avoid using value judgments in the wording, such as, "Children under the age of 12 *should* not drink alcohol." Instead state fact to avoid controversy. "It is harmful to health for children under the age of 12 to drink alcohol."
2. Avoid questions which use the words "always," "never," "all," or "none." Students are conditioned to answer false to these statements.
3. Avoid double negatives.
4. Avoid using compound sentences and long sentences.

Hints for grading true-false examinations:
1. Use a separate answer sheet instead of having students write their answers on the examina-

tion. Then the examinations can be used for different classes.

2. Rather than having students write t for true and f for false have them write T or + for true and F or - for false. It is easier to read these answers correctly. As an alternative, have a T and an F for each statement and have students circle their choice.

Multiple Choice Examinations

Advantages of multiple choice examinations:
1. There is a lower chance of guessing correctly than on true-false examinations.
2. It is easy to grade multiple choice examinations.
3. Students must critically examine several alternatives.

Disadvantages of multiple choice examinations:
1. It is time consuming to prepare them.
2. There must be several responses that are feasible for them to be valid.
3. Students may still guess at answers.

Hints in the construction of multiple choice examinations:
1. When writing the directions, use "Select the best answer" to protect against students finding reasons that more than one choice is correct.
2. Make each possible answer a worthy choice. When one or more of the choices can be ruled out right away, students are guided toward the correct choice without demonstrating mastery of knowledge.
3. Use four or five choices. More than five becomes too cumbersome and confusing and fewer than four increases the chance of a correct guess.

Hints for grading multiple choice examinations:
1. Have students write answers in capital letters. This minimizes errors in interpreting script.
2. Distribute an answer sheet upon which the student can circle the correct choice.

Matching Examinations

Advantages of matching examinations:
1. The scoring is easy and reliable.
2. Student guessing is minimized.
3. Students are required to discriminate in a more rigorous manner than on other kinds of examinations.
4. These tests are highly valid.

Disadvantages of matching examinations:
1. They can be difficult to construct.
2. They may take too long a period to complete.

3. The answers may be correct or incorrect in pairs.
4. There may be several answers for one question.

Hints for constructing matching examinations:
1. Do not include more than ten nor fewer than five or six items. Too many choices may lead to confusion and too few items may lead to "correct guessing."
2. The alternatives from which to choose should exceed the number of items by one or two. This eliminates the student automatically matching the remaining items if there is but one alternative left.

Hints for grading matching examinations:
1. A grading key can be made and placed next to student answers for quick grading.

Completion Examinations

A completion examination requires students to add missing information to a sentence fragment. Advantages of completion examinations:

1. This type of examination requires students to know all aspects of a subject.
2. It is difficult to guess on this type of examination.
3. This type of examination allows students to organize information.
4. It is easy to write this type of examination.

Disadvantages of completion examinations:
1. Several answers may correctly complete each item.
2. It takes more time to grade because of the number of possible correct answers.
3. Students will select answers they believe the teacher wants rather than ones they might give.

Hints for constructing completion examinations:
1. Word questions so that only one response will be correct. For example, "*Hashish* is more potent than marijuana" can be completed with other answers. However, "*Hashish* which is made from the resin of the hemp plant, is more potent than marijuana" is completed only with hashish.
2. Have students write answers on a separate sheet. Since completing items may fall any place on the question paper, such as the beginning, middle, or end of the sentence, grading can be time consuming. This also facilitates tallying the answers.

Hints for grading completion examinations:
1. When grading completion answers, place a line through the incorrect answer and not

through the question number. This prevents the student from changing the original answer and saying the item was misgraded.

2. If an answer is left blank by a student, place a line through it also. This prevents the student from filling in the blank when the examination is returned and saying the item was misgraded.

Evaluating the Teacher

You have been reading suggestions for evaluating the comprehensive school health curriculum and for evaluating student performance of behavioral objectives and life skills. Perhaps you have already begun to ask, "How will I be evaluated in my effectiveness?" There has been some research that has shown that your effectiveness is dependent upon what you *do* as well as upon how well you teach. The poem which follows speaks to the importance of your making a commitment to follow the life skills that were identified earlier in the chapter.

Teacher as Role Model

I'd rather see a sermon
　　than hear one any day;
I'd rather one should walk with me
　　than merely show the way.
The eyes a better pupil,
　　and more willing than the ear;
Fine counsel is confusing,
　　but examples always clear.

I soon can learn to do it,
　　if you'll let me see it done;
I can see your hands in action,
　　but your tongue too fast may run.
And the lectures you deliver
　　may be very fine and true.
But, I'd rather get my lesson
　　by observing what you do.
For I may misunderstand you
　　and the high advice you give,
But, there's no misunderstanding
　　how you act and how you live.

There is no doubt that students want to admire their teachers. They want to know that their teachers really believe and are committed to what they are saying. Therefore, an important aspect of teacher evaluation is the teacher's self-evaluation. This is not to imply that if your behavior is not perfect you will not be effective. What it means is that if *you* take responsibility for your health and follow the life skills identified in the chart on page 59, it will have a positive impact on your students. So take the time to regularly evaluate your performance of these life skills. If you are not engaging in specific life skills, use a health behavior contract to reinforce your habit of doing so. And share your commitment to practicing life skills and making health behavior contracts to form positive habits with your students. It demonstrates to them that you are committed to the process for healthful living.

Besides being a role model for students, you will want to demonstrate teaching effectiveness. A Likert Scale such as the following might be used to measure students' attitudes and beliefs about your teaching effectiveness.

Likert Scale to Measure Teacher Effectiveness

SA A N D SD
1. The teacher was interested in the subject matter.
2. The teacher motivated me to practice life skills.
3. The teacher had knowledge of health.
4. The teacher answered my questions.
5. The teacher communicated subject matter in a meaningful way.
6. The objectives for health were clear to me.
7. I knew which life skills were important for me to follow.
8. The tests that were given were fair.
9. The teaching strategies used helped me understand health information and practice life skills.
10. The assignments for this class contributed to my learning about health.

Additional comments: _____
_____
_____
_____
_____
_____
_____
_____
_____

You might also use a Semantic Differential to measure students' attitudes and beliefs about your teaching effectiveness. Examples of Semantic Differentials follow.

Semantic Differentials

Directions: I would like to learn how you describe our health education class. Below there is a heading. A list of pairs of words follows. Place a circle around the letter that describes how you feel about the heading.

Your Teacher

Caring	A B C D E	Uncaring
Well prepared	A B C D E	Not prepared
Healthy	A B C D E	Not healthy
Well informed	A B C D E	Not informed
Open minded	A B C D E	Opinionated

The Unit on Nutrition

Learned a lot	A B C D E	Did not learn much
Learned life skills	A B C D E	Did not learn life skills
Fair test	A B C D E	Unfair test
Good activities	A B C D E	Boring activities
Included family	A B C D E	Did not include family
Made me think	A B C D E	Did not make me think

Coments: _____
_____
_____
_____
_____
_____
_____
_____
_____
_____

References

1. Bloom, Benjamin S., et. al. (1956) *Taxonomy of Educational Objectives-The Classification of Educational Goals, Handbook II: Affective Domain*. New York: David McKay Company, Inc.

2. Gibran, Kahlil (1923, 1951) *The Prophet*. New York: Alfred A. Knopf. Inc.

3. Grunland, Norman E. (1971) *Measurement and Evaluation in Teaching*. New York: MacMillan, p.8.

4. Jourard, Sidney. (1971) *The Transparent Self*. New York: D. Van Nostrand.

5. Kibler, Robert J., and Larry Barker and David T. Miles. (1970) *Behavioral Objectives and Instruction*. Boston: Allyn and Bacon, Inc., 93-4.

Teaching about health is challenging and exciting. After all, our society is placing an increasing value on the importance of quality of life. And one achieves a quality of life through having a sound body, mind, and spirit.

THE CLASSROOM AS A LABORATORY FOR LEARNING LIFE SKILLS

As a teacher, you will have a significant impact on the health and well-being of hundreds, if not thousands of students. Because of your efforts, you will be able to influence students to adopt behaviors that will directly affect their health. This chapter is written to help you accomplish this very important task. This chapter is but an introduction to creativity. You can be as creative as you choose. But in order to be creative, you need the skills to use in the classroom setting. This chapter provides you with the basic kinds of strategies you can use to implement comprehensive school health education. Your classroom can become the laboratory for students to learn life skills. How does a young student escape from a fire? How can a student practice refusal skills when pressured to use illegal drugs? How can a student determine which kinds of foods are best for reducing the risk of developing heart disease? The facts that help answer these questions are important. But, knowing these facts is not enough. Students must use facts to take action. These actions or life skills are the main foci of comprehensive school health education. You are a key player in promoting life skill development.

THE IMPORTANCE OF HAVING A VARIETY OF INSTRUCTIONAL STRATEGIES

There have been many different names given to the process in which students participate in learning activities. Terms such as "methods of instruction," "learning activities," and "teaching techniques" are some that have been used. But the term most widely used by health educators today is "teaching strategy." A **teaching strategy** is a technique used by a facilitator or teacher to help a student 1. understand a particular concept and/or 2. practice a specific life skill. The strategy that you choose to use is dependent upon the objectives to be met. There is no such idea as "the best teaching strategy." A good teacher uses a variety of teaching strategies to meet any number of educational objectives.

Factors Determining the Selection of Teaching Strategies

There may be different kinds of teaching strategies that can work well with an objective. The strategy to be used depends on the desired outcome and the student's response. You might use a strategy that elicits an enthusiastic response among students. But, you may discover that another strategy used to cover the same objective may elicit higher level thinking skills when the same lesson is given. The outcome you desire helps you decide which strategy is best. Often, trial and error and teaching experience will help you determine which teaching strategy is most effective.

There are some general rules you can follow in determining what kind of teaching strategy to use.

1. The age of the learner is important in selecting a teaching strategy. The younger a learner, the less abstract the strategy used for presenting a concept. For example, you may use role play with sixth or seventh graders regarding the use of refusal skills when pressured to engage in a harmful practice. For primary grade students, you may read a story about a person who is pressured by friends at school to do something that is harmful. You can follow this by telling students that if someone at school tells them to do something that can be harmful, they should tell a teacher. This teaching strategy is more concrete than the first strategy that was used for sixth or seventh graders.

2. The behavioral objectives are critical in selecting a strategy. For example, you may want students

INSTRUCTIONAL STRATEGIES: MAKING THE HEALTH EDUCATION CLASSROOM EXCITING

to be able to demonstrate correctly the use of the abdominal thrust. Using a lecture only approach would not be as effective as having students work with partners to practice each step in performing the abdominal thrust.

3. The available resources help determine which strategy is best for reaching an objective. For example, students will react more favorably to learning about a concept when an appropriate video tape is shown than if you lecture and use no visuals throughout an entire presentation.

Teaching strategies can be varied and numerous. Some teaching strategies may be classified according to the type of teaching method used such as role play or lecture. Teaching strategies may be classified according to the instructional media used. Analogies using specific equipment may be used. For example, you can attach a hose to a faucet, turn on the water, and place your thumb at the opening of the hose to demonstrate that the force of water against the hose is analogous to the force exerted by blood against the walls of blood vessels. This demonstrates the concept that blood pressure readings are determined by how much pressure is exerted within arterial walls.

TYPES OF TEACHING STRATEGIES

While there are many different types of teaching strategies, the ones that will be described in this section will be categorized as being 1) individual and 2) group.

Individual and Group Strategies

Individual and group strategies consist of specific teaching strategies that process information through verbal interaction. These strategies may consist of those that the teacher implements or that students discuss. The strategies in this section will be defined. Following the definitions will be the strengths and weaknesses of each strategy. Finally, practical hints will be provided to help educators effectively use these strategies.

Lecture

Lecture is a verbal presentation to others with the possible use of aids such as overlays. The lecture method of teaching is considered the most universal form of presentation.

Strengths of Lecture
- An abundance of information can be presented at one time.
- A large group of people can be given the same information at one time.
- Many facts can be given in a relatively short period of time.

Weaknesses of Lecture
- Students cannot become actively involved.
- A lecture can become boring unless the presenter is a dynamic speaker.
- Students may not be able to show an ability to think creatively.
- It may be difficult to indicate if the students understand what is being presented.
- The students and the presenter will not be able to interact.
- If students are bored, there may be a propensity for an increase in disciplinary problems.
- Lecture does not allow for students to demonstrate life skills such as learning how to apply a splint in a first aid situation.

Helpful Hints for Using Lecture
- Make the delivery more interesting by inserting personal anecdotes, humor, or fascinating facts.
- Vary the voice so as to convey expression.
- If nervousness is present, avoid behaviors that accent this. For example, do not hold a single sheet of paper in front of you as it will waiver easily. Instead, hold the paper on top of some thing solid like a manila folder which is sturdy.
- If using a lectern, have your notes on single,

separate sheets so that you can slide each page from one side to the other instead of turning over a page which is a cause for distraction.

- When possible, do not stand behind a table or podium as students will relate more favorably to seeing a complete person as opposed to a person standing behind an object. Standing behind an object creates a distancing phenomenon.
- Be sure to look frequently at your audience, but do not stare more than a few seconds at one person as this can make the person feel uncomfortable.
- Always have a beginning, middle, and end to your lecture. Lectures should begin with a motivation such as a profound fact, statistic, quote, or personal experience. Then have a smooth transition to the middle, which will contain the major context of your lecture. Avoid transitions that are not smooth. For example, it is not a good idea to use a statement such as, "And now I'd like to talk about the signs of a fracture." Rather, you can say, "And how might a person know if he or she has suffered a fracture? Here are signs that may be present." When concluding a lecture, it is important to have have a meaningful ending. Perhaps you may refer to a statement made at the beginning and tie it in with the concluding remark.

Lecture/Discussion

A **lecture/discussion** is a teaching method in which a teacher allows for classroom interaction during a lecture. The lecture/discussion method is also referred to as large group discussion. The lecture/discussion method may be facilitated by the use of different instructional aids. Much of the information described in the lecture only method will also be applicable to the lecture/discussion method.

Strengths of Lecture/Discussion

- Students are allowed to interact with the teacher as well as with each other.
- It increases the ability of a student to think more creatively.
- Students have the opportunity to seek clarification of a concept or statement of fact.
- There is an opportunity to ascertain different points of view.
- Opinions other than those expressed by the teacher can be shared.

Weakness of Lecture/Discussion

- Certain students may dominate the discussion.
- The teacher may not keep the discussion on target.
- The teacher may not be able to cover all material.

Helpful Hints for Using Lecture/Discussion

- Be aware of those students taking notes about what you are saying. If students are writing what you are saying verbatum, give them time to complete their task. You can select one or more students to observe. Pause until you notice they have completed what they wanted and look up to you again. Then you can continue to lecture. This will indicate to you that the rest of the class probably is ready also. This will avoid students telling you to slow down.
- Avoid picking on students to answer questions if at all possible. Allow them to volunteer their answers if you ask a question. Suppose you ask a question and a student gives a response. You then have another follow-up question. Do not come back automatically to that same student asking for the answer. If the student does not know the answer, he or she may become embarrassed. Then this student will hesitate to answer another question. In a way, that student may feel punished for volunteering. Rather, allow the student the first opportunity to answer the follow-up question if he or she desires.
- A student may ask a question that is not germane to the lecture. What should you do? Do not tell the student you cannot answer it because that is not what is being discussed. Provide a short, simple answer and then indicate that you will discuss the answer further when you address that topic.
- Suppose a student asks you a question and you do not know the answer. You can tell the class you do not know the answer but that each person including you will try to find the correct answer and bring it to the next class. You may ask the class if anyone has the answer to the question. But you also need to be aware of what the answer is to be.
- Give students a prepared outline upon which they can take notes. This teaches them to be organized. Collect their notes to see how thorough they are. Students who take thorough notes usually do better in school.

Role Play

Role play is a spontaneous acting out of a social situation. One or several students can participate in a role play. Students can be given an opening scenario and you or the students can select who will play the parts you assign.

Strengths of Role Play

- A situation can be made to appear life-like for

the students.

- Students can be exposed to viewpoints that others may have in a situation although the viewpoints may be exaggerated.
- Role play can be effective in holding the attention of the class.
- Students can interact with each other on points of view they may not really hold. Yet, these points of view can bring an added dimension to discussion after the role play.
- Students can determine the factors they need to consider in making responsible decisions.
- Students can think creatively and not fear sharing their responses because they know the situation is not real.

Weaknesses of Role Play

- Students may become embarrassed during the role play.
- Students may think the role play is silly and not provide realistic responses.
- Some students may dominate others in a role play and not allow for differing opinions to be presented.
- Students may not carry the role play to the direction the teacher may want it to go.
- Students may find the role play realistic to the point where they become too involved due to a similar personal experience. As a result, they become wrapped up in the role play.
- Some students may find the role play a form of entertainment and may not be serious about it.
- It may be used as a fun task with no appropriate follow-up.
- Not many students may be given the opportunity to participate, thus limiting classroom involvement.

Helpful Hints for Using Role Play

- Always ask for volunteers rather than forcing students to participate. Some students may feel too embarrassed to participate. The wrong students may be selected if the role play reflects a real life situation for these students. This can be harmful and embarrassing to the student.
- Limit role play scenarios to about three minutes. If left too long, it can become boring and participants as well as observers lose their enthusiasm. Emphasize that there need not be any conclusions to the role play. The class can examine different conclusions for the role play.
- Use different techniques to modify the role play. For example, you can use role reversal. In **role reversal**, the role of one person is switched with the role of another in the middle of the role play as it continues. If a person does not know what to say and is silent, you can inter-

vene and give that person a statement and the role play continues.
- Focus on higher level thinking skills when the role play is completed. There are many ways you can do this. You can have a discussion with the entire class by asking numerous questions. Examples of questions you can ask include, "How would you have handled the situation if you were involved as...?" " Why or why didn't you think that ... was trying to exert peer pressure?" and "How would your parents have reacted if you were ... and smoked the cigarette?" Another way to follow up a role play is to divide the class into small groups and have them discuss specific questions. A representative from each group can provide a response to that group's answer to the rest of the class. You can then lead the class in a discussion.

Brainstorming

Brainstorming is a teaching technique in which a teacher elicits a number of responses for a problem that is to be solved. In this technique, there may be more than one correct answer so students can be spontaneous. The teacher can write all responses on the chalkboard.

Strengths of Brainstorming

- It allows students to express thoughts freely.
- Students can participate without feeling threatened.
- Creative responses can be received by the teacher.
- It can be used with different age groups.
- It allows what may appear to be impractical responses to have value.
- It fosters higher level thinking skills.

Weaknesses of Brainstorming

- Students may yell out answers and become disruptive.
- It may not work well with large groups.
- Can lose its value unless students have an understanding about the subject being discussed.

Helpful Hints for Using Brainstorming

- You can encourage classroom participation by telling students that they have only one chance to respond. They cannot respond again until all other students who wanted to contribute have had the opportunity.
- Provide the class with specific instructions about what they will be brainstorming.
- Accept all responses regardless of how worthwhile they may initially appear.

encies can take long to make, they can be overused, and can be distracting if the quality is poor.

Computers

Computers can play a significant role in comprehensive school health education. They can be used to facilitate instruction by serving as a way for students to practice decision making skills. Scenarios can be given and students can determine the healthful alternatives they can choose. Computers can also be used to help students respond to health inventories. One kind of inventory is the health risk appraisal. Students can use computers to ascertain their health status regarding susceptibility to diseases, accidents and illness. Computers can also be used in games so as to help students become familiar with health concepts. For example, computers may be used to help students identify the structure and function of different body systems. New software is constantly being developed in health education. Many companies have health education software to evaluate knowledge gained in the different areas of health. Test banks that correlate to different materials are also available by different commercial publishers.

There are many different ways a teacher of health can be creative in the classroom. The different instructional strategies and aids identified in this chapter will enable you to be a creative and dynamic teacher of health. After all, health education is one of the most important subjects a student can take in school. Good health serves as a basis for a solid foundation for a lifetime.

SPECIAL FEATURE: GAINING CLASSROOM CONTROL: A PREREQUISITE FOR IMPLEMENTING STRATEGIES

Most likely you have been trained by your university professors to implement numerous teaching strategies in your graduate or undergraduate training. Throughout many courses in the teacher education program, you have developed a broad content base so that you feel confident about your ability to present in-depth information that is current and relevant. You are enthusiastic, eager, and feel well-prepared.

You begin your teaching carreer and the unexpected happens. All of the methods, creative teaching strategies, and information you have garnered appear to be for naught. For as you try to teach, you find your students do not want to listen to you. Your students talk to each other while you try to teach, they refuse to follow your classroom instructions, and they talk back to you.

Welcome to the number one problem teachers face - handling discipline problems effectively. What can you do to handle difficult classroom situations?

Following are some typical scenarios that take place in classroom settings with suggested ways to intervene. The interventions are actual strategies that have worked.

Scenario #1. Throughout your teaching, Pat and Yvette continually carry on a conversation between themselves. They do not listen to what you are saying.

Interventions: One way to deal with this is to pause, remain quiet, and stare at them until they have ceased talking. You may ask them to stop talking by using an "I" message. For example, you may say, "When you talk to each other, it is disturbing and I become angry." If talking continues, you can assign separate seats to Pat and Yvette. If there are further problems, speak with them immediately after class and explain your expectations for classroom behavior.

Scenario #2: Matt is a student who has a tendency to act out toward you. He refuses to listen to you and answers back when you ask him to remove his hat. He has no hesitations about confronting you in front of the class.

Interventions: The first time Matt does something disturbing to you or the class, take action. For example, tell him you would like him to take off his hat as soon as he walks into the classroom. If he refuses, place him in a limit situation. A limit situation is a behavior that must be adhered to within a specific boundry. For example, "If you do not remove your hat, I will need to have you removed from this class." Avoid any confrontations in the class. Act swiftly and decisively. Let others know where you stand.

Scenario # 3: Rosalie refuses to do anything in your class. She refuses to participate in classroom activities and does not take notes. Often, she falls asleep in your class.

Interventions: As soon as you observe a pattern, it is important that it be addressed. After class, speak to Rosalie one-on-one. Explain that you are concerned about her lack of participation. Ask her if she would like to share any concerns she may have about the class. If nothing is resolved, explain that you will need to pursue further. You may need to contact a parent or guardian. You may need to contact a counselor at school.

There are many other behavioral problems that occur in schools. Some general tips to follow in creating a classroom as free as possible from behavioral problems are:

1. Follow through on your intentions. If you tell a student you will call a parent, do so. Saying you will do something and then not doing it will send a message to students that you do not do what you say and therefore, behavioral problems will worsen.

2. Deal with problems immediately. Failure to do so will give other students the idea that they too, can choose to engage in counterproductive activities.

3. Know your subject matter and be well-orga-

nized. Students show a great deal of respect for teachers who are well-prepared and organized. A teacher who shows interest and competence in what he or she is doing will be more respected than a teacher who is unprepared, poorly organized, and unenthusiastic.

4. Make your teaching exciting and create an environment in which students enjoy coming to class. Many students become discipline problems because they are bored. Exciting lessons promote a greater willingness to learn.

Section 2

Background Information and
Totally Awesome Strategies for Teaching Health

This Section is divided into ten chapters with each of the chapters focusing on one of the content areas in the comprehensive school health education curriculum: Mental and Emotional Well-Being, Family and Relationship Skills, Growth and Development, Nutrition, Personal Fitness, Substance Use and Abuse, Diseases and Disorders, Consumer Health, Safety and Injury Prevention, and Community and Environment. In each of the ten content areas for which a chapter is included, there is background information as well as twenty **"totally awesome strategies for teaching."** The background information is a discussion of current facts regarding the specific area of health identified. There is a focus on what facts are most important in preparing the teacher to teach the curriculum rather than having a volume of unnecessary information. Each of the **"totally awesome strategies for teaching"** is provided in a short lesson plan format. The area of health for which the strategy is appropriate is identified as well as the suggested grade level: elementary, middle school, junior high school, and/ or high school. When more than one grade level is identified, the authors recognized that the strategy could be slightly modified for use at different levels. For each strategy, there is an objective, life skill, and list of materials needed as well as a motivational approach for using the strategy and a means of evaluation. The motivation consists of step-by-step directions for using the strategy in the classroom. Each of the strategies has been field tested by the authors and is effective in involving students in developing life skills for health.

Mental Well-Being and Positive Adjustments is the area of health that examines ways to attain mental-emotional health, promote positive self-concept, make responsible decisions, express emotions in healthful ways, cope with stress, deal with depression, and prevent suicide.

Mental-Emotional Health

Mental-Emotional health is the condition of a person's mind and the ways that a person expresses feelings. The National Association of Mental Health defines mental-emotional health as the state of (1) being comfortable with yourself, (2) feeling good about your relationships with others, and (3) being able to meet the demands of life. The Teaching Master on page 145, "What Is Good Mental-Emotional Health?" can be used to assess mental-emotional health status.

Positive Self-Concept

The most important indicator of mental-emotional health is the person's self-concept. A **positive self-concept** is the feeling of being a worthwhile person. Having a positive self-concept is usually the product of having family members who provide support and encouragement, having good feelings about physical appearance and talents, being able to meet challenges, feeling a sense of achievement, and having healthful relationships with others.

A negative self-concept might be improved by establishing a close relationship with an adult. When having a trusting relationship with an adult is difficult, counseling is recommended. A trusting adult and/or a therapist can help by providing reassurance and support. Other ways to improve self-concept include identifying challenges that have been met and appreciating those successes, setting short term goals and feeling rewarded for accomplishing them, and spending time with close friends.

Responsible Decision Making

Living life in a responsible and disciplined manner contributes to mental-emotional health. The responsible decision making model can be used as a way of disciplining oneself. When a decision needs to be made, a person adheres to a step-by-step process in which he or she: 1) Clearly describes the situation, (2) Lists possible actions that can be taken, (3) Shares this list with a responsible adult who might make suggestions, (4) Carefully evaluates each possible action to learn if the results will be healthful, safe, legal, respectful of self and others, follow guidelines of responsible adults, and demonstrate good character and moral values, (5) Decides which action is responsible and most appropriate, and (6) Acts in responsible ways evaluating the results.

Being responsible and self-disciplined may involve the use of resistance skills to say NO to specific behaviors and situations. The effective use of resistance skills includes: (1) Using assertive behavior, (2) Avoiding the use of "No thank you," when asked to do something unhealthful, unsafe, illegal, disrespectful, or immoral, (3) Using nonverbal behavior that matches verbal behavior, (4) Influencing others to choose responsible behavior, (5) Avoiding situations in which there will be pressure to make harmful decisions, (6) Avoiding persons who choose harmful actions, and (7) Reporting pressure to engage in illegal behavior to appropriate authorities.

Healthful Expression of Emotions

Many of the diseases and disorders in the United States have a psychosomatic origination. "Psych" refers to the mind while "somatic" refers to the body. A person's attitudes and feelings (psych) influence the health of his or her body. For some persons, feelings of guilt, resentment, anger, frustration, and hostility are unacceptable. Rather than dealing with these feelings in healthful ways, they deny and repress these feelings.

MENTAL AND EMOTIONAL WELL-BEING

When these feelings are denied and repressed, bodily changes may occur which result in headaches, high blood pressure, stomachaches, heart disease, allergies, asthma, and the growth of cancerous cells in some body organs. Rather than denying feelings and repressing them, there are four questions that provide a framework for the healthful expression of feelings: (1) What is it that I am feeling? (2) Why do I feel this way? (3) What are some ways I might express this feeling? (4) Which ways of expressing this feeling are healthful?

Stress Management

Stress is the response of a person's mind or body to stressors. A **stressor** is a physical, mental-emotional, social, or environmental demand. According to Hans Seyle, a pioneer in stress physiology, the body responds to stress in three stages called the **general adaptation syndrome.** During the **alarm stage of GAS**, the body prepares for quick action as adrenaline is released into the bloodstream, heart rate and blood pressure increase, digestion slows, blood flows to muscles, respiration increases, pupils dilate, and hearing sharpens. The body is prepared to meet the demands of the stressor. As the demands are met, the resistance stage of GAS begins. During the **resistance stage of GAS**, pulse, breathing rate, and blood pressure return to normal. The pupils contract and muscles relax. If the demands from the stressor are met unsuccessfully, the GAS continues, and the exhaustion stage of GAS begins. During the **exhaustion stage of GAS,** the body becomes fatigued from overwork and a person becomes vulnerable to diseases.

People respond to stressors in different ways. **Eustress** is successful coping or a healthful response to a stressor. When a person experiences eustress, the resistance stage is effective in establishing homeostasis in the body because the demands of the stressor are met. **Distress** is unsuccessful coping or a harmful response to a stressor. The exhaustion stage often accompanies distress. For this reason, it is important to learn to identify stressors and to know ways to handle them to prevent distress.

Research indicates that the life events which are the most severe stressors for young people are death of a parent, death of a brother or sister, divorce of parents, marital separation of parents, death of a grandparent, hospitalization of a parent, remarriage of a parent to a stepparent, birth of a brother or sister, and loss of a job by a parent. Although these events may elicit distress because of their severity, it is now believed that young people experience distress most of the time from the accumulative effects of daily hassles. The daily hassles include concern about physical appearance, peer acceptance, homework assignments and tests, misplacing or losing belongings, and being the brunt of bullying or criticism.

Stress management skills are techniques that can be used to cope with stressors and to lessen the harmful effects of distress. Stress management skills used to cope with stressors include talking with responsible adults about difficult life events and daily hassles, using the responsible decision making model and resistance skills, and writing in a journal. Each of these techniques helps a person take action to relieve the cause of stress. Stress management skills that protect health include writing in a journal, exercising, being involved in faith experiences including prayer, eating a healthful diet, and spending time with caring persons.

Writing in a journal has been shown to protect health by elevating the number of Helper-T cells. **Helper-T cells** are a kind of white blood cell that fights pathogens and engulfs cancerous cells. Regular vigorous aerobic exercise increases the release of beta-endorphins. **Beta-endorphins** are substances produced by the brain that help relieve pain and create a feeling of well-being. Being involved in faith experiences including prayer has been shown to help immune system function including elevated levels of Helper-T cells. Having faith is often accompanied by an attitude that difficult times will pass. A healthful diet high in Vitamins A, B, and C and low in sugar and caffeine provides additional protection. Vitamin A provides protection against some types of cancer growths. Vitamin B keeps the nervous system healthy and vitamin C promotes immune system function. Sugar should be reduced as it uses up Vitamin B. Caffeine should be reduced as it further elicits the bodily changes induced by the GAS.

Depression

Depression is the feeling of being sad, unhappy, discouraged, and hopeless. Depression is the leading mental health problem in the United States. Approximately 4 to 6 million children and adolescents suffer from depression. Teenage girls have the highest incidence of any age group. The changes in health status and behavior that may signal depression in children and adolescents are: loss of sleep, loss of appetite, loss of energy, loss of concentration, untidy appearance, lack of enthusiasm, sadness, frequent crying, anxiety, anger, hostility, and withdrawal. Depressed youth also may withdraw from others and sleep most of the time.

Unfortunately, most depression in young people goes unnoticed and untreated. Depressed youth need medical attention to determine the cause and method of treatment. There is increasing evidence that many persons suffering from depression have an imbalance in brain biochemistry. In these cases, malfunctions in the normal processes that control the brain levels of certain neurotransmitters can lead to the onset of depression. There are new drugs to alleviate depession for persons who have an imbalance in brain biochemistry.

Youth who suffer from biochemical depression and youth who have no physiological cause for their depression both benefit from taking the following actions: (1) Sharing thoughts and feelings with at least one trusted adult, (2) Having a warm, affectionate relationship with family, (3) Making a list of things to do each day and attempting to accomplish several items on the list, (4) Dressing neatly and being well-groomed, (5) Making a list of strengths and reviewing them, (6) Engaging in vigorous aerobic exercise, (7) Planning social activities with friends, (8) Eating healthful, balanced meals, (9) Getting the appropriate amount of rest and sleep, (10) Journalling in a diary, (11) Participating in activities which promote faith.

Suicide

Suicide is the intentional taking of one's life. It is a leading cause of death in children, preteens, and adolescents. Suicide deaths have been reported in children as young as 5 and 6 years old. Younger children and preteens who are vulnerable to suicide are those who are treated poorly at home, desire to punish their parents, are worried that they will be severely punished for their rebellious behavior, are having difficulties in school, and/or have physical defects that worry them. Adolescents vulnerable to suicide are those who abuse alcohol and other drugs, have experienced the death of a parent or marital separation or divorce, have feelings of alienation from family and friends, fear independence, are the subject of ridicule or isolation from peers, and/or have difficulty in coping with bodily changes and sexuality.

Indications that a young person might be thinking about suicide include: a drastic change in personality, withdrawal from family and friends, loss of interest in personal appearance, loss of interest in schoolwork, difficulty getting along with peers and family members, use of chemicals such as alcohol and marijuana, change in sleeping and eating habits, giving away of personal possessions, and verbal or written statements about suicide or death.

Suicide prevention strategies are steps to follow when dealing with someone who demonstrates signs and symptoms of suicide intent. A person should always be taken seriously. Support and concern is needed. Respect for confidentiality should not be honored and a responsible adult should be immediately notified. If there is difficulty in contacting a specific responsible adult, call a suicide hotline, the local emergency number (9-1-1), or the police or fire department. Stay with the person until appropriate help arrives. After the crisis is over, recognize that this person will need continued support and encouragement.

Figure 5-1
**A person with good mental-emotional health has
a positive self-concept which is closely related
to achieving self-esteem and self-actualization
on Maslow's Hierarchy of Needs.**

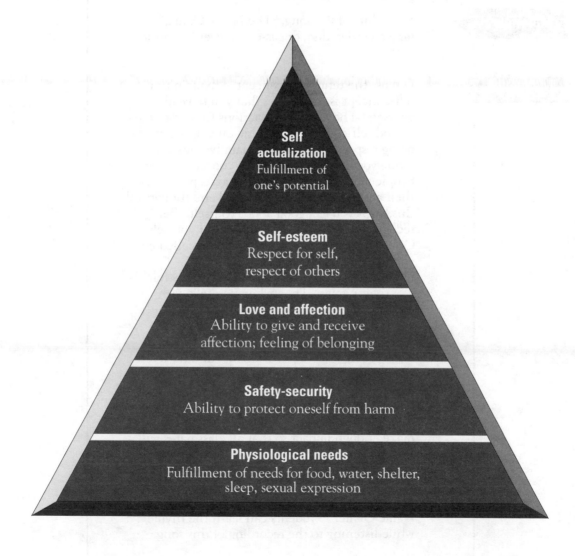

Self
actualization
Fulfillment of
one's potential

Self-esteem
Respect for self,
respect of others

Love and affection
Ability to give and receive
affection; feeling of belonging

Safety-security
Ability to protect oneself from harm

Physiological needs
Fulfillment of needs for food, water, shelter,
sleep, sexual expression

Name Game

Objective

Students will learn the names of each of their classmates and will tell why it is important to use names when speaking to others.

Life Skill

I will call persons by their names when I speak to them.

Materials

Recording of the song, "The Name Game," tape recorder, disc, or cassette player for music

Motivation

1 Discuss the term "self-concept." Explain that self-concept is the feeling that you have about yourself. There are many actions to take to have a good self-concept. Working on your strengths, being responsible, following family rules, and trying your best to improve self-concept. Other people also influence your self-concept. When their actions toward you are kind and thoughtful, this helps you feel good about yourself. Being recognized helps you feel good about yourself. One way of being recognized is to be called by your correct name. For this reason, it is important to listen carefully when others tell you their names. Then when you talk with another person, use this person's name when speaking.

2 Tell students that each of them will have a few minutes to teach their name to the class. They are to think of a very creative way. They might play a game or make up a rhyme to teach others their names. What is important is that they make enough impact so that all classmates will remember their name easily.

3 After each student has taught the class his/her name, play a recording of the song "The Name Game." Students can learn the rhyme while listening to the recording of this song.

4 Have students sit in a circle so that they can see all their classmates. Have students sing "The Name Game" beginning with one student's name and progressing around the circle. This is a fun way to review the names of all students in the class.

Evaluation

Have students volunteer to name every person in the class. Have students explain why it is important to call persons by their names when speaking with them.

Collage of Health

Objective

Students will define health, physical health, mental health, social health, wellness, healthful behaviors, and risk behaviors, and will examine their health status.

Life Skill

I will choose behaviors that improve my health status.

Materials

Posterboard, scissors, glue, magazines

Motivation

1 Review definitions needed to understand health and wellness. Health is the quality of life including physical, mental, and social well-being. Physical health is the condition of the body. Mental health is the condition of the mind and the style of expressing feelings and making decisions. Social health is the style of relating to others. Wellness is the quality of life resulting from decisions and behaviors. A health behavior is an action that promotes health and protects against illnesses and accidents. A risk behavior is an action that threatens health and increases the likelihood of illnesses and accidents.

2 Explain to students that they are to make a collage of their health. A collage is an artistic display in which materials are glued onto a surface. In this case, they are to cut out magazine pictures that are indicative of their physical, mental, and social health behaviors and glue them to the posterboard to make a personal collage of health. They are to include examples of both the healthful behaviors in which they engage and the risk behaviors in which they engage.

3 After students have finished their collages, give them a few minutes to analyze their work. They are to share their collages with the class and discuss their behaviors. They might share ways they can improve their wellness as well as ways they currently are promoting their wellness.

Have students draw a wellness scale as pictured. Near the high end of the wellness scale, have them list the healthful behaviors in which they engage. Near the lower end of the scale, have them identify risk behaviors they need to change. You may also want students to write definitions of health, physical health, mental health, social health, wellness, healthful behaviors, and risk behaviors.

Wellness Scale

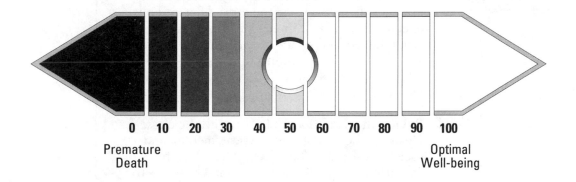

0   10   20   30   40   50   60   70   80   90   100

Premature
Death

Optimal
Well-being

I don't get enough sleep.
I skip breakfast.

I exercise each day.
I wear a safety belt in
an automobile.

The Attitude and Behavior Connection

Objective

Students will identify attitudes and behaviors that enhance physical, mental, and social health and they will explain ways in which these attitudes and behaviors influence the quality of life for others.

Life Skill

I will choose attitudes and behaviors that promote my health and the health of others.

Materials

Ball of red yarn, ball of yellow yarn, ball of green yarn, scissors

Motivation

1 Before beginning this strategy, you will need to make a ball of yarn using the three different balls of colored yarn. Cut three foot strips of yarn using the red, yellow and green yarn. Then make a new ball of yarn by connecting the strips of the different colors of yarn. Your new ball of yarn will be a ball which is red, yellow, and green.

2 Review the definitions of health with the class. Health is the sum of your physical, mental, and social well-being. Your physical health is the condition of your body. Your mental health is the condition of your mind and the ways in which you express your feelings. Your mental health also includes the ways in which you solve problems. Your social health is the quality of your relationships with others. You achieve good health by practicing healthful attitudes and behaviors.

3 Have students sit in a circle. Explain that you are going to form the attitude and behavior connection needed for good health for self and others. Explain that the red yarn represents physical health, the yellow yarn represents mental health, and the green yarn represents social health. Begin by wrapping a small piece of the end of the ball of yarn around your index finger. Check to see what color of yarn you have used. Suppose it is red representing physical health. State an attitude you have or a behavior that you practice that promotes your physical health. For example, you might say, "I get eight hours of sleep each night."

Then throw or roll the ball of yarn to a student and have the student wrap a small piece around his or her finger. The student checks to see what color of yarn is wrapped around his or her finger. Suppose it is green, the student mentions an attitude or behavior that promotes social health. For example, the student might say, "I respect the feelings of others." As the strategy continues, another student might respond with an attitude concerning mental health. This student might say, "I believe it is important to try my best at school." Repeat until every student has shared an attitude or a behavior.

4 Now ask students what they notice about themselves and the ball of yarn. They will notice that they are connected to their classmates by the yarn. Explain that the behaviors and attitudes about health that we each practice affects others. Have the class discuss ways that the behaviors and attitudes that were mentioned do this.

> **Evaluation**

Draw a health behavior triangle on the chalkboard with physical, mental, and social health at the three points. Have students give the definitions of the three kinds of health. At each point, have students write behaviors and attitudes that promote that kind of health.

Whole Person Health

Objective

Students will define healthful behaviors and risk behaviors and will explain how either kind of behavior affects the whole person in an holistic way.

Life Skill

I will choose healthful behaviors.

Materials

Two jars of water, red food coloring, blue food coloring

Motivation

1 Review definitions of health with students. Health is the sum of your physical, mental, and social being. Physical health is the condition of your body. Your mental health is the condition of your mind and the ways in which you express feelings. Your mental health is also the way in which you make decisions. Your social health is the quality of your relationships with others.

2 Explain that to be healthy, you must choose healthful behaviors and avoid risk behaviors. Healthful behaviors are actions that promote health and well-being for you and others. Risk behaviors are actions that might be harmful to you and others.

3 Have students give examples of healthful behaviors: eating a balanced breakfast, using effective communication skills, exercising daily, flossing teeth, and wearing a safety belt. Have students give examples of risk behaviors: hitchhiking, opening a door to a stranger, smoking a cigarette, eating a high fat diet, and riding in a car with someone who has been drinking too much.

4 Explain that all behavior effects us in many ways. Whole person health or holistic health states that any single behavior effects our total health and well-being. Use the following demonstration to illustrate this concept. Show the students the red and the blue food coloring. Explain that the red food coloring represents healthful behavior. You have chosen red because it is a life giving color just as the American Red Cross uses red. The blue food coloring represents risk behavior. Take one jar of water and put a drop of red food coloring in it. Mention that this represents a healthful behavior such as exercising every day. Shake the jar.

Ask students what has happened. They will mention that the red has spread and effected the entire jar of water. Explain that a healthful behavior has a total effect also. Give examples. The daily exercise reduces stress, helps control weight, and can be done with a friend.

5 Repeat this demonstration using a drop of blue food coloring in the other jar. The blue food coloring might represent the risk behavior of eating a high fat diet. This may increase weight, clog arteries, and increase the likelihood of cancer of the colon. Being overweight may effect self-esteem and relationship with others.

> Evaluation

Have students write a short paper in which they describe a healthful behavior to which they are committed and the many benefits they receive from participating in this behavior.

The Broken Record

Objective

Students will demonstrate the broken record technique when provided with sample situations to which they need to resist pressure and say NO clearly and firmly.

Life Skill

I will say NO when pressured to choose risk behaviors.

Materials

Old records, cardboard paper, construction paper markers, scissors

Motivation

1 Discuss the importance of making wise choices and responsible decisions. Explain that a responsible decision results in actions that are healthful, safe, and legal. It results in actions that show that you respect yourself and others and follow the guidelines of responsible adults. Explain that some young people make responsible decisions while others do not. Young people who make responsible decisions may encourage others to do the same. This is known as positive peer pressure. Young people who do not make responsible decisions may encourage others to make harmful choices. This is known as negative peer pressure. Explain that it is important to say NO when others try to encourage you to do something harmful.

2 Explain that refusal skills are ways young people can say NO to harmful choices. They can: look others in the eyes, speak with confidence, give reasons why they do not want to do something, use behavior to show they mean what they are saying, and leave the situation if pressure continues.

3 Explain that the broken record technique is a way of saying NO. This technique gets its name from a needle that remains in the same groove in a record, causing the words on the record to be repeated. When you use the broken record technique, you think of one reason you do not want to do something. You keep repeating this like a broken record each time you are pressured. For example, suppose you do not want to smoke a cigarette. Your reason is that you are on the track team and smoking cigarettes is not allowed. You say, "No, I do not want to smoke cigarettes because I am on the track team and there is a rule against smoking." When pressure continues, you keep repeating the same statement like a broken record.

4 Have students practice using the broken record technique by responding to these situations: 1) someone offers a drink of alcohol, 2) someone suggests hitchhiking, 3) someone suggests copying homework, 4) someone suggests smoking cigarettes or a joint. You can change the scenarios to fit situations most likely for your students.

5 Have students make records using the cardboard, colored construction paper, and markers. Near the center of the record where the title of the recording appears, have students write a typical pressure such as smoking cigarettes. Then in the grooves of the record, they are to write in circles as many times as possible, one reason why they would say NO to this situation or behavior.

Evaluation

Have students explain what a responsible decision is. Have them identify some refusal or say NO skills that they might use. Have them explain and demonstrate the broken record technique.

A Special Gift

Objective

Students will define self-concept, tell ways they are special, and explain how their special gifts benefit others.

Life Skill

I will act in ways that show I care about myself.

Materials

Shoebox, glue or tape, wrapping paper, mirror

Motivation

1 Construct a special gift box using the shoebox. Cover the shoebox with wrapping paper. Inside the shoebox, glue a small mirror to the inside lid. Have the box in front of the class, but do not tell anyone what is inside.

2 Ask students if they have ever gotten a special gift. Allow time for them to share stories about the special gifts they have received. Ask them how their gifts were wrapped. Explain that they probably did not know what the gift was until it was opened.

3 Explain that you have a gift box. There is something very special in the box. You are going to let them see what is special in the box but they are not to tell anyone what they see. Now open the gift box carefully so one student at a time sees what is inside.

4 Ask students what they saw. They will say "Me." Explain that they saw themselves in the gift box and that they each have gifts. Have students share their gifts. Talk about how these gifts are shared with others. For example, if a student has the gift of humor it helps others laugh.

Have students each repeat the following poem
and complete the last line.

"I looked in the mirror,
and what did I see?
I saw someone special.
It was me.
One way I am special is...."

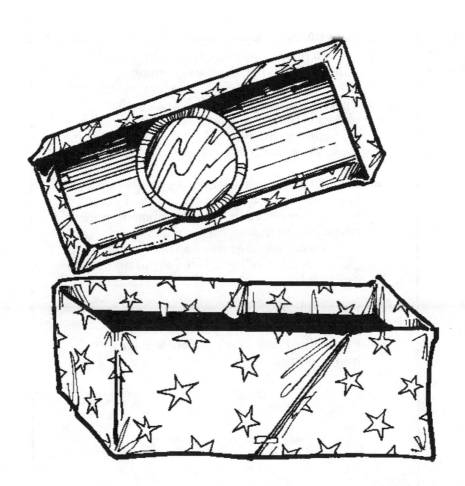

Personality Puzzle

Objective

Students will identify their strengths and interests and those they would like to develop.

Life Skill

I will develop new strengths and interests.

Materials

Variety of magazines, scissors, glue, cardboard paper

Motivation

1 Explain that strengths are things that they do well such as playing the piano. Strengths are also good qualities they have such as being a good friend. Interests are things you like to do and things you would like to be. Your strengths and interests help make your personality. Your personality is who you are.

2 Have students each make their own personality puzzle. They are to have a piece of cardboard paper. They can cut out pictures from magazines that represent their strengths and interests. They could also take paper and draw things to glue on to the cardboard. They are to fill the cardboard.

3 Have students use scissors to cut their sheets of cardboard paper into pieces to make a Personality Puzzle. Each student will have his/her own puzzle.

4 Then have students form pairs. They are to exchange their personality puzzle with their partner and put their partner's puzzle together. They can discuss their puzzles with one another. They can share their strengths and interests.

5 Then have each pair share about each other in front of the class. They are to share one strength and one interest of their partner.

Evaluation

Have students list three of their strengths and three of their interests. Have students tell a strength and an interest they would like to develop.

Thumbprint of Uniqueness

Objective

Students will tell ways in which they are unique and special and recognize ways in which others are unique and special.

Life Skill

I will choose actions that show I believe that I am special.

Materials

Index card for each student, markers or crayons, ink pad

Motivation

1 Give each student an index card. Ask each student to draw a picture of his or her body on the index card, but the body is not to have a head. After each student has drawn his or her body, have students place their thumbs on the ink pad and then make a thumbprint to represent the head. Have students write their names on the back of their card. Collect the cards and place them in a row on the chalkboard.

2 Use the cards to begin a discussion. How are the drawings of the children in the class similar? How are people similar? What needs do all people have?

3 How are the drawings of the children different? How are people different or unique?

4 Ask students how they would know which card belonged to them and to others. They would explain that the thumbprint could be used to tell which card belonged to whom. Explain that there is no one exactly like you. Each person is similar and different from others, but everyone is unique. Give students an opportunity to share two or three ways in which they are unique or special.

Give students a card that does not belong to
them. They can read the name of the student to
whom the card belongs. Then they can tell one
or two ways that this student is special and
return the card. Repeat for all students.

Journal of My Feelings

Objective

Students will explain changes that occur in the body when feelings are kept inside, diseases and disorders that might result, and ways in which journalling counteracts harmful changes and prevents diseases and disorders.

Life Skill

I will write my feelings in a journal when I feel stress.

Materials

Diary or notepad for each student, pens or pencils

Motivation

1 Discuss the stressors young people experience that affect their health and well-being. Some of these stressors might be: difficult peer relationships, difficulty in school, poor self-esteem, moving, having a death or divorce in the family, and worrying about an event. Make a list of these stressors on the chalkboard.

2 Explain to students that when stress continues for a period of time, there may be changes that occur in their bodies that effect their health status. They may have headaches and stomach-aches. They may have difficulty eating and sleeping and concentrating in school. There is something else that may happen. Normally body defenses protect you from becoming ill. But, when stress continues for long periods of time, the body defenses do not work as well. There are white blood cells in your body which usually surround and destroy pathogens that enter the body. These white blood cells are called helper-T cells. You can remember them because they are cells which "help" you stay healthy. But when you are under stress for a long time, the helper-T cell count is lowered. You do not have as many helper-T cells to keep you healthy.

3 Explain that there is something students can do for themselves when they feel pressure and stress. Researchers at The Ohio State University found that writing about feelings in a diary or journal caused changes to occur in the body. The helper-T cell count rises after writing about feelings.

Expressing feelings in detail can keep the number of helper-T cells higher for as long as two weeks.

4 Explain to students that for several weeks they are going to journal. Journalling is the term used that means you are writing about your feelings. To get the best results for your health and for your understanding of a situation, it is best to write out the answers to four questions: (1) What is it that I am feeling? (2) Why do I feel this way? (3) What are some ways I might express my feelings? (4) Which ways of expressing my feelings are healthful?

5 Discuss with students to whom they might turn to share their journals or diaries. Emphasize that the most important thing to do is to record all feelings when they journal. It is not necessary to share the journal with anyone else. However, sharing feelings with another trusted person further helps health.

Evaluation

Have students explain why they are more likely to have colds and flu during very stressful times. Have them describe how journalling will help them stay healthy.

When It Rains, It Pours

Objective

Students will identify causes of stress, signs and symptoms of stress, and healthful ways to respond to stress.

Life Skill

I will use stress management techniques to reduce the effects of stress.

Materials

Umbrella, tape, colored construction paper, markers

Motivation

1 Begin by explaining that stress is the way your mind or body responds to any demands. A stressor is a demand made upon the mind or body.

2 Talk about what happens to the body when there is stress. The body gets ready for a quick action to do something. Vision sharpens so that you see clearly. Your hearing gets better. There is an increase in the sugar in your blood to give you energy. Your heart beats faster so blood goes to your muscles. Your rate of breathing increases.

3 Using the colored construction paper, cut out large raindrops. Ask students to tell you stressors in their lives. Examples of the stressors might be: having an illness, taking a test, giving a speech, having a death in the family, having a divorce in the family, having a pet die, having a fight with someone about whom you care, doing poorly at something, having feelings hurt, moving, starting a new school, etc. Now write one of these stressors on each of the raindrops using the markers. Just write one or two words such as "pet dies," "move," "new school." Put the raindrops aside.

4 Ask two students to help you. Have them sit in chairs in front of the class. One will hold an umbrella while the other will not. Explain that the student holding the umbrella has learned what to do to stay healthy when there are stressors. Cut strips of construction paper. Ask students what the student who stays healthy does. Examples are: talk to family member, exercise, get rest and sleep, meditate, pray, eat healthful foods. Write each of these on a separate strip of paper and tape each strip to the umbrella.

Take the raindrops and drop them on the two students. Explain that both students feel stress, but the student with the umbrella has protection because this student has learned what to do to stay healthy during stress.

Have students define stress and stressor. Have them give at least five examples of stressors they experience. Have them tell three things that happen to their bodies when they feel stress. Have them tell three things they can do to stay healthy when they feel stress.

Soaking Up Stress

Objective

Students will identify causes of stress and healthful ways to reduce the effects of stress.

Life Skill

I will use stress management skills to reduce the effects of stress.

Materials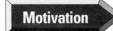

Sponge, pitcher of water something to place under the sponge when water is poured upon it

Motivation

1 You are going to begin by explaining to students that stress is the way your mind and body respond to demands. A stressor is a demand made upon the mind or body.

2 Tell students to think of different stressors that they have experienced. The stressors they will mention will depend partially upon their age and grade level. For example, younger students might mention going to school the first day or staying home alone. Older students might mention asking someone for a date. All age groups might mention having arguments with friends or family, having a death in the family, having a divorce in the family, taking a test, and moving.

3 Explain to students that the sponge represents their bodies. Each time a stressor is experienced, a demand is placed on the body. Mention a stressor and then pour a little water on the sponge. Then mention another stressor and pour more water on the sponge. Continue until the sponge is drenched. Explain that when you continue to feel the effects of many stressors your body absorbs or takes in too much stress.

4 Have a student hold the sponge and ask how it feels. It feels very heavy. When you absorb lots of stress your body feels heavy too. There is tension or heaviness in your muscles. You feel tired and drained and more likely to become ill.

5 Explain that it is not healthful to absorb too much stress. It is important to do something about stress as soon as you feel it. Talk about

what to do when you feel stress: talk to a
parent, exercise, get rest and sleep, eat
balanced meals, pray, meditate, write in a diary.

Then repeat the sponge and water experiment
differently. Have students tell a stressor and
pour water on the sponge. Then have students
tell a healthful action to take when there is
stress and squeeze the water out of the sponge.
Keep repeating this mentioning that everyone
has stressors but to stay healthful you take
healthful actions right away.

Evaluation

Have students define stress and stressors.
Have students give at least five examples of
stressors they experience. Have them tell
three things they can do to stay healthful when
they feel stress.

"Don't Worry, Be Happy!"

Objective

Students will identify the three essentials for happiness and will tell actions they can take to promote happiness in their lives.

Life Skill

I will work hard, spend time with friends, and set goals for happiness.

Materials

Recording of the song, "Don't worry, Be happy," tape recorder, disc or cassette player for music, poster paper, scissors, magazines, glue

Motivation

1 Write the following statement on the chalkboard. Joseph Addison said, "The three grand essentials to happiness are something to do, someone to love, and something to hope for." Then make a triangle on the chalkboard and write each of these at one of the points: something to do, someone to love, something to hope for. In the middle, write happiness.

2 Discuss happiness with students. Explain that happiness often involves choice. Each of us has control over happiness because we can choose to do things which promote happiness. Discuss each of the three points on the triangle. Having something to do promotes happiness. Give examples: playing on a sports team, having a hobby, volunteering to help others. Having someone to love promotes happiness. Give examples: spending time with family, having a close friend, having a pet. Having something to look forward to promotes happiness. Give examples: graduation from high school, a summer vacation, religion which gives meaning to the future.

3 Have students make a collage of happiness. On posterboard, they are to draw a large triangle. Then at the three points of the triangle, they can write: something to do, someone to love, something to hope for. They are to cut out pictures or draw pictures to represent these three areas. They may want to attach a picture of someone about whom they care near the point which says, "someone to love." While they are making their posters, you might play a recording of the song "Don't worry, be happy."

4 Have students share their completed posters explaining their choices for happiness in the three areas.

5 Referring back to the triangle, explain how these three areas give balance to life. Discuss what would happen if one side of the triangle were removed, the triangle would collapse. What happens to happiness when a person neglects one of these areas?

Evaluation Have students write a short paper titled, "Happiness is my choice."

Stressed Out

Objective	Students will identify signs and symptoms of stress.
Life Skill	I will use stress management techniques to reduce the effects of stress.
Materials	Paper and pencil

Motivation

1 You are going to place students in a stressful situation as soon as you walk into the classroom.

2 Tell students, "Take out a sheet of paper and number down the left hand side from 1-20. I told you that you were responsible for reading (whatever you are working upon currently). I am going to see if you completed this assignment. And by the way— this test is going to be worth fifty percent of your grade for the course."

3 Proceed to give students questions that will be almost impossible to answer. For example, you can say, "The first question has three parts. Name three effects of stress on the cerebral cortex." Choose another three difficult questions before stopping.

4 Tell students, "This is not a real test. However, when I told you that I was giving you a test, certain reactions occurred inside your body. What are some reactions that occurred?" Students will most likely mention increased heartbeat, sweating, dry mouth, etc.

5 Review information about the signs and symptoms of stress. The general adaptation syndrome or GAS is the three stage response of the body that occurs. The three stages are the alarm stage, the resistance stage, and the exhaustion stage. The alarm stage is the first response of the body to a stressor. During the alarm stage:

- adrenaline is secreted from the adrenal glands to get the body ready for quick action.
- the pupils or black part of the eyes widen.
- the sense of hearing sharpens.
- sugar is released from the liver to give energy.

- the breathing rate increases so more oxygen is taken in each minute.
- blood pressure and heart rate increase.
- digestion slows so blood flow can go to the muscles.

During the resistance stage, the body begins to return to normal. Under normal conditions, the changes that occurred during the alarm stage cease. But if stress continues, the resistance stage is not effective. The third stage of stress is exhaustion. During the exhaustion stage, the body has been working too hard and health is affected. The immune system is weakened and a person is more likely to acquire communicable diseases. Blood pressure increases putting more stress on the heart. Accidents are more likely to occur.

Evaluation

Have students identify the signs and symptoms of stress that they experienced during the alarm stage when you announced the test.

Ready To Burst

Objective

Students will identify causes of stress and ways to reduce the effects of stress.

Life Skill

I will use stress management techniques to reduce the effects of stress.

Materials

Balloon for each student
(Because balloons may be swallowed by birds and harm them, be certain that balloons are disposed of in a proper way.)

Motivation

1 Begin by explaining to students that stress is the way in which their minds and bodies respond to demands. When stress is experienced, the mind and body get ready to take quick action. Some of the changes that occur are:

- adrenaline is secreted by the adrenal glands to prepare for a response.
- the pupils dilate to help you see more clearly.
- the sense of hearing sharpens to warn you.
- the liver releases sugar to provide quick energy.
- breathing rate increases so that more oxygen is taken in each minute to go to the cells.
- the heart rate and blood pressure increase to assist in getting oxygen to cells.
- the process of digestion slows so that little oxygen is needed by these organs.
- more blood flow goes to muscles providing increased oxygen for work.

2 Explain that a stressor is a demand made upon the mind or body. Identify different stressors.

3 Now give each student a balloon and use the following illustration to discuss stressors and ways to reduce the effects of stress. Have students identify stressors they experience such as taking a test, arguing with peers, giving a speech in front of class, being behind in homework assignments, asking someone for a date, having a death or divorce in the family, etc. (You can think of stressors that are age appropriate depending upon the grade level you teach). Each time a stressor is mentioned have students blow a small amount of air in their balloons. Continue this part of the lesson until someone's balloon bursts. Then discuss the need to do something about stressors before "you feel ready to burst."

4 Discuss stress management skills. Stress management skills consist of healthful ways to reduce the effects of stressors. As soon as a stressor is experienced, it is important to do something about the stressor and to do something to prevent or lessen the harmful effects it may cause. Identify actions such as talking to a trusted adult, using responsible decision making, spending time with supportive friends, eating a healthful diet, cutting down on caffeine to reduce blood pressure, cutting down on sugar because it depletes Vitamin B needed for coping, exercising to use up adrenaline, and getting rest and sleep.

5 Now use the following illustration to show how to use stress management skills to control the effects of stressors. Have students identify a stressor and blow air into their balloons. Follow this by having students mention a stress management skill to use when this stressor occurs. Keep repeating by having students mention stressors then blowing in air and then mention stress management skills letting air out. Emphasize that no one is free of stressors in life, it is this continual adjustment that helps maintain health.

Evaluation

Have students list five common stressors in persons their age and stress management skills they would use for each.

Ready, Set... Relax!

Objective

Students will describe stress, the general adaptation syndrome, and the relaxation response.

Life Skill

I will use stress management techniques to reduce the effects of stress.

Materials

Two recordings of music- one with fast paced music, the other relaxing slow paced music, tape recorder to play music

Motivation

1 Review the definitions of stress, stressor, eustress, distress, and the general adaptation syndrome. Stress is the nonspecific response of the body to any demand made upon it. A stressor is the source of the demand. Eustress is a healthful response to a stressor. Distress is unsuccessful coping or a harmful response to a stressor. The general adaptation syndrome called GAS is the body's response to stress. GAS is divided into three stages: the alarm stage, the resistance stage, and the exhaustion stage. The alarm stage is the body's initial response to a stressor in which there is preparation for quick action. The resistance stage is the body's attempt to return to balance. If the resistance stage is unsuccessful in restoring balance, the exhaustion stage sets in. The exhaustion stage is the wearing down of the body as a result of prolonged stress.

2 Play the fast paced music. Discuss the students response to this music. If you have selected the music carefully, students may say that they want to dance or move about when they hear it. Explain that this is similar to the fight or flight reaction that is experienced when the alarm stage of GAS begins. The role of the sympathetic nervous system is to stimulate or energize the body for action. During the alarm stage, the following changes occur:

  •increased heart rate
  •increased blood pressure
  •increased breathing rate
  •increased blood flow to muscles

3 Play the slow paced music. Discuss the students response to this music. If you have selected the music carefully, students may say that they feel calmer and want to relax. Explain that this is similar to what the body attempts to do during the resistance stage of the GAS. The body wants to slow down the fast pace of the alarm stage and return body functions to normal. The parasympathetic nervous system takes over and its role is one of restoring homeostasis or balance. During the resistance stage, the following changes occur:

- decreased heart rate
- decreased blood pressure
- decreased body metabolism
- decreased breathing rate
- decreased blood flow to muscles

4 Explain to students that they can assist the body in restoring balance and in being relaxed. The relaxation response is the use of self-induced techniques to return the body to homeostasis.

5 The following technique can be used to trigger the relaxation response:
- Choose a quiet place with no distractions.
- Sit in a comfortable position.
- Shut your eyes
- Inhale slowly and deeply through your nose.
- As you exhale slowly blowing air out of your mouth, say the number "one" to yourself.
- Repeat for three to five minutes.

Evaluation

Ask the class to provide examples of three highly stressful situations which are situations that students their age might experience. Then have the class identify the stressor. Have them explain a response to this situation that might be classified as a eustress and a response that might be classified as a distress. Then have them explain what will happen during the GAS.

Defense Mechanisms Bingo

Directions:
Defense mechanisms are behaviors that you use to cope with emotions and S-O-L-V-E uncomfortable situations. There are many types of defense mechanisms: compensation, daydreaming, displacement, idealization, identification, projection, rationalization, reaction formation, regression, repression, sublimation, and substitution.

Under each of the five letters, S-O-L-V-E, write one of the twelve defense mechanisms. You cannot repeat the name of a defense mechanism under the same letter. For example, you cannot write daydreaming twice under S. However, you can repeat a defense mechanism under a different letter. You could have daydreaming under S and under O.

S	O	L	V	E

Defense Mechanisms

Compensation

A person tries to make up for his/her weaknesses by developing strengths in other areas.
Example: A student with a learning disability who struggles academically in school becomes a leader in the art club.

Daydreaming

A person escapes unpleasant, boring, or frustrating situations by imagining that he or she is doing something else.
Example: A student is very shy and does not talk much with peers at school but imagines that he or she is voted homecoming king or queen.

Displacement

A person transfers the emotions he or she feels from the original situation or object to another situation or object.
Example: A student is angry at a teacher for something that has happened at school and returns home after school and yells at his/her mother.

Idealization

A person places an overexagerrated value on someone or something.
Example: A student admires the team coach so much that he or she cannot see that this person is human and has faults as do others.

Identification

A person tries to assume the qualitites of someone that is admired.
Example: A student wants to be like a sports figure that is admired and begins to eat the foods that this person advertises in hopes of being just like this person.

Projection

A person shifts the blame and/or responsibility for his/her actions or thoughts to another person.
Example: A student does poorly on a test and then states that the teacher wrote an unfair test.

Rationalization

A person gives an acceptable reason for behavior in a certain way rather than the true reason.
Example: A student is unprepared for a test and wants to stay home from school. The student tells his/her parents that he/she is not feeling well.

Reaction formation

A person demonstrates behavior that is contradictory or opposite of his/her nature.
Example: A student is very selfish but tries to hide this quality by offering others special things.

get dressed.
- Try to get exercise and fresh air each day.

4 Explain that sometimes problems of living become so difficult that normal responses to life situations are interrupted and a person is left with behaviors that are not conducive to positive mental health. According to The National Association for Mental Health, these are the danger signals:

- A general and lasting feeling of hopelessness and despair.
- Inability to concentrate, making reading, writing, and conversation difficult.
- Changes in physical activity like eating, sleeping, or exercise.
- A loss of self-esteem which brings continual questioning of personal worth.
- Withdrawal from others, not by choice, but from an immense fear of rejection of others.
- Threats or attempts to commit suicide.
- Extreme sensitivity to words and actions of others, and general irritability.
- Misdirected anger and difficulty in handling most feelings.
- Feelings of guilt and self blame.

5 Show the students a copy of a car owner's manual. Inside the manual it will most likely say "important operating, maintenance, and service information." Have students make a coping kit with the title MENTAL HEALTH: OWNER'S MANUAL. The coping kit or mental health manual should provide instructions for maintaining and promoting good mental health. It should also include information on danger signals that the owner needs service or professional help.

Evaluation

Check the MENTAL HEALTH: OWNER'S MANUAL for characteristics of good mental health, ways to cope with depressed feelings, and signs that professional help is needed.

You may also want students to write definitions of health, physical health, mental health, social health, wellness, healthful behaviors, and risk behaviors.

What is Good Mental-Emotional Health ?

Directions: Put a check in front of each statement that describes you. This handout is reprinted from the National Association fo Mental Health, *Mental Health is 1, 2, 3*. Washington, D.C.: National Association for Mental Health, 1968.

_____ 1. I feel comfortable with myself.

_____ 2. I am not bowled over by my own emotions- by my fears, anger, jealousy, guilt, or worries.

_____ 3. I can take life's disappointments in their stride.

_____ 4. I have a tolerant, easygoing attitude toward myself as well as others; I can laugh at myself.

_____ 5. I neither underestimate nor overestimate my abilities.

_____ 6. I can accept my own shortcomings.

_____ 7. I have self-respect.

_____ 8. I feel able to deal with most situations that come my way.

_____ 9. I get satisfaction from the simple, everyday pleasures.

_____ 10. I feel right about other people.

_____ 11. I am able to give love and to consider the interests of others.

_____ 12. I have personal relationships that are satisfying and lasting.

_____ 13. I expect to like and trust others, and take it for granted that others will like and trust me.

_____ 14. I respect the many differences I find in people.

_____ 15. I do not push people around, nor do I allow myself to be pushed around.

_____ 16. I can feel I am part of a group.

_____ 17. I feel a sense of responsibility to my neighbors and fellow persons.

_____ 18. I am able to meet the demands of life.

_____ 19. I do something about my problems as they arise.

_____ 20. I accept my responsibilities.

_____ 21. I shape my environment whenever possible; I adjust to it whenever necessary.

_____ 22. I plan ahead, but do not fear the future.

_____ 23. I welcome new experiences and new ideas.

_____ 24. I make use of my natural capacities.

_____ 25. I set realistic goals for myself.

_____ 26. I am able to think for myself and make my own decisions.

_____ 27. I put my best effort into what I do, and get satisfaction out of doing it.

Suicide Prevention Hotline

Objective

Students will recognize signs that indicate warnings of suicide and will identify suicide prevention strategies.

Life Skill

I will get help for myself or for any friend who shows signs of being suicidal.

Materials

Index cards, pens or pencils, local phone numbers for suicide prevention hotlines

Motivation

1 Introduce the topic of suicide. Suicide is the intended taking of one's own life. It is the second leading cause of death in teenagers and young adults and now a leading cause of death in children. Most suicides are attempts at getting help and may be prevented if persons are in touch with the signs that indicate a suicide attempt might be made. These signs include:

- withdrawing from family, friends, and activities
- giving away prized possessions
- talking about getting even with parents or other significant persons
- losing interest in personal appearance and grooming
- having a drastic change in personality
- changing normal patterns of eating and/or sleeping
- having difficulty getting along with peers
- increasing use of chemicals such as alcohol, marijuana, crack, cocaine
- talking about committing suicide
- discussing one's death

2 Discuss what young people can do if they recognize these signs in others. Steps they can take include:

- Paying attention to these signs rather than ignoring them hoping you are wrong.
- Do not listen to others who do not believe that a person is thinking about suicide.
- Tell a trusted adult rather than worrying about breaking the confidence of a friend. This is

too difficult to handle yourself.
- Stay with someone who shows signs of suicidal behavior until a trusted adult arrives to handle the situation.
- Listen to the person and encourage the person to talk about feelings.
- Encourage the person to seek professional help.
- Be supportive by showing the person you care and pointing out the person's strengths.

3 Give each student an index card. Discuss the importance of having a support network to turn to in difficult times. On one side of the index card, have students write the names and phone numbers of their personal support network. You might suggest that they include: (l) two family members (2) two close friends (3) a trusted adult outside the family (4) a trusted adult at school (S) a person who is a member of their religious faith- minister, priest, rabbi Students who are not able to identify persons in these categories should be encouraged to work on developing a broader based support network. Explain that having and turning to a support network can be helpful during crisis situations and is an important strategy in dealing with the difficulties that may precipitate suicidal feelings.

4 On the opposite side of the card, have students write the names of hotlines and places for emergency help in their communities along with the phone numbers. Where appropriate, write names of persons to contact.

Evaluation

Have a group of students devise a scenario in which a young person shows signs of depression and suicidal behavior. The class can then identify the signs of suicidal behavior and describe steps to take.

Family and Relationship Skills is the area of health that examines loving functional families, changes in family relationships, dysfunctional families, abuse within families, communication skills, relationships with same and opposite sex, dating and sexual decision making, and marriage and parenthood.

Loving Functional Families

Loving functional families are those in which there are guidelines set for responsible behavior, consequences for inappropriate behavior, an atmosphere of trust, an open expression of affection, positive communication, and evidence of cooperation. In loving functional families, there is no evidence of abuse, violence, or chemical dependency. Children raised in these families receive adequate guidance, attention, and affection and as a result, develop a strong sense of self and a positive self-esteem. They are appropriately guided and disciplined enabling them to develop a sense of responsibility. They learn skills for relating in healthful and responsible ways and are able to use these skills in their friendship and dating relationships and later in marriage and parenthood.

Changes in Family Relationships

It is not surprising that changes in family relationships are viewed as being very stressful for children, adolescents, and their parents/guardians. Marital separation and divorce have a profound effect on the security and safety that children and adolescents need to have as they grow and develop physically, mentally, emotionally, socially, and spiritually.

The reactions to marital separation and divorce vary depending on the age of the child or adolescent. Preschool children usually react with fear and become preoccupied with what will happen to them. Children who are six to eight years old express sadness and are likely to have crying and/or sobbing spells. They experience conflicts in their loyalty to parents. Chil-

dren who are nine to twelve years old are often angry with parents. They may bargain with parents in an attempt to get them to reconcile. When no reconciliation occurs, they may act out their anger through inappropriate behavior at home and school. Often, they are not aware that their actions against others are really an expression of their anger about their family situation. Help may be needed. Twelve-year-olds usually respond by demonstrating a shaken sense of identity. They are particularly vulnerable because they have their own issues of sexual identity at this time and they need the effective role modelling of both parents. However, they usually side with one parent or the other which causes them to lose emotional closeness with the other parent. As a result, there is much confusion. Later, they may choose inappropriate sexual behavior as a way of coping with their shaken identity. Teenagers often respond to parental separation and/or divorce with delinquency, depression, psychological disturbance, expressions of hostility, and poor social adjustment. They are usually embarassed and feel this embarassment around peers. This may lead to feelings of low self-esteem.

Some children and adolescents adjust more easily to parental separation and divorce than others. What seems to make a difference? Research findings indicate that psychological separation is more difficult to adjust to than is physical separation. In other words, if parents remain emotionally and psychologically close even though they are not living with a child, the adjustment is easier. Children and adolescents who indicate the greatest adjustment problems are those who feel psychologically abandoned. Those who make more healthful adjustments usually do not like the separation and divorce but they still feel parents are close to them.

Feelings of abandonment versus feelings of closeness also appear to be vital in adjusting to parental dating, remarriage, and joining a stepfamily. Young children find parental dating disruptive if they believe they will be abandoned if the parent connects into a new relationship. This is especially true if the new relationship demands a

FAMILY AND RELATIONSHIP SKILLS

great deal of time, thereby reducing time spent with parent and child. Adolescents usually have difficulty with parents dating because they are at the developmental stage where this is appropriate behavior for them. In order to sort out their own feelings about opposite sex relationships, they had hoped that their parents would be in a comfortable and stable relationship. Again, much dialogue is needed between parent and child for a healthful adjustment to be made.

Much research has focused on remarriage and the formation of the stepfamily. Parents may believe that if their new relationship is comfortable and loving, children will have these same feelings about the stepfamily. However, research findings indicate that it may take seven years for children and adolescents to feel a comfortable bond with the new family unit. Young people tend to have an easier time adjusting if their natural parents spend some quality time alone with them and provide them much emotional support.

Dysfunctional Families

Dysfunctional families are those in which no guidelines for responsible behavior or consequences for inappropriate behavior exist, and there is distrust, lack of affection, and lack of cooperation. Children and

Dysfunctional Family Relationships

Characteristics of Persons with Co-Dependence

Messages learned in Dysfunctional Families that contribute to co-dependence

- It is not alright to talk about family problems.
- I must present a positive family image to others.
- I cannot change what is happening.
- It is safer to keep my feelings to myself.
- Others need not treat me with respect.
- I cannot let others know how I feel.
- It is better to be serious than playful.

Contributing causes or Root of Family "Dis"-function

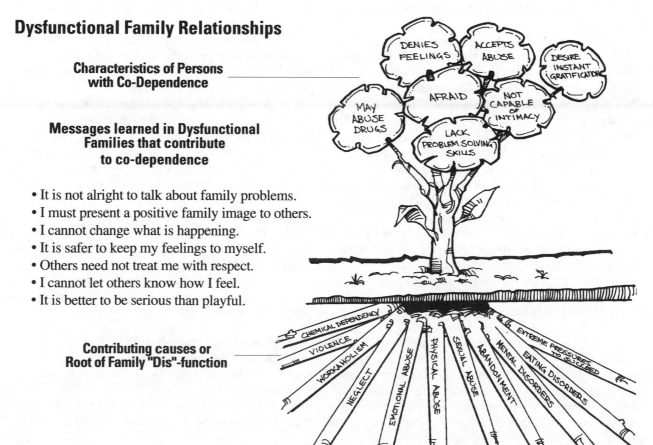

adolescents in these families do not learn to delay gratification and struggle unsuccessfully to solve problems. The term dysfunctional was first used to describe families in which there was alcoholism. The alcoholic behavior of one family member and the reactive behaviors of other family members contributed to family "dis"-function. Today, all families with some or all of the characteristics previously mentioned are identified as dysfunctional. Some contributing causes to family "dis"-function are: chemical dependency, violence, workaholism, neglect, emotional abuse, physical abuse, sexual abuse, abandonment, mental disorders, eating disorders, and extreme pressures to succeed.

In dysfunctional families, family members begin to interact in harmful and inappropriate ways rather than in healthful and responsible ways. Some or all family members show signs of co-dependence. **Co-dependence** is a mental disorder in which a person loses personal identity and is unaware of personal thoughts and feelings. The messages persons with co-dependence have learned from their families include: 1) It is not alright to talk about the problems the family has, 2) It is important to present a positive image of the family to others even if this image is not accurate, 3) It is better to continue in "dis"-function than to make changes, 4) It is safer to keep my feelings to myself, 5) It is unrealistic to believe that others should treat me with respect, 6) It is better to be dishonest because if others knew the truth they would not accept me, 7) It is important to be serious, not playful, 8) It is important to be safe and not trust others.

These messages destroy the ability to form healthful relationships with those outside the family. Unfortunately, these messages also contribute to attempts at coping via risk-taking behavior. Alcohol, other drugs, and sex experimentation are much more common in children and adolescents who have difficult family relationships. The alcohol and drug use may be an attempt to numb the painful feelings these youth are experiencing. The sexual experimentation is often an attempt to compensate for affection that is lacking at home. These children and adolescents often are willing to take risks to receive temporary relief from pain rather than deal with the difficult and painful issues that face them. Recovery from co-dependence always involves dealing with painful issues and learning to express feelings and get needs met in healthful ways.

Abuse Within Families

Family violence and abuse are unpleasant topics, yet statistics indicate that they are common. At least fifty percent of married couples report using violence during an argument at least once during their marriages. Twenty-five percent of youth under the age of 18 have been abused with a family member being the abuser eighty-five to ninety percent of the time.

A **battered spouse** is a person in a committed relationship that is physically or emotionally abused by the partner. The most common abusers are males who were abused as children themselves, grew up with low self-esteem, and repeated patterns of behavior they had learned. The victims are usually females who grew up in dysfunctional families and as a result had low self-esteem and poor relationship skills. They usually did not learn to expect the respect of others and often feel deserving of abuse. The entire family, both partners and their children, suffer from battering that takes place. In many instances, the victim and the children must be away from the abuser in order for the family to be helped. There are shelters available to provide safety until help can be obtained. There are twenty-four hour hotlines for both victims, abusers, and children. Recovery involves counseling for all family members.

Child abuse is the maltreatment of a child under the age of 18. There are at least four kinds of abuse: physical abuse, neglect, emotional abuse, and sexual abuse. **Physical abuse** is maltreatment that harms the body. Signs of physical abuse include bruises, burns, cuts, missing teeth, broken bones, and internal injuries. **Neglect** is maltreatment that involves lack of proper care and guidance. Signs include malnourishment, poor health, and illnesses related to being inadequately clothed for the weather. **Emotional abuse** is maltreatment that involves assault in a nonphysical way. Examples of emotional abuse include constant criticism and withdrawal of affection. Signs of emotional abuse include poor peer relationships, distrust, excessive fear, and low self-esteem. **Sexual abuse** is maltreatment that involves inappropriate sexual behavior between an adult and a child. Signs of sexual abuse include poor peer relationships and sexual acting out in inappropriate ways. Youth who have been sexually abused may also show physical signs such as squirming in their seats because of harm to vaginal and/or rectal tissue.

By law, all cases of suspected child abuse must be reported by school personnel to appropriate authorities. Children and teenagers who have been abused need counseling and reassurance. Often, they believe they are at fault for the abuse and feel guilty and ashamed. They need to be reassured that no one has the right to abuse them. They need help in developing positive self-esteem to break the abuse cycle. If the abuse cycle is not broken, abused youth are likely to become adult abusers or victims.

Communication Skills

Communication is the sharing of feelings, thoughts, and information with another person. Inability to communicate has been linked to many psychosomatic diseases and disorders.

I-messages are statements used to express feelings. I-messages need to contain a reference to (1) a specific behavior, (2) the effect of that behavior on you, and (3) the feeling you have as a result. **You messages** are statements that attempt to blame and shame another person rather than express feelings. Suppose a person wants to express feelings about a family member being late for dinner. An I-message might be, "When you were late for dinner (behavior), my dinner became cold (effect of behavior) and I was angry (feeling). A you-message might be, "You are thoughtless and rude to be late." The I-message expresses feelings while the you-message expresses blame and shame.

Active listening is a type of listening in which a person is reassured his or her message is heard and understood. **Feedback** is a way of acknowledging that a person has paid attention to the nonverbal and verbal behavior of another person. Using good manners and taking turns talking also promote healthful communication.

Relationships With Same and Opposite Sex

Healthful communication is the foundation for both same and opposite sex relationships. It has been said that relationships with both sexes should be based upon friendships. Friendships that promote health are ones in which there are good communication skills, trust, honesty, compassion, support, adherence to laws and values, and mutual respect.

Dating and Sexual Decision Making

A primary developmental task of adolescence is to use communication skills and friendship skills that have been learned in dating relationships. When adolescents have had a healthful and intimate family relationship, they are better prepared for this task. Parental/guardian guidance is especially important at this time. When adolescents are mature enough to date, it is beneficial for parents/guardians to set clear guidelines and expectations for behavior. It is also helpful for parents/guardians to help their adolescents set clear guidelines and expectations for the behaviors of those whom they chose to date. The transition into dating is much smoother and more natural when there is this dialogue.

This dialogue also should include a discussion about sexual feelings and sexual behavior. During adolescence, youth are experiencing sexual feelings that result from a strong physical and/or emotional attraction to another person. They need to understand that these feelings are accompanied by bodily changes. Females need to know that strong sexual feelings increase blood flow to the genital area and increase lubrication in the vagina. Males need to know that strong sexual feelings increase blood flow to the genital area causing the penis to become erect. A lubricating fluid is secreted from the tip of the penis.

Parents/guardians can explain that the expression of physical affection intensifies sexual feelings. Since over 90 percent of parents/guardians want their teenagers to abstain from sexual intercourse, a frank discussion about setting limits is important. The majority of teenagers who abstain from sexual intercourse say that they do so because "it is against my parents'/guardians' guidelines and my religious beliefs." Although parents/guardians can discuss other benefits such as protection from HIV infection and infection from sexually transmitted diseases and protection from teenage marriage and parenthood, a primary focus should be on values and religious beliefs. There are other ways to help adolescents adhere to abstinence. They can be encouraged to spend time with their families, be involved in school activities, talk to parents and other trusted adults about their sexuality, remove themselves from situations that are tempting, select friends who also choose abstinence, date persons who do not pressure them, and avoid alcohol and other drugs that lower inhibitions and increase the likelihood of making a decision that will later be regretted.

Marriage and Parenthood

In a recent survey, happily married couples were asked what the key ingredient was that kept their marriage satisfactory. The respondents answered "friendship" a majority of the time. Age of marriage, education, values, religious backgrounds, and financial stability also are key factors. Persons who marry after they are twenty years old have a much higher success rate for their marriages than those who marry earlier. They also are more likely to feel satisfied being a parent. Other key factors in satisfying parenthood appear to be having had education about the growth and development of a baby and child, having a clear idea of what constitutes the difference between abuse and discipline, and being financially able to afford child care for the pursuit of leisure activities.

Building A Firm Foundation

Objective

Students will identify and practice skills for building lasting and meaningful family relationships.

Life Skill

I will treat family members in loving and caring ways.

Materials

Large building blocks, paint, paintbrushes

Motivation

1 Discuss the importance of belonging to a family. A family can provide acceptance, love, and support. A family provides a place where you can learn, grow, develop, and share. Each family member has a responsibility to other family members to be the best family member that (s)he can be.

2 Have a set of large building blocks. Write or paint one of the following words on each block:

caring	loving
listens	loyal
shares	chores
manners	helps
warm	cheerful
respects	responsible
honest	trustworthy
interests	spends time

3 Discuss each of the blocks asking the class to tell how the words on the blocks relate to being the best family member that a person can be.

4 Have students build a pyramid with the blocks. They have to select the blocks for the bottom of the pyramid that are needed for a firm foundation and build up. Students can explain why they placed the blocks as they did.

5 Remove one of the blocks from the foundation. What happens? What happens when family members do not put forth their best efforts in their family relationships?

Have students pretend that there is a contest to select a person who is an outstanding family member. Have them write an ad announcing the contest and how to nominate a family member. They must write a clear description of how nominations will be judged.

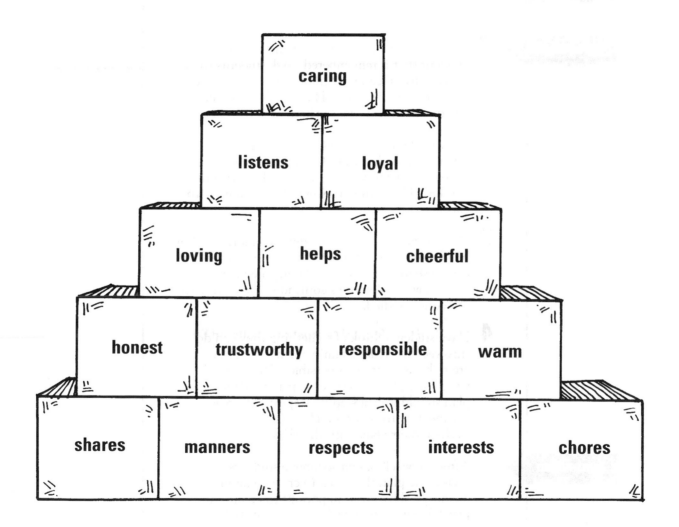

4 Set up a greeting card section of a store someplace in your classroom. Allow students to browse and look at the greeting cards. Each student might select a card that another student has designed that is of particular interest. Have a class discussion about the greeting cards students selected from those made by classmates. What feelings were expressed in the card? Why were these feelings appropriate to share? Why is it important to share life events with family and friends? What are other important ways to share feelings with family and friends?

Evaluation

Give students a list of life events that might be shared with family and/or friends. Have them identify kinds of feelings that might be shared and reasons why it is important to share feelings.

Family Connection

Objective

Students will describe how family members influence the health of other family members.

Life Skill

I will choose behaviors that have a healthful influence on my family.

Materials

Two jars of water, red food coloring, blue food coloring, Teaching Master, "Family Wellness Scale," on page 159.

Motivation

1 Use the Teaching Master, "Family Wellness Scale," page 159, to show how members of families can engage in wellness behaviors or healthful behaviors and risk behaviors. Wellness behaviors or healthful behaviors are actions that promote health and prevent injuries and illnesses. Risk behaviors are actions that threaten health and increase the likelihood of injuries and illnesses.

2 Take a jar of water. Explain that the jar of water represents the family unit. Take the red food coloring. The red food coloring represents the healthful behavior of one family member. Have students give examples of healthful behaviors that a family member might choose such as exercising every day, eating balanced meals, driving an automobile safely, and answering the phone safely. Put a drop of the red food coloring into the jar of water. Soon it will color the water in the jar. Ask students what has happened. Have students explain how healthful behaviors of one family member can effect the family unit.

3 Take the other jar of water. Take the blue food coloring. Explain that the blue food coloring represents the risk behavior of one family member. Have students give examples of risk behaviors that a family member might choose such as drinking too much alcohol, smoking cigarettes, eating too many fattening foods, and forgetting to lock the doors to the house. Put a drop of the blue food coloring into the jar. Ask students what has happened. Have students explain how risk behaviors of one family member can effect the family unit.

The Fire of Co-Dependence

Objective

Students will describe what is meant by dysfunctional family, its causes, characteristics, and ways its cycle can be changed.

Life Skill

I will seek help from a family member or other trusting and responsible adult if I am experiencing signs of co-dependence.

Materials

Construction paper, scissors, tape, markers

Motivation

1 Explain that not all families have loving, healthful, and responsible relationships. A dysfunctional family is a family in which the emotional, physical, and social needs of family members are not met in healthful ways. Explain that the term dysfunctional family was first used to describe families in which there was chemical dependence. Professionals who worked with families in which there was chemical dependency, particularly alcoholism, discovered that not only was the person who was chemically dependent suffering from the disease but also others in the family showed signs of poor functioning in relationships. Now we know that there are many causes of dysfunctional families other than chemical dependency. Some situations within families that may result in dysfunctional families are:

- eating disorders
- sexual abuse
- neglect
- abandonment
- physical abuse
- emotional abuse
- workaholism
- lack of clear values
- chemical dependence

2 Persons who live in dysfunctional families often suffer from a condition called co-dependence. Co-dependence is a condition in which a person becomes so dependent on another person that he or she loses touch with personal thoughts and feelings. A person who suffers from co-dependence is called co-dependent. Some of the characteristics of persons with co-dependence are:

- accepts abuse from others
- clings to others
- has difficulty sharing feelings
- criticizes others
- makes up excuses for poor behavior of others
- feels afraid
- does not tell the truth
- does not trust others
- becomes the family hero
- becomes the family clown

3 Use the construction paper and markers to make the fire and logs depicted in the illustration. The fire should be made of red construction paper. On the flames of the fire, print the causes of dysfunctional families: eating disorders, sexual abuse, neglect, abandonment, physical abuse, emotional abuse, workaholism, lack of clear values, chemical dependence.

4 Use the construction paper and markers to make logs to place under the fire. On separate logs write: accepts abuse from others, clings to others, has difficulty sharing feelings, criticizes others, makes up excuses for the poor behavior of others, feels afraid, does not tell truth, does not trust others, becomes the family hero, becomes the family clown.

5 Tape the fire on the chalkboard with the logs placed under it. Discuss the relationship between the two. The fire is the person who has the underlying problem creating the dysfunctional family. For example, the fire might represent a father with alcoholism. The logs represent the behaviors of the persons who live in that family. These persons begin to show ways of coping which do not promote healthful relationships. They actually add fuel to the fire. For example, in the family having the father with alcoholism, the mother might not tell the truth and call in sick for the father when he is too drunk to work. The teenager might cling to a boyfriend or girlfriend as a source of affection. Another teenager in the family might allow the father to abuse her/him when he is drinking. The logs add fuel to the flame. The fire and the logs depend upon each other. Begin to take the logs away and discuss what happens. Discuss what might happen if the flames in the fire die down. All members must change for the family to become healthy.

Use the following short essay quiz: (1) Define dysfunctional family. (2) List five causes of dysfunctional families. (3) List five characteristics of co-dependence. (4) Describe the relationships of family members within a dysfunctional family.

Family Soaps

Objective

Students will identify values that promote lasting and meaningful family relationships and will describe the influence of the media on family values.

Life Skill

I will watch television programs and movies and read books and magazines that promote healthful family values.

Materials

Newspaper section showing television programs, or a TV guide

Motivation

1 Introduce the topic of family values. A value is something that is desirable or important to you. Have students browse through the newspaper section showing television programs and the TV guide to show television programs. List five or six shows on the chalkboard in which family life is depicted. Ask students to identify some of the values that are portrayed in these shows. In many cases, the values will not be those that promote lasting and meaningful family relationships.

2 Divide students into groups to create Family Soaps. Each group is to create a new Family Soap that will appear on television. They are to create a title and a theme for the show. They are to identify at least three values that promote lasting and meaningful family relationships that will be in the theme. They can decide how many characters will be in the show. They are to make a two minute advertisement to air on television announcing the first episode of their Family Soap. They are also to make a newspaper ad for their television Family Soap.

3 Have students perform their two minute advertisements for their Family Soaps. Discuss each of the Family Soaps. Would each Soap be appealing?

Create a bulletin board of the newspaper announcements for the Family Soaps. Compare and contrast these with some of the currently watched Soaps and Family television shows.

Have students identify five values that promote meaningful and lasting family relationships. Have them identify current programs that support these values.

Family Soaps

Older and Wiser

Objective

Students will identify special needs of aging family members and will tell ways that they can show empathy and understanding.

Life Skill

I will show respect, love, and understanding for older family members.

Materials

Petroleum jelly, pair of old glasses, wooden tongue depressors, tape, cassette recording of muffled sounds, cassette recorder

Motivation

1 Discuss aging. Relate the gifts of aging to the older, beautiful trees in the community. As trees get older, they have more branches and their trunks are larger. As persons get older, they have had many more experiences. They have much more to share with others.

2 Explain that as people get older there are physical changes as well. Just as the branches on trees become more brittle and break more easily, the body undergoes changes with aging as well.

3 Take an old pair of glasses and smear petroleum jelly on them. Ask a student to wear them. Then ask the student to read a book or to look at something in the distance. Explain that persons who are older sometimes have vision problems and cannot see as easily. Some older persons have cataracts that must be corrected.

4 Have students cover their ears with their hands. Then play a recording of muffled sounds. Ask students how they felt. It should be very stressful for them. Then have them uncover their ears. Speak clearly to them. Discuss hearing and persons with a hearing loss. Mention that it is important to speak clearly and look directly at the person to whom you are speaking.

Take the tongue depressors and tape. Ask for a student volunteer. Put the tongue depressor behind one finger and then tape two fingers together. Ask the student to try to do simple tasks like tying shoes or eating with a fork using this hand. Explain that arthritis is common in older persons and it results in lack of joint movement. Discuss the patience that is needed when an older family member has arthritis.

Evaluation

Have students write papers on "The Special Gifts and Special Needs of Older Persons."

Celebrity Impersonations

Objective

Students will define and give examples of nonverbal communication.

Life Skill

I will use nonverbal behavior that matches my verbal behavior to clearly communicate with others.

Materials

None

Motivation

1 Discuss nonverbal communication. Nonverbal communication involves using your behavior rather than words to express what you are feeling. Give examples of nonverbal communication: kissing, hugging, tapping the foot, winking, shaking hands, frowning, putting thumbs down, looking up, looking away, shaking the head yes or no, and crossing the arms.

2 Have students select different celebrities that are known for making gestures that are nonverbal. Tell students not to tell classmates the celebrity that they have selected. Have students take turns doing their celebrity impersonations. Classmates must guess the celebrity they are impersonating from the nonverbal communication they use.

3 Have students discuss their own use of nonverbal communication. How can nonverbal communication clarify communication between people? How might nonverbal communication be confusing?

Evaluation

Have students identify five different ways that nonverbal communication is used to convey feelings and describe which feeling is conveyed in each of the ways identified.

Relationship Diary

Objective

Students will examine their personal relationships and evaluate the healthful or destructive effects of these relationships.

Life Skill

I will continually evaluate my relationships to be certain they are healthful and make changes when I find a relationship(s) destructive.

Materials

Diary or notepad for students, pen or pencil

Motivation

1 Review I messages. I messages are messages that convey (1) a behavior, (2) the effect of the behavior, (3) and the feelings that result. Give examples of I messages:

When you were late for the movie (the behavior), we missed the beginning (the effect of the behavior) and I was angry (the feelings that resulted).

When I studied hard for my test (the behavior), I answered the questions correctly (the effects of the behavior) and I felt good about myself (the feelings that resulted).

2 Have students write examples of I messages on the chalkboard.

3 Explain that they are going to examine their personal relationships by keeping a diary in which they record I messages that describe the behaviors, effects, and feelings that occur when they are around others. For example, today one of the students played tennis with a friend. Tonight she would write in her diary:

When I played tennis with Sarah (behavior), I got plenty of exercise (effects of the behavior) and I felt energetic (the feelings that resulted).

The time spent between these two persons seemed to be positive. Provide another example. Suppose a student called a friend on the phone. They spent the hour gossiping about someone at school. Tonight this student might write in her diary:

When I gossiped with Joe for an hour on the phone (behavior), I wasted valuable time (effects of that behavior) and I felt badly about myself (feelings that resulted.

4 Have students keep their diaries for one week. They are to record at least one I message each day. They can discuss the relationship further if they choose to do so. At the end of the week, have students examine the I messages written to describe what occurred in their relationships.

Evaluation

Based on their diaries, have students identify ways in which relationships contribute to their physical, mental, and social health and ways in which relationships might be destructive to physical, mental, or social health.

MY RELATIONSHIP DIARY

I MESSAGE

BEHAVIOR	EFFECT	FEELING
When I studied with Sarah	I got all my homework done.	I felt proud.

My relationship with Sarah helps my mental health. I complete my school work and my self-esteem is good.

Friendship Want Ad

Objective

Students will identify qualities they admire in friends and friendship qualities they want to develop.

Life Skill

I will develop and maintain healthful friendships.

Materials

Sample of a want ad from the newspaper, markers

Motivation

1 Discuss friendship. A friend is someone you know well and like. Ask students what qualities they believe to be important in friendship. Some of the qualities they might mention are: being honest, having a sense of humor, making responsible decisions, having common interests, avoiding gossiping about others, being loyal, being well-groomed, being a good listener, being kind and sensitive, using good manners, and being trustworthy.

2 Show students a sample of a want ad from the newspaper. Explain that a want ad is a description of something that a person is trying to find. To locate what is desired, the want ad must be very clear. For example, if the want ad is for a housekeeper who will care for an elderly person, specifics are given. The want ad might describe the exact hours the housekeeper will work. The want ad might mention characteristics that will help the housekeeper relate to the elderly person. The housekeeper may need to feed this person. This person might be in a wheelchair and want to be helped on walks twice a day to get fresh air. The closer the description as to what is desired, the more likely there will be a good match between the elderly person and the housekeeper.

3 Have students create want ads for a friend. The want ads should be very specific. They should mention characteristics that are desired such as loyalty, honesty, and ability to listen. They should mention common interests to be shared such as specific sports, movies, dancing, hobbies, etc. Students can use paper and markers to make their want ads. The want ads should resemble wants ads for the newspaper.

4 Create a bulletin board for the want ads. The bulletin board should be designed to resemble a newspaper. The newspaper headline might be "Friendship Press." Students might think of other appropriate names. Have students place their want ads on the bulletin board. Each want ad should be assigned a number. The number should appear on the lower right hand corner of the want ad for identification purposes. Students must remember their want ad identification number.

5 Have students read the want ads written to their classmates. Each student can select one or two want ads to which they will respond. They are to write a letter explaining why they are suitable to respond to the ads they selected. Collect the responses and give them to the persons who wrote the ads. Ask students what they learned from this strategey. What qualities and interests do they have which make them desirable as friends for others? What qualities and interests do they desire in friends?

Evaluation

Review the qualities and interests desired in friendship. Then have the class sit in a circle. One student begins by saying, "I'm going to select a friend and my friend will——." The student will complete the sentence, perhaps saying "my friend will be loyal." The next student repeats what the first student said and adds another quality. "I'm going to select a friend and my friend will be loyal and trustworthy." Continue around the circle.

CLARKSVILLE DAILY

1991

Want Ads

Best Friend Wanted!

Looking for someone I can trust,
who likes to talk and take walks.
Prefer someone who likes sports.
Special consideration given to someone
with good manners.

Friendship Recipe

Objective

Students will identify ingredients needed in healthful and responsible friendships and rank order these in order of importance to them.

Life Skill

I will behave in healthful and responsible ways with friends.

Materials

Index cards, colored markers, file box, sample cookie recipes

Motivation

1 Discuss friendship. A friend is someone you know well and like. Ask students what a good friend is. Students may say a good friend is caring, thoughtful, friendly, warm, cheerful, kind, loyal, trustworthy, honest, sincere, well-mannered, well-groomed, and responsible. Using the chalkboard, make a list of the words the students use to describe a good friend.

2 Show the students a recipe for making cookies. The cookie recipe will have a list of the ingredients needed and the amounts of each ingredient. Then there will be directions for putting the ingredients together.

3 Explain to students that they are to write a friendship recipe using the cookie recipe as a guideline. They are to list the ingredients needed for friendship. They are to tell the amount of each ingredient that is needed. They must put the ingredient they value most in the largest amount. Then they are to finish their recipes by writing a few directions for putting the ingredients for friendship together.

4 Collect the recipes and put them in a file box of friendship recipes. Select a few of the recipes to discuss. Have students comment on the ingredients and on the amounts of the ingredients selected for the recipe.

Evaluation

After students have examined the recipes of the class, have them write a recipe that would describe themselves as a friend.

FRIENDSHIP RECIPE

INGREDIENTS:
DASH OF HUMOR
1/3 C HONESTY
1 C LOYALTY
2 tsps. CHEERFULNESS
1 Tbs. MANNERS

DIRECTIONS:
BLEND HUMOR WITH CHEERFULNESS.
FOLD IN HONESTY AND LOYALTY.
ALLOW TO SIMMER FOR TWO
MONTHS. TOP WITH MANNERS.

Friendship Tree

Objective

Students will identify the qualities needed for good friendship and the persons who helped them develop these qualities.

Life Skill

I will model the friendship qualities of adults who have healthful and responsible friendships.

Materials

Poster paper, crayons, markers or paint, construction paper

Motivation

1 Discuss friendship. A friend is someone you know well and like. Discuss making and keeping friends. Discuss qualities that are desirable for good friendship. Some of these qualities might be: honesty, kindness, sincerity, humor, responsibility, discipline, generosity, sensitivity, manners, trustworthiness.

2 Discuss persons who have helped them develop the qualities needed for friendship. For example, a parent might have helped them learn responsibility. They might have learned trustworthiness from a scout leader and honesty from a coach.

3 Have students make a friendship tree using poster paper, crayons, markers, or paint. The roots of the tree should each be labelled with the name of someone who helped them develop the qualities needed for good friendship. On the branches of the tree, have them write the qualities needed for good friendship. Have the class discuss the friendship trees they have made.

4 Have students select one of the persons who helped them develop the qualities of good friendship. Have them make this person a greeting card about friendship that expresses their gratitude or thankfulness.

Evaluation

Have students complete the sentence "A friend is someone who..."

Don't Judge a Book by its Cover

Objective

Students will identify characteritstics that are desirable in healthful and responsible dating.

Life Skill

I will identify qualities that are desirable in a person whom I choose to date and I will look for these qualities when I am making plans to date someone.

Materials

Two books, brown wrapping paper, markers, magazine pictures, glue

Motivation

1 Cover each of the books with brown wrapping paper. Then decorate one of the covers very glitzy and appealing. Decorate the other cover in a somewhat attractive manner but not as attractive as the other book cover. You may want to ask some of your students to cover the two books rather than doing it yourself.

2 Place a sheet of paper inside each of the two books. On the sheet of paper inside the glitzy book, write several characteristics of a teenager with some being desirable, but others not being desirable. Your list might be something like this: smokes cigarettes, is friendly, is attractive, plays on an athletic team, is self-centered, gossips about his/her dates, is dishonest. On the sheet of paper inside the book with the not so glitzy cover, write only desirable characteristics such as: well-mannered, honest, kind, supportive, trustworthy, well-groomed. You might also assign this task to some of the students. Of course, they cannot share what they have done with the rest of the class.

3 Show the two books to the class. Have them select which book they find desirable based on the cover only.

4 Explain that you have just sold them a"date." They selected their date based on outside appearances only. Now they will learn more about the characteristics of the person they have selected. Open the two books and share the lists that are inside. Are they pleased with their selection?

5 Discuss characteristics they find desirable in a good date.

Evaluation

Have students describe what they believe they can tell from the first impression of a person. Then have them describe what qualities and characteristics might not be noticeable on a first impression.

Can you judge a book by its cover?

My Relationships, My Future

Objective

Students will identify goals they wish to accomplish and choices that might prevent these goals from being reached.

Life Skill

I will set goals and make a plan to reach them which includes making healthful and responsible choices.

Materials

Broomstick

Motivation

1 Select a student to do a demonstration for classmates. Placing the stick end on the finger, this student is to try to balance the bottom of the broomstick while looking down at the bottom of the stick.

2 Now have the student repeat this demonstration only this time the student should look at the top of the broomstick while trying to balance it. The broomstick should balance for a longer time period while the student looks up at the top of the stick than while (s)he was looking at the bottom.

3 Explain that looking at the bottom of the broomstick was similiar to making decisions based upon the present without looking ahead to the future. For example, choosing to use drugs now is a decision with little regard for what that might mean in the future.

4 Have students give examples of goals that they have in their future. Some of these goals might be to attend a vocational school or college, to get a good job, to support themselves financially, to graduate from high school, etc. Discuss choices that might interfere with these goals such as teenage marriage, teenage parenthood, use of drugs, sexual involvement, cheating on tests, etc.

Evaluation

Have students write a short paper describing their goals and how they plan to accomplish them. Have them mention health-related choices that would interfere with their goals.

Temptation

Objective

Students will identify ways to avoid being tempted to become involved in risk behaviors and risk situations when pressured by peers.

Life Skill

I will say NO when pressured by peers to engage in risk behaviors and risk situations.

Materials

Tootsie Roll for each student

Motivation

1 Use the following demonstration to illustrate peer pressure to your students. Divide the class into three groups. The first group is the risk behavior group. Explain that a risk behavior is an action that might be harmful to you or others. Give each person in the risk behavior group a Tootsie Roll. The second group is the risk situation group. Explain that a risk situation is a situation in which another person's behavior threatens your health. Give the risk situation group a Tootsie Roll. The third group is the healthful behavior group. This group does not get a Tootsie Roll.

2 Now explain peer pressure. Peer pressure is the influence persons your age use to encourage you to make the decisions they want you to make. Explain that the first group is to eat one of their Tootsie Rolls in front of the second while they encourage the second group to do the same. They are to be as convincing as possible to the second group. After several minutes, stop to see if anyone in group two ate a Tootsie Roll. Discuss the kinds of reasons that group one used to pressure group two.

3 Now have the students in group two who did not eat their Tootsie Roll, unwrap it, and take a small bite. Then they are to hold the remaining part of the Tootsie Roll in their hand near their mouth without eating it. Again, group one is to pressure group two to eat the Tootsie Roll. After several minutes, stop and ask persons in group two if they were more tempted to eat the Tootsie Roll before they unwrapped it or after they had unwrapped it and taken a small bite.

4 Take aside group three so that groups one and two will not hear the directions that you are going to give them. Tell group three to say "NO, I do not want to eat the Tootsie Roll" each time they are pressured. They are not to touch the Tootsie Roll. After they are pressured three times, they are to move away from the person offering them the Tootsie Roll. Now give groups one and two Tootsie Rolls that they can offer group three. Instruct them to pressure group three to try to eat the Tootsie Rolls.

5 Discuss the results of this experiment. When group one pressured group two, what convincing techniques were used? After persons in group two unwrapped their Tootsie Rolls and took a bite, was it more tempting to continue eating the Tootsie Roll? Explain that it usually is. This is why limits need to be set on most behaviors to avoid easily doing something you previously said you would not do. For example, taking a sip of a beer may lead to drinking, taking a puff of a cigarette may lead to smoking, and petting may lead to sexual intercourse. Discuss group three. Group three avoided the risk behavior by firmly saying "NO." But this group also avoided being tempted. No one touched the Tootsie Roll. Group members got away from the risk situation.

Evaluation

Have students define peer pressure, risk behaviors, and risk situations. Have students tell ways to avoid engaging in risk behaviors and risk situations.

Magnetic Attraction

Objective
Students will differentiate between relationships that are healthful and responsible and relationships which are destructive and irresponsible.

Life Skill
I will behave in healthful and responsible ways with friends.

Materials
Two magnets

Motivation

1 Draw a continuum on the chalkboard. On one end of the continuum, write healthful and responsible relationships. On the other end of the continuum, write destructive and irresponsible relationships. Explain to students that you have drawn a relationship continuum similar to a wellness scale. There are destructive relationships and there are healthful relationships. Just as you must choose certain behaviors to promote your physical and mental well-being, you must also choose certain behaviors to promote the well-being of your relationships.

2 Healthful relationships contain certain ingredients. There is good communication. There is an open and honest sharing of feelings. There is a sense of fairness. In a healthful relationship, two persons each assume responsibility for the relationship. Persons treat each other with respect. There are clear values in healthful relationships.

3 Destructive relationships lack the ingredients found in healthful relationships. Much of the time, persons attracted to destructive relationships have been involved in these relationships within their families. They may have grown up in families in which feelings were not shared, honesty was lacking, and there was a lack of clear values. They may not have felt valued and secure in their home life. There may have been a lack of physical affection or some kind of abuse.

4 Use the two magnets to show the attraction between persons who have been involved in destructive relationships in their families. Explain that the first magnet is a teenage boy whose father abused him and his mother. As a result, this boy learns to be abusive. Explain that the second magnet is a teenage girl who was sexually abused by her father. She believes she is not worthy. Put the magnets near each other and they will pull together. Ask the class to explain why this teenage boy and girl might be attracted to each other.

5 Give another situation using the magnets. One of the magnets represents a teenage boy who is neglected by his parents. As a result, he feels abandoned and has not learned a clear set of values. The other magnet represents a teenage girl whose father and mother are divorced. She has no emotional relationship with her father. Put the magnets together. Ask the class to explain why this teenage boy and girl are attracted to each other. Suggest that the teenage boy pressures the girl to have sex with him. He says, "If you love me, you will." He threatens to break the relationship off, if she does not have sex. Why might the girl say "yes" and stay in the relationship?

Evaluation

Have students make up two scenarios to show the attraction that pulls a relationship together. One scenario should describe the attraction of persons in a healthful relationship. The other should describe the attraction of persons in a destructive relationship.

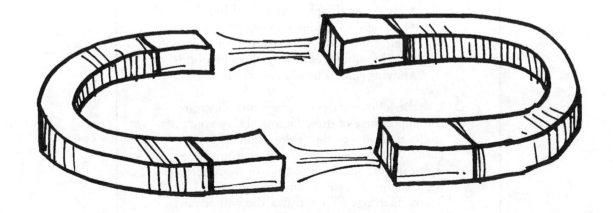

Staying Connected

Objective

The students will identify factors that increase the likelihood of a successful, satisfying, and lasting marriage.

Life Skill

I will set and reach goals and develop skills that will prepare me for successful, satisfying, and lasting marriage.

Materials

Ball of yarn

Motivation

1 Introduce the topic of marriage. Have students discuss the expectations they have for relationships and marriage.

2 Have students identify factors that they believe will increase the likelihood of a successful, satisfying, and lasting marriage. Some of these are:

- having clearly defined goals
- being of similar age
- being at least twenty years old
- knowing each other for at least a year
- having similar hobbies
- being independent from parents
- having similar values
- being physically attracted
- having similar views about children
- having premarital counseling or classes
- having similar philosophies of life
- having similar views about sex
- being able to communicate with one another
- having similar educational backgrounds
- having similar family backgrounds

3 Use the following demonstration to illustrate the importance of these factors. Have your students sit in a circle. Take a ball of yarn. Wrap the end of the string around your index finger. Mention one factor that increases the likelihood of successful, satisfying, and lasting marriage. Then throw the ball of yarn to a student in the circle. This student wraps a piece of the yarn around his/her index finger and states another factor that increases the likelihood of successful, satisfying, and lasting marriage. Continue until each student has wrapped the yarn around his/her finger and stated a factor that increases the likelihood of successful, satisfying, and lasting marriage.

4 Ask the students what the ball of yarn has done. The ball of yarn has connected everyone in the circle. Make the analogy that the factors they have mentioned help connect a couple and keep them together. Marriages are more likely to be successful, satisfying, and lasting when these factors are present.

Evaluation

Have students list ten factors which increase the likelihood of successful, satisfying, and lasting marriage and rank order these beginning with the one they believe to be most important.

Do As I Do

Objective

Students will identify parenting skills that are helpful in raising children with positive self-esteem.

Life Skill

I will treat others with respect.

Materials

Teaching Master, "Children Learn What They Live" on page 189.

Motivation

1 Discuss the saying "Do as I say, not as I do." Change the saying and discuss "Do as I do, and as I say." Which of these sayings is more realistic? Why?

2 Use The Teaching Master, "Children Learn What They Live," on page 189. Have the students read this together. Then divide the class into ten groups. Assign each of the groups one of the first ten lines from this saying. Each group is to develop a short skit in which a parent or parents teach children the behavior that is referred to in the line that was assigned.

3 Have the groups of students perform their skits. After each skit, discuss a parenting skill that helps in raising children with positive self-esteem who feel accepted and loved.

4 Have students recall a lesson that they learned from a parent, parents, or other significant adult that was a result of loving, responsible behavior in which "do as I do" was demonstrated.

Evaluation

Have students write a short paragraph on the responsibilities of parenthood emphasizing the skills children learn by modelling their parents' behavior.

Children Learn What They Live

If a child lives with criticism, (s)he learns to condemn.

If a child lives with hostility, (s)he learns to fight.

If a child lives with ridicule, (s)he learns to be shy.

If a child lives with shame, (s)he learns to feel guilty.

If a child lives with tolerance, (s)he learns to be patient.

If a child lives with encouragement, (s)he learns confidence.

If a child lives with praise, (s)he learns to appreciate.

If a child lives with fairness, (s)he learns justice.

If a child lives with security, (s)he learns to have faith.

If a child lives with approval, (s)he learns to like himself.

If a child lives with acceptance, and friendship,

(S)he learns to find love in the world.

Dorothy Law Nolte

Growth and Development is the area of health that focuses on information and life skills related to the body systems as well as the different kinds of changes that result from conception through death.

A major aspect in the health education curriculum for growth and development is that of body systems. There are a number of body systems, the understanding of which is important in understanding physical health.

Skeletal System

The **skeletal system** is the system of the body that is composed of the different bones and joints. The skeletal system serves as a framework. There are 206 bones in the human body. The different bones in the body determine how the different body parts move. **Ball-and-socket joints** allow circular movements. **Hinge joints** allow for open and shut movements.

Bones in the body are connected by ligaments. **Ligaments** are tough cords made of fibers that allow bones connected to each other to move. Most joints need a sort of lubricant between them so that they can move at the joints. This lubricant or fluid is called **synovial fluid.** The **spinal column** is a very important set of 33 bones that extends from the base of the head down to the hip region. The **spinal cord** is a delicate set of nerves that runs inside the spinal column. The spinal column protects the spinal cord.

Another part of the skeletal system that also is related to the nerves inside the body is the skull. The skull serves as the encasement for the brain. The skull is also known as the **cranium**, consisting of 16 large, flat, hard bones.

The skeletal system serves many purposes inside the body. Red blood cells are produced in long bones such as the femur. Some bones help protect different body organs. For example, the ribs help protect the lungs and heart.

Bones in the skeletal system must be kept healthy. Exercise helps keep weight bearing bones strong. Foods such as milk help provide calcium which is necessary for bone growth and strength. Maintaining good posture will also help keep the skeletal system healthy.

Muscular System

The **muscular system** is the body system that is made up of all the muscles in the body. The muscular system works closely with the skeletal system to help a person move.

Many muscles in the body are attached to bones by strong tissues called **tendons.** When movement occurs, the muscles will contract and extend to produce movement. To produce these movements, the muscles work in pairs. That is, when one muscle such as the biceps muscle on the upper arm contracts to bend the arm at the elbow, muscles on the upper arm contract to straighten the arm. Whenever one muscle contracts, another will also expand.

There are over 600 muscles in the body. These muscles can be voluntary or involuntary. **Voluntary muscles** are muscles that a person can control. For example, muscles in the arm are controlled so that the arm will move when you desire a certain movement. **Involuntary muscles** are muscles that you do not control. For example, the heart muscle will work automatically.

It is important for the muscular system to be maintained properly. A well-rounded program of physical exercise including aerobic activities improves muscle tone. Warm-up exercises prevent muscle injury.

Circulatory System

The **circulatory system** is the body system that consists of the blood, blood vessels, and heart. Blood is composed of **plasma** which is a liquid made of 90 percent water. There are blood cells in plasma. The three major types of blood cells are white blood cells, red blood cells, and platelets. The greatest number of blood cells are red blood cells which live about 100 days. Dead red blood cells are removed from the body by the

GROWTH AND DEVELOPMENT

7

spleen. **White blood cells** help keep a person healthy by engulfing and destroying pathogens. **Platelets** are cells that help blood clot.

There are three major types of blood vessels. **Arteries** are blood vessels that carry blood away from the heart. **Veins** are blood vessels that carry blood to the heart. **Capillaries** are tiny blood vessels that connect arteries to veins.

The circulatory system helps the body function healthfully by bringing nutrients to the different tissues in the body and carrying away the waste produced after the nutrients are used. The circulatory system is the main vehicle by which oxygen is distributed throughout the body.

There are many healthful behaviors to follow to keep the circulatory system healthy. Avoid foods that are high in saturated fats so as to reduce the risks of plaque buildup in the arteries. Avoid cigarette smoking as this behavior is a leading cause of heart disease. Engage in aerobic exercise for at least 20 minutes, three times per week at target heart rate to keep the heart muscle strong. People who have high blood pressure should take steps to control it. High blood pressure increases the risk of developing heart disease. Through regular physical checkups, problems such as high blood pressure can be diagnosed and interventions can be implemented.

Respiratory System

The **respiratory system** is the body system that enables a person to use the oxygen and other gases in the air necessary for survival. The respiratory system disposes of waste gases such as carbon dioxide.

The major organs of the respiratory system are the lungs. When a person inhales, air moves through the mouth and/or nose into the trachea. The **trachea** is also known as the windpipe. Hairlike structures in the throat called **cilia** trap foreign matter when they enter the air passage. Air then flows to the bronchi that extend into smaller branches called **bronchioles.**

Lining the surface of the inside of the lungs are air sacs called **alveoli.** Oxygen moves from the alveoli into blood that circles it. The blood picks up the oxygen and carries it throughout the body. When a person exhales, the waste products, most notably carbon dioxide, are released by the lungs to the outside of the body.

The process of breathing results from changes inside the chest cavity. When a person inhales, the chest expands. The rib muscles contract as does the **diaphragm,** a muscle that separates the chest and abdominal regions. When air is forced out of the lungs, the rib muscles relax. They move downward and inward. The diaphragm also relaxes so that air will be able to be forced from the lungs.

To protect the respiratory system, it is best not to smoke as smoking causes the alveoli to lose their ability to function. As a result, oxygen cannot be exchanged as it should to the bloodstream. Smoking is also the primary cause of two major lung diseases, lung cancer and emphysema. It is also important to avoid different forms of air pollution. Something most important is exposure to radon. **Radon** is a radioactive gas given off in the earth that is a possible cause of 20,000 cases of lung cancer annually.

Digestive System

The **digestive system** is the system of the body that breaks down food so that nutrients can be absorbed by the cells in the body. Digestion begins in the mouth where food is chemically broken down by saliva. Food then moves to the **esophagus**, a tube that runs from the mouth to the stomach. From the esophagus, food moves to the stomach where it it broken down by gastric juices. A sphincter muscle then permits the broken down food to move to the small intestine. The **small intestine** is an organ, about 22 feet long, that breaks down food in its final stages. It is through the **villi**, tiny projections in the walls of the small intestines, where nutrients are absorbed into the circulatory system and carried throughout the body.

The **large intestine** is the organ that receives undigested material from the small intestine. After further changes, this undigested material moves to the rectum where it is stored and eliminated from the body.

The digestive system works closely with the **excretory system**, a body system made up of organs that help the body get rid of wastes. The kidneys are the major organs of the excretory system that filter water, salts, and other wastes. These wastes combine with urea to form urine.

The digestive and excretory systems can be kept in good condition by drinking the equivalent of 6-8 glasses of water each day. As stated in Chapter 8, adequate amounts of fiber in the diet each day are needed for a daily bowel movement. Recommendations by the Physicians Committee for Responsible Medicine in 1991 stressed the importance of making fruits, vegetables, and grains the basis of a sound diet that would also improve the health of the digestive system.

Reproductive System

The **reproductive system** is the body system that plays an integral role in the development of offspring. The main parts of the female reproductive system include the ovaries, uterus, Fallopian tubes, and vagina. The **ovaries** are responsible for the development of the ova or egg cells and produce estrogen and progesterone, the female sex hormones. These hormones are responsible for the changes that occur in the female body during puberty. **Puberty** is the stage of development during which males and females become capable of reproducing. The **uterus** is the muscular organ in which a developing baby will grow during pregnancy. It is the lining of the inside of the uterus that sheds during menstruation.

Connected to each side of the uterus is a Fallopian tube. The **Fallopian tube** is an organ with ducts that open into the uterus. The ovary releases an egg cell into the Fallopian tube where it travels to the uterus. If an egg cell is fertilized within the Fallopian tube, it will travel to the uterus where it attaches to the wall and develops for about nine months.

The **vagina**, or birth canal is the female organ through which a baby passes during the birth process. The vagina is also the organ used for sexual intercourse.

The main organs of the male reproductive system include the testes, penis, urethra, vas deferens, prostate, and seminal vesicles. The **testes** are the reproductive organs that produce sperm cells and the male hormone, testosterone. The penis is the reproductive organ through which semen and urine pass. Semen and urine pass through an opening in the penis called the **urethra**. When sperm are produced in the testes, they are carried through the male reproductive system via the **vas deferens.** The **prostate** is a gland that produces fluid for sperm. **Seminal vesicles** are glands that secrete fluids to help sperm travel. Males and females need to be concerned about the health of the reproductive systems. Women need annual Pap smears and monthly breast self-examinations. After age 40, a woman needs a mammogram. Men need to perform regular testicular self-examinations. After 40, they need a rectal exam to check the prostate.

Nervous system

The **nervous system** is the body system consisting of the brain, spinal cord, and the many branching nerves. The **central nervous system** is the part of the nervous system made up of the brain and spinal cord. The three major parts of the brain include the cerebrum, the cerebellum, and medulla. The **cerebrum** is the part of the brain that controls thinking and memory. The **cerebellum** is the part of the brain that controls coordination and muscle activity. The **medulla** is the part of the brain that controls involuntary actions such as heartbeat.

The nervous system can be kept healthy by engaging in regular exercise and eating foods that have the proper nutrients. Wearing a safety belt in a car will help protect the nervous system during an accident.

Growth and Development

The process of growth and development begins when an egg cell is fertilized by a sperm cell in the Fallopian tube. A woman will experience any number of signs to indicate she is pregnant. These include a missed period, nausea upon awakening, an increase in size and tenderness in the breasts, and darkening of the areola tissue that surrounds the nipples. In addition, she may experience frequent urination and an increase in the size of the abdomen.

After birth, life continues as many changes occur throughout the life cycle. As babies grow and develop toward childhood, they become more physically, socially, mentally, and intellectually mature. Puberty will occur in females most often between the ages of 11 and 13 and in males between the ages of 13-15. Boys and girls will enter adolescence at around age 12 and be considered adolescents until about age 19. During adolescence, secondary sex characteristics appear and result in a growth spurt.

By about age 20, most men and women are legally independent and begin to establish their foundations for adulthood. Education, schooling, family changes, and career challenges occur. Throughout this process, a person will continue to age. Through the aging process, the different body parts begin to wear. By the age of 65, most adults will be in good enough health to be independent of other's care and be able to maintain active lifestyles. But, maintaining an activeful lifestyle during old age will be dependent upon the health behaviors followed in youth. People have the ability, in most cases, to contol their health. Heart disease is the leading cause of death in old age. Yet, many of the lifestyle behaviors can be modified so that heart disease is delayed. Cancer is the second leading cause of death in old age. Like heart disease, many cases of cancer can be delayed, or even prevented by engaging in healthful behaviors now. For example, most cases of lung cancer can be prevented by not smoking.

Eventually everyone will face death. A person is considered clinically dead when there is a lack of heartbeat and breathing, no nervous system functioning, and the presence of rigor mortis. Death indicates the end of the life cycle.

Teeth With a Bite

Objective

Students will describe the three main purposes of teeth.

Life Skill

I will protect my teeth by eating healthful foods, brushing and flossing, and wearing a safety belt when travelling in a car.

Materials

Carrot or other hard and healthful food, magazine photo of person with wide smile

Motivation

1 Tell the class you are going to review the three most important purposes of teeth. Have a student come to the front of the room and ask him/her to take a bite of a carrot. Then tell the student to pretend (s)he has no teeth. This is accomplished by having the student pucker his/her lips over the front teeth. Then ask the student to bite the carrot. (The student will not be able to bite the carrot.) Explain to the class that the student simulated not having teeth. Ask the class, "What can you tell me is one purpose of teeth?" (To bite food.)

2 Discuss the second purpose of teeth. Show the students a picture of a person who has a wide smile with bright, white teeth. Ask students, "What do you think of this person's appearance?" (The person has a nice smile and a nice appearance.) Take a black marker and color one or two teeth black. Then ask the class again, "How does this person look?" (This person is not as attractive as before.) Ask, "What is another purpose of teeth?" (To help us look good.) It is important to emphasize that some students, if they are in the lower grades, may be losing their teeth. Explain that this is normal since they are losing their baby teeth. You are concerned that people practice healthful habits that promote healthy adult teeth.

3 Cover the third purpose of teeth. Tell students you want them to say the following tongue-twister. "She sells sea shells by the sea shore." Have the class repeat this with you. Then have them repeat the phrase, but this time they are to pucker the lips over the teeth. Their responses will not be clear. Ask, "What is another purpose of teeth?" (To speak clearly.)

4 Discuss ways to care for and protect teeth. Eat foods that keep teeth strong. Milk products contain calcium to harden teeth. Brush and floss daily. Wear a mouthguard for appropriate activities. Always wear a safety belt in a car.

Evaluation ➤ Ask students to identify the three purposes of teeth. (To bite, for appearance, and to speak clearly.)

"She sells seashells by the seashore."

Go With the Flow

Objective

Students will trace the flow of blood through the heart.

Life Skill

I will exercise regularly to improve blood flow and strengthen my heart muscle.

Materials

Diagram, "The Flow of Blood Through The Heart" on page 199, masking tape, a chalkboard eraser

Motivation

1 Provide students with the Diagram, "The Flow of Blood Through The Heart." Students can work in groups of five or more. They are to copy the picture of the heart on the Diagram onto the floor using masking tape. However, students are not to place the arrows that show the flow of blood nor are they to write the parts of the heart through which blood flows.

2 Divide the heart into quadrants. The top left is worth 4 points, top right is worth 3 points, bottom left is worth 2 points, and the bottom right is worth 1 point. Draw a line about five to ten feet from the bottom of the heart.

3 Students stand behind the line and toss a chalkboard eraser at one of the quadrants. To score the points identified in the quadrant within which the eraser lands, students must hop through the heart in the same direction through which blood flows. As they hop through the heart, they must name the part of the heart through which they hop. When they get to the eraser, they must pick it up, continuing to hop, and continuing to name the parts of the heart.

4 You can work this activity in two teams. You can do it by speed, so that there is stiffer competition. Naming a part incorrectly will result in not getting the points.

5 Identify ways to care for the heart such as engaging in regular exercise, eating healthful foods, and handling stress in healthful ways.

Compute the number of students in the class who identify all parts of the heart correctly as they pass through. You may choose to do this for more than one round and compare how scores improve.

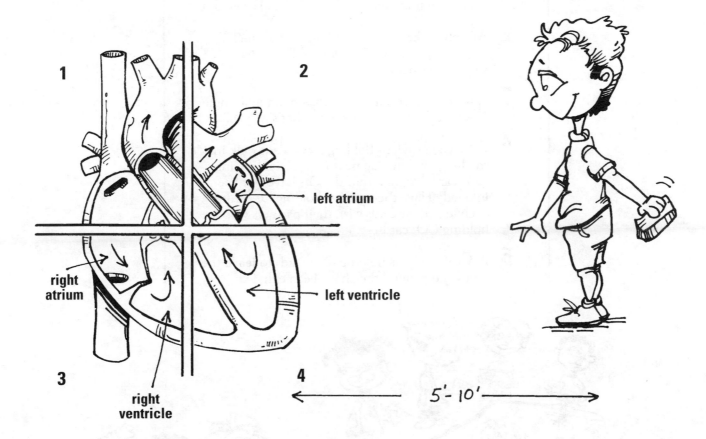

1

2

left atrium

right atrium

left ventricle

3

4

right ventricle

5'- 10'

"O Two My CO$_2$

Objective	Students will explain how the exchange of oxygen and carbon dioxide occurs inside the lungs.
Life Skill	I will not smoke cigarettes.
Materials	3"x5" index cards that say O$_2$, 3"x5" index cards that say CO$_2$, masking tape

Motivation

1 Using the masking tape, draw an outline of the lung on the floor. Draw just one lung but have it large enough so that half the class can stand around it.

2 After half the class is standing around the lung, have them hold 3"x5" index cards that have "CO$_2$" written on them.

3 Have the other half of the class stand in a single line holding 3"x5" index cards that say "O$_2$."

4 Have each student holding an O$_2$ card walk inside the lungs and line up next to a person holding a CO$_2$ card. Explain that the O$_2$s have just been inhaled. Have the students holding O$_2$ cards exchange their cards with their partners who are holding CO$_2$ cards.

5 Ask the students holding CO$_2$ cards to leave the lungs and pretend they have been exhaled.

Ask the class to describe what happens to oxygen and carbon dioxide when a person inhales and exhales. (During inhalation, the oxygen is exchanged with the carbon dioxide so that a lower percentage of oxygen leaves the lungs along with an increased percentage of carbon dioxide. As oxygen is used in the body, it is exchanged with carbon dioxide. The carbon dioxide is considered the waste gas that was converted from the oxygen.)

You Can't Control That Reflex

Objective

Students will demonstrate how a reflex is an involuntary action.

Life Skill

I will follow behaviors to prevent injury.

Materials

A sheet of cellophane paper about two feet long, a sheet of paper crumpled into a ball

Motivation

1 Introduce the word "involuntary." Explain that involuntary means something that you cannot control; it happens automatically.

2 Tell students that there are bodily functions that are involuntary. Some examples of these include heartbeat, blinking, and reflex actions.

3 The following activity will demonstrate for students an example of a reflex action. Take a sheet of cellophane paper and have a student hold the paper about six inches in front of his or her eyes. Crumble a sheet of paper into a ball. Have the student face the class. Tell the class to observe what will happen as you throw the ball at the cellophane paper which is held in front of the person's eyes. The class will notice that the student blinked.

4 Explain that the blinking was an example of a reflex action. The student automatically blinked as the ball was thrown. The blinking was an automatic reaction or reflex in response to protecting one's self from possible harm. Blinking is an involuntary action.

Evaluation

Have students give examples of how reflex actions have enabled them to keep protected. One example can be when falling off a bicycle, hands were placed on the ground to help break the fall.

Say, "Blocked Blood Vessels" Five Times

Objective

Students will describe why blocked blood vessels reduce blood flow through the heart.

Life Skill

I will avoid eating foods such as those containing large amounts of animal fats so as to avoid the buildup of unnecessary plaque in my blood vessels.

Materials

Two cardboard inner tubes from paper towels, clay, marbles

Motivation

1 Explain to students that the cardboard tubes represent blood vessels in the heart. Have one tube clear and explain that it represents a blood vessel without plaque build-up. Plaque is the fatty deposits inside the blood vessel. Line the other tube with clay. Tell the class the clay represents the plaque inside the walls of a blood vessel.

2 Call two students to the front of the class. Give each student about 20 marbles. Indicate that the marbles represent oxygen-carrying blood cells. Lay the cardboard tubes so that one side is tilted about an inch from the surface of the desk. Have each student begin at the same time and roll the marbles through the cardboard tube. The marbles that are rolled through the cardboard tube with clay around the inside will not flow as rapidly as the marbles through the unobstructed cardboard tube.

Ask students to make a conclusion about what they have just observed. (Blood vessels that are clogged have a reduced blood flow within. This means that the different parts of the body may not get enough oxygen adequately.) Explain that the tube is a cross section of a blood vessel. Have them hold both blood vessels to the light and look through them. They will see that there is a wider hole through the cardboard tube that is not blocked than through the cardboard tube that has deposits. Explain that the wider the opening, the greater the amount of blood that can flow through.

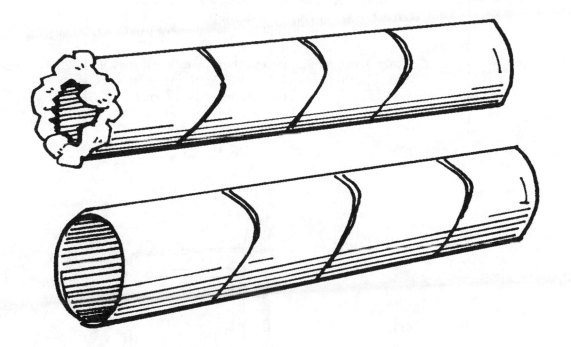

Draw Your Own Analogy

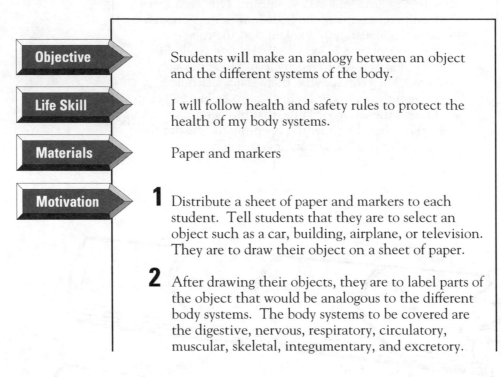

Objective

Students will make an analogy between an object and the different systems of the body.

Life Skill

I will follow health and safety rules to protect the health of my body systems.

Materials

Paper and markers

Motivation

1 Distribute a sheet of paper and markers to each student. Tell students that they are to select an object such as a car, building, airplane, or television. They are to draw their object on a sheet of paper.

2 After drawing their objects, they are to label parts of the object that would be analogous to the different body systems. The body systems to be covered are the digestive, nervous, respiratory, circulatory, muscular, skeletal, integumentary, and excretory.

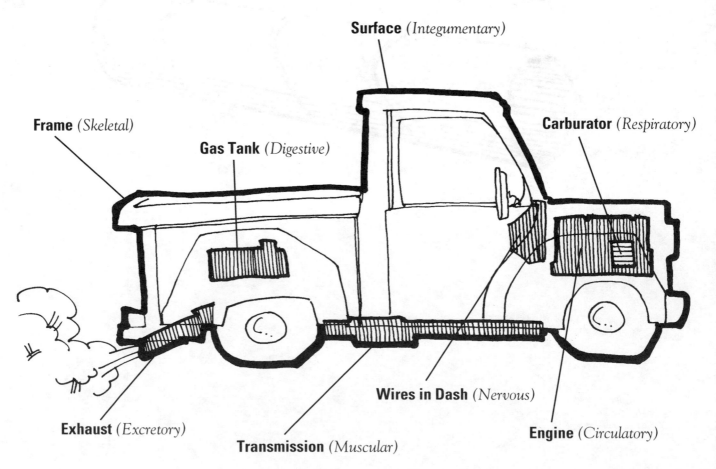

Surface (*Integumentary*)

Frame (*Skeletal*)

Gas Tank (*Digestive*)

Carburator (*Respiratory*)

Wires in Dash (*Nervous*)

Exhaust (*Excretory*)

Transmission (*Muscular*)

Engine (*Circulatory*)

3 You can use the example of the car on the bottom of this page.

4 Ask students to explain how to keep the body systems healthy.

Have each student present their drawings to the class. They are to identify how they labeled parts and give their reasons why they made the labels they chose.

Body Part Put Up

Objective

Students will name and locate different organs within the body.

Life Skill

I will practice healthful behaviors to keep my body systems healthy.

Materials

Felt board, body parts in different felt colors, Teaching Master , "Internal Body Organs," on page 209.

Motivation

1 Tell the class it will learn about different parts of the body. For this activity, you can use felt and cut out different internal parts of the body. You can cut out organs in the shape of those labeled on the bottom of this page.

2 Also cut out a large outline of the human body within which the organs can fit. Attach the outline of the body to the felt board.

3 Distribute different body organs to the students. Distribute a copy of the Teaching Master, "Internal Body Organs." Have students look at the Master and place their body organs in the correct place on the felt body. As they place the body organ on the body, they are to name the body organ for the class.

Evaluation

Have students repeat the same task but this time, they cannot look at the Teaching Master for guidance.

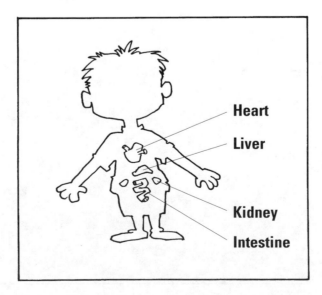

Heart

Liver

Kidney

Intestine

Internal Body Organs

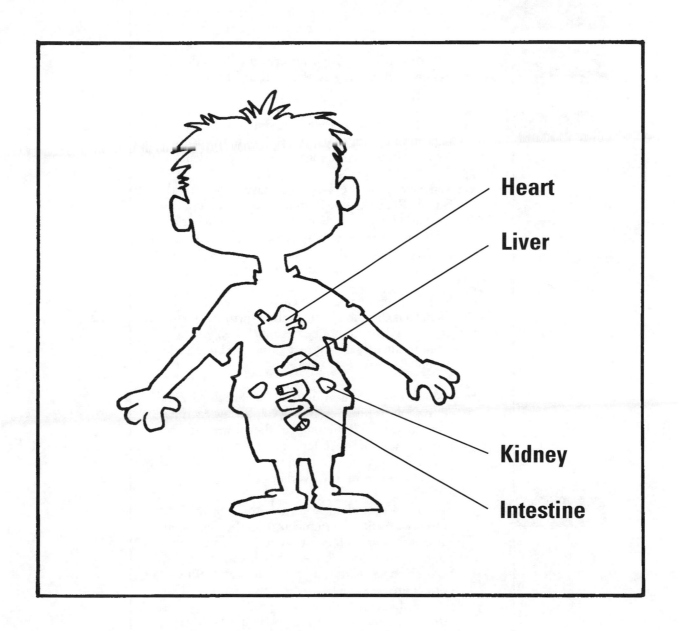

Heart

Liver

Kidney

Intestine

Reproduce My System

Objective

Students will identify parts of the male and female reproductive systems.

Life Skill

I will ask a responsible adult any questions I have about the organs of the reproductive system.

Materials

Teaching Master, "Male and Female Reproductive Systems," transparency of Teaching Master

Motivation

1 Explain that the reproductive system is a very important system in the body. Often, this is the system whose parts are least known by students.

2 Make a copy of the Teaching Master, "Male and Female Reproductive Systems." Give students a copy and have them write the correct number of each part identified. After you have had students do this, collect each paper. Tell students that their names should not appear on their papers.

3 Redistribute the papers to each student and tell them that they do not have their own. This will enable students to not be hesitant when you ask them to identify the correct parts based upon the papers they have.

4 Using a health education text, label each part and state what its function is. As you review each part, have students tell the number they think it is and the functions of the different parts. Students can follow you as you work from the overlay. Fill in the correct answers on the overlay.

Evaluation

See how well students were able to label the different parts. Write the numbers from the papers on the board. For each question, write the number correct. For example, say, "How many of you are holding papers with ten correct answers? Nine correct answers? Eight correct answers?" etc. Do this for the female and male reproductive systems. After you tally the answers, you will most likely need to indicate that there is much that students do not know.

You can use this same idea by giving a post-test at a later time and comparing scores.

Male and Female Reproductive Systems

Vaginal opening   _____
Urethra   _____
Pubic bone   _____
Urinary bladder   _____
Ovary   _____
Cervix   _____
Rectum   _____
Fallopian tube   _____
Vagina   _____
Uterus   _____

Seminal vesicle   _____
Scrotum   _____
Penis   _____
Rectum   _____
Urinary bladder   _____
Pubic bone   _____
Prostate gland   _____
Epididymis   _____

Happy Birth Day

Objective

Students will observe the process of birth by viewing a simulation of the passage of a baby through the birth canal.

Life Skill

I will ask my parent any questions I have about the birth of a baby.

Materials

One sock, a stuffed small animal that can fit through the opening of the sock

Motivation

1 Hold a sock up to the front of the class and explain that the sock represents the uterus and the birth canal through which a baby will pass during the birth process.

2 Describe the birth process by describing that the part of the sock in which the baby develops is called the uterus. Explain that contractions are pushing the baby down the birth canal. The opening of the sock expands so that the head of the baby can begin to pass through. This is analogous to the stretching of the vagina. Emphasize how just as the opening of the sock can stretch to accommodate the baby, so can the opening of the vagina.

3 You may choose to use scissors to perform an episiotomy on the sock. You can explain that this is done so that the sock will not rip. On a woman, this is done so that the muscles around the vaginal opening do not tear and cause permanent damage.

4 You can modify this activity by using the front of the sock as the uterus and the opening through which the baby will pass as the cervix. Explain that the cervix opens to allow the baby to pass. The opening of the cervix is measured in centimeters. You can use the tips of your fingers to show dilation of the cervix.

Evaluation

Invite a student to the front of the class and use the sock and doll to describe the birth process.

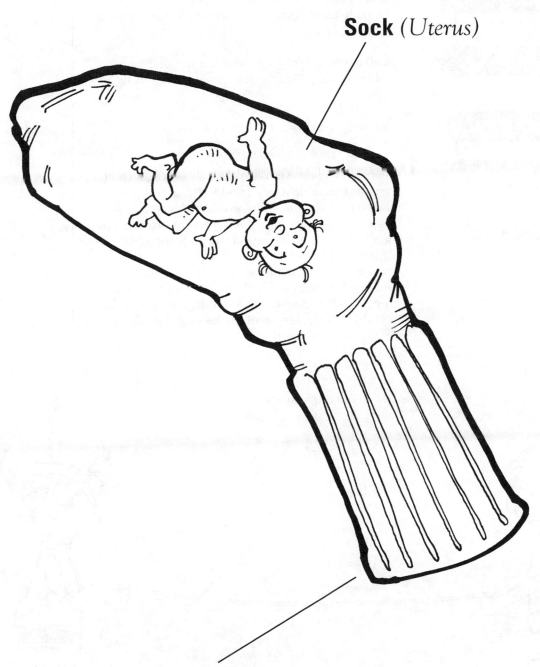

Sock (*Uterus*)

Neck of Sock (*Birth Canal*)

String-Along Intestines

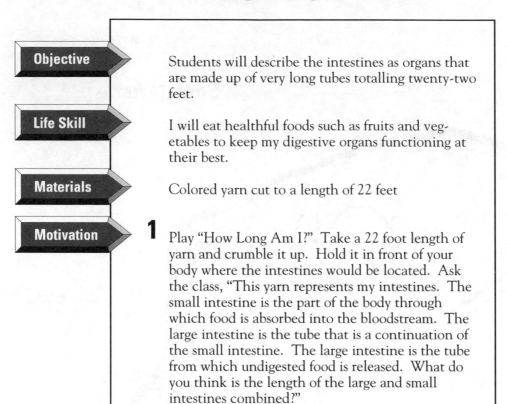

Objective

Students will describe the intestines as organs that are made up of very long tubes totalling twenty-two feet.

Life Skill

I will eat healthful foods such as fruits and vegetables to keep my digestive organs functioning at their best.

Materials

Colored yarn cut to a length of 22 feet

Motivation

1 Play "How Long Am I?" Take a 22 foot length of yarn and crumble it up. Hold it in front of your body where the intestines would be located. Ask the class, "This yarn represents my intestines. The small intestine is the part of the body through which food is absorbed into the bloodstream. The large intestine is the tube that is a continuation of the small intestine. The large intestine is the tube from which undigested food is released. What do you think is the length of the large and small intestines combined?"

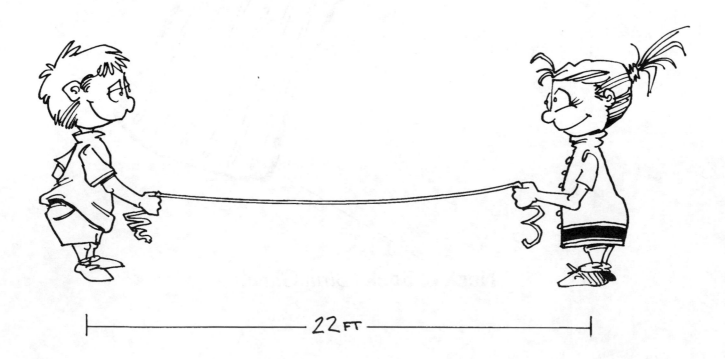

22 FT

2 Have students work in pairs. They are to stand away from each other at a distance they think is the length of the intestines. Have different teams compete with each other to determine who is standing apart the correct distance.

3 Take the crumpled yarn and hand it to a student. Have the student hold one end and stand away from you until the yarn is completely stretched. Observe which student team is standing a distance that most closely represents the length of the intestines. Explain that the length of the intestines is 22 feet. Have students observe how long 22 feet is.

Evaluation

Ask students to discuss why the intestines are so long. (The longer the intestines, the greater the surface area through which nutrients from food can be absorbed into the bloodstream.)

We're Here to Pump You Up

Objective

Students will explain why a strong heart muscle is needed to lower resting heartbeat rate.

Life Skill

I will not engage in activities such as smoking that are harmful to my heart.

Materials

Motivation

1 With students seated, have them hold their hands above their heads.

2 Give students the following instructions:

- Begin with your fingers spread wide apart. At the count of one, make a fist as tightly as possible. This will represent the contraction of the heart. The contraction of the heart muscle indicates the heart at work.
- At the count of two, open the fingers wide. This represents the heart while at rest.
- For a period of one minute, have students open and shut their fists at one second intervals. Open (one second), shut (one second), etc.

3 At the end of one minute, ask students how their fingers felt. (Most students will say that their fingers began to tire.) Explain that unlike fingers, the heart needs to keep working at all times to pump blood to the body. Blood carries oxygen.

4 Explain that during exercise, the heart can beat two to three times faster than while at rest. More blood must be pumped because more oxygen is needed. Have students do the same thing, but this time have them open and close their fists to a pace of 120 beats per minute. Then have students do the same thing at a pace of 180 beats per minute. After completing this task, have students describe their feelings of being tired.

Evaluation

Tell students that if they smoke, the heartbeat rate increases as many as 20 beats per minute while at rest. Do this activity so that there is a 20 beat per minute increase. Ask students to make an analogy about how smoking may affect the heart. (It can cause the heart to work harder than it needs, thereby causing strain.) Have students describe why having a strong heart is helpful in athletics.

Move Your Muscle

Objective

Students will differentiate between muscle contraction and muscle relaxation.

Life Skill

I will engage in exercises to bend and stretch my muscles.

Materials

Balloon, preferably a long one

Motivation

1 Introduce the concept that a muscle in a contracted state will shorten and become wider. Have students extend their arms and feel their bicep muscle. When they do this, they should have their palms facing the ceiling. They can feel the bicep muscle by placing their fingers half-way between the elbow and shoulder. The muscle will appear flat.

2 Have the students bend their arms at the elbow joint. Another way of saying this is to ask them to "make a muscle." As they make a muscle, have them observe what happens. (The muscle pops up. This results from the muscle contracting, thereby becoming shorter.)

3 Take a balloon and blow it up. Grab both ends and stretch it. Have students observe that the balloon becomes elongated and thin. Explain that the balloon represents a muscle.

4 Tell the students that the balloon is now going to contract. Allow students to observe what happens to the balloon.

Evaluation

Have students describe why the balloon became wider? (It became wider because it shortened.) Have students identify what happens when a muscle in the body extends. (The muscle becomes shorter.)

Boney Maroney

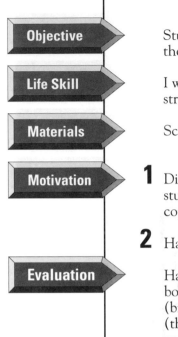

Objective

Students will identify how the major bones inside the body make up the human skeleton.

Life Skill

I will eat foods that contain vitamin D to strengthen my bones.

Materials

Scissor to cut out bones, glue

Motivation

1 Distribute a copy of the bone puzzle below. Have students cut out the bones and place them in the correct way to form the human skeleton.

2 Have students share their puzzles with the class.

Evaluation

Have students name the appropriate bones. The bones they will assemble are: skull (head), sternum (breast bone), radius (thick bone above wrist), ulna (thin bone above wrist), humerus (long bone on upper part of arm), clavicle (shoulder bone), femur, (top part of leg), tibia (long bone below knee), fibula (thin, long bone below knee) patella, (knee cap).

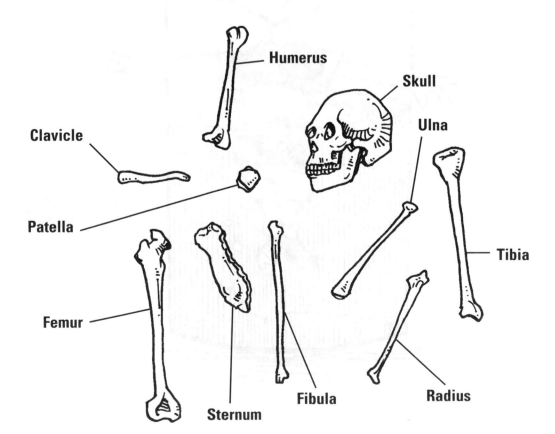

Trace Me

Objective ▶ Students will be able to draw and identify the major bones on a life-size outline of the body.

Life Skill ▶ I will eat foods containing vitamin D to strengthen my bones.

Materials ▶ Large sheets of brown butcher paper that are the size of the human body, white chalk

Motivation ▶

1 Tell students you would like them to work with a partner. The students will be paired into groups of two.

2 Give each person a sheet of paper. Taking turns, first one person will lie back down on the paper. The partner will outline the person's body on the sheet of paper using a piece of chalk. Then have the students switch and draw the other partner.

3 Each person is to take his/her sheet of paper and write his/her name on the bottom in large letters. Students should then fill in the major bones of the body using the chalk. The bones can be colored white. Each student will have a picture of his/her body with the bones drawn. The diagram on the bottom of Page 224 can be used as a guide. Each bone on the body can be labeled as per the picture on this page.

Evaluation ▶ Select one drawing and cover each of the names of the bones. Have students identify the names of each bone to which you point.

Line Up By Size

Objective

Students will describe how their bodies change as they grow.

Life Skill

I will follow a healthful diet to help my body grow.

Materials

Cord, clothespins or paper clasps, socks of different sizes

Motivation

1 Using clothesline or string, attach each end so that it is fastened to the wall or another object. Explain to the students that this clothesline represents a line of growth.

2 Come to class with socks of different sizes. You should have socks that people of all ages wear. You can have socks that fit infants through adults. Arrange the socks by size with the smallest on the left. Attach a tag to each sock which identifies the approximate age the person who wears the sock may be.

3 Have students observe the different socks and describe what differs about each. Students will notice the most obvious - that the socks increase in size as a person grows older. What also will be observable is that at a certain age, the socks no longer are bigger.

4 Explain to students that the body changes physically as a person grows. The socks represent how the feet grow in size. Explain that many other body parts change in size as a person grows older. Other parts that change include the arms, shoulders, and hips. Students can identify other parts that can change. Body parts will stop growing after a person completes puberty.

5 Explain that growth occurs in many ways other than physical. Students can brainstorm some of the ways a person changes both mentally and socially throughout the life cycle.

Evaluation

Have students bring an old shirt from home. This shirt should be significantly smaller than one that fits them now. Have students try on the shirts in class and tell others how their bodies have changed over the past number of years.

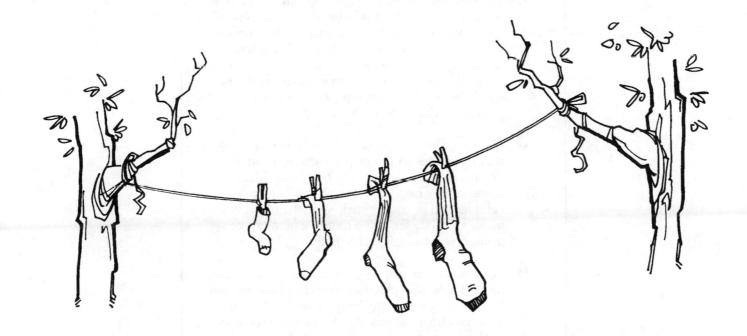

Mapping Your Body

Objective

Students will describe the flow of blood through arteries, veins, and capillaries.

Life Skill

I will reduce my intake of fat.

Materials

An old map, poster paper

Motivation

1 On a sheet of poster paper, outline the human body. Draw the head, hands, feet, and body. Show the body to the class.

2 Take an old road map. Your map can be one that shows local roads or it may be one that is from a national road atlas. Cut the map so that it fits the shape of the body you have drawn. If you wish, you can draw the outline of the body on the map instead of on the poster paper. Then you can cut the map and paste it on the poster paper. Show students the picture of what is now a body map.

3 Show students the picture of the body map. Explain that the routes on the map are analagous to the different blood vessels in the body. Just like the routes on the map serve as a place where motor vehicles can be transported, so do the blood vessels inside the body serve as a route for blood to be transported throughout the body.

4 You can use the map to explain that there are major routes for motor vehicles to travel. There are major blood vessels inside the body in which blood travels. You can choose to talk about how veins serve as routes for blood to be carried to the heart while arteries are blood vessels that carry blood away from the heart. Discuss the concept that arteries, just like roads, need to be kept clear for movement through them. Plaque that blocks the arteries is analogous to a traffic accident that blocks roads. In both cases, there are blocked routes.

5 You can draw pictures of some of the major organs in the body. For example, you can draw the heart, lungs, and brain. Students can trace the flow of blood on the map to these organs. The flow of blood can be in arteries or veins.

Have students color blood vessels from the heart in red and veins in blue. They are to connect these blood vessels to any other part of the body such as the hands, brain, or legs. They are to trace which are arteries and which are veins. They are to tell why they are arteries or veins. (The arteries carry blood away from the heart while the veins carry blood to the heart.)

The Body Systems Game

Objective

Students will categorize different body organs into the body systems to which they belong.

Life Skill

I will practice behaviors that keep my body systems healthy.

Materials

3" x 5" index cards, tape

Motivation

1 To prepare for this activity, you will need 25, 3" x 5" index cards. On each card you are to print the following body systems and their associated parts. Print the names of the body systems in RED. The other parts will be written in blue or black.

- *circulatory system* - heart, arteries, veins, blood
- *digestive system* - liver, small intestines, stomach, large intestines
- *respiratory system* - lungs, bronchial tubes, alveoli, bronchi
- *skeletal system* - sternum, radius, ulna, tibia,
- *nervous system* - axon, dendrite, neuron, brain

2 Tell students they are going to be playing a game. Explain that students are to come up to the front of the room and you will tape a name of a body system or a part of a body system to their backs. Tell students they are to guess what is on their backs. They can ask questions that receive only a YES or NO response and they can ask only one question per person. When they guess what is on their backs, they are to tape the card to their chests. This will indicate they guessed their parts. But, they are still to help others guess their parts.

3 After about five minutes, stop and have the students tape their parts on their chests. Then tell students they are to remain nonverbal. Tell them that they all belong to one of five groups. Without talking, they are to form their like groups. (Students should group by body system.) At the end, students will team up with a RED card and the body parts that go with that card.

4 Tell students they are to work with their group and develop a five-line jingle that tells how to keep their assigned body system healthy. Explain that they are not limited to using the names of the parts of that system. After 15 minutes, students are to present their jingles to the front of the class.

5 This activity can be modified so that more or fewer cards can be added to each group depending upon the number of students in the class. For students in lower grades, pictures can be used. This activity can be used for different areas of health. For example, it can be used in nutrition by identifying food groups and specific foods that fall within each food group.

Evaluation

Have students identify two health facts from each presentation of a body system.

T Cell - B Cell

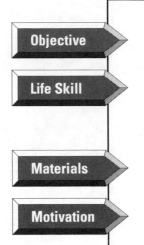

Objective

Students will describe the functions of T cells and B cells in the immune system.

Life Skill

I will protect my immune system by getting rest and sleep, having a good attitude, using stress management skills, and having a source of vitamin C in my daily diet.

Materials

Posters labeled T cell, B cell, antibody, and germ

Motivation

1 Explain to the class they are going to discuss how the immune system protects people from germs that enter the body. Explain that when a germ enters the body, T cells recognize that this germ has entered. The T cells send out a signal to bring on B cells. B cells produce antibodies for that particular germ. Then the body is protected against that germ for as long as a lifetime.

2 Tell the class that they will act out what happens when a germ enters the body. Give students posters that say T cell, B cell, antibody, and germ. Have students pretend they are inside the body. A germ enters the body. T cell says, "There is someone in here who does not belong here. We need help from B cell." B cell comes along and produces an antibody. Antibody pushes the germ outside the body. Antibody protects the person from illness that can be caused by the germ.

3 You can choose to modify this by teaching what happens when the AIDS virus, or HIV, enters the body. Explain that when HIV is in the body, the T cells are destroyed and B cells no longer can come to the rescue. Antibodies will no longer be able to be produced. Eventually, the effectiveness of the immune system is destroyed.

4 Explain to students that they can help keep their immune systems healthy by eating healthful foods, getting rest and sleep, having a good attitude, and having a source of vitamin C in the daily diet.

The entire class can participate in the activity by making a poster for each student. Posters will consist of the T cell, B cell, germ, and antibody. You can give directions for T cells to signal B cells and for antibodies to be formed. The germs will be pushed from the body by the antibodies.

Nutrition is the area of health that examines nutrients, the seven dietary guidelines, diet and health, diet and cancer, diet and heart disease, weight management, and eating disorders.

Nutrients

Nutrients are chemical substances in foods that provide energy and materials for the growth, maintenance, and repair of body cells. There are six main kinds of nutrients: proteins, carbohydrates, fats, vitamins, minerals, and water. **Proteins** are nutrients that are essential for the growth, development, and repair of all body tissues. **Amino acids** are the building blocks of proteins. There are twenty-two different amino acids needed for good health. Fourteen amino acids are made by the body while eight are not. The **essential amino acids** are the eight amino acids that must be derived from food that is eaten. **Complete proteins** are those that contain all eight essential amino acids. Fish, steak, and poultry are examples. **Incomplete proteins** are proteins that do not contain all eight essential amino acids. Beans, legumes, nuts, and grains are examples. Incomplete proteins must be eaten in combination to get the needed amino acids.

Carbohydrates are nutrients that provide the main source of energy for the body. **Simple carbohydrates** are carbohydrates that enter the body rapidly to supply quick energy. They are found in sugar, fruits, honey, cookies, and pies. **Complex carbohydrates** are carbohydrates such as starches and fiber that provide long-lasting energy. Pasta and bread are good examples. **Fats** are nutrients that provide a source of energy and carry vitamins to body cells. **Saturated fats** are fats found in animal meats and dairy products. Hamburger, steak, cheese, and whole milk are examples. **Unsaturated fats** are fats found in fish, poultry, nuts, seeds, olive oil, corn oil, and turkey. **Cholesterol** is a fatty substance made by the body and found in animal meats and dairy products. It makes up five percent of the fat in the body and when in excess in the bloodstream can form plaque on the artery walls.

Vitamins are nutrients that facilitate chemical reactions in the body. **Fat-soluble vitamins**, A, D, E, and K, are vitamins that can be stored in the body. **Water-soluble vitamins,** B complex and C, are vitamins that cannot be stored and are needed as part of the diet each day. **Minerals** are nutrients that regulate chemical reactions in the body. **Macrominerals** such as calcium, chlorine, magnesium, phosphorus, potassium, and sulfur, are minerals that are needed in large amounts. **Trace minerals** such as copper, fluorine, iodine, iron, and zinc are minerals needed in small amounts.

Water is a nutrient that helps make up blood, helps the process of digestion, and regulates body temperature. About 60 percent of the body is made up of water. The equivalent of six to eight glasses of water is needed each day.

A United States Recommended Dietary Allowance has been established for the nutrients needed by the body. **Recommended Dietary Allowances** are the levels of intake of essential nutrients considered, in the judgement of the Committee on Dietary Allowances of the Food and Nutrition Board of the National Academy of Sciences, to be adequate to meet the known nutritional needs of practically all healthy persons.

Seven Dietary Guidelines

Seven out of ten of the leading causes of death can be linked to diet. The **seven dietary guidelines** are recommendations for diet choices made by the United States Department of Agriculture and the Department of Health and Human Services. (1) *Eat a variety of foods.* Traditionally, there have been four food groups: milk group, meat group, fruit and vegetable group, and grain group. The configuration for appropriate servings has been two servings of meat a day, two of dairy products, six of grains and five of fruits and vegetables. This configuration is the topic of much debate today. The United States Department of Agriculture wants to reconfigure the groups to emphasize the importance of

8

NUTRITION

grains and fruits and vegetables with a corresponding de-emphasis on meat and dairy products. The USDA created "The Eating Right Pyramid" which promoted (1) 6-11 servings of bread, cereal, rice, and pastas, (2) 3-5 servings of vegetables, (3) 2-4 servings of fruits, (4) 2-3 servings of milk, yogurt, and cheese, (5) 2-3 servings of meat, poultry, fish, dry beans, eggs, and nuts, and (6) fats, oils, and sweets used sparingly. Thus far, the "Eating Right Pyramid" is still being examined and has not been released from the USDA with their recommendations. However, these recommendations are consistent with research indicating guidelines for reducing cancer and cardiovascular diseases with careful eating habits. The recommended intake of each of the nutrients is 30% fat, 12% protein, 48% complex carbohydrates, and 10% sugar. *(2) Maintain a healthful weight.* Desirable weight is the weight and body composition that is recommended for a person's age, height, sex, and body build. Being overweight has been linked to the development of heart disease, diabetes, and cancer. *(3) Choose a diet low in fat, saturated fat, and cholesterol.* **Atherosclerosis** is a disease in which fat deposits harden and form plaque on artery walls. A low-fat diet and exercise help prevent this buildup. Recently, a high-fat diet has been linked to cancers of the breast, colon, and prostate. *(4) Choose a diet with plenty of vegetables, fruits, and grain products.* New evidence indicates that fruits and vegetables actively protect against cancer and heart disease. There appears to be an excess of free radicals, oxygen compounds produced as a result of normal metabolism, that travel throughout the body doing damage and initiating both cancer and atherosclerosis. The best defense against these free radicals appears to be nutrients known as anti-oxidants. The anti-oxidants neutralize the effects of the free radicals. Anti-oxidants are found in the mineral silenium, vitamin E, and betacarotene, which is vitamin A in the body. Fruits and vegetables are rich sources of these anti-oxidants. Thus, what you eat (saturated fats) as well as what you don't eat (fruits and vegetables) can play a factor in your risk of developing heart disease

and/or cancer. Grains are important because they contain fiber, a substance which passes through the body promoting a daily bowel movement. Having a daily bowel movement decreases the risk of colon and rectal cancer. *(5) Use sugar only in moderation.* A high sugar diet can be linked to heart disease, obesity, and tooth decay. *(6) Use salt and sodium only in moderation.* The average American consumes 4-7 grams of sodium per day. Five grams are equal to about one teaspoon. An intake of 6 grams has been linked to increased blood pressure. *(7) Drink alcohol only in moderation.* Moderation is defined as drinking 1 ounce of pure alcohol or less per day. Pregnant women should not drink alcohol at all.

Diet and Health

The National Academy of Sciences released *Diet and Health: Implications for Reducing Chronic Disease Risk* in 1989. The recommendations of this group were similar. (1) Reduce total fat intake to 30% or less of calories. Reduce saturated fat to less than 10% of calories, and the intake of cholesterol to less than 300 mg daily. (2) Every day eat five or more servings of a combination of vegetables and fruits, especially green and yellow vegetables and citrus fruits. Increase intake of starches and other complex carbohydrates by eating six or more daily servings of a combination of breads, cereals, and legumes. (3) Maintain protein intake at moderate levels. (4) Balance food intake and physical activity to maintain appropriate body weight. (5) Do not drink alcoholic beverages. For those who choose to drink, limit consumption to the equivalent of less than 1 ounce of pure alcohol in a single day. Pregnant women should never drink. (6) Limit total daily intake of salt to 6 grams or less. (7) Maintain adequate calcium intake. (8) Avoid taking dietary supplements in excess of the RDA in any one day. (9) Maintain an optimal level of fluoride, particulary during primary and secondary years of growth.

Diet and Cancer

The American Cancer Society suggests the dietary guidelines to reduce the risk of cancer: (1) Avoid obesity. Persons who are 40% overweight have an increased risk of colon, breast, and uterine cancers. (2) Reduce total fat intake. High fat intake is related to breast, colon, and prostate cancers. (3) Eat high-fiber foods. This reduces the risk of colon and rectal cancers. (4) Eat foods rich in vitamins A and C. This reduces the risk of developing cancers of the larynx, esophagus, and lung. (5) Eat cruciferous vegetables such as cabbage, broccoli, and brussels sprouts. This reduces the risk of cancers of the digestive organs. (6) Eat limited amounts of salt-cured, smoked, and nitrite-cured foods. This reduces the risk of cancers of the stomach and esophagus. (7) Limit the intake of alcohol. This reduces the risk of cancers of the mouth, larynx, throat, liver, esophagus, and stomach.

Diet and Heart Disease

The American Heart Association suggests guidelines for preparing meals at home or eating at a restaurant: (1) Serve margarine in place of butter. (2) Serve skimmed milk rather than whole milk. (3) Trim visible fat from meat and remove skin from poultry. (4) Broil, bake, steam, or poach meat, fish, or poultry. (5) Limit portion size to four to six ounces of cooked meat, fish, or poultry. (6) Leave all butter, gravy, or sauce off your main dish or side dish. (7) Serve fresh fruit or fruit in light syrup, (8) Prepare food without adding salt.

Weight Management

Weight management is a plan to maintain desirable weight. Desirable weight is a healthful weight based upon a person's body composition, height, age, and sex. A weight management plan is based on caloric intake being balanced with caloric expenditure. A caloric intake of 3500 calories more than caloric expenditure results in a weight gain of one pound of body fat. A caloric expenditure of 3500 calories more than caloric intake results in a weight loss of one pound of body fat. The most healthful way to lose weight is to establish a program whereby an increase in caloric expenditure through exercise and a reduction in caloric intake burns an additional 1000 Calories per day for a two pound weight loss each week. When attempting to lose weight, the dietary guidelines should be followed. Increasing the amounts of fruits and vegetables in the diet is helpful.

Eating Disorders

Eating disorders are food-related dysfunctions in which a person changes eating habits in a way which is harmful to the mind and body. Therefore, eating disorders are classified as diseases of the mind as well as the body. **Anorexia nervosa** is an eating disorder in which a person is preoccupied with being excessively thin. The Anorexia Nervosa and Related Eating Disorders Organization (ANRED) estimates that 1 out of 100 females aged 12 to 18 have this disorder. Onset is usually just before or after puberty. The female is usually perfectionistic and a people-pleaser. She attempts to please everyone else at the expense of herself and loses her identity. This is coupled with her difficulty in accepting her sexuality and the fat deposits in the breasts and buttocks that normally accompany puberty. In order to gain the lost control of her life that she is experiencing, she attempts to gain control of her weight. She starves herself, exercises to the point of exhaustion, and uses diuretics and laxatives for further weight loss. Her behavior results in drastic loss of body fat, damage to the liver and kidneys, and irregular heart beat. These signs are usually accompanied by depression. Untreated, anorexia nervosa results in a death rate of 15-21%.

Bulimia is an eating disorder in which a person has uncontrollable urges to eat excessively and then goes to sleep or more commonly, engages in self-induced vomiting. Bulimia is most common in females and usually begins in early or middle adolescence. It is known as the secret eating disorder because the person with it makes great attempts to hide it from others. The binges usually occur during intense emotions such as anger, depression, fear, or loneliness. They are a way of coping. After the binge of 1,000 to 10,000 Calories, the female with bulimia usually experiences guilt and induces vomiting. Laxatives and diuretics also may be used. This is followed with a feeling of relief and/or euphoria. The vomiting causes damage to the esophagus, teeth, and gums. There may be stomach, liver, and kidney damage. Depletion of potassium can lead to irregular heart beat. Persons with bulimia as well as anorexia nervosa need medical and psychological help. They need help with their self-esteem, coping skills, and sexuality. They usually require medical treatment for health problems associated with starvation, vomiting, and the use of laxatives and diuretics.

Diet Mobile

Objective

Students will identify the seven dietary guidelines and will explain ways that they can meet these guidelines.

Life Skill

I will choose foods that meet the dietary guidelines.

Materials

Poster board, magazines, glue, string or yarn, scissors, hole puncher

Motivation

1 Review the dietary guidelines with students. They are:

- Eat a variety of foods.
- Maintain a healthful weight.
- Choose a diet low in fat, saturated fat, and cholesterol.
- Choose a diet with plenty of vegetables, fruits, and grain products.
- Use sugar only in moderation.
- Use salt and sodium only in moderation.
- Drink only in moderation as an adult.

Note: You may choose only to work with the first six dietary guidelines and not include the seventh for this activity.

2 Discuss ways to meet the dietary guidelines. The corresponding ways might be:
- Eat foods from each of the food groups each day emphasizing foods from the fruit and vegetable and grain groups.
- Eat fewer foods and exercise to lose weight and eat more healthful foods to gain weight.
- Cut down on fatty foods such as ice cream and foods that are fried.
- Eat more vegetables such as green beans, salads, broccoli; eat more fruits such as apples, pears, and oranges; eat more grain products such as cereal, rice, whole wheat bread.
- Limit sugar to naturally occurring sugar such as the sugars in fruit; avoid adding sugar to cereals and fruits.
- Avoid salting food or eating foods with lots of salt such as salted pretzels.
- If an adult, drink very little alcohol.

- When a team scores a touchdown, it receives six points. The opposing team then "gets the ball."

- The team with the most points at the end wins the game.

- Optional: the team that scores the touchdown could be given another food; if the entire team answers with the correct food group, it earns the extra point after the touchdown.

Evaluation

Have students plan a daily menu with a breakfast, lunch, and dinner with servings from the healthful food groups. Check to see that plenty of fruits, vegetables, and grains were included.

Basic 4 Baseball

Objective Students will identify foods that belong to the healthful food groups.

Life Skill I will eat a balanced diet.

Materials Chalkboard and chalk

Motivation

1 Review the healthful food groups and the kinds of foods that belong to each group. Emphasize the importance of eating plenty of fruits, vegetables, and grains.

2 Draw a baseball diamond on the chalkboard. Make symbols to represent the runners (Example: make four red circles and four blue squares).

3 To Play

- Choose sides; assign each team a color or symbol.

- Toss a coin to determine which team will bat first.

- First player on the pitching team pitches the ball by asking the first player on the batting team to which food group a specific food belongs. (Example: "Milk belongs in the_____ group.")

- To advance to first base, the first batter must answer correctly. If the first batter answers incorrectly, the pitcher must then name the correct food group for the batter to be out. If the batter answers incorrectly, and the pitcher also answers incorrectly, the batter walks to first base.

- The batting team continues playing until it has three outs.

- When a team has three outs, the opposing team comes to bat.

- The team with the most runs at the end of nine innings wins the game.

Variations:

- Add foods that would score a double, triple, or home run.

- Students could actually move around designated bases on the diamond instead of using symbols.

Evaluation

Have students plan a daily menu with a breakfast, lunch, and dinner using the correct number of servings from the healthful food groups.

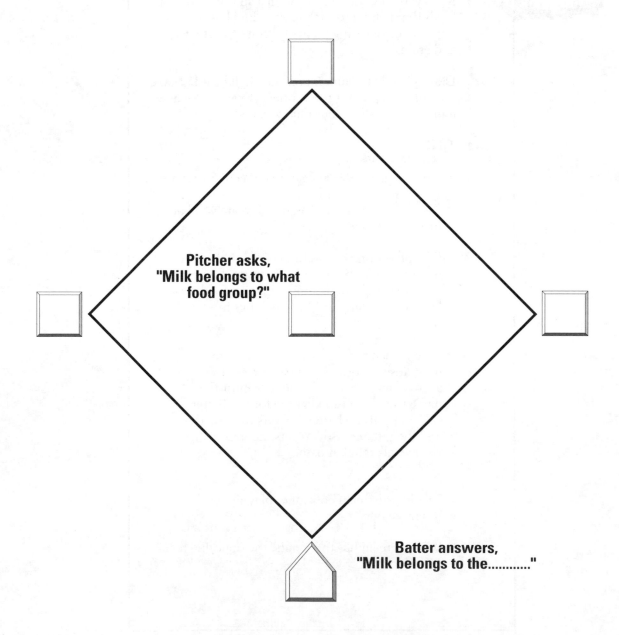

**Pitcher asks,
"Milk belongs to what
food group?"**

**Batter answers,
"Milk belongs to the............"**

Nutrition Relay

Objective

Students will identify foods that belong to the healthful food groups and the others group.

Life Skill

I will eat a balanced diet.

Materials

Ten grocery bags, empty cartons or packages of foods, pictures of foods

Motivation

1 Review the healthful food groups and the others group and the foods that belong to each group.

2 To play

- Divide the class into two teams.

- Each team gets a grocery bag with an equal number of sample foods or pictures of foods. Each item in the bag belonging to Team No. 1 has a "1" marked on it. All items in the Team No. 2 bag have a "2" on them.

- At a point equally distant from both teams are five empty grocery bags, each labeled with one of the food groups.

- At the call "Go!" the race begins. The first student of each team grabs an item in the proper food group bag. The student runs back to the team and tags the next person in line, who repeats the action. This continues with both teams until one team finishes first.

- The first place team gets fifteen points. The second place team gets ten points. In a tie game, each team gets fifteen points.

- The food group bags are now checked to be sure the items in them belong there. For each item placed in the wrong bag by a certain team, the other team gets two additional points. Thus, Team No. 1 may have finished first, but has three incorrect items. Team No. 2 having no incorrect items, would then get six additional points, giving it a total of sixteen, and they win the game.

• If each team has an equal number of incorrect items, the teams cancel out and no additional points are given.

Evaluation

Have students make a grocery list to buy foods they enjoy from each of the healthful food groups. Have them list five foods they enjoy from the others group that they should limit.

- Elementary (modified)
- Middle/Junior High
- High School

Sugar Cube Count

Objective

Students will identify foods that are high in sugar.

Life Skill

I will limit the amount of sugar I eat.

Materials

Posterboard, magazine pictures, scissors, glue, markers, eight ounce clear plastic glass, sugar cubes or sugar, teaspoon, Teaching Master, "Sugar Cube Count" on page 246.

Motivation

1 Use an eight ounce clear plastic glass. Have students place either five sugar cubes into the glass or five teaspoons of sugar. Explain to the class that this is how much sugar there is in this size of a soft drink.

2 Discuss the dietary guideline which says to use sugar only in moderation. Using too much sugar may cause cavities and overweight. It may increase the risk of heart disease.

3 Ask students to identify foods they believe are high in sugar. Show students the Teaching Master "Sugar Cube Count" on page 246 and review the amount of sugar in common snacks.

Have students help you make a Sugar Cube Chart. Have them cut out pictures of the foods from the Teaching Master. Glue these to the left side on posterboard. To the right of each, draw the correct number of sugar cubes to represent the amount of sugar in each food.

Evaluation

Have students complete the following open ended statement. I will follow the dietary guideline for using less sugar by_____

Sugar Cube Count

Food or Snack	Amount of Snack	Amount of Sugar in Teaspoons
Chewing Gum	1 stick	1/2
Average cookie	1	1-3
Jams and jellies	1 tablespoon	2 1/2-3
Soft drink	8 ounces	5
Cocoa	6 ounces	4
Ice cream	1/8 quart	5-6
Apple pie	1/6 of 9"pie	12
Devil's food cake	1/12 of 9"cake	15
Gelatin dessert	1/2 cup	4 1/2
Raisins	4 1/2 tablespoons	4
Chocolate pudding	1/2 cup	4
Orange juice	1/2 cup	2
Grapefruit	1/2 medium	3 1/2
Milk chocolate bar	1 ounce	8
Chocolate syrup	2 tablespoons	4
Cake type of doughnut	1	6

Calorimeter

Objective

Students will define Calorie and tell how Calories are measured.

Life Skill

I will eat the number of Calories I need to maintain my desirable weight.

Materials

Pamphlet or chart showing foods and Calories, 3 cup can, black paint, cork, 2 gram Brazil nut, pin, test tube, candle, Centigrade thermometer, matches.

Motivation

1 Have students with the help of the teacher, construct a calorimeter to measure the energy in a given food. The source of directions for constructing the calorimeter was Edith M. Selberg and Louise A Neal. *Discovering Science in the Elementary School.* Reading, Massachusetts: Addison Wesley, 1970, pp. 232-233.

2 A 3 cup can is sprayed with black paint and two openings are cut in it before the class period begins. One hole is cut in the bottom of the can to hold the test tube, and another hole is cut in the side of the can large enough to hold a cork to which a 2 gram nut (Brazil or walnut) is attached with a pin.

3 The teacher blackens the end of the test tube in order to cause it to absorb more heat. (A candle could be used). The tube is then inserted through the hole and the student pours 8 milliliters of water into the test tube.

4 Using a centigrade thermometer, the student measures the temperature of the water and records it. The thermometer is removed carefully, and the nut is lighted by the teacher with a match. It is allowed to burn until nothing remains, but the ash.

5 As soon as possible after the nut is consumed by the flames, another reading is taken of the water to measure the heat energy the water absorbed. This reading is recorded and the differences are noted on this chart. For example:

	1st reading	2nd reading	3rd reading
	24°C	44°C	20°C

6 The student makes the computations by multiplying the water times the increase in heat, i.e., 8ml(gm) water x 20* difference gives the total of 160. Therefore, each gram of nut produced 80 Calories of heat.

7 The student should be able to state that a Calorie is the amount of heat required to raise the temperature of 1 gram or ml of water one degree centigrade.

Evaluation

Have students write the definition of Calorie and tell how Calories are measured.

Watch That Fat!

Objective

Students will tell ways to meet the dietary guideline that states "choose a diet that is low in fat, saturated fat, and cholesterol."

Life Skill

I will limit the amount of fat I eat.

Materials

Paper towels, greasy French fries, baked potato, potato chips, hot air popped corn, oil popped corn that is buttered

Motivation

1 Review the dietary guidelines.

1. Eat a variety of foods.
2. Maintain a healthful weight.
3. Choose a diet low in fat, saturated fat, and cholesterol.
4. Choose a diet with plenty of vegetables, fruits, and whole grains.
5. Use sugar only in moderation.
6. Use salt/sodium only in moderation.
7. If you are an adult, drink alcohol only in moderation.

2 To illustrate dietary guideline #3, use the following demonstration. Place a paper towel on the table in front of students. Place greasy French fries on the paper towel. Allow them to sit for a minute. Remove them and ask students what has happened. There will be oil left on the paper towel. Explain that when you eat fried foods, the grease or oils in which they are fried stick to your artery walls just as the oil stayed on the paper.

3 Use another paper towel. Place potato chips on the paper towel. Allow them to sit for a minute. Remove them and ask students what has happened. They will see again that there is a film of oil left. Mention that potato chips also are high in fats which can clog arteries.

4 Use another paper towel. Place a baked potato on the paper towel. Allow the potato to sit for a minute. Remove the potato and students will see that there is no film of oil. Explain that potatoes are not high in fats. They are actually

As a class, write a story called "A Trip to The Grocery Store." Have students discuss the kinds of foods they buy at the grocery store and where they are located. An optional suggestion: Make copies of the story to send home to parents and/or guardians for family discussion.

Guess That Snack

Objective

Students will identify healthful snacks in each of the healthful food groups.

Life Skill

I will eat healthful snacks.

Materials

Large paper grocery bags, scissors, colored markers or crayons

Motivation

1 Review the healthful food groups and the kinds of foods that belong to each.

2 Divide the class into groups of four. Give each student a grocery bag large enough to fit over the student's head. Each group is to illustrate a food from each of the four healthful food groups. For example, one student might draw an apple on the bag to show the fruit and vegetable group. Have the students cut out eyes on each bag.

Apple
Fruit and Vegetable Group

Ice Cream Cone
Milk Group

Bread
Grain Group

Chicken Drumstick
Meat Group

3 Mix the bags up so that the student does not have his or her own bag. Have the students close their eyes and then put the bags over their heads. The students cannot see the bags on their own heads although they can see out.

4 Each student is to ask other students questions that can be answered by yes or no to help guess what food (s)he is. When the student guesses what food (s)he is, (s)he must tell to what group the food belongs before removing the bag from his/her head.

Evaluation

After the learning activity, collect all the bags. Students must identify the food group to which the snack on each bag belongs.

Name That Food

Objective ▶ Students will identify foods by their sizes and textures and will categorize them into their correct food groups.

Life Skill ▶ I will eat a balanced diet.

Materials ▶ Large bag, variety of different foods that can be handled by students-figs, radishes, etc., blindfolds

Motivation ▶

1 Place all the different foods into a large bag. Show the bag to the class. Explain that students are going to take turns putting their hands into the bag and selecting a food while they are blindfolded. They are to feel the food and try to guess what it is. Optional: they might ask the class questions about the food that can be answered yes or no.

2 Place all of the foods in front of the class. Explain to students that the foods belong to five groups. Have the students put the foods into five groups. They should tell what the five groups are and why they put each food into each group.

3 Review the four healthful food groups and the others group.

- *Milk group* is milk and foods made with milk. These foods help you have strong bones and teeth.
- *Meat group* is beef, poultry, fish, eggs, and nuts. These foods keep your muscles strong and help you grow.
- *Fruit and vegetable group* is apples, grapes, carrots, cauliflower, broccoli, beans, and other fruits and vegetables. These foods help you grow and keep your eyes, skin, and hair healthy.
- *Grain group* foods include wheat, oats, rice, barley, rye, breads and cereals. These foods provide energy and help you have daily bowel movements.

- *Others group* consists of foods which are high in fats, sugars, and salt. Pretzels, potato chips, soft drinks, candy, cakes, and pies are in this group.

Have students plan a packed lunch in which they choose a variety of foods from the healthful food groups. Emphasize the importance of including several servings of fruits, vegetables, and grains.

Make A Meal

Objective

Students will plan meals that contain plenty of servings of fruits, vegetables, and grains and meet the seven dietary guidelines.

Life Skill

I will choose foods that meet dietary guidelines.

Materials

Paper plates, scissors, glue, crayons, napkins, plastic forks, plastic spoons, plastic knives, plastic cups, magazines showing foods

Motivation

1 Review the healthful food groups with students. These are the milk group, meat group, fruit and vegetable group, and grain group. Emphasize to students the importance of choosing low-fat foods from the milk group and including beans, fish, poultry, and legumes and limiting red meat from the meat group. Also, emphasize the importance of eating plenty of fruits, vegetables, and grains. Explain that fruits, vegetables, and grains are helpful in protecting against cancer and heart disease.

2 Review the dietary guidelines with students.

  • Eat a variety of foods.
  • Maintain a healthful weight.
  • Choose a diet low in fat, saturated fat, and cholesterol.
  • Choose a diet with plenty of vegetables, fruits, and grain products.
  • Use sugar only in moderation.
  • Use salt/sodium only in moderation.
  • If an adult, drink alcoholic beverages only in moderation.
    (optional to cover this guideline).

3 Divide students into groups of four. Each group should have four paper plates, plenty of magazines with pictures of foods, glue, and scissors. Each group is to plan three meals for a day and one snack. On the back of the four paper plates they are to write: breakfast, lunch, dinner, and snack. Then on the front side of the paper plate, they are to glue pictures of the foods they have selected for the three meals and the snacks. Have them select low-fat foods as choices from the milk group and fish, beans, legumes, or poultry as choices from the meat group. Also, have them find several kinds of fruits, vegetables, and grains for their meals and snacks.

4 After students have finished their meals and glued them to the plates, have each student put a plate in front of himself/herself. Teach students to set the table correctly using the napkins and plastic cups, forks, knives, and spoons. Discuss table manners.

Evaluation

Have each group share their three meals and snack. They can share reasons why they selected low-fat foods from the milk group and beans, fish, poultry, or legumes from the meat group. They can tell reasons for including plenty of fruits, vegetables, and grains. Have each student share a dietary guideline that was followed when planning the meals and snacks.

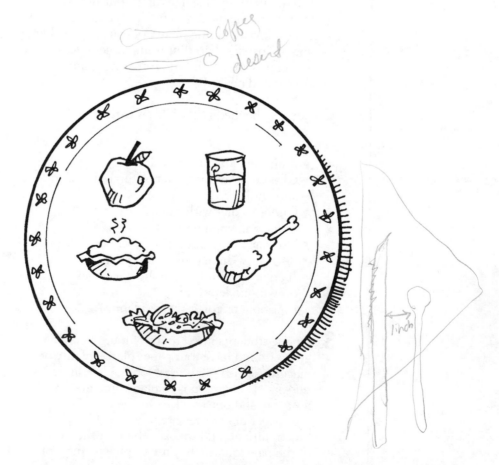

Fast Foods

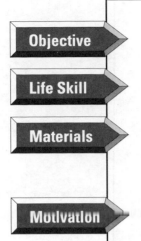

Objective

Students will identify healthful foods they can order at fast food restaurants.

Life Skill

I will follow dietary guidelines when eating at fast food restaurants.

Materials

Teaching Master, "Nutrition in Fast Foods," on page 261, tape recorder, recording of commercials for foods at fast food restaurants, menus from fast food restaurants

Motivation

1 Play the commercials for foods at fast food restaurants. Ask students which foods they enjoy the most. Have them list on paper the foods from a fast food restaurant that they might enjoy eating for lunch.

2 Review the dietary guidelines with students.

- Eat a variety of foods.
- Maintain a healthful weight.
- Choose a diet low in fat, saturated fat, and cholesterol.
- Choose a diet with plenty of vegetables, fruits, and grain products.
- Use sugar only in moderation.
- Use salt/sodium only in moderation.
- If an adult, drink alcohol only in moderation.

3 Use the Teaching Master, "Nutrition in Fast Foods," for review. Have students find the foods they wanted to order on the chart to learn how much fat and sodium are in them. Also, examine the caloric count.

4 Provide students with copies of menus from fast food restaurants. If the fast food restaurants in your community do not have paper menus to take home, ask selected students to visit these restaurants prior to teaching this lesson and copy the food selections on a sheet of paper to share with the class.

5 Have students decide if there are choices that are healthful at the fast food restaurants in their community. What healthful meals might they order?

Have students make pamphlets that give guidelines for eating healthful foods at fast food restaurants in their community. They should have a clever title for their pamphlets. They should mention the healthful food groups and dietary guidelines. They should mention selections that are available at different fast food restaurants that persons frequent.

Nutrition in Fast Foods

Item	Calories	Protein (g)	Carbohydrates (g)	Fats (g)	Sodium (mg)
McDonald's Big Mac	541	26	39	31	962
Burger King Whopper	606	29	51	32	909
Burger Chef Hamburger	258	11	24	13	393
Dairy Queen Cheese Dog	330	15	24	19	N.A.*
Taco Bell Taco	186	15	14	8	79
Pizza Hut Thin 'N Crispy Cheese Pizza (1/2 of 10-in. pie)	450	25	54	15	N.A.*
Pizza Hut Thick 'N Chewy Pepperoni Pizza (1/2 of 10-in. pie)	560	31	68	18	N.A.*
Arthur Treacher's Fish Sandwich	440	16	68	18	836
Burger King Whaler	486	18	64	46	735
McDonald's Filet-O-Fish	402	15	34	23	709
Long John Silver's Fish (2 pieces)	318	19	19	19	N.A.*
Kentucky Fried Chicken Original Recipe Dinner (3 pieces chicken)	830	52	56	46	2285
Kentucky Fried Chicken Extra Crispy Dinner (3 pieces chicken)	950	52	63	54	1915
McDonald's Egg McMuffin	352	18	26	20	914
Burger King French Fries	214	3	28	10	5
Arthur Treacher's Coleslaw	123	1	11	8	266
Dairy Queen Onion Rings	300	6	33	17	N.A.*
McDonald's Apple Pie	300	2	31	19	414
Burger King Vanilla Shake	332	11	50	11	156
McDonald's Chocolate Shake	364	11	60	9	329
Dairy Queen Banana Split	540	10	91	5	N.A.*

Data supplied by the companies to the Senate Select Committee on Nutrition and Human Needs. *N.A. = not available

Fruit and Vegetable Recipe Cards

Objective

Students will identify fruits and vegetables and the vitamins and minerals that are found in them.

Life Skill

I will eat at least five servings of fruits and vegetables each day.

Materials

Index cards, recipe books, magazines and newspapers with recipes, file box for index cards

Motivation

1 Discuss the dietary guidelines and the guidelines from the American Institute for Cancer Research. The dietary guidelines suggest that a person "choose a diet with plenty of vegetables, fruits, and grains." The American Institute for Cancer Research recommends at least five to six servings of fruits and vegetables a day.

2 Have students identify as many fruits and vegetables as they can. Fruits include: apples, bananas, blackberries, blueberries, cantaloupe, coconut, cranberries, grapefruit, kiwi, lemons, limes, musk melon, oranges, pears, pineapples, raspberries, strawberries, tomatoes, and watermelon. Vegetables include: artichokes, asparagus, beans(green), beans(lima), beans(navy), beans(waxed), beets, broccoli, brussels sprouts, cabbage, carrots, cauliflower, celery, chard, corn, cucumber, dandelion greens, eggplant, kohlrabi, leeks, lettuce, mushrooms, okra, onion, parsnips, peas, peppers, potatoes, radishes, rutabagas, sauerkraut, spinach, squash, sweet potatoes, tomatoes, turnips, yams, and zucchini.

3 Have students copy this list on a sheet of paper. Using their health textbooks or other references, they are to identify the vitamins and minerals found in each.

4 Divide students into groups to browse through recipe books, magazines, and newspaper clippings to find recipes for foods made with a variety of fruits and vegetables. Give each group ten index cards. They can copy the recipes that look appealing to them on the recipe cards.

5 Have the groups share the recipes they selected with the other groups. Collect all of the index cards and place them into the file box. Have each student select one recipe card to share with his or her family. The student should select a recipe that his or her family has not tried.

Evaluation

Have students identify six fruits and vegetables that they would enjoy eating tomorrow. Have them identify the vitamins and minerals found in each.

What Vitamin Am I?

Objective ▷ Students will be able to identify the sources, functions, and deficiencies for various vitamins.

Life Skill ▷ I will eat a balanced diet that contains the vitamins needed for optimal health.

Materials ▷ Post-its, marker

Motivation ▷ **1** Review facts about vitamins.

Vitamin A. *Sources*-carrots, sweet potatoes, liver, yams; *Functions*-night vision, bone formation; *Deficiency*-rough skin, night blindness, bone growth failure.

Thiamine. *Sources*-nuts, fortified cereals, peas, beans, pasta; *Functions*- normal appetite, digestion, healthy nervous system; *Deficiency*-muscle weakness, leg cramps, poor memory.

Riboflavin. *Sources*-whole milk, cottage cheese, eggs, yogurt; *Functions*-metabolism, energy production, healthy eyes and skin; *Deficiency*-cracks in the mouth, sore tongue, visual disturbance.

Niacin. *Sources*-fortified cereals, liver, fish, peanuts; *Functions*-normal digestion, appetite, use of carbohydrates, healthy skin and nervous system; *Deficiency*-diarrhea, skin disorders.

Vitamin B6. *Sources*-whole grain cereals, liver, red meat; *Functions*-helps form red blood cells, metabolism of carbohydrates, fats, and proteins; *Deficiency*-anemia, skin disorders, nervous disturbances.

Folic Acid. *Sources*-whole grain bread, broccoli, lean beef; *Functions*-blood formation, enzyme function; *Deficiency*-anemia.

Ascorbic Acid. *Sources*-oranges, lemons, limes, tomatoes. *Functions*-helps body resist infection, strengthens blood vessels, forms cement to hold cells together; *Deficiency*-loose teeth, gum disease, scurvy, bruising.

<u>Calciferol.</u> *Sources*-fortified dairy products, tuna, sunlight, fish liver oils; *Functions*-helps body use calcium and phosphorus to strengthen bones and teeth; *Deficiency*-soft bones, rickets, soft teeth.

<u>Tocopherols.</u> *Sources*-eggyolks, wheat germ, corn oil, vegetable oil; *Functions*-keeps oxygen from destroying Vitamin A; *Deficiency*- breakdown of red blood cells.

2 Write the names of each of the vitamins on Post-its. Make enough Post-its so that each student will have one. Do not show them to students. Have the students form a line. Place a Post-it with the name of a vitamin written on it on the back of each student.

3 The students are to guess what vitamin they are. They can ask other students questions that can be answered "yes" or "no." For example, a student might have the Post-it which says "ascorbic acid." This student does not know what vitamin is written on the Post-it on his/her back. The student asks a classmate, "Am I found in squash?" The classmate answers "no." The student asks another classmate, "Am I found in limes?" This classmate answers "yes." The student thinks he/she knows which vitamin is written on the Post-it and asks, "Am I ascorbic acid?" The classmate says, "Yes."

4 When a student guesses the vitamin correctly, he or she puts the Post-it on his or her front. The student continues helping other classmates guess what vitamins they are.

When all students have correctly guessed which vitamin they are, they are to form a group with classmates who are the same vitamin. The group is to make up a song or jingle about their vitamin that tells its sources, functions, and deficiency.

Evaluation

Mineral Match Game

Objective

Students will be able to identify sources, functions, deficiencies, and relevant facts about various minerals.

Life Skill

I will eat a balanced diet that contains the minerals I need for optimal health.

Materials

Paper, marker for each student

Motivation

1 Review facts about minerals.

Calcium. *Sources*-milk, cheese, cottage cheese, yogurt; *Functions*-strong bones and teeth, regular heartbeat, iron metabolism, healthy nervous system; *Deficiency*-osteoporosis, rickets; *Facts*-to be absorbed vitamin D is needed, most abundant mineral in the body.

Chlorine. *Sources*-table salt; *Functions*- aids in digestion, keeps the body limber; *Deficiency*-loss of hair and teeth; *Facts:* helps the liver remove waste.

Iodine. *Sources*-iodized table salt, kelp, seafood; *Functions*-energy, mental alertness, growth, aids in manufacture of thyroid; *Deficiency*-goiter, hypothyroidism; *Facts*-thyroid gland has two-thirds of the body's iodine.

Iron. *Sources*-oatmeal, red meat, liver, egg yolk; *Functions*-forms red blood cells, growth, prevents fatigue; *Deficiency*-anemia; *Facts*- women lose iron during menstrual periods, needed for use of B vitamins.

Magnesium. *Sources*-grapefruit, apples, dark green vegetables, lemons, nuts; *Functions*-fights depression, prevents heart attacks, promotes healthy teeth; *Deficiency*-depression, insomnia, nervousness; *Facts*-helps relieve stress, lacking in persons with alcoholism.

Phosphorus. *Sources*-whole grains, eggs, nuts, fish, poultry; *Functions*-healthy gums and teeth, growth and repair of cells; *Deficiency*-rickets;

Facts-helps maintain regular heart rate, present in all cells.

Potassium. *Sources*-oranges, bananas, green leafy vegetables; *Functions*-reduces blood pressure, helps oxygen flow to brain, helps with waste removal from body; *Deficiency*-edema, low blood sugar; *Facts*-regulates the body's water balance, stress can cause a deficiency.

Sodium. *Sources*-carrots, beets, shellfish; *Functions*-helps nerve and muscles function, prevents heat prostration; *Deficiency*-difficulty digesting enzymes; *Facts*-high intake depletes potassium, high intake may increase blood pressure.

Sulfur. *Sources*-eggs, fish, lean beef, cabbage; *Functions*-healthy hair and skin, helps B vitamins with metabolism, fights bacterial infections; *Deficiency*-unknown; *Facts*-skin problems treated with sulfur creams.

Zinc. *Sources*-wheat germ, eggs, lamb chops; *Functions*-growth, mental alertness, helps decrease cholesterol deposits; *Deficiency*-hardening of the arteries; *Facts*- useful in treating brain disorders.

2 Divide the class into teams of five to play mineral match. Have each team choose a name. Write the names of the teams on the chalkboard. Each student needs a marker and paper.

3 To play mineral match, you are to ask questions to the class and each student is to write an answer on his or her paper without knowing the answer that his or her teammates are writing. For example, you might ask, "What is a food that is a good source of potassium?" Every student writes an answer.

4 To get the team scores for mineral match, team members hold their papers up and you check to see how many matches there are. For example, two students might have written "banana," one student might have written "orange juice," and two other students might have written "green leafy vegetables." This team has two matches so the team receives four points. Now suppose three of the students had said "banana" and two had said "green leafy vegetables." They would be rewarded five points. Record the points for each team next to their names on the chalkboard. Continue playing while you review information about minerals by asking questions.

Have students list foods that they ate the previous day. Have them identify the minerals in the foods. Discuss whether their diets are rich in minerals.

I'm Going to the Grocery Store to Buy Vegetables

Objective

Students will name vegetables that can be eaten to meet dietary guidelines.

Life Skill

I will eat at least three servings of vegetables each day.

Materials

None

Motivation

1 Have students simulate the game, "I'm going on a trip and I'm going to take..." In this simulation, they are going to substitute the words, "I'm going to the grocery store and I'm going to buy..." The first student begins by naming a vegetable that he or she might buy, for example, broccoli. The next student continues by saying, "I'm going to the grocery store and I'm going to buy broccoli and ... corn." Continue with each student repeating in correct order the vegetables other students have named and adding a vegetable to the list. Some vegetables that might be named include: artichokes, asparagus, green beans, lima beans, navy beans, waxed beans, beets, broccoli, brussels sprouts, cabbage, carrots, cauliflower, celery, chard, corn, cucumber, dandelion greens, eggplant, kale, kohlrabi, leeks, lettuce, mushrooms, okra, onion, parsnips, peas, peppers, potatoes, radishes, rutabagas, sauerkraut, spinach, squash, sweet potatoes, tomatoes, turnips, yams, and zucchini.

2 Mention dietary guideline #4 to students. This guideline states, "Choose a diet with plenty of vegetables, fruits, and grain products." It has been suggested that persons eat five servings from the fruit and vegetable group each day with at least three servings being vegetables and two servings being fruits.

Evaluation

Have students make a list of vegetables their families might eat for dinner for one week. Then have them make a grocery list of the vegetables they would need to buy. Emphasize the need for variety to obtain adequate vitamins and minerals. Have students share their lists with their families.

Going on a picnic

Thin Is In

Objective

Students will discuss eating disorders, anorexia nervosa, and bulimia and will identify pressures to be thin.

Life Skill

I will have a plan for weight management that is based on a realistic and healthful body image.

Materials

Magazines, tape recorder

Motivation

1 Review information about eating disorders. An eating disorder is a food related dysfunction in which a person changes eating habits in a way which is harmful to the mind and body. Anorexia nervosa is an eating disorder in which a person is preoccupied with being excessively thin. Bulimia is an eating disorder in which a person has uncontrollable urges to eat excessively then goes to sleep or most likely, engages in self-induced vomiting. Both anorexia nervosa and bulimia are most common in females who are perfectionists, have low self-esteem, and have an unrealistic body image. These eating disorders have serious consequences. Persons with anorexia nervosa and bulimia frequently use diuretics and laxatives to lower their body weight. This can deplete the body of water and potassium. Too little potassium affects heart beat rate. Excessive use of diuretics to force urination damages kidneys. Persons with bulimia frequently engage in self-induced vomiting which causes tearing and bleeding of the gums, stomach, and esophagus. Both persons with anorexia nervosa and bulimia have low self-esteem and frequent bouts of depression. Psychological as well as medical help is needed.

2 Have students analyze magazines to find examples of pressures on teenagers to be thin. Students also might record commercials and advertisements from radio and television with these pressures to share with their classmates.

3 Divide the class into groups to develop and perform skits which illustrate pressures on teenagers to have a perfect body. Some of the skits can focus on pressures on females to be very thin. Others might focus on the pressures the males feel they have on them for a specific body image.

4 After students perform their skits for their classmates, discuss ways in which these pressures affect the self-concepts of teenagers. Have students discuss what it means to have a realistic body image.

Evaluation

Have students pretend that they are a physician who is a columnist for a teenage magazine. They have received the following letter from a concerned teenager to which they must write a response.

> Dear Doctor: It is almost bathing suit weather and I don't like the way my body looks in my bikini. I have been starving myself and taking diuretics and laxatives to lose as much weight as possible, but I'm still not satisfied. Any tips for extra weight loss? Pudgy

Healthy Heart Guide To Eating Out

Objective

Students will identify restaurants in their community that follow the American Heart Association Guidelines for Eating Out.

Life Skill

I will eat at restaurants which appear in the American Heart Association Dining-Out Guide or I will call a restaurant ahead and ask if they will prepare my food using the AHA guidelines.

Materials

American Heart Association Dining-Out Guide for your community, and newspaper, magazine, or telephone book listing of restaurants in your community

Motivation

1 Explain that the American Heart Association is committed to helping people eat foods which promote heart health. Because of their interest, they have examined foods prepared at restaurants, hotels, and on airlines. They have made recommendations as to how foods might be prepared. The AHA suggests eating at restaurants that are willing to:

- serve margarine rather than butter with the meal.
- serve skimmed milk rather than whole milk.
- prepare food using vegetable oil (corn, soy, sunflower, safflower) or margarine made with vegetable oil rather than butter.
- trim visible fat off meat or skin off poultry.
- broil, bake, steam, or poach meat, fish, or poultry rather than saute or deep fry.
- limit portion size to four to six ounces of cooked meat, fish, or poultry.
- leave all butter, gravy, or sauce off an entree or side dish.
- serve fresh fruit or fruit in light syrup for dessert.
- prepare a dish without added salt or monosodium glutamate (MSG).
- accommodate special requests if made in advance by telephone or in person.
- have a special seating area for nonsmokers.

2 Have students examine newspaper, magazine, or telephone book listings of restaurants in their community. If there is an American Heart Association Dining Out Guide for your community, have them check to see which restaurants appear in this Guide. Then have them make a list of the restaurants which do not appear in the Guide. The students can assign themselves one or more of the restaurants on the list. They are to call the restaurant and ask if they might have food prepared to meet the AHA guidelines (you can write the above list on the chalkboard and they can copy it for reference). Have them write down the response of the person with whom they speak from the restaurant. Have students share findings with classmates.

Evaluation

Give students a quiz in which they are asked to (1) identify at least six ways foods might be prepared to meet American Heart Association Guidelines and (2) list at least five restaurants in their community that will agree to follow these guidelines.

Create A Cancer Prevention Commercial

Objective

Students will identify the American Cancer Society dietary guidelines for reducing the risk of cancer.

Life Skill

I will avoid obesity, cut down on total fat intake, eat more high-fiber foods, eat foods rich in vitamins A and C, eat cruciferous vegetables, and limit my intake of salt-cured, smoked, and nitrite-cured foods.

Materials

Foods or empty food containers: margarine, high-fiber cereal, whole grain bread, carrot, spinach, peach, orange, grapefruit, cabbage, broccoli, brussels sprouts, bacon, hot dog; construction paper, colored pencils or markers

Motivation

1 Explain to students that many researchers believe that at least thirty-five percent of cancers are related to diet. The American Cancer Society has identified dietary guidelines that may help to reduce the risk of cancer. These guidelines are as follows:

Avoid obesity. The risk of breast, colon, and uterine cancers increases if you are 40% above your recommended weight. A physician can help you make and follow a sensible weight management plan.

Cut down on total fat intake. Recent evidence indicates that a diet high in fat, especially animal fats, increases the likelihood of breast, colon, and prostate cancers. Decreasing intake of fatty foods also helps control weight.

Eat more high-fiber foods. Studies suggest that eating a high-fiber diet helps to reduce the risk of colon cancer. Eating a variety of high-fiber foods also may help control weight as these foods may be substituted for fats. Many fruits and vegetables are high-fiber foods and provide minerals and vitamins.

Include foods rich in vitamins A and C in your daily diet. These two vitamins are believed to lower the risk of cancers of the larynx, esophagus, and the lung. Vitamin A is found in deep yellow fresh vegetables such as squash and sweet potatoes. It is also in fruits such as cantaloupe, apricots, and peaches. Vitamin C is found in citrus fruits such as oranges, grapefruits, limes, and lemons.

Include cruciferous vegetables in your diet. Cabbage, cauliflower, brussels sprouts, and broccoli are cruciferous vegetables. These vegetables release indoles which help protect against cancer.

Eat limited amounts of salt-cured, smoked, and nitrite-cured foods. By-products in these foods are linked to cancers of the stomach and esophagus.

Avoid alcohol. Heavy alcohol drinkers have an increased risk of cancers of the mouth, larynx, throat, esophagus, and stomach.

2 Divide students into groups to create cancer prevention commercials. They are to create a commercial that promotes eating or not eating a specific food. For example, one of the commercials might promote drinking orange juice. Students might give a clever name to the brand of orange juice. The commercial should say in a clever way that drinking orange juice may lower the risk of cancers of the larynx, esophagus, and lung.

3 Have students perform their commercials for classmates.

Evaluation

Have students make pamphlets that identify the dietary guidelines for reducing the risk of cancer using the construction paper, colored pencils, and markers.

Count Those Calories

Objective

Students will explain how to balance caloric intake with caloric expenditure to maintain weight, gain weight, and reduce weight.

Life Skill

I will maintain my desirable weight.

Materials

Desirable weight chart for teenagers

Motivation

1 Discuss weight management. Weight management is a plan to maintain desirable weight. Weight management is based on caloric intake (foods) and caloric expenditure (energy needed for daily activities and exercise). Use the chalkboard to write the following facts. Explain each.

3500 Calories = 1 pound of fat
500 extra Calories eaten per day for a week (seven days) = 1 pound weight gain in a week
500 extra Calories burned per day for a week (seven days) = 1 pound weight loss in a week

2 Have students compute the number of Calories that they need each day. To do this, they are to multiply their ideal weight times the activity code which describes them. The activity codes appear below:

Couch Potato (code = 13). I spend most of my time watching TV and doing school work. I do not move about much.

Less than Lazy (code = 14). I walk slowly and do household chores. I stand and move my arms now and then.

Maybe Mover (code = 15). I am a moderate mover. I stand and move about to do activities such as cleaning my room. I enjoy walking moderately fast.

Enthusiastic about Activity (code = 16). I like heavy work and vigorous movement. I walk quickly and exercise for fun.

Moving Lifestyle (code = 17). I spend most of my time in activities that are physically demanding. I have a regular vigorous exercise program such as running.

Evaluation

After students have computed the number of Calories they need each day to maintain their ideal weights, have them compute how many Calories they need if they wanted to lose 2 pounds of fat per week. Then have them compute how many Calories they need if they wanted to gain two pounds per week.

Personal Fitness is the area of health that examines the components of physical fitness, the benefits of physical fitness, how to make a physical fitness plan, kinds of exercises to include in a physical fitness plan, training principles to follow, and guidelines for the prevention of injuries.

The Components of Physical Fitness

Physical fitness is the condition of the body as a result of participating in exercises that promote muscular strength, muscular endurance, flexibility, cardiovascular endurance, and a healthful percentage of body fat. **Muscular strength** is the amount of force the muscles can exert as they are used to lift, pull, and push. **Muscular endurance** is the ability to use muscles for an extended period of time. **Flexibility** is the ability to bend and move the body in different ways. **Cardiovascular endurance** is the ability to do activities which require oxygen for an extended period of time. **Healthful body composition** is a high ratio of lean tissue to fat tissue.

A person who has achieved a level of muscular strength, muscular endurance, flexibility, and cardiovascular endurance and who has a healthful body composition is **physically fit.** There are different tests to measure physical fitness, but two tests, The President's Challenge and The AAHPERD Physical Best, are commonly used in schools. The President's Challenge includes five tests: curl-ups, pull-ups, v-sit reach, one-mile walk/run, and shuttle run. The Physical Best also includes five tests: modified sit-ups, pull-ups, sit and reach, one-mile walk/run, and body composition testing. Curl-ups and modified sit-ups measure abdominal muscular strength and endurance. Pull-ups measure arm and shoulder muscular strength and endurance. The v-sit reach and the sit and reach measure the flexibility of the lower back and thighs. The one-mile walk/run measures cardiovascular endurance while the shuttle run measures leg muscle strength and endurance. A skinfold measurement is used to measure the amount of body fat to determine body composition. Students can earn awards for achieving specific levels of

fitness on the President's Challenge and the Physical Best. The awards are a patch that can be sewn on a shirt or jacket. Adults can earn a patch from the President's Council on Physical Fitness and Sports for participating in sports activities which promote fitness. Patches are given for a variety of sports. The participant keeps a log of the activities, the intensity and the duration, and submits them when specific criteria are met.

Benefits of Physical Fitness

There are numerous health benefits derived from obtaining a desirable level of physical fitness. Being physically fit promotes cardiovascular health, reduces the incidence of cancer, helps to control the effects of harmful stress, promotes weight management, and improves the strength and condition of bones, muscles, and joints.

Figure 9-1
Calculating Heart Rate

A   **B**

You can take your heart rate (a) at your wrist, or (b) at one of the carotid arteries in your neck.

PERSONAL FITNESS

9

There are numerous ways in which being physically fit can promote cardiovascular health. When a person exercises, the heart muscle becomes stronger. This has a positive effect on cardiac output. **Cardiac output** is the amount of blood pumped by the heart to the body each minute. Another way of saying this is, cardiac output is equal to the heart rate multiplied by stroke volume. **Heart rate** is the number of times that the heart beats each minute forcing blood into the arteries. **Stroke volume** is the amount of blood the heart pumps with each beat. To become physically fit, a person engages in exercises that promote cardiovascular endurance. These exercises strengthen the heart muscle enabling the heart to pump more blood with each beat. This lowers resting heart rate and allows the heart an opportunity to rest between beats. This is accompanied by a reduction in blood pressure which means there is less wear and tear on artery walls.

Exercises that promote cardiovascular endurance have an additional benefit in promoting cardiovascular health. Participating in these exercises for at least twenty minutes, three days per week, increases the ratio of high density lipoproteins in the bloodstream to low density lipoproteins in the bloodstream. **Lipoproteins** are fats in the bloodstream. **High-density lipoproteins** or **HDLs** are fats that transport excess cholesterol to the liver for removal from the body. **Low-density lipoproteins** are fats that form deposits on the artery walls and contribute to the development of atherosclerosis.

Many people are aware of the health benefits of exercise with regard to cardiovascular disease while not as many are aware of the health benefits with regard to cancer. A study at the Harvard School of Public Health revealed that females age 10-12 who participated in team sports at least twice a week for two hours had a lower incidence of breast and colon cancer when they were older. This is believed to be due to the positive influence that regular exercise has on the menstrual cycle and the effect that it has on promoting regular bowel movements. There is an additional way in which exercise may reduce the risk of cancer. One of the risk factors for cancer is being overweight. Persons who exercise regularly are better able to control their weight.

Regular exercise also benefits persons who have or have had cancer. Researchers have found that persons undergoing treatment for cancer were better able to

Figure 9-2
Stretching to Increase Flexibility

Before stretching, run in place to gradually increase body temperature. This prevents injury. Do a minimum of five repetitions of each exercise: (a) foot pull, (b) wall stretch, (c) seated toe touch, and (d) knee-chest pull.

tolerate their treatment and maintained a more optimistic attitude if they were involved in an exercise program. Regular exercise also benefited those patients who had surgery and needed to regain muscular strength. Exercising with others also was beneficial as it provided for fellowship and support while simultaneously deriving health benefits.

Participating in an exercise program for physical fitness helps reduce the harmful effects of stress. During the alarm stage of the general adaptation syndrome, adrenaline and sugar are released into the bloodstream to prepare for a quick response to the stressor. Staying in the alarm state for periods of time is harmful as adrenaline increases heart beat rate and blood pressure and depletes vitamin B needed for a healthful nervous system and vitamin C needed for a healthful immune system. And increased blood sugar increases the likelihood of heart disease. Exercise will use up the adrenaline and the blood sugar helping the body to move out of the alarm stage of stress and return to homeostasis. Regular exercise also helps reduce stress by generating overall feelings of well-being. After a person participates in an exercise program for at least 25 minutes, three times per week for seven to ten weeks, his or her body will release beta-endorphins during exercise and continue to release these substances for 90 minutes following completion of exercise. **Beta-endorphins** are substances produced in the brain that help reduce pain and create a feeling of well being. These substances have been linked to the "runner's high" that some runners report having after running at a steady pace for 25 minutes or more.

Participating in an exercise program for fitness helps with weight management in a number of ways. The **energy equation** states that caloric intake needs to equal caloric expenditure for weight maintenance. With regard to children and adolescence, overweight has been linked to inactivity rather than overeating. A regular program of exercise changes the energy equation. During exercise, more calories are expended. Research indicates that the metabolic rate continues to be increased for up to six hours following exercise. Regular exercise influences the appetite by affecting the hypothalmus, a part of the brain. As a result, persons who exercise regularly tend to eat less. Regular exercise also effects body composition by decreasing the percentage of body fat and increasing the amount of lean tissue. A person has more muscle tone thereby looking trimmer.

Participating in an exercise program for fitness improves the strength and condition of bones, muscles, and joints. The weight bearing bones become more dense as a result of regular exercise. As a person ages, (s)he is less likely to develop osteoporosis. **Osteoporosis** is a disease in which the bones become brittle and break easily. Regular exercise improves the strength and condition of muscles. Persons with strong muscles are less likely to become injured when lifting, pulling, or pushing objects. They are more likely to maintain healthful sitting, standing, and walking posture and they are less vulnerable to back pain as they age. The joints also benefit from regular exercise. **Osteoarthritis** is a condition in which there is erosion in the moveable parts of a joint. Regular exercise in which the joints are moved through the full range of motion reduces the effects of this condition in old age.

The Physical Fitness Plan

Because of the many health benefits derived from being physically fit, it is recommended that all persons develop a complete plan for physical fitness that contains 1) exercises for warming up, 2) exercises for flexibility, 3) exercises for cardiovascular endurance and body composition, 4) exercises for muscular strength and endurance, and 5) exercises for cooling down. A person might make a health behavior contract for each of these five parts of the physical fitness plan. Keeping a record of progress and results is important.

Kinds of Exercises

There are different kinds of exercises that can be used when making the physical fitness plan. A person can choose from a variety of aerobic, anaerobic, isokinetic, isometric, and isotonic exercises. An **aerobic exercise** is one in which oxygen is required continually for an extended period of time. These exercises must be performed at target heart rate for at least twenty minutes, three times per week. **Target heart rate** is between 60 and 90 percent of the difference between resting heart rate and maximum heart rate. **Maximum heart rate** is 220 minus your age. Aerobic dancing, swimming distances, running distances, bicycling distances, and walking distances are examples of aerobic exercises.

An **anaerobic exercise** is one in which the body demands more oxygen than is available and a person begins to pant for air. Playing basketball, running sprints, playing soccer, and playing tag are examples of anaerobic exercises. An **isometric exercise** is one in which a muscle is tightened for about five to six seconds and there is no body movement. Pushing against a wall would be an example. An **isokinetic exercise** is one in which a weight is moved through a full range of motion. The exercise machines at health centers and in training rooms provide for isokinetic exercise. An **isotonic exercise** is one in which there is a muscle contraction and a movement of body parts. Lifting weights and chinning are examples of isotonic exercise

Training Principles

When participating in a physical fitness plan, it is important to pay attention to training principles. **Training principles** are guidelines to follow to derive the maximum benefits from an exercise plan. The **principle of warming up** involves three to five minutes of light exercise to gradually begin increased blood flow to prepare joints and muscles for harder exercise. The **principle of cooling down** involves three to five minutes of reduced exercise to slow the heart beat rate and body temperature down and to return blood flow to the heart. The **principle of specificity** involves selecting a specific exercise or activity to provide a specific benefit. The **principle of overload** involves increasing activity levels to develop an increased fitness level. The **principle of progression** involves planning a fitness program in which the intensity and duration of exercise are gradually increased. The **principle of frequency** involves exercising frequently enough to derive the desired benefits.

Common Conditions and Injuries

It is helpful to know something about the most common conditions and injuries that accompany exercise and sport programs. These are: athlete's foot, blisters, bruises, joint injuries, muscle cramps, muscle soreness, muscle strain, side aches, sprains, and stress fractures. **Athlete's foot** is a fungal infection that grows between the toes when feet are not kept dry. It can be treated with a powder or ointment that kills the fungus. **Blisters** are an accumulation of fluid between the layers of the skin that are usually caused from friction from poorly fitting shoes or improper use of equipment. Small blisters should be covered and a first aid cream applied. Large blisters should be lanced by a physician and covered. **Bruises** are discolorations from hemor-

rhaging resulting from blows to the muscles or bones. Applying ice helps reduce bleeding and swelling. **Joint injuries** are injuries to the tissues that surround the joints. Poorly fitting shoes and jarring during exercise contribute to joint injuries. Applications of ice and a period of rest are recommended. **Muscle cramps** are sharp pains that occur when muscles contract involuntarily usually because muscles have not been stretched before hard exercise. Stretching and massaging the muscle can alleviate the soreness. **Muscle strain** is injury and hemorrhaging in muscle tendons that is accompanied by a loss of muscular strength. Applying ice, stretching, and resting the muscle from hard exercise are recommended. **Side aches** are dull sharp pains in the side that occur when there has been inadequate warm up. Because side aches indicate too much too soon, slowing down or taking a break is helpful. **Sprains** are injuries to ligaments that usually occur from twisting particularly the knees and ankles. Applying ice and resting are recommended. **Stress fractures** are hairline breaks in a bone caused by undue stress on or blow to a bone. Stress fractures can be serious, especially if the fracture is through a large segment of the bone. But often, the fracture is not detectable on an x-ray. Some runners suffer stress fractures to bones in the leg or foot due to the pounding on the bones caused by running. The treatment for stress fractures depends on the severity and the area that is affected. Sometimes a cast is placed around the injured body part.

STRRR—ETCH!

Objective

Students will demonstrate stretching exercises which promote flexbility.

Life Skill

I will do stretching exercises for ten to fifteen minutes a day to promote flexibility.

Materials

Spaghetti noodles, pan, water, heating source

Motivation

1 To demonstrate the importance of flexibility, perform the following experiment for students. Cook a few spaghetti noodles. Show students a cooked spaghetti noodle and an uncooked spaghetti noodle. Have a student bend each. The cooked spaghetti noodle will bend in different ways with ease. The uncooked spaghetti noodle will snap when bent.

2 Explain that the cooked spaghetti noodle represents muscles that have been stretched or warmed up. Muscles that have been stretched are flexible. Flexibility is being able to move the joints and muscles through a full range of motion. (For elementary students, flexibility is being able to bend and move in different directions). The uncooked spaghetti noodles represent muscles that have not been warmed up or stretched. When they are moved in different directions, they snap. This might be similar to having a muscle strain because muscles are not stretched. Then, when they are exercised, they lack flexibility and they can be injured.

3 Discuss exercises that help stretch the muscles to keep them flexible. Some examples might be touching the toes with the knees slightly bent to stretch the hamstrings, the muscles in the calves of the legs. Doing wind mills in which the arms make wide circles, stretches the muscles in the upper arms and shoulders. Jumping jacks stretch muscles in the legs as well as the arms and shoulders.

Evaluation

Have students make a health behavior contract in which they write a life skill and make a plan for stretching for 10 to 15 minutes per day.

Perfect Pump Up

Objective

Students will define heart rate, stroke volume, and cardiac output and describe the importance of regular exercise to strengthen the heart muscle.

Life Skill

I will engage in exercises which strengthen my heart muscle for at least 20 minutes three times per week.

Materials

Basketball, pump, needle for pump

Motivation

1 Write the following equation on the chalkboard.

Cardiac output= your heart rate x stroke volume.

Explain that heart rate is the number of times that the heart beats each minute forcing blood into the arteries. Stroke volume is the amount of blood the heart pumps with each beat.

2 Demonstrate the different equations for cardiac output using the basketball, needle, and pump. Pump air into the basketball with quick, short, strokes. Explain that this is one equation for cardiac output. In this equation, cardiac output is maintained from a fast heart rate and a low stroke volume.

3 Now pump air into the basketball using long, powerful strokes. Explain that this is another equation for cardiac output. The pumping action is more forceful so the heart beats less often. When the heart beats, there is a higher stroke volume because more blood is pumped.

4 Compare the two equations for cardiac output. Explain that when the heart rate is fast and the stroke volume is low, a person tires faster. For good health, it is important to lower the resting heart rate and increase the amount of blood pumped with each beat.

5 Discuss the kinds of exercises the make the heart muscle strong. These exercises include swimming, running, walking, bicycling, roller skating, ice skating, etc. These exercises must be done for at least twenty continuous minutes three days per week. They will make the heart muscle strong. A strong heart muscle pumps more blood with each beat. For this reason, a person with a strong heart muscle will have a lower resting heart beat rate.

Evaluation

Have students write the equation for cardiac output. Then have them explain what the cardiac output of someone who was not physically fit might be compared to someone who was physically fit.

Twister

Objective

Students will describe how varicose veins impede blood flow and ways to prevent varicose veins.

Life Skill

I will exercise my leg muscles each day.

Materials

Twisted straw, straight straw, water, glass

Motivation

1 Discuss varicose veins. Varicose veins are bluish, bulging veins usually occurring in the legs where blood returning to the heart has to flow against the pull of gravity. Usually, one-way valves in the leg veins prevent blood from draining backward into the legs. However, if the valves in the leg veins become weakened, blood tends to accumulate in the leg, distending the veins and producing visible varicosities.

2 Demonstrate varicose veins using the two straws. First, have a student try to sip water through the twisted straw. The student will need to suck with force to bring the water through the straw. The water does not flow smoothly. It has a tendency to stay in the glass unless force is used. When a person has varicose veins, blood pressure increases to force blood flow back to the heart. Second, have the student sip water through the straight straw. It is easy to sip the water because there is no obstruction.

3 Discuss ways to prevent varicose veins. One
way is to avoid any cutting off of circulation
which puts pressure on veins. Sitting with legs
crossed puts pressure on veins and should be
avoided. Another way to help prevent varicose
veins is to choose exercises to strengthen the
leg muscles. Exercises such as running, walking,
bicycling, and skating make leg muscles strong.
Strong leg muscles push against veins moving blood
back to the heart.

Evaluation

Have students define varicose veins, tell ways
to prevent them, and write a health behavior
contract in which they write a life skill and
plan for exercising leg muscles.

Move That Fat

Objective

Students will define atherosclerosis, high density lipoproteins, low density lipoproteins, and cholesterol and tell ways to reduce cholesterol in the blood.

Life Skill

I will engage in aerobic exercises for at least twenty minutes three times per week.

Materials

Jar with a lid, water, red food coloring, mineral oil, index cards

Motivation

1 Discuss the health benefits of exercise. Regular exercise helps tone muscle, maintain weight, reduce stress, and reduce the likelihood of injury. In addition, regular exercise may help to prevent heart disease and cancer. Regular vigorous exercise helps prevent atherosclerosis. Atherosclerosis is a disease of the blood vessels in which fat deposits and plaque forms on artery walls narrowing the passageway for blood.

2 Explain that reducing the amount of cholesterol in the blood may help in preventing atherosclerosis.

3 Perform the following experiment. Fill a jar half-way with water. Then add several drops of food coloring. Put the lid on the jar and shake. The water will turn red and resemble blood. Pour the water out. The jar will be clear.

4 Fill the jar half-way with water again. Add mineral oil so that the jar is three-quarters full. Add several drops of red food coloring. Put the lid on the jar and shake. Explain that the mineral oil is cholesterol that is circulating in the blood. Let the jar sit for a while. Then pour out the mixture. The jar will have a film around the inside because of the mineral oil. Explain that cholesterol also is sticky and lines the inner wall of the artery.

5 Discuss the benefits of exercise in reducing cholesterol in the blood. Regular vigorous exercise increases the number of the high-density lipoproteins in the blood and reduces the number of low density lipoproteins in the blood. The HDLs reduce blood cholesterol by carrying it to the liver where it is broken down and excreted. The LDLs carry cholesterol to cells.

6 Identify regular vigorous exercises which increase HDLs and reduce LDLs. They are running, swimming, bicycling, walking, roller skating, ice skating, snow skiing, etc. These exercises must be done at a steady pace for at least twenty minutes three times a week.

Evaluation

Give students an index card. Have them write facts they have just learned. Then have them repeat the experiment done in class for their families. They are to share the facts written on their index cards with their families as they do the experiment.

Sports Flash

Objective

Students will describe the health benefits of regular vigorous exercise.

Life Skill

I will engage in vigorous exercise for at least twenty continuous minutes at least three times per week.

Materials

Tape recorder

Motivation

1 Review important information about the health benefits of exercise.

Exercise and Nutrition. Athletes who participate in long distance events have been known to practice carbohydrate loading. Carbohydrate loading is the practice of eating a diet high in complex carbohydrates beginning a week before an event. This practice is believed to increase the amount of stored energy in the body. This practice may result in weight gain, abnormal heartbeat, and swollen, painful muscles. There has not been much evidence that it increases energy during the long distance event.

Exercise and Cancer. Cancer researchers have found that persons having chemotherapy tolerate this treatment much better if they are engaging in a regular exercise program. Researchers also have other interesting findings regarding exercise and cancer. A study at the Harvard School of Public Health revealed that females ages 10-12 who participated in team sports at least twice a week for two hours had a lower incidence of breast and colon cancer when they were older. Researchers also believe that exercise is a vital way to maintain desirable weight. Being overweight is considered a risk factor for developing cancer.

Exercise and Osteoarthritis. Osteoarthritis is a condition in which there is erosion in the moveable parts of a joint. Regular exercise in which the joints are moved through the full range of motion reduces the effects of this condition in old age.

Exercise and Osteoporosis. Osteoporosis is a disease in which the bones become brittle and break easily. Diet and exercise can help keep bones from becoming brittle. Foods and beverages containing the mineral calcium are important as calcium strengthens bones. Regular vigorous exercise is important as this helps keep bones dense.

Exercise and Stress Management. When a person engages in vigorous exercises for at least twenty minutes three times per week for a six week period, substances that reduce stress are released into the bloodstream. One of these substances is called beta-endorphins. Beta-endorphins are substances that are natural pain relievers and give a person a sense of well-being. Another of these substances is norepinephrine. Norepinephrine is a substance that transmits brain messages along certain nerves and gives a person a feeling of well-being. These substances can create feelings of well-being for as long as 90 minutes after exercise.

2 Divide the class into five groups. Each group is to prepare a two minute sports flash for radio. The sports flash is to be a motivational news brief that provides facts about the health benefits of exercise. Have each group record their sports flash using the tape recorder.

3 Pretend that a sports flash is going to be played every day Monday through Friday for the following week. Play one sports flash each day.

Evaluation

Have students pretend that they are responsible for a sixth sports flash that summarizes the five sports flashes that were aired during the week. They are to write a script for this summary sports flash.

Clogged Arteries

Objective

Students will tell ways in which regular exercise helps to keep arteries clear.

Life Skill

I will do exercises that make my heart strong for at least twenty minutes three times a week.

Materials

Test tube, shortening, yellow food coloring, small spoon

Motivation

1 Discuss the ways in which regular exercise helps the body. Regular exercise can help you stay at a healthful weight, keep your muscles toned, keep you from feeling harmful stress, help your bones to grow, and help you to get a good night's sleep.

2 Explain that there is another way that regular exercise can help the body. Regular exercise helps to move fats out of the bloodstream. Then these fats will not stick to the arteries.

3 Show the test tube. Tell students the test tube will be an artery. Arteries are blood vessels through which blood flows. Take a small spoon of shortening. Put yellow food coloring on it. Put the shortening into the test tube. Tell students the shortening with the yellow food coloring is fat. Explain that when they eat fats that might be in foods like butter, hamburger, and cheese, these fats go into the bloodstream.

4 Name exercises that help move this fat out of the bloodstream. Explain to students that exercises that make the heart muscle strong also keep the arteries clear of fat. Some exercises that do this are walking, running, bicycling, jumping rope, skipping, roller skating, and swimming. These exercises should be done three times a week. It is best to do them for at least twenty minutes.

Evaluation

Have students draw a large heart. Inside the heart they are to write the names of exercises that strengthen the heart and keep the arteries clear. For younger students, have them draw pictures of the exercises.

Smooth Flow

Objective

Students will discuss ways that blood pressure can be reduced.

Life Skill

I will do exercises that strengthen my heart muscle for at least twenty minutes three times a week.

Materials

Tubes from empty paper towel rolls, small opening straws, large opening straws, paper cups, frostie drink

Motivation

1 Explain to students that they are going to learn about their hearts and about blood flow. Have students use tubes from used paper towel rolls. They can listen to one another's heart beating by using the tubes in the same way a stethoscope is used.

2 Explain that when the heart beats, it pushes blood into the arteries. Blood pressure is the force of blood against the walls of the arteries. Ask students to think about the kitchen faucet. Suppose they turn the water on slightly and they put their hand under the water. How forceful would the water feel? The water would not be forceful because it is not moving with much pressure. Now suppose the water was turned up as high as possible. How forceful would the water feel? The water would be very forceful as it is moving faster and harder because there is much pressure. High blood pressure is similiar. The blood moves faster and harder putting more pressure against the artery walls.

3 Put some thick frostie drink into paper cups. Have students drink a sip of frostie with the large opening straws. Explain that the straws were like the arteries and the frostie was blood. The blood moved easily through the arteries.

4 Explain to students that sometimes arteries get clogged and they are not big enough for blood to move through easily. Have them sip the thick frostie drink using the small (narrow) opening straws. They will see how much more difficult it is to sip the frostie. They had to suck with more force. When arteries are narrow, blood pressure increases.

5 Explain that diet and exercise are important in keeping arteries clear. When fats are eaten, they might stick to artery walls making arteries narrow or smaller. Regular exercise helps to move the fat from the arteries so it does not stick to artery walls.

Evaluation

Make a "Be Good To Your Heart" bulletin board. Cut out a large heart. Have students draw or cut out pictures of activities that strengthen the heart muscle and reduce blood pressure- walking, running, swimming, bicycling, skating, rope jumping. Have students place the pictures on the bulletin board and explain how arteries get clogged and why exercise is important.

Save Your Heart

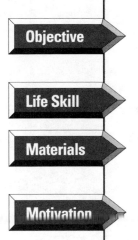

Objective

Students will discuss cardiac output and compute the number of heart beats that can be saved by lowering resting heart beat rate.

Life Skill

I will engage in aerobic exercise for at least twenty minutes three times per week.

Materials

Copies of Teaching Master, "Save Your Heart," on page 299, optional: calculator

Motivation

1 Discuss the benefits of aerobic exercise with students. Aerobic means "with air." Aerobic exercises are those that are done at a continuous pace for twenty minutes. While you are engaged in aerobic exercise, you are breathing regularly and should be able to carry on a conversation. This is why aerobic exercises are "with air." You do not get out of breath. Examples of aerobic exercises are walking, running, rope jumping, bicycling, ice skating, roller skating, swimming, and skiing continuously at a steady pace. Aerobic exercises make the heart muscle stronger.

2 Discuss the benefits of a strong heart muscle. Explain that the heart muscle is like all other muscles. As a result of doing aerobic exercises, the heart muscle becomes larger and stronger. When the heart muscle contracts, it does so with more force.

3 Explain cardiac output. Cardiac output is equal to heart beat rate times stroke volume. Heart beat rate is the number of times the heart beats per minute to supply oxygen to the body's cells. Stroke volume is the amount of blood pumped with each beat. Suppose a person who is physically fit from doing aerobic exercises to strengthen the heart muscle is compared to someone who is not physically fit. The physically fit person will have a stronger heart muscle. In order to pump oxygen to the cells, the resting heart beat rate will be lower and the stroke volume greater than in a physically unfit person.

The heart muscle is larger and stronger, therefore, the heart pumps more blood with each beat. This gives the heart more rest before it needs to beat again.

4 Give each student a copy of The Teaching Master, "Save Your Heart." The answers to the computations the students need to do are as follows:

Resting
Heart Rate 70x60=<u>4200</u> x24=<u>100,800</u> x7=<u>705,600</u> x52=<u>36,691,200</u>

Minus(-) 67x60=<u>4020</u> x24=<u>96,480</u> x7=<u>675,360</u> x52=<u>35,118,720</u>

Heart Beats
Saved   Hour=<u>180</u> Day=<u>4,320</u> Week=<u>30,240</u> Year=<u>1,572,480</u>

Evaluation

Have students make a pamphlet which describes how exercises "Save Your Heart" by lowering resting heart beat rate which provides more rest for the heart between beats.

Save Your Heart

Regular aerobic exercises such as swimming, walking, running, rope jumping, bicycling, roller skating, ice skating, and skiing help to strengthen your heart muscle. They influence the cardiac output equation. Cardiac output is equal to heart rate times stroke volume. Heart rate is the number of times your heart beats each minute to supply oxygen to your body's cells. Stroke volume is the amount of blood pumped with each time the heart beats. When the heart muscle becomes stronger, heart beat rate decreases and stroke volume increases. This has a healthful effect on the heart. The heart does not have to beat as often to pump the same amount of blood to the body. When the resting heart beat rate decreases, the heart gets more rest between beats. You "save your heart" by doing aerobic exercises to make your heart muscle strong and lower your resting heart beat rate.

Suppose you lowered your resting heart beat rate by only three beats per minute from 70 to 67. Complete the chart below to learn how many heart beats you might save in an hour, day, week, and year.

Resting Heart Rate	70x60=_____	x24_____	x7_____	x52_____
MInus(-)	67x60=_____	x24_____	x7_____	x52_____
Heart Beats Saved	Hour=_____	Day=_____	Week=_____	Year=_____

For the next week, plan to do aerobic exercises at least three times. Remember to do them for at least twenty minutes. Write down the three exercises you did next to each of the tennis shoes below. It is alright to do the same exercise all three times.

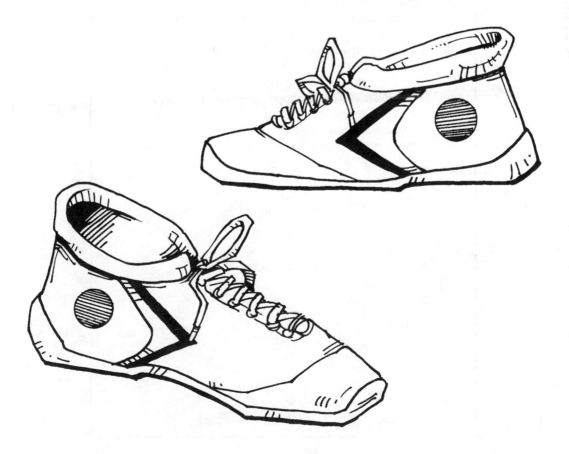

Strong Heart, Weak Heart

Objective

Students will describe why it is important to do exercises that make the heart muscle strong.

Life Skill

I will do exercises that make my heart strong for at least twenty minutes three times a week.

Materials

Poster paper, crayons or markers

Motivation

1 Discuss the heart. Explain that the heart is a muscle. Like other muscles, it gets stronger with exercise.

2 Have the students make a clenched fist. Then have them pound their fists on their desks. Pound at a rate of about 72 beats per minute. Explain that the fist represents their heart. The heart is a muscle. It is pushing blood out each time it beats or pounds.

3 Now talk about exercises that make the heart muscle strong. Explain that you cannot see the heart muscle, but there are ways to know that this muscle is getting exercise. When you are exercising the heart muscle, it pumps faster. What are some exercises that make the heart pump faster? Have students name some. Bicycling, running, rope jumping, skipping, hopping, swimming, ice skating, and roller skating are good examples. Explain that these exercises need to be done for about twenty minutes without stopping. They need to be done about three times a week.

4 Now have students make a fist again. But, this time they are to make a clenched fist and then put the other hand around the clenched fist. Explain that this is a strong heart because the heart muscle is stronger from doing heart exercises. Have students pound their fists on the table. Have them pound slower and harder. Explain that the heart is not pumping as often. Each time the heart pumps more blood is going to body cells than before.

Evaluation

Give students posterboard, crayons, and/or markers. Have them draw themselves doing an exercise to make their heart stronger. Have them share their posters with the class. They can tell what they have learned about exercise and the heart.

Puffed Up

> **Objective**

Students discuss reasons why it is dangerous to use anabolic steroids.

> **Life Skill**

I will not use anabolic steroids and I will report persons who offer these to me to responsible adults and legal authorities.

> **Materials**

Balloons, pins

> **Motivation**

1 Discuss anabolic steroids. Anabolic steroids are synthetic derivatives of the male hormone testosterone that stimulates increased muscle growth. They are usually injected with a needle by persons who want to be stronger for a sport or have a more muscular appearance.

2 Give each student a balloon. Discuss anabolic steroid use. Explain that you are a teenager on the football team who wants to receive praise from teammates. You want to have as many tackles in a game as possible. Instead of working within your natural limits, you allow someone to talk you into injecting anabolic steroids. Have students blow some air into their balloons. Explain that your muscles got somewhat bigger and you were pleased so you injected anabolic steroids again. Have students blow some air into their balloons. Now explain that you are feeling that this is an easy way to improve your muscular strength and you like the way you look, too. Have students blow more air into their balloons.

3 Now explain to students that you were rather short-sighted. You wanted to improve your strength, look better, make more tackles, and gain further recognition, but you did not think ahead. Have students use the pins to break the balloons.

4 Discuss the scientific evidence that indicates that anabolic steroid use is dangerous. In teenage boys, these drugs cause the testes to shrink in size, sperm production to stop, and hair to fall out. They can cause the male to become very aggressive and violent. In teenage girls, there may be abnormal growth of hair on the face, breasts, and chest. The clitoris enlarges and menstruation stops. Long term side effects include kidney damage, liver cancer, and high blood pressure. When a person stops taking anabolic steroids, there are usually withdrawal symptoms including severe depression.

5 Discuss the link between anabolic steroid use and infection with HIV, the virus that causes AIDS. Infection with HIV might result from sharing an infected needle to inject the anabolic steroids.

Evaluation

Explain to students that drug testing involves testing for anabolic steroids. Have them pretend that they are coaching an athletic team. They are going to give a three minute speech on the dangers of anabolic steroids to the players on the team. What will they say? How will they motivate the players to accept their natural body limitations? How might they encourage players to report persons who encourage teenagers to use anabolic steroids?

Sit Tall

Objective

Students will explain why it is important to have correct posture.

Life Skill

I will sit at my desk with correct posture.

Materials

Classroom desks, balloons, scissors, marker, roll of paper, tape

Motivation

1 Discuss posture. Posture is the way you hold your body when you sit, stand, and move.

2 Have a student lie on his/her back on the floor on the roll of paper. Trace the student's body. Cut it out. Blow up balloons. Tape the balloons to the body outline. Explain that the balloons are different body organs. They might be the stomach, heart, liver, etc. Place the body outline with attached balloons at one of the student's desks. Bend the body outline over showing slouching posture. This will put pressure on the balloons.

3 Have students explain what happens when the body is bent over. There is not much room for the body organs. Blood cannot flow as easily to the organs. Explain that the person does not look and feel as good either.

4 Explain that strong muscles help to keep the body in correct posture while they sit at their desks. Have students sit with their feet flat on the floor. Then have them place their hands palms down on their chairs next to their hips. They are to push down while counting to six. Then they are to relax. They will be sitting with correct posture. They have just participated in an exercise that makes the muscles used for correct sitting posture strong.

Evaluation

Have students define posture, name ways that correct posture improves health, and demonstrate an exercise to help sitting posture.

Fitness Concentration

| **Objective** | Students will identify and define six kinds of fitness skills, five types of fitness, and five kinds of exercises. |

| **Life Skill** | I will make and follow a plan in which I participate in a variety of exercises to help me develop physical fitness and fitness skills. |

| **Materials** | Index cards, markers |

| **Motivation** | **1** Review the five types of fitness, six kinds of fitness skills, and five kinds of exercises. |

Five Types of Fitness

- Muscular strength is the amount of force the muscles can exert.
- Muscular endurance is the ability to use the muscles for an extended period of time.
- Flexibility is the ability to bend and move the body in different ways.
- Cardiovascular endurance is the ability to do activities that require oxygen for an extended period of time.
- Healthful body composition is a high ratio of lean tissue to fat tissue.

Six Kinds of Fitness Skills

- Agility is the ability to change your position or direction quickly.
- Balance is the ability to keep from falling.
- Coordination is the ability to use two or more body parts at the same time to do a task.
- Power is the ability to use muscular strength to do an activity.
- Reaction time is the length of time you require to move after you have heard a signal.
- Speed is the ability to move quickly.

Five Kinds of Exercise

- An aerobic exercise is one in which oxygen is required continually for an extended period of time.
- An anaerobic exercise is one in which the body demands more oxygen than is available and you begin to pant for air.
- An isokinetic exercise is one in which you move a weight through a full range of motion.
- An isometric exercise is one in which you tighten your muscles for five to six seconds without body movement.
- An isotonic exercise is one in which there is a muscle contraction and a movement of body part(s).

2 Have students work in pairs to make a set of Fitness Concentration cards. Each set will have 32 cards. Sixteen of the cards will have terms written on them and the other sixteen cards will have the corresponding definitions written on them.

3 Have students play Fitness Concentration in pairs. They are to shuffle their set of sixteen cards and place them face down. Each student takes a turn turning over two cards attempting to match the term with the correct definition. If there is a match, the student keeps the two cards and attempts to make another match. If there is no match, the student loses his/her turn and the other student attempts to make a match. Play continues until all cards have been claimed by one of the two players. The player with the most cards is the winner.

Evaluation

A matching quiz can be used to learn if students can correctly match the 16 terms with their definitions.

Warm Up

Objective

Students will explain why it is important to warm up before doing aerobic exercises.

Life Skill

I will warm up for ten to fifteen minutes before I do exercises to make my heart strong.

Materials

Stick of licorice that has been frozen, stick of licorice at room temperature

Motivation

1 Use the two sticks of licorice to help students understand the importance of warm up before exercise. Ask a student to touch both pieces of licorice and to tell the difference between the two. The student will say that one is cold while the other is not.

2 Tell students these two pieces of licorice are like muscles. One stick is like muscles that are warmed up before exercise and the other stick of licorice is like muscles that are cool because they have not been warmed. Have one of the students twist and bend the warmed licorice. Explain that muscles that have been warmed up are ready to move easily. Have one of the students twist and bend the cold licorice. It will not twist and bend easily. Explain that it might even snap. When muscles are not warmed up, they may become injured, also.

3 Explain how muscles get warmed up. By gradually doing exercises during warm up, blood flows to the muscles. This warms them up and gets them ready for harder exercise.

4 Have students do warm up exercises from the President's Challenge, obtained from the President's Council on Physical Fitness and Sports, Washington, D.C. 20001.

* *Deep Breather*. Stand tall with knees slightly bent. Rise on the toes and slowly circle the arms inward and upward, until the arms are straight overhead. Inhale deeply. Continue circling the arms backward and

downward while lowering the heels and exhaling. This exercise should be done slowly and smoothly. Repeat five times.

- *Swinging March.* Stand up straight with feet shoulder-width apart, hands at the sides. Alternate right and left arms in forward circle motions as if doing the forward "crawl" swimming stroke. At the same time, lift the opposite knee so that when the right arm is circling forward the left knee is raised; the right knee is raised while left arm is moving forward. Do 10 complete circles with each arm, and then switch arms to do the "backstroke." Repeat 10 full circles with each arm.

Evaluation

Have students identify exercises that they enjoy that are strenuous, such as bicycling. Have students tell ways they might warm up before the exercises they identified.

Lean and Mean

| Objective | Students will explain body composition and discuss why exercise and healthful diet are better than starvation for weight loss. |

Life Skill — I will eat healthful foods that are low in Calories and exercise to lose weight.

Materials — Balloons, pins, cellophane tape

Motivation

1 Blow up two balloons. Place a piece of cellophane tape on one of the balloons. Use a pin. Take the balloon without the tape. Explain to students that some persons who want to lose weight starve themselves. Place the pin in the balloon and it will burst. Explain that this leads to quick weight loss. Now take the other balloon. Place the pin in the cellophane tape. Explain to students that other persons who want to lose weight eat a healthful diet. Show them that some air is coming out of the balloon, but not much. Then stick the pin into the cellophane tape again. Explain that these persons continue their diets over a period of time. They want to lose approximately two pounds a week. Then stick the pin into the cellophane tape again. Explain that these persons also exercise regularly. This adds to the weight loss. Ask which style of losing weight is most healthful and why? Who is most likely to keep weight off?

2 Introduce the topic of body composition. Body composition is the percentage of fat tissue and lean tissue that makes up the body. Fat tissue is found beneath the skin and around the internal organs. The percentage of the female body that is stored fat is about 22 to 25%. The percentage of the male body that is stored fat is about 16 to 19%. Females need more stored fat around their breasts and buttocks to protect organs in the reproductive system. Lean tissue consists of muscles, bones, cartilage, connective tissue, nerves, skin, and internal organs.

3 Explain that persons who are physically fit and in optimal health decrease their amount of fat tissue and increase their amount of lean tissue. Persons who starve themselves as a method of weight reduction lose lean tissue. Persons who lose weight slowly and who exercise regularly decrease their amount of fat tissue and increase their amount of lean tissue. In addition to dieting in a more healthful way, these persons look and feel better because they are toning their bodies.

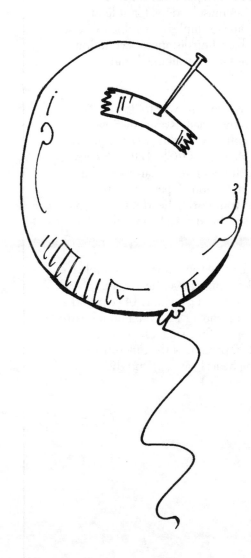

Evaluation

Divide students into groups to design advertisements for healthful weight loss. Their advertisements need to contain facts about body composition. They can think of clever names for weight loss groups.

On Target

Objective	Students will compute their target heart rate.
Life Skill	I will engage in aerobic exercise for at least twenty minutes three times per week at my target heart rate.
Materials	None

Motivation

1 Discuss aerobic exercise. Aerobic exercises are those that require a steady flow of oxygen to body cells for an extended period of time. This is why these exercises must be done for at least twenty minutes. Some examples of aerobic exercises are aerobic dance, bicycling distances, swimming distances, skating distances, walking distances, and cross-country skiing.

2 Explain that there is a specific way to do aerobic exercises so that there is a steady flow of oxygen to body cells. According to the American College of Sports Medicine (ACSM), aerobic exercises must be performed at your target heart rate. Target heart rate is between 60 and 90 percent of the difference between your resting heart rate and your maximum heart rate. Maximum heart rate is 220 minus your age.

3 On the chalkboard, write the following example to illustrate how to determine target heart rate. Use the example of a teenager who is 14 years old and has a resting heart rate of 72. Maximum heart rate is 220 minus 14 or 206. Target heart rate is between 60 and 90 percent of the difference between the resting heart beat (72) and the maximum heart rate (206).

206(maximum heart rate)-72 (resting heart rate)=134

.60 x 134 = 80.4 + 72(resting heart rate) = 152.4

.90 x 134 = 120.6 + 72(resting heart rate) = 192.6

Target heart rate = 152.4 to 192.6 beats per minute

Evaluation

Have students compute their own target heart rates using the formula provided in the example.

If The Shoe Fits

Objective

Students will discuss the importance of wearing appropriate clothing for exercise.

Life Skill

I will wear appropriate tennis shoes and socks that absorb moisture when I exercise.

Materials

Sports tape, wooden board splints, athletic magazines, poster board, scissors, glue, students wearing tennis shoes and socks

Motivation

1 Have one student volunteer. Take the wooden splint board and tape it to the bottom of the foot using the sports tape. Ask the student to try to stand on his/her toes. The student will not be able to do this because it will be uncomfortable. Ask the student to pivot as if he or she was going to move to hit a tennis ball or kick a soccer ball. Again, this is very difficult. Now ask a student who is wearing tennis shoes and socks to stand on toes and to pivot. This student will be able to do this easily.

2 Discuss the importance of wearing appropriate clothing for exercise and sport. Appropriate clothing is comfortable and helps prevent injury by supporting some part of the body. Mention that some people try to participate in exercise and sport without proper shoes. As in the demonstration, they are unable to move as they might. They also might injure parts of their body when they do not have proper support.

3 Discuss other kinds of clothing for exercise and sport. It is always important to wear socks with tennis shoes because socks absorb moisture helping to keep the feet dry. When there is too much moisture between the toes, pathogens have a place to grow. It is always important to dress for the weather when exercising. Clothes help keep the body warmer or cooler depending on the weather. Light colored clothes should be worn when it is very hot. Layered clothes should be worn when it is very cold.

4 Have students make a poster collage of clothes for exercise. They can cut out pictures from the sports magazines and glue them on the poster board.

Evaluation

Have students share their poster collage of clothes for exercise and sport with the class. Have them point to different clothing items and tell why they might be worn.

Mouth Protectors

Objective

Students will discuss the importance of wearing a mouth protector when playing sports.

Life Skill

I will wear a mouth protector when playing sports in which I might have an injury to the teeth, lips, cheeks, or tongue.

Materials

Shoebox, scissors, cellophane wrap, tennis ball, optional: various mouth protectors

Motivation

1 Use a shoebox to make a model of the mouth. Cut teeth in one of the sides of the shoebox. Demonstrate injuries to the teeth using the shoebox mouth and the tennis balls. Toss the tennis ball at the mouth so it strikes the teeth. Explain to students that the number one injury during sports and games is injury to the mouth.

2 Wrap cellophane around the shoebox mouth. Now toss the tennis ball at the mouth and teeth. The cellophane will block the contact between the tennis ball and the teeth. Emphasize the importance of wearing something to protect the mouth and teeth from injury during sports.

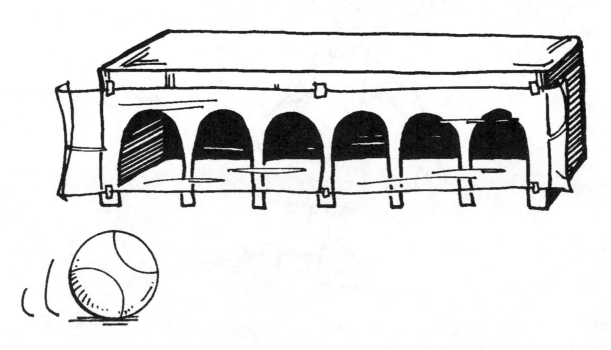

3 Discuss mouth protectors. A mouth protector is a device that helps prevent injury to the mouth, teeth, lips, cheeks, and tongue. There are three kinds of mouth protectors. The stock mouth protector can be purchased at a sports store. It comes in different shapes and sizes. It cannot be adjusted. The mouth-formed protector is made by a dentist and shaped to a person's mouth. It is very comfortable because it was made for the person. The custom-made mouth protector is also made by a dentist. This is the most exact kind. A dentist first mades a mold of the person's teeth. Then the mouth protector is made by putting material over this model. Then the mouth protector will be very exact.

Evaluation

Have students discuss possible ways they might get an injury to the mouth, teeth, lips, cheeks, and tongue. For example, they might get kicked in the mouth playing soccer or a ball might hit their mouth while playing baseball. Have students identify sports they enjoy or think they will enjoy in the future. How will a mouth protector help for each sport?

I-Guard

Objective

Students will discuss the importance of wearing eye guards to protect eyes when playing sports.

Life Skill

I will wear eye guards for sports in which there is a danger of my eyes being injured.

Materials

Two hard boiled eggs, crayon, marble, glass of water, cellophane wrap, magazines, posterboard, glue, paints, crayons, markers

Motivation

1 Use the crayon to draw an eye on each of the hard boiled eggs. Place one of the hard boiled eggs in water. Explain that this is similar to the real eye being in the eye socket and being cushioned with fluids. Drop a marble on the eye so that the hard boiled egg cracks. Explain that it is easy to have an injury when something strikes the eye. The eye can become bruised or the parts of the eye can become detached.

2 Remove the cracked hard boiled egg from the glass of water. Place the other hard boiled egg in the glass of water. Cover the glass with cellophane wrap. Drop the marble so that it hits the cellophane wrap. Explain that the eye is protected and will not become injured.

3 Discuss the importance of wearing eye guards for certain sports. In sports such as racket ball, the ball is traveling fast and from different angles on the court. As players move about, it is difficult to move in time to dodge a ball that is traveling toward the eyes.

Evaluation

Have students make a bulletin board of eyes that they have cut out from magazines or have them draw different eyes on posterboard. Using markers, have them draw eye guards to cover the eyes. Then have them discuss the importance of wearing eye guards for sports.

Balloon Toss

Objective

Students will identify exercises that strengthen different muscle groups.

Life Skill

I will exercise daily to make my muscles stronger.

Materials

Large balloon, roll of paper, marker, crayons

Motivation

1 Discuss exercise. Explain that exercise is moving body muscles to make them stronger. Identify different muscles such as arm muscles, leg muscles, shoulder muscles, and heart muscles. Explain that there are exercises to make all of these muscles strong.

2 Have students sit in a circle. Pass the balloon to each student via the air. When it comes to the student, the student names an exercise (s)he likes to do and hits the balloon to another student who names an exercise (s)he likes to do and hits the balloon to another student, etc. Have students name as many exercises as possible. Some exercises they might name are: running, bicycling, playing badminton, playing tennis, swimming, roller skating, ice skating, skiing, dancing, playing tag, playing kickball, playing baseball, playing basketball, walking, and rope jumping.

3 After students have named many different exercises, have them tell which muscles become stronger when doing each exercise. Discuss the importance of doing a number of exercises so that arm, leg, shoulder, and back muscles as well as the heart muscle become strong.

Use a roll of paper. Have one student lie on the paper and trace the outline of this student's body. Then have students use crayons to draw pictures of exercises for different muscle groups. For example, they might draw a tennis racket on the arm to indicate that the arm muscles are strengthened by playing tennis. They might draw a bicycle where the heart would be to indicate that the heart muscle is strengthened by bicycling.

Sports Expert

Objective

Students will identify common exercise and sport injuries and tell ways to train properly to prevent them.

Life Skill

I will prevent exercise injuries by knowing my body limitations, following safety rules, and training carefully.

Materials

Copies of Teaching Master, "Preventing Exercise Injuries", on page 325.

Motivation

1 Review the five kinds of exercise that might be done to develop physical fitness. *Isometric exercises* are exercises in which muscles are tightened for about five to ten seconds without any corresponding movement of a body part. *Isotonic exercises* are exercises in which there is contraction of a muscle or muscle group with a corresponding movement of a body part. *Isokinetic exercises* are exercises in which weight is moved through an entire range of motion to strengthen muscles. *Aerobic exercises* are exercises in which oxygen is supplied to muscles for an extended period of time. *Anaerobic exercises* are exercises in which there is oxygen debt because the exercise requires more oxygen than is supplied to the body.

2 Review the kinds of injuries that persons might sustain from exercising. *Athlete's foot* is a fungal infection that grows between the toes when feet are not kept dry. *Blisters* are an accumulation of fluid between the layers of skin that are usually caused from friction from poorly fitting shoes or improper use of equipment. *Bruises* are discolorations from hemorrhaging resulting from blows to the muscles or bones. *Joint injuries* are injuries to the tissues that surround the joints that usually result from poorly fitting shoes and jarring the body during exercise. *Muscle cramps* are sharp pains that occur when muscles contract involuntarily usually because muscles have not been stretched before hard exercise. *Muscle soreness* is a dull pain that is felt after exercising muscles that have not been exercised for awhile. *Muscle strain* is injury and hemorrhaging in muscle tendons that is accompanied by a loss of muscular strength. *Side aches* are pains in the side that occur when there has been inadequate warm up. *Sprains* are injuries to ligaments that usually occur from twisting particularly the knee and ankle. *Stress fractures* are minor breaks in the bones that usually result from overuse or a blow.

3 Discuss the importance of training. The *principle of warming up* involves three to five minutes of light exercise to gradually begin increased blood flow to prepare joints and muscles for harder exercise. The *principle of cooling down* involves three to five minutes of reduced exercise to slow the heart beat rate and temperature down and to return blood flow to the heart. The *principle of specificity* involves selecting a specific exercise or activity to provide a specific benefit. The *principle of overload* involves increasing activity levels to develop an increased fitness level. The *principle of progression* involves planning a fitness program in which the intensity and duration of exercise is gradually increased. The *principle of frequency* involves exercising frequently enough to derive the desired benefits.

4 Examine other exercise related information that helps a person train and keeps a person injury free during exercise. *Physical profiling* is an analysis of the kinds of exercises that are best suited for your body. *Biomechanics* is an analysis of how the body moves during exercise. The *RICE treatment* is a procedure for treating injuries that involves resting the injured part, applying ice, applying compression, and elevating the injured part.

5 Give students a copy of Teaching Master, "Preventing Exercise Injuries, on page 325." They are going to be a sports expert. First, follow the directions on the teaching master and write the terms in each of the spaces provided. Then you are going to write the definitions for each of the terms on index cards. Shuffle the cards and place them face down in a pile. Begin by turning the first card over and reading the definition that appears on the card. Students are to place a 1 in the box in which the word appears. You are to label this card with a 1. Continue with card 2 by reading the definition, labelling the card, and having students place a 2 in the box in which the term for the defined word appears. This procedure is continued until one student is a Sports Expert having five boxes in a row completed up or down or vertically. Then check the definitions from the cards that are labelled with the numbers students have written by the terms to be certain students made the correct matches.

Evaluation

A matching test can be given in which students match definitions with terms.

Preventing Exercise Injuries

Directions: Write each of the words listed below in one of the boxes under "Sport." Do not write them in order, but scramble them so that they will appear in different order from your classmates. Then your teacher will read a definition and give you a corresponding number for the definition. Write the number for the definition in the box in which the term appears. You are a sports expert when you have written numbers in five boxes in a row up and down or vertically.

Aerobic exercises
Anaerobic exercises
Athlete's foot
Biomechanics
Blisters
Bruises
Isokinetic exercises
Isometric exercises
Isotonic exercises
Joint injuries
Muscle cramps
Muscle soreness

Muscle strain
Physical profiling
Principle of cooling down
Principle of frequency
Principle of overload
Principle of progression
Principle of specificity
Principle of warming up
RICE treatment
Side ache
Sprain
Stress fracture

S	P	O	R	T

Substance Use and Abuse is that area of health that deals with the different types of chemical substances that can be used and abused. Some of these drugs may be controlled substances such as cocaine and heroin. Alcohol and tobacco are other drugs that fall under this area of health. Regardless of the type of drug used or abused, all drugs will fall under stimulants, depressants, cannabis, hallucinogens, narcotics, inhalants and designer drugs.

Stimulants

Stimulants are drugs that increase the activity of the central nervous system. Stimulants can be called uppers because they cause an increase in heartbeat rate, blood pressure, and brain function.

One of the most common types of stimulants used is caffeine. **Caffeine** is a legal drug that is found in chocolate, coffee, tea, and some aspirin products. Just how harmful caffeine in the form of coffee is has not been concluded. As few as two-and-one-half cups of coffee per day elicits the stress response causing adrenaline and sugar to be released into the bloodstream. Some reports indicate that excessive coffee consumption, meaning ten or more cups per day, can lead to anxiety, diarrhea, restlessness, loss of sleep, and headaches. There have been some indications that excess use of coffee can result in fibrocystic breast condition in women, but that has yet to be proven.

Amphetamines are stimulants that were used at one time as diet pills by people who wanted to lose weight. They are no longer used as diet pills because of the harmful effects that can result. On occasion, amphetamines are used to treat medical conditions such as **narcolepsy**, a condition in which a person has an uncontrollable desire to fall asleep. Amphetamines are also used on occasion as a treatment for **hyperactivity** or higher than normal physical restlessness. Amphetamines help a person who is hyperactive by neutralizing insignificant stimuli in the body.

One of the most significant of the stimulants is cocaine. **Cocaine** is a stimulant drug derived from the coca shrub. When taken, cocaine produces a "rush," or feeling of excitement. This feeling can last from five to thirty minutes. Afterwards, severe depression can occur. Continuous use of cocaine can lead to weight loss, insomnia, and anxiety. Through chronic snorting of cocaine, the lining of the nose can become damaged. This is why chronic cocaine users can often be seen sniffing and rubbing their nose.

For years, it was believed that chronic use of cocaine could cause **psychological dependence** or a mental need for a drug. It is now believed that use of cocaine can result in **physical dependence**, a physical need for a drug. Regular use of cocaine results in tolerance. **Tolerance** is the need to increase the dosage of a drug in order to experience an effect. The frightening aspect of cocaine is its different effects on people who may take the same dosage. Cocaine can cause an unusual interference in signals within the heart chambers, sometimes resulting in heart failure and death. Exactly why this occurs is not known. Studies indicate that cocaine taken along with alcohol is extremely dangerous. To maintain potency when smoked, cocaine may be **freebased** or prepared with volatile substances such as ether.

Crack is another form of cocaine that results from purification with baking soda and water. Crack has been described as looking like slivers of soap but with a hard texture.

Depressants

Depressants are drugs that slow down the workings of the central nervous system. Use of depressants can result in psychological and physical dependence and development of tolerance. **Barbiturates** are depressant drugs that are used to induce sleep and relieve tension. When used in small dosages, barbiturates can cause a decrease in the ability to be responsive and loss of muscle coordination. With increased dosage, they can result in slurred speech, decreased breathing rate, slowed heartbeat, and possible unconsciousness and death.

Barbiturates have played a role in about one-third

SUBSTANCE USE AND ABUSE

10

of all drug-related deaths in the United States. They are extremely dangerous when taken with alcohol. Once a person is physically dependent on barbiturates, medical supervision is needed for withdrawal.

Cannabis

Cannabis is a mixture of crushed leaves and flowers of the cannabis plant. **Marijuana,** the most popular of the cannabis products, is usually smoked in the form of a cigarette or joint. The effects of marijuana are dependent on the amount of its active ingredient, **tetrahydrocannabinol,** or **THC**. In low doses, marijuana use can result in altered perceptions, increased heartbeat rate, and dry mouth and throat. Marijuana affects the nervous system by impairing coordination. Blood pressure can be increased. Use of marijuana can impair the functioning of the immune system thereby leaving a person more susceptible to infections. There is some thought that marijuana can suppress ovulation and alter hormone levels in females. There is speculation that males may suffer impaired fertility. Perhaps one of the more significant results of marijuana use is the development of amotivational syndrome. **Amotivational syndrome** is a lack of desire by people to become motivated to perform daily responsibilities.

Hallucinogens

Hallucinogens are a group of drugs that interfere with a person's ability to use the senses properly. **Peyote** and **mescaline** are two types of hallucinogens that may produce hallucinations including bright lights and geometric designs. **LSD** is a hallucinogen that produces hallucinations including bright colors and altered perceptions of what is real. The effects of LSD may last for as long as 12 hours. The physical effects produced by LSD include increased heartbeat rate and body temperature, headache, and nausea. If a person has a bad trip, anxiety and distorted thoughts may occur.

PCP is a hallucinogen that may be manufactured as a tablet or capsule but it can also be smoked, swallowed, or sniffed. The greatest danger of PCP is its resulting in what is known as **behavioral toxicity** which is the transformation of normal people into insane persons who become violent. These people may get sudden bursts of energy and feel as if they have superior strength. The unpredictability of PCP makes it a very dangerous drug. Large amounts of PCP can result in convulsions, heart failure, and stroke.

Narcotics

Narcotics are opiate drugs that depress the central nervous system. Narcotics are used medically to relieve pain but they are also highly addictive.

Opium is a natural derivative of the opium poppy plant that may be smoked or sniffed as a powder. The two substances that can be extracted from opium are morphine and codeine. **Morphine** is a drug that is used to control pain. When it is prescribed, a patient begins to have an altered perception of pain. Usually, the relief of the pain is due more to the perception than the actual physical effect.

Codeine is produced from morphine. Although it is weaker than morphine, it still can be used as a painkiller. However, codeine is most often used as a liquid for relieving coughs.

Heroin is a narcotic drug that has no medicinal value. In most cases, heroin is injected intravenously. Perhaps one of the greatest concerns today associated with intravenous heroin use is its propensity for transmitting HIV. This is especially a concern since many heroin users share needles and often the needle has blood with HIV on it from an infected person and then is used by another person who then becomes infected.

A person who is dependent on heroin may suffer weight loss, lethargy, and loss of sexual appetite. If a person is denied heroin, withdrawal may occur. Symptoms of withdrawal include chills, fever, sweating, and severe aches and pains.

Inhalants

Inhalants are chemicals that produce vapors resulting in psychoactive effects. The more common inhalants include aerosols, airplane glue, cleaning fluids, and petroleum products such as kerosene. **Nitrous oxide** also known as laughing gas, is another inhalant that is abused.

Physical effects of inhalants include a slowing down of the body activities and a loss of inhibition. Some people believe that use of inhalants is not dangerous. But, serious medical complications can result. Liver failure, kidney failure, respiratory impairment, blood abnormalities, and heart arrythmias can occur.

Amyl nitrate is an inhalant used by heart patients under close medical supervision. When used illegally without medical supervision, side effects such as decreased blood pressure, headache, and dizziness may occur. Another similar inhalant, **butyl nitrate,** causes similar reactions.

Designer Drugs

Designer drugs are a group of drugs that are made in labs to imitate well-known drugs. They fall into their own classification. They are manufactured from raw materials that are easily available. Designer drugs are particularly dangerous because they can be far more dangerous than the drugs they imitate. People who use designer drugs do not know what they are taking into their bodies and thus leave themselves to unknown side effects.

MDMA, also known as **"ecstacy"** is somewhat related to mescaline and amphetamines. It is a drug with no known medicinal value and is very dangerous. Effects of this drug include insomnia, muscle aches, fatigue, and an inability to concentrate. There is a possibility MDMA causes brain damage.

Anabolic Steroids

Perhaps one of drugs of major concern to school-age students is anabolic steroids. **Anabolic steroids** are synthetic derivatives of the male hormone testosterone. The people who have been using anabolic steroids have been those who want to build body mass to improve strength and appearance. Anabolic steroids are very dangerous. They can cause heart disease, liver disease, cancer, kidney disease, and severe depression. In males, they can cause the testicles to enlarge, impotence, and infertility. In females, steroids may cause a deepened voice, breast reduction, beard growth, and cessation of menstruation. People who use anabolic steroids can become aggressive, paranoid, and violent.

Anabolic steroids have been used by professional and amateur athletes to improve athletic performance. However, drug testing for the presence of anabolic steroids has resulted in a decreased use by athletes. Athletes who test positive for anabolic steroids can be banned from competing for life.

Alcohol

Alcohol is a major drug of use and abuse in the United States. **Ethyl alcohol** is the alcohol that is consumable. It is produced by a process called **fermentation**. Fermentation is a form of processing using grains with ethyl alcohol.

Whether or not alcohol will have an effect on a person will be dependent on a number of factors. These include the alcohol concentration in a drink, the rate at which the alcohol is consumed in the body, the amount of alcohol consumed, the amount of food in the stomach, and the genetic make-up of the person. The use of alcohol is a particular concern, especially among young drivers. Young drivers do not have the experience in compensating for the effects of alcohol. They are inexperienced drivers to begin with so that alcohol impairment is accentuated. Young drivers take more risks and they generally weigh less than adults which means the alcohol will affect them easier.

Of particular concern is drinking alcohol during pregnancy. Pregnant women are advised not to drink at all during their pregnancy. Heavy use of alcohol can result in fetal alcohol syndrome in pregnant women. **Fetal alcohol syndrome** is a condition in which abnormalities in a newborn result from the mother's drinking alcohol during pregnancy. Among these abnormalities are small eye slits, small head circumference, and mental retardation. These effects are long lasting.

There are other risks to health due to drinking alcohol. Heavy drinkers have an increased risk of developing cancer. The sites most often affected include the mouth, espohagus, larynx, tongue, stomach, liver, pancreas, colon, and rectum. The emotional problems related to alcohol abuse are many. These problems affect the individual, family, and society.

Tobacco

Tobacco use is a leading cause of disability and death in the United States and worldwide. There are 3,800 known compounds in tobacco. These compounds become condensed and form **tars**, a brown, sticky cancer causing agent that lines the lungs of smokers. Recently, cigarette smoking has been linked to leukemia.

The **nicotine** in cigarettes, a stimulant drug that causes the heart to overwork, is extremely dangerous. A person who smokes a pack a day will take 70,000 puffs on a cigarette a year. The nicotine as well as other chemicals taken into the body is enormous. In fact, so great can be the consumption of nicotine that people can suffer nicotine poisoning. Beginning smokers can experience nicotine poisoning consisting of dizziness, rapid pulse, cold, clammy skin, and nausea.

The use of smokeless tobacco has been a concern among the adolescent group. Young people may think that smokeless tobacco is harmless because smoke is not drawn into the lungs. But use of smokeless tobacco is extremely dangerous. Whether the smokeless tobacco is in the form of **snuff**, a powdered form of tobacco, or **chewing**, in a plug or loose form, it is hazardous. It rots the teeth because it causes the roots of the teeth to be exposed, it causes the enamel of the teeth to be worn. Use of smokeless tobacco can cause **leukoplakia**, a white, patchy lesion that can lead to cancer. Leukoplakia is found on the lining of the inside of the cheek. There are some indications that use of smokeless tobacco is responsible for the development of cancer in other sites of the body.

Blacktop for Lungs

Objective

Students will describe what happens to the surface of the lungs when exposed to cigarette smoke.

Life Skill

I will not smoke cigarettes.

Materials

Plastic baggie, straw, cotton, rubber band

Motivation

1 Explain to students that they will observe how harmful ingredients from cigarette smoke can harm the lungs. They will observe how tar from the smoke inhaled from cigarettes can line the lungs. This interferes with the ability to breathe. Tars also are carcinogens and thus, increase a person's risk for developing lung cancer.

2 Place a few balls of cotton inside a clear plastic baggie. Have a straw stick out of the opening of the baggie. Wrap the baggie around the straw and tighten the baggie around the straw with a rubber band. Explain that the baggie represents the outside of a lung. The cotton represents the alveoli, or air sacs, that line the surface of the lungs. The straw serves as the airway or trachea, that leads to the lungs.

3 You can perform this part of the experiment by blowing smoke into the baggie. Emphasize to students that you are not inhaling the cigarette so as to avoid any smoke getting into your lungs. After each puff of smoke you blow into the baggie, squeeze the bag so that the smoke leaves. Repeat this several times.

4 Have students observe the color of the cotton. Ask them what they observe. (The cotton turns brown.) Ask students what this indicates. (The tar from the cigarette smoke accumulated on the cotton. Inside the lungs, smoke accumulates on the alveoli making the exchange of gases inside the lungs difficult as well as coating the lungs with tar, thereby increasing the risk of developing lung cancer.)

Hold a clean cottonball next to the cotton inside the plastic baggie. Have students describe why a clean cottonball, if it represented the surface of the lung, would be more functional that the one that is dark. (The dark one is lined with tar and the tar would block the air passages inside the lungs.) Have students discuss why smoking cigarettes is harmful to health.

Your Reaction Time

Objective

Students will describe the effects of alcohol on reaction time.

Life Skill

I will not drink alcohol.

Materials

Yardstick, glass of cold water

Motivation

1 Introduce the term "reaction time." Explain that reaction time is the ability to respond to a stimulus from the time it is recognized.

2 Explain that it is important to have a quick reaction time to help protect the body from injury. For example, when riding a bike, a person may notice a that another person has just stepped in front of the bicycle. It is important to be able to stop the bike quickly to avoid running into the person. Explain that certain drugs such as alcohol slow reaction time. This results in an increase in accidents.

3 The following experiment shows how reaction time can be slowed. Ask a volunteer to hold his/her thumb and forefinger spread apart so that the bottom of a yardstick is at the level of these fingers. You are to tell the student you will release the yardstick. As soon as the yardstick is released, tell the student to grab it with the two fingers. After doing this, have the class notice how many inches of the yardstick passed before it was grabbed.

4 Have the student hold his/her fingers in the bowl of cold water for one minute. Repeat releasing the yardstick with the student grabbing it as soon as possible. The class will observe that more of the yardstick slipped than when performed without holding the hand in cold water. Explain that the cold water helped slow reaction time.

5 Explain that drugs such as alcohol slow reaction time. Ask students to analyze why people who drink alcohol have more accidents while under the influence than people who do not drink alcohol. Explain that alcohol slows reaction time and a person cannot respond as quickly to a situation.

Evaluation

Have students identify how activities they perform can be affected by having a slower reaction time. Tell why it is important to avoid drinking alcohol.

Cigarette Tips

Objective
Students will provide at least three reasons why cigarette smoking is harmful to health.

Life Skill
I will not smoke cigarettes.

Materials
Old shoe boxes, white sheets of paper, tape

Motivation

1 Explain to students that they will share with others in the class why cigarette smoking is harmful to health. They will also develop sayings to discourage others from ever starting to smoke.

2 Take a shoe box and have it decorated as if it were a large cigarette pack. The students can do the decorations. It should be decorated so that the cover has a saying that shows cigarettes are harmful. Students can help in the decorations by cutting pictures from magazines and combining these pictures so that there is a creative saying or picture that depicts smoking as not an "in thing" to do.

3 Provide each student a sheet of white paper. Tell students they are to write a statement that indicates why smoking is harmful They can also have the option of writing a jingle about the dangers of cigarette smoking or why one should never smoke.

4 After students write their statements, they are to roll the sheet of paper into what appears to be a long cigarette. Use tape to attach the paper at the edge so that it remains closed. The paper will now look like a cigarette.

5 Place the newly made cigarettes into the shoe box (cigarette box). Have each student pick a "cigarette tip" from the box and read it to the class.

Evaluation

Brainstorm the different facts that students remembered from this activity. Write the facts on the chalkboard. Do not repeat like answers. Have students identify three reasons why cigarette smoking is harmful to the body.

Warning: Cigarette Smoking is Harmful to Your Health

Objective

Students will develop warning labels that indicate how cigarette smoking is harmful to health.

Life Skill

I will not smoke cigarettes.

Materials

Strips of paper, shoe box.

Motivation

1 If easily available, bring sample packages of cigarettes into class. Have students read the warning labels on the side of some of these packages. These warnings were developed and supported by the U.S. Surgeon General. There are four major warnings:

"Quitting smoking now greatly reduces serious risks to your health."
"Cigarette smoke contains carbon monoxide."
"Smoking by pregnant women may result in fetal injury, premature birth, and low birth weight."
"Smoking causes lung cancer, heart disease, emphysema, and may complicate pregnancy."

2 Tell students they will have the opportunity to create their own warnings. But this time, students are to use their language arts skills and develop a two line jingle that depicts the harmful effects of cigarette smoking on the body.

3 After students complete this task, they are to place the warnings on the side of the shoe box. They can then decorate the shoe box so that it resembles a cigarette package. However, the package will represent a display that shows how cigarettes are harmful.

Evaluation

Have students write three ways cigarette smoking is harmful. Information should be obtained from the creative jingles students developed.

"Speed-Up, Slow-Down"

Objective

Students will describe the effects of stimulants and depressants on the body.

Life Skill

I will not use illegal stimulants or depressants.

Materials

Record player or tape of any kind of popular song

Motivation

1 Explain to students they are going to examine the effects of different kinds of drugs on the body. One kind of drug is called stimulants. A stimulant is a drug that speeds the actions of the body. Another kind of drug is a depressant. Depressants are drugs that slow the actions of the body. Examples of stimulants are cocaine, caffeine in coffee and cola drinks, and amphetamines. Examples of depressants are alcohol, heroin, and barbiturates.

2 Tell students they will listen to a record. The first record represents stimulants. Play the record, but instead of playing it at the speed required, increase the speed. Then indicate that this record was representative of stimulants. Then play the same record again, but this time on a lower speed than required. Explain that this record represented depressants.

3 Ask students to describe their reactions when they heard the records played at two different speeds. Explain that these speeds represented how a person might behave when using stimulants or depressants. Have students make analogies how people might behave when using stimulants and depressants. Explain that the use of these drugs illegally is extremely dangerous. Stimulants can speed up the body actions so fast that heart failure can result due to over stimulation. Depressants can slow the workings of the body, mainly the heart, so that the heart can stop beating.

Evaluation

Have students share how stimulants and depressants can affect everyday activities. Have students provide different examples of how stimulants affect the body.

Drugs: A Lost Cause

Objective Students will identify at least three personal losses that might result from illegal drug use.

Life Skill I will not use illegal drugs.

Materials 3" by 5" index cards

Motivation

1 Distribute three index cards to each student. Have students think of three things in their lives that are most important to them. They are to write one item on each card. Students can identify items or people including friends or family.

2 Ask several students to volunteer sharing their lists. After several students have shared their items of importance, walk up to several other students including those who have shared their lists. Have the students to whom you have walked up hand you their cards. When you take the cards, give students a card in exchange. The card you will hand them will have the word "drug" written on it.

3 Ask students how they would feel if they were to lose the items they had listed on their cards. Most students will indicate they feel hurt. They may also say they would have a difficult time compensating for the loss. Tell students that they had a drug card after they had given up their prized possessions. Explain that when one becomes involved in illegal drug use, they risk losing many things in their lives that are considered prized possessions.

4 Have students discuss how drugs can cause losses such as friends and perhaps, sometimes family members, money, educational opportunities, and other items of value.

Evaluation Have students identify ways they can avoid using drugs so that they can keep their prized possessions. Students can share their answers with class members. You can also have students share how their lives may change if they were dependent on drugs.

Drugs: A Mixed Bag

Objective

Students will define designer drugs and describe why they are dangerous.

Life Skill

I will not use designer drugs if they are offered to me.

Materials

Various foods in packages such as candy bars but have different products in the packages such as soap, pencils, or erasers

Motivation

1 Select several packages that contain food. These packages may contain healthful snacks such as granola or cereals. Replace the inside of the packages with substances that are not eatable. For example, instead of cereal inside the boxes, you may place rubber erasers.

2 Call a student up to the front of the class and show this student the package. Indicate to the student that you will give him/her a taste of what is inside the package. You can say, "In fact, I will give you this package and you can eat as much as you want from what is inside of it. You will love what you will eat. Would you like to have this package?" Most likely the student will say, "Yes."

3 After you give the student the package, ask him/her to open it and show the class what has been chosen to eat. The class will notice that what was pulled from the package was not eatable.

4 Explain that sometimes people take drugs based upon what someone tells them the drug is or what they perceive the drug may be. Designer drugs are drugs that are supposed to imitate the effects of certain well-known drugs. Designer drugs may be made in a home lab. Because there is no inspection of the composition of the drug, the ingredients can be harmful, if not deadly. Yet people take designer drugs when they do not know anything about the composition of that drug. Emphasize to students that they should never accept an offer to use any kind of drug including designer drugs if offered by another person.

Have students identify conditions under which they should accept any kind of medicine. For example, students can take medicine under a physician's prescription or by a responsible adult who has permission to dispense a medication. You can also have students describe how designer drugs can be dangerous to them.

Yucky Lung

Objective

Students will explain how the ingredients in cigarette smoke damage the lungs and cause lung disease.

Life Skill

I will not smoke cigarettes.

Materials

Either a large cut-out outline of a lung or a plain sponge sheetcake in the shape of a lung that is baked at home, a knife used to spread food, a concoction of messy, dark ingredients such as mud or dirty oil that is in a jar.

Motivation

1 Have either an outline of a lung made of poster paper or even better, a layer of spongecake that is just one sheet thick. Show the class the outline of the lung and tell them this lung is healthy. It is healthy because its owner does not smoke and does exercise.

2 Show the class the jar with the unsightly ingredients inside. Among these ingredients will be mud or any other mixtures that students will find offensive. Tell students what is inside the jar. In a nonchalant manner, use the knife to spread the ingredients from the jar on to the lung. As you are doing this, tell students that the ingredients you are spreading represent the tar in cigarettes that line the surface of the lungs of people who smoke.

3 As you do this, students will make comments like, "Yuck." Then walk around the room with the "yucky" lung and have students observe it. Emphasize that this lung was exposed to cigarette smoke and that the tars in the cigarette smoke cause the surface of the lungs to turn black.

Evaluation

Have students explain why lungs that are coated with tar promote lung disease. (The tars contain carcinogens, or cancer-causing agents. Tars also prevent the gases from exchanging easily inside the lungs.)

Stuck Like Glue

Objective

Students will define physical and psychological dependency and identify ways persons who are drug dependent can get help.

Life Skill

I will not use illegal drugs.

Materials

Rubber glove, sheet of paper, quick-drying glue

Motivation

1 While in front of the class, place a rubber glove on one hand. On the tip of the glove, place a quick-drying glue. Then take a sheet of paper. The word "drug" should be written on the sheet of paper. Attach the paper to the glove and allow it to form a bond to the glove.

2 Explain to students that the sheet of paper represents drugs. Tell students that the drug is attached to you. Try to remove the drug from your glove by shaking your hand. You might want to ask several students to try to gently tug the sheet of paper from the drug. The paper will stick to the glove. It cannot be removed.

3 Ask students to draw a conclusion about the connection between starting to use drugs and then trying to discontinue their use. Students should observe that once a person takes certain kinds of drugs for a period of time, (s)he develops a dependence on that drug. Indicate that dependency means a need to have something. A physical dependency for a drug is a bodily need for a drug. A psychological dependency is a mental need for a drug. All drugs can cause psychological dependence. Many drugs can cause physical dependence. Just as it was difficult to get rid of the "drug" from the glove, so is it difficult to stop using a drug once dependency has developed. Medical help is often needed.

4 You can take another sheet of paper and write the word "family" on it. Then tear this sheet in half. Explain that drugs can be a cause of family breakups. Have students describe how drug use interferes with family relationships.

You may discuss ways in which people who are dependent on drugs can take steps to free themselves with the help of family, friends, and medical personnel. Identify available community resources.

Have students define physical and psychological dependency. They can identify ways they can avoid becoming involved with drugs and thus not worry about drug dependency. For example, students can discuss the importance of communication skills with parents and becoming involved in healthful activities such as after-school events.

No Matter How Hard You Try, There's Still Some Left

Objective

Students will discuss why fat soluble drugs such as marijuana have long term dangers that may not as yet be known.

Life Skill

I will not use marijuana.

Materials

Bowl of water, a sponge

Motivation

1 Students may not realize that marijuana is a fat soluble drug. A fat soluble drug is a drug that can remain in the body tissues, specifically fat tissue, for an extended period of time.

2 To demonstrate the concept that certain drugs are fat soluble, take a sponge and allow it to become saturated in a bowl of water. Then have a student remove the sponge and squeeeze the water from it. The class will observe that most of the water has been removed from the sponge.

3 Now you take the sponge and squeeze it even harder. The class will notice that even more water was removed. There was still water stored inside the sponge. Even after you squeeze the sponge, there continues to be water inside. The water can be equated to marijuana that can be stored in the brain for periods of time.

4 Explain that marijuana is a fat soluble drug. When taken into the body, THC, the active ingredient in marijuana is distributed throughout the body, including the brain, by the blood. Since the THC in marijuana is stored in fat cells, it can remain inside the body for 30 days. Researchers are studying the effects of THC remaining inside the brain cells for extended periods of time. It could be that there are more harmful effects of marijuana than originally thought.

Evaluation

Have students describe why marijuana can be detected in the body a few weeks after it has been used. (It remains in the fat cells in the body because it is fat soluble.)

One Plus One Equal Three

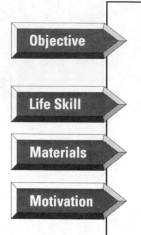

Objective

Students will explain the synergistic effect and identify reasons why two drugs should not be taken at the same time.

Life Skill

I will not take two medications together unless cleared by a physician.

Materials

Two glasses, water, vinegar, baking soda

Motivation

1 Explain to students that certain drugs can produce synergistic effects. A synergistic effect of a drug is an effect that is accentuated more by the combination of two or more of a like drug than an effect that is produced if the same drugs were taken individually. For example, a person who drinks alcohol and also takes a barbiturate will receive a much greater effect than each of these drugs individually can produce. Both alcohol and barbiturates are depressants. To clarify, instead of $1 + 1 = 2$, $1 + 1 = 3$.

2 Demonstrate a synergistic effect by performing the following experiment. Take a glass and inside, pour one cup of water. Then pour another cup of water and have students observe the level of the water. Explain that one cup plus one cup produced a glass holding two cups of water.

3 Place one cup of vinegar in a glass. Take two tablespoons of baking soda and dissolve it in one cup of water. Tell students that one glass of water represents alcohol and the other represents barbiturates. Explain that according to the experiment you did in Step One above, the ingredients in one glass added to the ingredients of the other glass will amount to a level of two cups. Now you will add the glass containing the water and baking soda to the glass of vinegar. Make sure you have a bowl below the glass or do it over a sink. When you mix the ingredients from the two glasses, the ingredients overflow. One plus one did not equal two. Instead, it equalled three. This is an example of a synergistic effect.

Have students discuss why physicians often want to know if a person is already taking a medication before writing a prescription for a drug. (Certain drugs, when combined, will produce a synergistic effect. The physician should be aware if a person is taking another drug to avoid possible serious effects.)

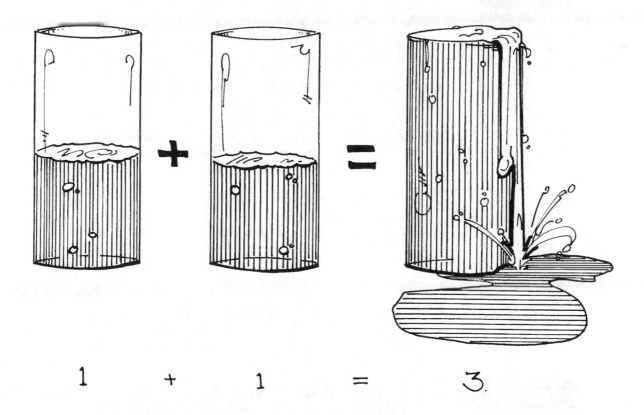

1   +   1   =   3.

Phew! It Stinks

Objective

Students will identify ways that cigarette smoking detracts from personal appearance.

Life Skill

I will not smoke cigarettes.

Materials

Onion

Motivation

1 Take an onion and rub it between your palms before you enter class. As you enter the class, begin your lesson. Do not act as if anything is wrong. Continue to give the lesson. Ignore anything that students are saying about you.

2 Observe the behavior of the students in the class. You will notice that they are laughing and giggling. They may be talking to each other. After a while, stop the lesson. Have students share the thoughts they had about you. They will say things like, "You smelled." or "I didn't want to be around you."

3 Explain that the odor of the onion caused others not to be around you. Explain that there are many different kinds of odors people may have that are not too pleasant. One example of an odor is that of tobacco smoke. Explain that when people smoke a cigarette, they exhibit an unpleasant odor.

4 Explain that people who smoke will have the unpleasant odor of tobacco on their clothing, breath, and hair. This is only one of the negative effects of smoking on personal hygiene.

Evaluation

Have students describe how they perceive people would react to them if they smoked cigarettes and had a repulsive odor on their hair, clothing, and breath.

Candy or Drug?

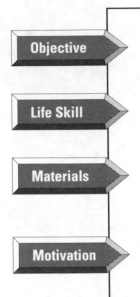

Objective

Students will explain the difficulties in distinguishing between pills and capsules which are drugs and candies that resemble these drugs.

Life Skill

I will not eat or drink anything without knowing what it is and without knowing the person who gives it to me.

Materials

Poster paper, glue, four over-the-counter (OTC) capsules or tablets and four types of candies that can pass as being drug tablets or capsules when not inside their packages

Motivation

1 On a large poster paper, glue four OTC drug tablets or capsules and four kinds of candies that can pass as drugs. Mix the order of these substances so that not all of the same kind are together.

2 Under each substance, write either the word drug or candy to indicate what that substance is. Cover what you have written with a strip of paper.

3 Show your poster to the class and tell students to imagine that they are walking down the street and someone offers them one of the substances. Explain that this person said the substance being offered is candy. Have students look at the substances on the poster and have them identify which are candy and which are drugs. You can assign numbers to each of the substances to aid students in identifying them. Students can write their answers on a sheet of paper.

4 After students have completed this task, review their answers. Most likely, students will have trouble differentiating between the drugs and the candy. Use this experience to emphasize to students they should not accept anything someone gives them to eat unless they know what that substance is.

Have students participate in a role play in which one person tries to persuade another to accept a piece of candy. The person who is being asked to accept the candy does not know if the substance really is a candy. Have the class discuss reasons why the person should not accept the candy and what that person can do to reinforce his/her decision to say NO.

One in Four

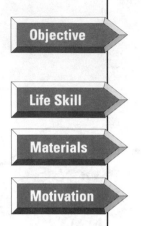

Objective

Students will describe the prevalence of alcoholism within families and the ways which this disease affects family life.

Life Skill

I will seek help if someone in my family has a drinking problem that is affecting me.

Materials

White index cards for 75 percent of the class and color index cards for 25 percent of the class

Motivation

1 Have enough index cards so that each student in the class can have one. You should have enough white index cards for 75 percent of the students in the class and color index cards for 25 percent of the students in the class. Thus, if you have 20 students in your class, you should have fifteen white index cards and five color index cards. The color cards represent the percentage of families who are affected by drinking (25%) in the United States.

2 Mix the white and color cards together. As students walk into the classroom, hand each a card. Do not tell them why you are handing them a card. After everyone has received a card, mention that you are going to discuss a health problem that is significant today. Ask students that are holding a color index card to stand.

3 As students holding color index cards are standing, tell the class that the number of students in this class that are standing represents the percentage of families in the United States that are affected by a particular health problem. Have the class guess what this health problem is (alcoholism). If they have trouble, give them hints. Some examples are: "This problem is related to a drug." or "This is a kind of disease."

4 You can use this activity to introduce the class to a discussion about the effects of alcohol on society and families.

Have students write pamphlets describing the prevalence of alcoholism in families, the effects on the family, and places in the community in which help can be received.

A Solid Foundation

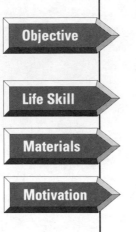

Objective

Students will describe ways in which drug use destroys the values upon which the foundation of life is built.

Life Skill

I will not use illegal drugs.

Materials

Toy blocks, paper, tape

Motivation

1 On small sheets of paper, write the following: family members, friends, activities with family, grades at school, athletic teams, relationships with teachers, study habits, and any other items you feel are important for establishing a foundation for achieving good health. Attach one item to a toy block.

2 Explain to the class the concept that all things need a foundation upon which other things can be built. Use the idea of a building. A building cannot be constructed without a solid base which may consist of cinderblock or cement. A wood frame for a building is build on the cement which acts as the foundation. Then other things can be added on top of the frame until a building is complete.

3 Explain that everyone needs a foundation for life. Take each block and build upon it. Explain that the blocks represent a foundation for good health. Among the things needed in this foundation for good health are relationships with family members, good friends, and good study habits. The foundation of blocks grows and helps the foundation remain solid.

4 Take a block that has the word "drugs" written on a sheet of paper that is attached to it. Push this block hard against the bottom of the others. The class will notice that the foundation collapsed. Use this to discuss why drug use can cause the foundation of life to collapse and thus, cause a life to fall apart.

Discuss how drugs impact upon the foundations of life. You can choose some integral parts of a foundation such as family. Then have the class discuss how one person in a family who uses drugs can cause instability in that family. After students have discussed how drugs can ruin a foundation, you can discuss how a foundation can be rebuilt if it has crumbled.

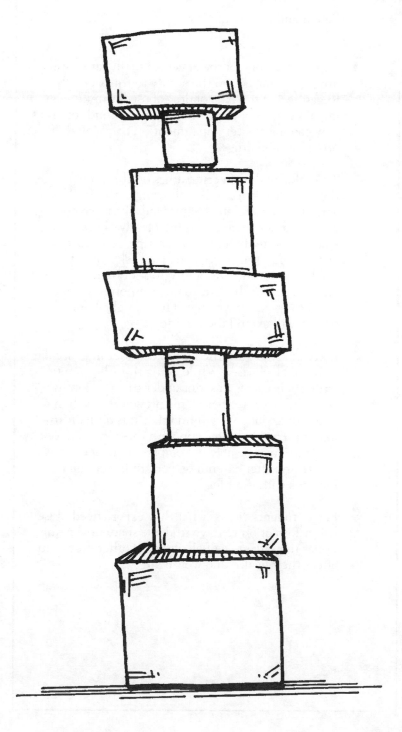

Trying to Think Straight

Objective

Students will describe how drug use impairs thinking.

Life Skill

I will not use illegal drugs.

Materials

Pencil and a sheet of paper

Motivation

1 Explain that one of the effects of taking any kind of drug is the impact on the ability to think clearly. Regardless of the type of drug abused, thinking is impaired when a drug is taken. Some kinds of drugs may cause a greater impairment on thinking than other kinds of drugs.

2 To replicate the effects of drugs on thinking, have the students perform the following activity. This activity will simulate what it feels like to be confused and not be able to think clearly. First, have students write their names in script on a sheet of paper. After they have done this, ask students to hold one foot straight out in front of them. They are to hold out the foot that corresponds to the hand they use for writing. Thus, a right-handed person will extend the right foot.

3 Have students turn their extended foot in a circular fashion, clockwise. While doing this, they are to write their names in script under the position in which they wrote their name previously. When doing this, students will find that it is difficult to maintain a circular motion with the extended foot. They will also be able to compare their signatures before and after extending, performing circular motions with their foot.

4 Have students discuss what they experienced. Use this information to have students share how being under the influence of alcohol and other drugs can affect their health and well-being.

Have students identify what impact drugs would have on their ability to perform daily activities which they must perform with the ability to think clearly.

You Can't Convince Me

Objective

Students will use refusal skills to resist the temptation to use drugs.

Life Skill

I will say NO when pressured to use illegal drugs.

Materials

Index cards with instructions

Motivation

1 This activity is designed for your students to work in groups of five. You are to design index cards so that each person in a group will have one index card. Four of the index cards per group will have the following written, "Pretend you are at a party drinking alcohol and you want to convince the one person in the group who is not drinking to join the others and drink." One card per group will say, "You are at a party with your friends and they all are drinking. They want to convince you to drink also, but you do not want to drink."

2 Divide the class into the groups of five and distribute the index cards. Tell students they are to play the roles on the cards that they have received. Allow the groups about five minutes to play their roles.

3 Have the class come together to discuss what happened in their respective groups. Students should respond to the following questions:

- What did people say to try to convince the nondrinker to drink?
- How persuasive were the drinkers?
- How valid were some of the arguments given to persuade a person to drink?
- What tactics did the nondrinker use to resist drinking?
- What options could the nondrinker have used that were not used?

Evaluation

Have students make a list of the kinds of refusal skills a person can use to resist drinking or using other kinds of illegal drugs.

Paralyzed Cilia

Objective

Students will describe why people who smoke suffer an increased risk to respiratory infections.

Life Skill

I will not smoke cigarettes.

Materials

Glitter, glue, paper

Motivation

1 Introduce the concept that people who smoke cigarettes run an increased risk of upper respiratory infections. This is a result of paralysis of the cilia due to the harmful ingredients contained in cigarette smoke. When the cilia become paralyzed, they cannot sweep foreign particles from the respiratory tract effectively. Thus, the foreign substances enter the lungs easily.

2 Draw an outline of the windpipe and the lungs on a sheet of poster paper. Spread glitter inside the windpipe. Explain that this air passage is that of a nonsmoker. The glitter represents foreign elements such as germs. Blow the germs so that they fall off the poster. Explain that the cilia are working effectively and that the germs were easily removed from the air passage.

3 Spread glue or rubber cement on the inside of the air passage. Then sprinkle glue on the cilia. Explain to the class that this is the air passage of a smoker. The cilia become paralyzed. Blow the glitter so as to remove it from the air passage. A good part of the glitter sticks to the air passage. Explain that the cilia could not remove many of the germs from the air passage. The germs remain in the air passage and can move down to the lungs.

Evaluation

Have students describe why people who smoke have more upper respiratory infections than people who do not smoke. (The cilia become paralyzed. Pathogens that cause disease are not easily removed from the air passage and thus, can then cause illness.)

Gasping for Air

Objective ▸ Students will describe what it feels like to have emphysema.

Life Skill ▸ I will not smoke cigarettes.

Materials ▸ A straw for each student in the class

Motivation ▸

1 Provide each student with a straw. Each straw should be wrapped in its original paper.

2 After students have their straws, ask them to remove the wrapping. Then ask them to pinch their nostrils closed so that they cannot inhale or exhale through their nose. Ask each student to place a straw in his/her mouth. Each student is to keep his/her nostrils pinched closed while inhaling and exhaling through the straw. Explain that if any difficulty exists with breathing, they can stop the activity at any time. Students are to breathe through the straw for a one minute period.

3 If you wish to make breathing more difficult, you can have students also try this activity by using a coffee stirrer instead of a straw as the stirrer has narrower holes.

4 After students have completed the activity, ask them to describe what it was like to breathe through the straw. Students will tell that they had a difficult time breathing. Explain that this is what it feels like to breathe when a person has emphysema. And almost all cases of emphysema are due to cigarette smoking.

Evaluation

Ask students to describe what it might feel like to breathe in the above manner every day, 24 hours per day. Then have them describe how they would feel if they had to breathe in this manner and tried to perform activities such as climbing stairs or running fast to catch a bus. Students will indicate that this is not an enjoyable way to exist.

The Root of the Matter

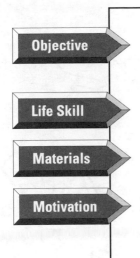

Objective

Students will describe ways in which using illegal drugs will interfere with physical, mental-emotional, and family-social health.

Life Skill

I will not use illegal drugs.

Materials

Paper and pencil

Motivation

1 Distribute a sheet of paper with a picture of a tree. The tree should have large leaves with roots at the bottom of the tree. Have students fill each leaf with something positive. For example, students will write, strong family, good athlete, like math, great friends, etc.

2 Have students draw a picture of any kind of drug and place it at a root. Then have students describe what would happen to the leaves on the tree of drugs were to get absorbed through the roots and travel up through the tree. They might say poor school performance, arguments with parents, difficult peer relationships, and chemical dependency.

3 Facilitate a discussion about how drugs act as a means to ruin the positives in a person's life. Students can use this opportunity to describe how they can avoid getting into a situation in which drugs may be present.

Evaluation

Have students brainstorm ways they can increase the number of "positive leaves" on their trees.

Diseases and Disorders is the area of health that deals with the prevention, causes, signs and symptoms, and treatment of infectious and noninfectious diseases and disorders. Of particular concern in this area of health are the two leading causes of death - cardiovascular disease and cancer. Another area of importance in this area of health, and of particular concern to school districts, is AIDS.

Cardiovascular Disease

Cardiovascular disease is disease of the heart and blood vessels. The most common forms of cardiovascular disease include **arteriosclerosis** which is hardening of the arteries, **angina pectoris** which is chest pain due to narrowed blood vessels in the heart, **myocardial infarction** or heart attack, **arrhythmia** or irregular heartbeat, **hypertension** or high blood pressure, and stroke, a break or block in a blood vessel in the brain.

Risk factors for developing heart disease can be categorized into one of two groups risks that an individual cannot control and risks that an individual can control.

There are three risks that are not voluntarily controlled: sex, race, and age.

Sex. Men have a higher risk of developing cardiovascular disease than do women. This is at least true up until the age of forty. It is rare for a woman to have a heart attack before she reaches menopause. But once a woman reaches the age of 65, heart disease becomes the number one cause of death.

Race. African Americans are two times more likely than whites to develop high blood pressure. And an increased blood pressure means an increased risk of developing heart disease. African Americans also have a greater family history of developing heart disease.

Age. The older a person, the greater the risk of developing heart disease. About 80 percent of people who develop heart disease do so after age 65.

There are many risks that can be controlled.

Smoking. The United States Surgeon General believes that cigarette smoking is the single most preventable cause of death in the United States. Smokers have a significantly higher risk of developing cardiovascular disease than do nonsmokers. And a smoker who does have a heart attack has an increased chance of dying from a heart attack than does a nonsmoker. The reason smoking is a risk factor is that the ingredients in the smoke of a burning cigarette affect the heart in particular. Nicotine in smoke causes the heart to pump more often. Carbon monoxide in the smoke displaces the oxygen in the bloodstream. The heart is denied adequate amounts of oxygen. Cigarette smoke also harms the inside of the coronary arteries so that cholesterol can build up easier. This results in narrowed arteries and restricted blood flow.

Diet. Diet plays a significant role in how healthy the heart is. Foods high in cholesterol precipitate increases in the buildup of **plaque** or fatty deposits in the coronary arteries. It is recommended that a person keeps blood cholesterol within a healthful range. Total cholesterol is recommended to be below 200 mg of total cholesterol per deciliter of blood (mg/dl). A person who has a total cholesterol level of between 201-239 is considered borderline and thus at moderate risk of developing heart disease. Levels of over 240 are considered high and dietary and/or medical interventions are needed.

Diet is also a factor in the amount of fats (lipids) in the bloodstream. These lipids are called lipoproteins. There are two kinds of lipoproteins in the body. High-density lipoproteins (HDLs) are the "good substances" since they pick up excess cholesterol and carry it back to the liver for removal from the body. The higher the HDLs in the body, the lower the risk of developing heart disease. People who exercise regularly increase their HDL levels.

Low density-lipoproteins (LDLs) are the "bad substances" in the blood that form deposits on the arterial walls. The higher the LDL reading, the greater the risk of developing heart disease. What is most important to understand about HDLs and LDLs is their ratio to total

DISEASES AND DISORDERS

cholesterol. The higher the ratio of HDL to total cholesterol, the lower the heart attack risk. A man is at increased risk if the percentage of HDL is less than 20 percent. For a woman, an HDL ratio of lower than 25 percent places her at risk. The best way to control cholesterol is by reducing intake of foods high in fat.

Hypertension. Hypertension forces the heart to work harder than it should. The heart must force blood into arteries with increased resistance. Thus, the heart can become diseased too easily. Also, the arteries may become diseased and burst.

Lack of exercise. Exercise helps a person maintain a desirable body weight, increases HDL levels, and lowers blood pressure. Regular aerobic exercise is important in reducing the risk of heart disease.

Obesity. Having a high percentage of body fat and being obese increase a person's risk for developing heart disease. The heart must work harder if a person is overfat and obese than if a person has a lean body and a desirable weight.

People who have heart disease can be treated successfully. Drugs such as calcium blockers can lower blood pressure and control arrythmias. **Beta-blockers** are drugs that can slow the heartbeat rate and reduce the force of the heart's contractions.

One of the more common treatments of heart disease is coronary bypass surgery. **Coronary bypass surgery** is an operation in which a vein from another part of the body, most often the leg, is grafted into a coronary artery so that blood is detoured around a blockage. However, coronary bypass surgery is not a panacea since a large number of people who have this surgery develop blockages up to ten years later.

Another method for treating a blocked coronary artery is the use of balloon angioplasty. **Balloon angioplasty** is a procedure in which an artery is unclogged by catheterization. A dye is injected into the arteries so that the clog shows up on a monitor. A balloon is then inflated so that the artery is widened. The balloon is then deflated so that normal blood flow can resume.

Cancer

Cancer is the second leading cause of death in the United States. **Cancer** is considered a group of diseases in which there is uncontrolled multiplication of abnormal cells in the body. Often, the development of cancer is manifest in the growth of malignant tumors. A **malignant tumor** is a cancerous tumor. This is in contrast to a **benign tumor** which is a noncancerous tumor.

Why a normal cell develops into a cancerous cell is not known. There may be a combination of factors involved such as viruses, chemicals, radiation, or a combination of these or other elements. There is some evidence that the development of cancer may have some commonalities.

Heredity. There seems to be a link that some kinds of cancers are related to a person's genetic make-up. Cancer of the breast, ovary, pancreas, and colon appears to run in families.

Viruses. There is some link between viruses and the development of certain kinds of cancers such as leukemias.

Tobacco. People who smoke cigarettes and use smokeless tobacco have an increased risk of developing cancer. Cigarette smoke contains carcinogens and is therefore related to the development of lung cancer.

Ultraviolet radiation. There is a definite link between exposure to ultraviolet radiation whether from the sun's rays or tanning beds and the development of cancer, particularly skin cancer, the most common form of cancer. Most skin cancers can be successfully treated if diagnosed early. Examples are basal and squamous cell carcinomas. But there is now evidence that exposure to ultraviolet radiation is responsible for **malignant melanoma**, the most serious of the skin cancers. Malignant melanoma is highly invasive so that early detection and immediate treatment is required if it is to be curable.

One sign of malignant melanoma is a change in the color of a lesion. The color may be in multiple shades of brown or black, red, white, and blue, and spread to the surrounding skin. There may be an enlargement of the lesion. The shape of the lesion may change so that the surrounding border may develop an irregular shape. The lesion may appear raised and scaling, and may ooz. Crusting may result. If there is itching and pain as well as a softening or other change in texture, medical help is indicated.

The best method of handling cancer is to practice prevention. Among the methods of prevention include having **mammograms** or special x-rays of the breast if you are a woman. There should be one baseline x-ray between the ages of 35-39 and then one every one to two years between ages 40-49. A yearly mammogram should be given after age 50. All women who are sexually active or who have reached 18 years of age should have a Pap test and pelvic exam yearly. After the age of forty, a person should have a digital rectal examination each year and a procto exam, after two initial negative tests one year apart, every three to five five years after fifty.

If a person is diagnosed as having cancer, there are different treatment methods available. Surgery is the most common treatment method for cancer. If tumors are confined to a particular site, surgery can be used independently to accomplish a cure.

A large number of people who are diagnosed as having cancer will receive radiotherapy. **Radiotherapy** is the treatment of cancer via the use of radiation. In this treatment method, x-rays are used to stop the spread of cancer cells by killing them.

For other people, chemotherapy is the method of treatment. **Chemotherapy** is the use of drugs to kill cancer cells inside the body. Using chemotherapy has many different side effects. These can include nausea, hair loss, weight loss, and fatigue. Many people may receive experimental drugs that may cause side effects resulting in serious conditions. However, this may be the best alternative if other drugs do not work. But in many cases, a combination of treatments are used. Chemotherapy might be combined with radiotherapy and/or surgery.

AIDS

AIDS is a syndrome that results in a breakdown of the immune system, thereby leaving a person susceptible to the development of opportunistic infections. An **opportunistic infection** is a disease or infection that would probably not have the opportunity to exist if a person's immune system were healthy. But a person who is infected with **HIV**, the virus that causes AIDS, is at risk for opportunistic infections.

To understand how HIV affects the body, one must understand how the immune system functions. The body has helper T cells and B cells. When a pathogen enters the body, helper T cells become aware that something has invaded the bloodstream. The helper T cells signal the B cells who, in turn, produce antibodies. **Antibodies** are proteins that destroy or neutralize foreign substances such as pathogens. Antibodies can make pathogens susceptible to macrophages. **Macrophages** are white blood cells that destroy pathogens. But when HIV gets into the body, the helper T cells are attacked and destroyed. The helper T cells can no longer signal the B cells for help. Therefore, more and more helper T cells are destroyed so that the body is no longer able to protect itself from pathogens leaving a person susceptible to the development of opportunistic infections. There are three major ways HIV can be transmitted from an infected person to an uninfected person. Each method of transmission involves HIV entering the bloodstream. If there is a break in the skin, HIV can infect a person through intimate sexual contact such as penile-vaginal intercourse or anal intercourse. Infected semen or blood can enter the bloodstream of a sexual partner through the break in the skin. Another mode of transmission is through sharing HIV-contaminated needles. If an HIV-infected drug user uses a needle to inject drugs, then gives this needle to another IV drug user, infected blood on the needle can enter the bloodstream of the other user, thereby infecting this person. The third most common mode of transmission is through pregnancy. An HIV-infected mother can pass HIV through the bloodstream to her developing baby.

There is no cure for HIV infection. Once a person is infected, the infection will remain for a lifetime. A drug known as **AZT** can relieve the signs and symptoms of AIDS, but this drug is not a cure. The best method for preventing AIDS is avoiding risk behaviors that lead to HIV infection. These include avoiding the use of illegal IV drugs and abstaining from sexual contact. People who enter into and remain in a monogamous relationship with a person who has not been infected and avoid other risk behaviors will not become infected with HIV. Contrary to what many people have misinterpreted in the literature, HIV is easy to get if one engages in risk behaviors.

Recently, there has been concern raised about transmitting HIV through receiving organ transplants. Although transmission of HIV has occurred via organ donations, new testing procedures have just about eliminated this from happening.

Spread It Out

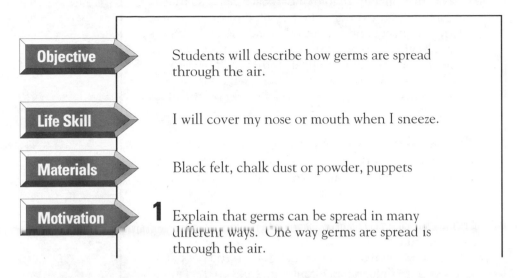

Objective	Students will describe how germs are spread through the air.
Life Skill	I will cover my nose or mouth when I sneeze.
Materials	Black felt, chalk dust or powder, puppets
Motivation	**1** Explain that germs can be spread in many different ways. One way germs are spread is through the air.

2 To demonstrate how germs are spread through the air, take black felt and hang it in front of the room. Use two puppets. Hold one in each hand so that each faces the other. Place chalk dust or powder in the mouth of one puppet. Pretend the two puppets are having a conversation with each other. Sneeze at the mouth of one puppet so that the powder or chalk dust from its mouth is sprinkled on the felt. Students will notice the powder marks on the black felt.

3 Explain that the specks of powder represent germs. Tell the class that the other puppet is breathing in or inhaling the germs. When the germs get in the body of the other puppet, that puppet can also become ill.

4 Ask students to explain how the germs could have been prevented from spreading when the puppet sneezed. (The puppet could have covered its mouth and nose when sneezing so that the germs would not spread through the air.)

Evaluation

Have students explain ways to prevent the spread of germs when coughing or sneezing.

HIV: You Have Entered

Objective

Students will describe how HIV can be transmitted from an infected person to an uninfected person through sharing a needle for IV drug use.

Life Skill

I will not use illegal intravenous drugs.

Materials

Two glasses filled half-way with water, cellophane wrapping paper, food coloring

Motivation

1   Explain to the class that they will learn about one way HIV, the virus that causes AIDS, can enter the body.

2   Have two glasses filled half-way with water resting on your desk. Cover each glass with plastic cellophane wrapping paper. Explain that the water represents blood inside a blood vessel. The cellophane wrapping paper represents the skin. Show the class that you have food coloring. Explain that the food coloring represents HIV.

3   On the first glass, place several drops of the coloring on the cellophane. Ask students what happened to the color of the water. (The water did not change color.) Ask the students why the water did not change color. The skin (cellophane wrapping) did not have any break in it. The coloring (HIV) was not able to enter the bloodstream (water). The blood did not become infected.

4   On the second glass of water, place a slit in the cellophane. Then place several drops of coloring (HIV) through the cellophane. Ask the class to observe what happened to the water. (It turned red.) HIV passed through the broken skin. The blood became infected.

5 Ask, "Can the water return to its original color?" (No.) Once HIV gets inside the body, will it ever be removed? (No. Once HIV enters the body, it remains inside for life.)

Evaluation

Using the information presented, have students describe how HIV can enter the body when a needle used by an infected person is used by another person.

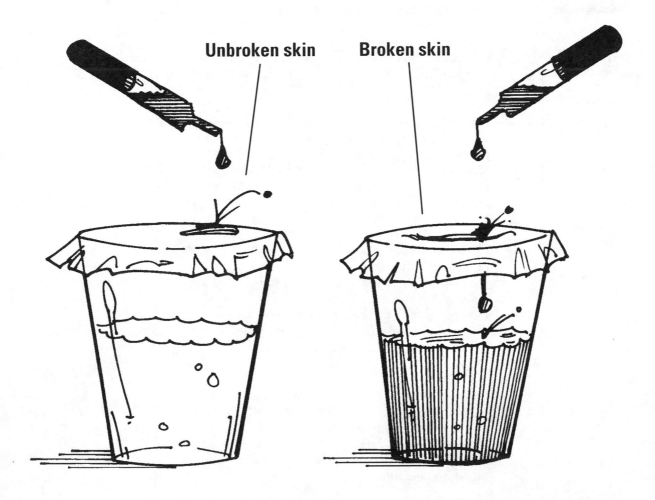

Unbroken skin   **Broken skin**

Your Handshake is Glittering

Objective

Students will discuss how germs are spread through direct physical contact.

Life Skill

I will wash my hands with soap and water to prevent the spread of germs.

Materials

Glitter

Motivation

1 Place a small amount of glitter on your hand, spread it around, and shake the hand of a student. Then have that student shake the hand of another student. Have the next student shake hands with one more student.

2 Have each student who received a handshake look at his or her hand. Each student who received a handshake will have glitter on his/her hand. Explain that the glitter represents germs. Explain that the germs from you were spread to others in the class. Explain that you did not need to shake a person's hand in order for that person to get your germs.

3 Explain that if a person's hands are placed by the mouth or if the hands are used to rub the eyes, the germs can enter the body and the person can become infected with an illness. Most often, germs, particularly those responsible for causing the common cold, are spread by touch. For this reason, it is important to wash hands frequently, especially before eating.

Evaluation

Hand a student a pencil. Have the students play detective and determine how the pencil can be the source of germs and cause another person in the class to catch a cold.

Washing With Soap

Objective

Students will discuss the importance of using soap when washing hands.

Life Skill

I will wash my hands with soap and water to prevent the spread of germs.

Materials

Soap, bowl of water, sand, petroleum jelly

Motivation

1 Find out how many students use soap each time they wash their hands. Explain that it is important to use soap every time when washing hands because soap will help remove germs more easily if used than if not used. Explain that soap helps break down the oil on the surface of skin. If only water is used, the germs and other foreign matter on the hands will not break away from the oil.

2 This experiment will show how soap is important in washing hands. Rub petroleum jelly on your hands. Explain that the petroleum jelly represents oil on the skin. Place sand on your hand. The sand represents dirt and germs. Wash your hands in the bowl of water. Have the class notice how much sand remains on the hand.

3 Repeat what you have done in Step 2 but this time, wash your hands using soap. Ask students what they have observed. (The hands are cleaner now than before.)

Evaluation

Ask students to describe why less sand remained on the hands when they were washed with the soap. (Soap helped break down the oil on the skin, thereby resulting in the sand to be more easily removed.)

Team Defense

Objective

Students will describe how the body's natural defenses help protect it from disease.

Life Skill

I will get adequate sleep and rest to help keep my body defenses strong.

Materials

Large poster paper, string

Motivation

1 Explain to students that they will be learning about ways the body works to keep protected from pathogens or harmful organisms.

2 Use different color poster paper and cut four posters in the shape of t-shirts. Explain that the shirts represent football jerseys. The shirts will have sleeves and a cut-out semicircle around the neck. Attach string from one part of the neck area to the other part, so that students can place the string around their necks. Thus, they can wear the shirt like a billboard. Label each of the shirts using markers, with the following titles: antibody, skin, white blood cell, and T cell.

3 Assign students to write facts about each title of a shirt. The facts can be taped on a sheet of paper to the inside of the shirts.

4 Select four students to come to the front of the room. Each will wear a shirt. Pretend that this is the defense of a football team whose players are being introduced before a game. Each player is to step forward and introduce the part of the body's defense system that appears on the front label. They are to state facts about their part of the defense system. The teacher serves as the announcer who states the player's name. For example, the announcer will say, "Now introducing Number 32, Skin." Skin will say, "I'm Number 32, Skin. My job today is to not break down so that any pathogen that tries to get by me will be blocked. If I do the right things, no one will break through my line of defense." Have other students do the same.

Take a sheet of paper and crumple it into a ball. Have a student throw the ball against one of the four shirts so that the ball bounces off. Then have students describe why the ball bounced off by indicating how that particular defense served as protection for the body.

Simulating Cerebral Palsy

Objective

Students will describe ways in which cerebral palsy affects a person's ability to coordinate muscular movement.

Life Skill

I will include classmates who have cerebral palsy and other disorders in social activities.

Materials

A textbook to be placed between the knees

Motivation

1 Explain that there are many different kinds of disorders that may limit a person's ability to perform all tasks easily. One such disorder is cerebral palsy. Cerebral palsy is a nervous system disorder in which muscle coordination is impaired. The exact cause of cerebral palsy is not known in most cases. Some people have cerebral palsy due to an injury to the brain during birth.

2 People who have cerebral palsy may have trouble walking. To simulate what it might feel like having cerebral palsy, ask students to take a book and place it between their knees. Then have them walk around the room without letting go of the book. Students will walk in a manner similar to that of a person who has cerebral palsy.

3 Have students observe others as they walk around the room. Ask them to describe how certain tasks may be difficult to perform. Discuss why people who have cerebral palsy may be able to perform at an even higher optimal level than someone who does not have this condition.

Evaluation

Have students share ways cerebral palsy may interfere with performing certain activities. Identify ways to include persons with cerebral palsy in social activities.

A Flowing Idea

Objective

Students will describe how a narrowed artery in the heart reduces blood flow.

Life Skill

I will reduce my intake of fats.

Materials

Two cardboard tubes from the the inside of bathroom tissue, clay, marbles

Motivation

1 Take the inside cardboard tubes from two bathroom tissues. Explain to students that these represent arteries inside the heart. Line one with clay. Explain that the one with clay has a narrower opening than the other. The narrowed opening represents an artery that has plaque built up inside of it. Plaque is fatty deposits that can line arteries. Plaque causes a reduced flow of blood.

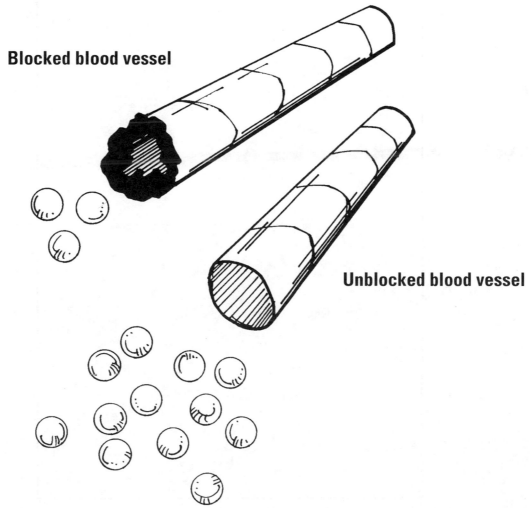

Blocked blood vessel

Unblocked blood vessel

2 Call two students to the front of the room. Give each 25 marbles. Tell the class that the marbles represent red blood cells. Red blood cells carry oxygen to the different parts of the body.

3 Lay the cardboard tubes on the desk but tilted slightly down. Have students roll the marbles through the tubes. Have the class observe through which tube the marbles passed quickly. The marbles that passed through the tube without the plaque made it through more quickly than the marbles that passed through the tube with the plaque.

Evaluation

Have students describe what this experiment says about the buildup of plaque in arteries inside the heart. (Plaque causes a reduced blood flow. Oxygenated blood may not be pumped quickly enough by a heart whose blood vessels are diseased by a build-up of plaque.)

Coronary Blockage

Objective

Students will describe how a blocked coronary artery results in a heart attack.

Life Skill

I will achieve a healthful weight, follow a healthful diet, exercise, and avoid smoking to avoid developing coronary artery disease.

Materials

Glass of water, straw, gum

Motivation

1 Explain to students that heart disease is the leading cause of death in the United States. There are many risk factors for heart disease. Some risk factors cannot be changed. These include heredity, male sex, and increased age. Some risk factors for developing heart disease can be changed. Among these are cigarette smoking, high blood pressure, and blood cholesterol levels. Other contributing factors for heart disease include diabetes, obesity, physical inactivity, and stress.

2 Explain that a heart attack results when a coronary or heart artery becomes blocked. When this occurs, the heart muscle cannot receive blood. Part of the heart muscle can die. A heart attack can be fatal.

3 To demonstrate what happens during a heart attack, have a student drink water through a straw. The water represents blood while the straw represents a coronary artery. As the student drinks through the straw, the class will notice that the water (blood) flows through the straw easily. Have the student soften a piece of gum by chewing on it. Place the gum at the bottom of the glass with water. Then have the student stick the straw on the gum. The student is then to try sipping water through the straw. No water will go through the straw. The gum served as a blockage in the coronary artery. No blood could go through the artery.

Have students describe why a heart muscle can die based upon what they have just observed. (The heart muscle was deprived of blood and could not receive oxygen. This caused the heart muscle to die.)

Just Like Leather

Objective

Students will discuss how prolonged exposure to the sun can cause the skin to toughen and wrinkle prematurely as a person ages.

Life Skill

I will reduce my exposure to the sun by staying in shaded areas, wearing sunblock, and moving indoors if exposure to the sun has been too long.

Materials

Any leather object such as a football or a leather jacket

Motivation

1 Explain that overexposure to the sun is responsible for an increased risk of developing skin cancer. Most cases of skin cancer are caused by the sun. The American Cancer Society recommends that people protect themselves from overexposure to the sun. Sunscreens and sunblocks are recommended as well as covering up the body.

2 It is also known that people who are overexposed to the sun develop skin that is unnecessarily tough. Select a student to come to the front of the room and close his/her eyes. Then have the student touch the inside of a person's arm. The arm will feel smooth. Then have the student feel the skin of a football made of leather or another leather object. The student will indicate that this object feels rough. Explain that exposure to the sun causes the skin to have a leathery feel.

3 Explain that overexposure to the sun also causes the skin to wrinkle prematurely. Show students a smooth sheet of paper. Tell the class this sheet of paper represents smooth skin. Take the sheet of paper, crumple it into a ball, and then unfold it. Explain that exposure to the sun will cause the skin to wrinkle prematurely.

Evaluation

Have students brainstorm ideas for behaviors they can practice to prevent overexposure to the sun. They should present ideas such as staying in shaded areas, wearing sun block, or doing outdoor activities when the sun is not at its strongest (before 10:00 AM and after 3:00 PM.)

Family Feud Disease

Objective

Students will identify the the major kinds of communicable and noncommunicable diseases.

Life Skill

I will seek prompt treatment for signs and symptoms of communicable disease.

Materials

Poster paper

Motivation

1 This activity will follow the rules of the TV game show Family Feud. You can divide the class into groups of five with two groups of five playing together. The topic will focus on different kinds of diseases. You can select topics and make a list of five facts about the particular topic. You can write the list on a poster board and cover all the answers, assigning point values to each.

2 Invite two teams to the front of the room. You can have each team give itself a team name. The name may reflect a disease or disorder. For example, a team may name itself the Chronic Illnesses.

3 Among the kinds of topics you can choose are "Kinds of STDs." You may ask, "Name five major STDs." You can flip a coin to determine which family goes first or you can do it similar to the way it's done on the game show by having one representative from a family come to the front of the room. The first to answer a question is awarded the rest of the questions for his/her family.

4 As with the rules on TV, teams continue answering the questions. If a question is missed, the other team gets a turn and can win all the points by answering a missed question. You can modify this game in any way you wish.

5 Other topics can be: signs and symptoms of specific STDs, preventing STDs, or medications used to treat STDs.

Evaluation

Have students compile the facts as stated during each game. For example, students will list signs and symptoms of specific STDs.

Block That Sun

Objective

Students will describe how certain products help protect the skin from the effects of the sun.

Life Skill

I will wear sunscreen or sunblock when I expect to be exposed to the effects of the sun for a long period of time.

Materials

Petroleum jelly, an index card

Motivation

1 Explain that the harmful rays of the sun are called ultraviolet rays. To block these harmful rays, a person should apply sunscreen. The lighter a person's skin, the higher the sun protection factor (SPF) needed in a sunscreen. Thus, a person with very fair skin should use a product with an SPF of 30 while a person with light, brown skin should use a product with an SPF of 15.

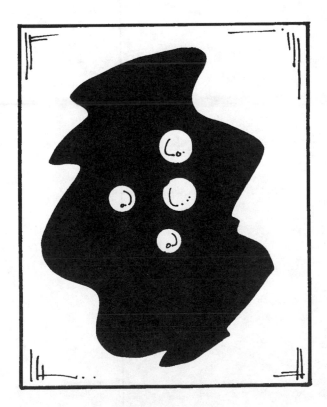

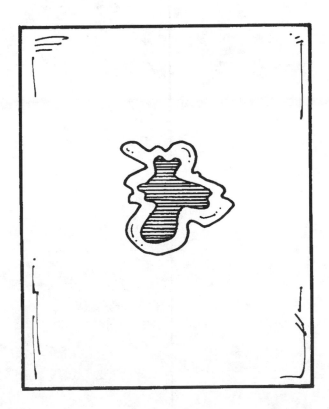

2 To identify how sunscreens work, take an index card and on half of it, spread a layer of petroleum jelly. Leave the other half of the card clear. The petroleum jelly represents sunscreen while the index card represents skin. Take a drop of water and place it on top of the part of the index card that is covered with petroleum jelly. Explain that the drop of water represents the sun's ultraviolet rays.

3 Have the class observe what happens to the drop of water. (It remains on top of the petroleum jelly and does not penetrate into the index card.) Then have the class observe what happens when you place a drop of water on the part of the index card that is not protected by the petroleum jelly. (The drop of water penetrates into the index card.)

Evaluation

Have the class draw a conclusion about the purpose of using sunscreen when exposed to the sun. (Sunscreen helps protect the skin from the harmful rays of the sun.)

A Rotten Core

Objective

Students will describe the importance of the skin in protecting the body from germs.

Life Skill

I will care for my skin so that it is clean and unbroken.

Materials

Apple, knife, food coloring

Motivation

1 Explain that when the skin remains unbroken, it is very difficult for microorganisms to penetrate and enter the body.

2 Take an apple and place it on the desk. Have students observe that the skin on the apple is not broken. Then take a knife and slice the apple. Have students describe the appearance of the inside of the apple. They will indicate that it is not discolored and looks fresh.

3 Continue with your lesson while the apple remains exposed to the air. After about fifteen minutes, have students observe the apple. They will notice that the apple begins to turn brown. Have students explain what this means. (The apple is becoming spoiled because the skin is broken and the inside of the apple is no longer protected.)

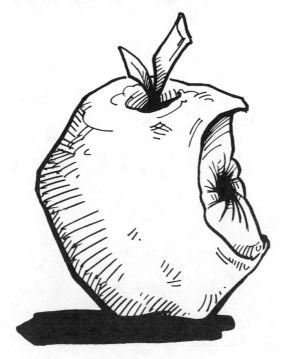

4 You can also demonstrate how the skin protects the apple by cutting a small hole on the top of the apple. Take food coloring and place a few drops on the skinned part of the apple. The class will notice that the food coloring did not penetrate the apple. Now take several drops of food coloring and place it in the hole you cut. Allow the apple to sit for about one-half hour. Then slice the apple through the cut where the food coloring was placed. Have students observe what happened. (The food coloring began to spread through the apple.)

Evaluation

Ask students to describe why skin is important and what happens once a pathogen gets inside the body. (Skin helps keep the body protected from pathogens. When pathogens enter the body, they can spread to other parts of the body in a manner in which the food coloring spread to other parts of the apple.)

Manual Dexterity

Objective

Students will describe the frustration involved in performing a task without having appropriate motor skills.

Life Skill

I will be sensitive to persons who have specific needs and handicaps.

Materials

None

Motivation

1 Explain that there are many different kinds of handicaps that people may have. In some kinds of handicaps, people may not be able to use their muscles to the greatest degree possible or they may need help in performing certain tasks.

2 The following task will enable students to identify the difficulties involved in performing a task that most people consider easy. Tell students they are to try to tie their shoes. However, they are to have one limitation. They are to try to tie their shoelace without using their thumbs. Allow students the opportunity to perform this task without any time limit.

3 Discuss with students the difficulties involved with performing this task. Have students describe what feelings they experienced. They will mention that they became extremely frustrated even though they had plenty of time to perform this task.

Evaluation

Discuss with students what they can do to overcome frustrations. They can discuss the importance of helping others who may have difficulties due to handicaps.

Wheel of Misfortune

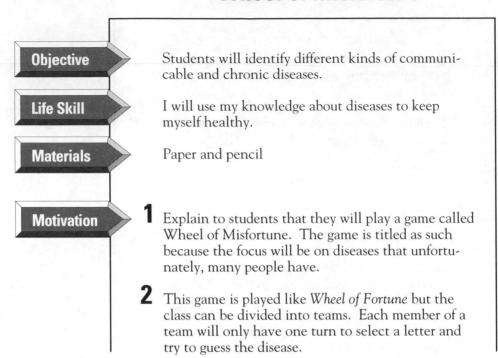

Objective

Students will identify different kinds of communicable and chronic diseases.

Life Skill

I will use my knowledge about diseases to keep myself healthy.

Materials

Paper and pencil

Motivation

1 Explain to students that they will play a game called Wheel of Misfortune. The game is titled as such because the focus will be on diseases that unfortunately, many people have.

2 This game is played like *Wheel of Fortune* but the class can be divided into teams. Each member of a team will only have one turn to select a letter and try to guess the disease.

3 Use the front of the room to place your letters. Take sheets of paper and write one letter per sheet of paper. Your words may be the names of diseases or disorders such as mononucleosis, chlamydia, cystic fibrosis, or any other words you cover in your class. You can also use sayings. For example, you may say, "A phrase which focuses on prevention." (Wash your hands.)

4 You can play several rounds of this game and declare the team that names the most correct answers as the winner.

Evaluation

Use the information from the games to develop a post test. For each word or phrase you use, have students answer a related question on a test.

A Spray of Germs

Objective

Students will describe how germs can be dispersed throughout a room and spread through the air.

Life Skill

I will cover my mouth and nose with a tissue when I cough or sneeze to prevent germs from spreading.

Materials

A spray deodorant can

Motivation

1 Explain to students that there are always germs around them. They are on objects that are touched. They are inside water that a person would drink. They are in the air that a person breathes.

2 Explain that many kinds of germs are spread throughout the air we breathe. Yet, these germs may not be observable. They may not be seen. They may not produce an odor. Yet, these germs are in the air.

3 To demonstrate that germs may be present in the air, take a can of room deodorizer. Spray it in the air. Tell students to imagine that you have pumped germs in the air. Students will observe the germs when the spray is initially pumped, but they will not see the mist after a while. Explain that the scent they will smell will be indicative that there are still germs in the air. In this case, the germs are observable.

4 Show students how covering one's nose and mouth when sneezing can prevent germs from getting into the air. Using the spray deodorant, cover the opening of the nozzel with a cloth. The cloth represents a handkerchief. When the spray is directed into the cloth, the mist is prevented from entering the air. Students will not be able to smell the scent from the spray. They will not be able to see the mist in the air.

Evaluation

Have students discuss how the germs in the air can enter a person's body. (When a person inhales, the germs enter the lungs. They move into the bloodstream from the lungs.)

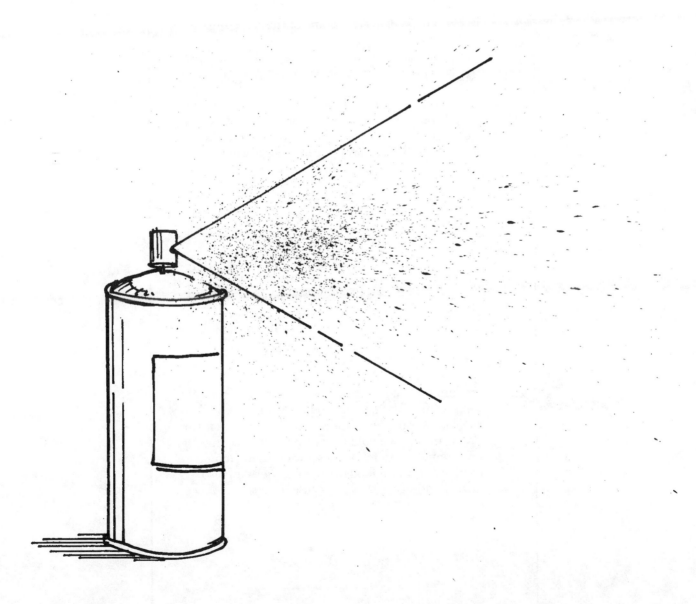

Sens-ible

Objective

Students will describe how the senses help protect the body from illness.

Life Skill

I will not eat food that looks or smells spoiled.

Materials

A container of milk that has turned sour, a slice of cheese that has been exposed to room temperature and has mold formed on it

Motivation

1 Explain to students that some of the sense organs can help protect people from illness. The senses of smell, taste, and sight, provide us with hints about the safety of certain products we eat.

2 Demonstrate how the senses of smell and taste help us to keep from eating foods that can cause illness. Tell students you would like them to smell a container of milk that has not been refrigerated. As you hold the container of milk, students will become aware of the unpleasant odor. Sometimes spoiled milk can only be detected by its sour taste. This is an example of how taste and smell can help protect us.

3 The sense of sight also helps prevent illness from spoiled food. Show the class a slice of cheese that is spoiled. Students will notice the mold that has formed when the cheese was not refrigerated. Tell students they should avoid cheese that has mold growing on it as it is an indication it is spoiled and can cause illness if eaten.

Evaluation

Explain to students that there is a saying, "Eat cold foods when they are cold and eat warm foods when they are warm." Ask students to describe what this saying means. (If cold foods are left in a warm environment, bacteria can grow on them and cause spoilage. If warm foods turn cold, they can also attract pathogens that can cause illness.)

Blurred Vision

Objective

Students will describe the need to correct impaired vision.

Life Skill

I will have regular eye examinations and will seek prompt treatment for visual disturbances.

Materials

Slide projector with any kind of slide

Motivation

1 One of the most common types of vision problems is astigmatism. Astigmatism is blurred vision at any distance. It is caused by an irregularly shaped cornea. A student who has astigmatism may hold reading material close to the eyes, squint, or frown.

2 Have students experience what it feels like to have astigmatism. Turn on a slide projector and flash a slide on a screen. Turn the lens on the projector so that the picture is out of focus. Explain to students that if they had astigmatism, vision would appear blurred like the picture in the slide.

3 Discuss the implications of astigmatism to health. Explain that a person who has astigmatism and does nothing to correct this condition, may be at increased risk to having an accident or suffering unexpected injury.

Evaluation

Have students think about the many activities in which they are involved daily. Have them describe how having astigmatism can interfere with these activities. For example, a student who plays baseball may not be able to see clearly a ball that is thrown and may suffer needless injury.

Lights Out

Objective

Students will describe how pathogens and particles in the air get into the lungs.

Life Skill

I will avoid exposure to polluted air when possible.

Materials

Slide projector, two jars filled with cotton, a lid for one jar

Motivation

1 Explain to students that there are always pathogens in the air we breathe. Most of the time, these pathogens cannot be seen.

2 To provide students with a glimpse of the degree to which the air is filled with dust and possible pathogens, close the lights in the room. Turn on the slide projector and have students describe what they see where the light is shining. Students will notice dust in the air.

3 To show that dust accumulates over a period of time, fill two glasses with cotton balls. Cover one of the glasses with a lid. Leave the other glass uncovered. Place the glasses somewhere in the room. If you choose, you can place the glasses outside the room. Observe the cotton in the glasses after a week. Students will notice that the uncovered cotton has specks of dirt evident, but the cotton in the covered glass is clean.

Have students conclude why the cotton in the jar that is covered was cleaner than the cotton in the uncovered jar. (The cotton in the uncovered jar was exposed to the air. The air has particulates, or specks of dirt.) Ask students what assumptions can be made about this experiment and health. People who may have lung problems can aggravate their conditions by exposure to dirty air.

Bend Your Joint

Objective

Students will describe why a person who has arthritis has difficulty bending at the joints.

Life Skill

I will be sensitive to the needs of a person who has arthritis.

Materials

None

Motivation

1 Explain that arthritis is a condition in which inflammation at the joints makes it difficult to bend. Explain to students that they have joints throughout their bodies. There are joints at the knee, hip, elbow, fingers, and toes, to name a few.

2 Explain that the class will experience what it feels like to have arthritis. Divide the class into two groups. The first group will be participants and the second group will be observers. Tell the first group you are going to ask them to stand at their seats. The second group must observe the first group stand. However, you will place criteria on how people will stand. The people who will stand are to pretend they have arthritis that affects the knees. Therefore, when they stand, they must try to do so while keeping the knees straight. When you have them stand, have the other group observe them.

3 Have the first group now sit. But in sitting, the knees must remain as stiff as possible. Have the second group observe the first group sit. Then have the class switch roles so that the observers become participants, and vice versa.

Evaluation

Have students share how the persons with arthritis sat and stood. They should be able to make analogies to people who are older and cannot sit and stand easily. Explain that while arthritis is mostly a condition associated with older people, it also, on occasion, affects young people.

Hearing Impaired

Objective

Students will describe how hearing helps protect health.

Life Skill

I will avoid loud noises.

Materials

None

Motivation

1 Begin a lesson by getting in front of the room and telling the class a phrase. However, you will not say the phrase orally. You will lip sound what you are saying. Lip sound the following statement: "Please help me. My home is on fire."

2 Ask students to interpret what you have said. Most likely, students will not be able to tell you what you said. Tell the students you said, "Please help me. My house is on fire." Explain that people who are hearing impaired will have the same experience as the class. They will see lips move, but not hear sound. However, people who are hearing impaired may be able to interpret what people are saying by observing lip movement. People who are hearing impaired use sign language to communicate with others.

3 Discuss the importance of the sense of hearing to health. Ask the class to provide examples of how the sense of hearing can help keep a person protected. Some ways hearing helps to keep people healthy is through hearing oncoming traffic, through receiving important instructions, and sending important information over the telephone.

4 Discuss the ways hearing can be protected. Avoid loud noises. Lower the volume emitted through headphones if there is a vibration felt. Do not clean the ears by placing cotton swabs deep into them.

Have students become aware of the importance of sound when they are at school. Have students pretend what an average school day would be like for them if they were not able to hear. Discuss how learning would be affected. How would they communicate with friends? What would it be like to participate in athletic activities?

Evaluation

Have students identify ways their hearing protects them during their daily activities.

Consumer Health is the area of health which focuses on being a responsible consumer by budgeting time and money carefully, analyzing advertisements, differentiating between healthful products, services and quackery, reporting quackery to consumer protectors, taking responsibility for personal health management, and having knowledge of health care providers, health care facilities, and health insurance plans.

Budgeting Time and Money

A **consumer** is a person who spends time and money on products and services. It is estimated that more than 50 cents of every dollar are spent on health products and services. Thus, the health industry is big business. Many dollars are spent in efforts to influence consumers to spend their time and money on specific health products and services.

Most consumers acknowledge that they want to be protected from wasting their money. Yet, responsible consumership also focuses on the wise use of one's time. A **time management plan** is a plan that indicates how time will be spent on daily activities and leisure. An effective time management plan includes blocks of time set aside to promote physical, mental-emotional, family-social, and spiritual health. To make a time management plan, a person identifies all daily activities on a calendar showing the hours of the day. Then a person might examine the activities and assess whether or not attention has been paid to all areas of well-being. Persons who manage their time well and who attempt to balance their time and include activities to promote all areas of health, tend to be healthier and happier and report fewer harmful effects from stress.

Having a budget and living within that budget also tends to influence health, happiness, and stress level. A **budget** is a plan which shows income, expenses, and savings. A wise consumer makes a budget and lives within that budget. This person attempts to buy the best products and services affordable with the given resources. Some suggestions include: gather information about a product or service before purchasing, engage in comparative shopping, insist on formal contracts and dated receipts and keep them in a file, and obtain written instructions and warranties on the use of products or services.

Advertisements

Advertising companies pay large sums of money to influence consumers to buy their products and services. There are ten different kinds of appeals they use to be convincing. Ads using **bandwagon appeal** try to convince you that everyone wants a particular product or service and you should too. Ads with **brand loyalty appeal** tell you that a specific brand is better than the rest. You would be cheating yourself to use anything but this brand. Ads with **false image appeal** convince you that you will be a certain way if you use the product even though you really won't. Persons who want a specific image might buy a product or service hoping that it will help them create that image. Ads with **glittering generalities** contain statements that greatly exaggerate the benefits of the product. Ads with **humor appeal** use a slogan, jingle, or cartoon to catch and keep your attention. Ads with **progress appeal** tell you that a product is a new and better product than one you used to see advertised. Ads with **reward appeal** tell you that you will receive a special prize or gift if you buy a product. Ads using **scientific evidence appeal** give you the results of survey or laboratory tests to provide confidence in a product. Ads with **snob appeal** convince you that you are worthy of a product or service because it is the best. Ads with **testimony appeal** include a promotion by a well-known person who says a product or service is the best one for you. A wise consumer is able to differentiate between a product and service that is needed and is a responsible use of time and money and one that might be purchased because of an advertising appeal.

CONSUMER HEALTH

Quacks and Quackery

The practice of promoting and/or selling useless products and services is known as **quackery** or **consumer fraud**. The person who markets inaccurate health information, unreliable health care, or useless health products, is referred to as a **quack** or **fraud**. A quack or fraud may promote products or services by promising quick cures, miracles, and/or new formulas of which no one has heard. This person may sell door-to-door or by telephone rather than in conventional ways. The consumer may be provided with testimonials from persons who claim that several illnesses or ailments were remedied by a product or service. Responsible consumers should avoid purchases in these instances as almost always consumer fraud is indicated.

Consumer Protectors

Because the health industry is such big business and the potential harm to persons is great, there are a variety of federal, state, and local agencies as well as professional associations who serve as consumer protectors. Professional associations help the consumer by monitoring the credentials of their members and their actions. The **American Medical Association** or **AMA** is an association that sets standards for the education and conduct of medical physicians. The AMA has a Department of Investigation and a Department of Health Education to assist the consumer and to investigate complaints. The **American Dental Association** or **ADA** is an association that sets standards for the education and conduct of dentists.

There are other kinds of consumer protectors. The **Better Business Bureau** is a nonprofit, voluntary, self-regulating organization that monitors unfair competition and misleading advertisements for private firms. Although this organization has no legal power, businesses want to have a favorable reputation and usually comply with their recommendations. The **Consumers' Research** and **Consumers' Union** are private groups that test products and provide ratings for consumers to make comparisons with regard to price, performance, and safety. Both groups are supported by private donations and by the sale of their publications.

State and local agencies and associations also are valuable consumer protectors. The **state health department** usually has a consumer affairs office that investigates complaints and takes action when harmful products or services are sold in the state. The **local or city health department** may also have a consumer affairs office that investigates complaints and takes action when harmful products or services are sold at the city or local level.

The federal government plays a vital role in consumer protection. The **Food and Drug Administration** or **FDA** is a federal agency within the Department of Health and Human Services that tests the safety and effectiveness of medical devices and new drugs and the safety and purity of cosmetics and foods. The **Federal Trade Commission** is an independent agency that monitors the advertising of foods, drugs, cosmetics, devices, and advertising that appears on television. The **United States Postal Service** protects the public when products, devices, and services are sold through the mail. The **Office of Consumer Affairs** serves as the liason between the President and all consumers. This office coordinates investigations into consumer problems, coordinates research, and conducts seminars to inform the public.

Personal Health Management

Personal health management is a term used to describe a process whereby the individual assumes responsibility for keeping a detailed personal health history and family health history, carefully chooses competent medical and dental care, and investigates health facilities and health insurance policies. Persons who choose to be involved in personal health management are in partnership with their physicians and dentists rather than giving primary responsibility to them. They choose to be educated thoroughly and to make comparisons before making choices.

Health Care Providers

Consumers seek health care providers for screening, preventive measures, consultation, diagnosis, and treatment. Selecting a competent health care provider is an important task. After an initial visit, several questions can be asked: Was I comfortable with this person? Was I able to communicate? Were all my questions answered in an understandable and reassuring way? Did this person show concern for my well-being? Does this person seem interested in having me as a client? Is this person's training and specialty area a match for my needs? Is this person associated with professional associations or hospitals that are credible? Is this person's policies for payment compatible with my ability to pay? What are the hours that this person is available? Will my needs be met if there is an emergency? Will I receive prompt responses to my telephone calls?

Health Care Facilities

There are a variety of facilities of which consumers need to be aware. **Private hospitals** are hospital facilities owned by private individuals and operated for profit. They are not supported with tax dollars, thus they are usually used by persons who are able to pay for all services. **Public hospitals** are governmental or tax-supported hospitals. These hospitals usually provide services to low-income persons as well as others. They are frequently teaching hospitals. **Voluntary hospitals** are nonprofit, public institutions usually owned by the community. They are supported by patient fees and contributions. Religious groups, fraternal groups, and charitable organizations often run them. A current trend is for these hospitals to have wellness centers.

Prior to using health care facilities, responsible consumers learn about them. They learn the exact services performed and the costs for those services. They check into methods of payment. They make comparisons to using other types of facilities.

Health Insurance Plans

Americans spend in excess of 625 billion dollars on health care. Consumers pay for health care directly out of their pockets, through local, state, and federal taxes, and through health insurance. **Health insurance** is a financial agreement between an insurance company and an individual or group for the payment of health care. The consumer pays a premium to the insurance company for a health insurance policy and in turn the health insurance company pays for specific benefits. Health insurance policies differ in their coverage making it necessary for consumers to be well-informed prior to purchasing a policy and prior to expecting benefits to be paid for specific health care. Usually, there is a **deductible**, an amount to be paid by the policy holder before the health insurance company makes any payment. Usually there are **fixed indemnity benefits**, specified amounts that are paid for specific procedures. Often, there are **exclusions**, certain items and services that are not covered by the health insurance policy.

Because of rising health care costs, there has been an emergence of health maintenance organizations. **Health maintenance organizations** or **HMOs** are health care delivery plans in which subscribers prepay a fixed monthly fee for coverage from health care providers. HMOs usually provide comprehensive health care as well as preventive care. This arrangement encourages persons to use health care providers as they are paying for services. The health care providers work together allowing for cost containment. One drawback of the HMO is the lack of personal patient/health care provider relationship. The patient sees many different health care providers rather than developing a constant relationship with one.

The government is also involved in paying for health care. **Medicare** is a governmental health insurance in which persons contribute during their working years in exchange for some of their health care costs being covered after age 65. **Medicaid** is a governmental health insurance plan in which persons receiving other types of public assistance receive medical and hospital coverage. There is no age requirement for medicare.

Health Specialists Concentration

Objective

Students will be able to identify medical health specialists.

Life Skill

I will seek prompt medical care when I have symptoms for which I need a checkup.

Materials

Large sheet of heavy display board, poster board, construction paper, small exacto knife

Motivation

1 One way to help students become familiar with health specialists and the kinds of general services they offer is through a Health Specialists Concentration game. The materials consist of a gameboard with twenty compartments. In ten random compartments, there are the names of various health specialists; and in the remaining ten, there are brief descriptions of the nature of the specialists' services. Each compartment has a numbered cover card which conceals the pertinent information. In addition, there is a judge's sheet with the correct combination of specialists and services identified.

Construction of the gameboard is relatively simple and inexpensive. Use a large sheet of heavy display board to make the gameboard sturdy. Poster board can be used for the twenty health specialists and brief description cards, and construction paper can be used for the twenty cover cards. Use a small exacto knife to make slits in the display board to hold the game cards. A sample key appears below. A variation for use of this game with primary children would be to use pictures, for example, for an eye doctor, an eye; for a dentist, a tooth, etc.

Numbers	Specialist	Description of work
5/20	Cardiologist	Heart specialist
11/18	Dentist	General care of teeth
3/19	Dermatologist	Skin specialist
1/16	General Practitioner	General health care
4/7	Obstetrician	Cares for mother before baby is born
2/10	Ophthalmologist	Corrects vision problems/ can perform eye surgery

6/13	Optometrist	Corrects vision problems
8/14	Oral Surgeon	Pulls teeth/performs mouth surgery
12/17	Orthodontist	Straightens teeth
9/15	Pediatrician	Children's doctor

Ideally, there would be sufficient boards for everyone in the class to be involved in a team of three. If you had thirty students in your class, you would need ten gameboards. Since there are so many different kinds of health specialists, each gameboard can be different, although there can be some repetition. In this way, the game can be used for several rounds before the students have a chance to learn all the health specialists.

2 For each gameboard, there are two players and one judge. The rules for the game are simple. Order of play can be determined by having the judge write a number between one and ten and allowing each player to choose two numbers from the board. The cover cards are removed, revealing two pieces of information. If there is no match, the cover cards are returned to their original positions on the gameboard and the second player takes a turn.

3 The game is terminated when all cover cards are removed from the board. The winner is the player who holds the most cover cards at the end of the game. In case of a tie, the player who received the last two cover cards loses.

4 When students have completed the game, review information. A health specialist is a person who has additional training in a specific area. A symptom is a change in a body function from a normal pattern. Symptoms which indicate a person needs a checkup include: shortness of breath for no reason, loss of appetite, cold symptoms for more than a week, blood in the urine or bowel movement, constant cough, a fever of 100 degrees Fahrenheit, swelling or stiffness in joints, severe pain, frequent or painful urination, sudden weight gain or loss, dizziness or fainting, any warning signs of cancer, and any warning signs of heart attack or stroke.

Evaluation

Have students list (or state orally) the definition of symptom and the symptoms that indicate a checkup is needed. Then have them list (or state orally) the names of five health specialists and what they do.

Don't Forget To Floss

Objective

Students will discuss the importance of flossing teeth each day.

Life Skill

I will floss my teeth each day.

Materials

Shoebox for each student, scissors, yarn, gumdrops, paper and markers

Motivation

1 Have students use the cardboard shoeboxes to construct a mouth full of teeth (see illustration). They should leave some cardboard at the bottom of the teeth to represent the gums. Make certain that students cut a separation between each tooth.

2 Discuss care of the teeth. Explain that when a person eats, small pieces of food get caught between the teeth. These small pieces of food that collect near the gums combine with germs in the mouth to form a substance called plaque. Plaque can be described as a sticky material that forms on teeth. When it is not removed daily, it hardens and may cause cavitites. A cavity is a hole in a tooth caused by the germs in the plaque. Brushing teeth helps remove some of the pieces of food and plaque, but brushing teeth won't remove it all. Flossing is a way to remove the pieces of food and plaque. Dental floss is a special thin thread that is used to clean between the teeth.

3 Demonstrate correct flossing using the yarn and the cardboard teeth in the shoebox. Show students how to wrap the floss around their fingers. Show a gentle motion whereby the floss is slid down between the teeth, wrapped around a tooth, and brought up to remove pieces of food and plaque. Put a small piece of the gumdrop between two of the cardboard teeth. Use the dental floss to re-move it.

4 Have students demonstrate flossing using their
shoebox replicas of teeth. Give them pieces of
gumdrops to place between teeth for extra practice.

Have students draw seven teeth on a sheet of paper.
Each of the teeth represents one day of the week.
For the next week, they are to make a smiley face
on one of the teeth for each day that they floss.

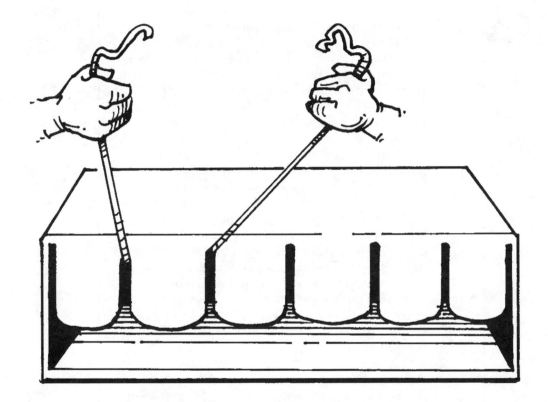

Name That Food

Objective

Students will explain why it is important to read and compare food labels when buying foods.

Life Skill

I will read food labels to learn the ingredients in foods.

Materials

Teaching Master, page 411, "Name That Food," three grocery bags, Good and Plenty candy, Coffee-mate, Kal Kan Whiskas cat food, several food labels

Motivation

1 Tell students you are going to play, "Name That Food."

2 Show Teaching Master, "Name That Food," page 411. You also may distribute a copy of this master to each student. Tell them that they have two tasks. (1) They are to imagine being on a deserted island with these three foods. They are to pick the one they would eat. (2) They are to decide what the food is (not the brand name). Give students five minutes to complete these two tasks.

3 Ask students to indicate by a show of hands, "Who chose food number one?" Repeat the same question for the other two foods and record answers on the chalkboard. Most likely the overwhelming majority of students will select food number 3.

4 Have the three foods each in a grocery bag on your desk. Beginning with food number 1, ask students to indicate what food they think is in the bag. Ask why they answered as they did.

5 After students give answers for what is in bag #1, pull out this food (Good and Plenty). Do the same for bag #2 (Carnation Coffee-mate). Say, "And now, the choice made by this class." Pull the food from bag #3. Tell students that they chose Kal Kan Whiskas cat food.

5 Explain the importance of reading food labels when buying foods. The ingredients in the food are listed with the ingredient that is greatest in amount being listed first.

Evaluation

Ask students why it is important to read food labels. Show them several food labels. Have them tell you what ingredients are in each food and which ingredient appears in the greatest amount.

Name That

1

sugar, corn, syrup, wheat flour, molasses, carmel color, licorice extract, corn starch, salt, artificial colors (including yellow 6), resinous glaze, anise oil, carnuba wax, artificial flavors

2

corn syrup solids, partially hydrogenated vegetable oil, (may contain one or more of the following: oils-coconut, cottonseed, palm, palm kernel, safflower, or soybean), sodium caseinate, mono- and diglycerides (prevent oil separation), dipotassium phosphate, artificial flavor, and annato color

3

tuna, water sufficient for processing, vegetable oil, dicalcium phosphate, sodium tripolyphosphate, tricalcium phosphate, sodium chloride, Vitamin A, B_1, B_6, E and D_3 supplements, zinc sulfate, menadione sodium bisulfide, manganous sulfate, sodium nitrite, folic acid

Your Nose Knows Not The Price

Objective

Students will explain the importance of comparing the price and ingredients when purchasing health products.

Life Skill

I will compare the price and ingredients when purchasing health products.

Materials

Teaching Master, on page 414, "Your Nose Knows Not The Difference," supermarket nasal spray, brand name nasal spray

Motivation

1 Begin this activity by asking students, "Suppose I told you that I could sell you Product X for $6.79 or I could sell you product Y for $1.99. Both products are exactly alike with regard to their ingredients. Which would you buy?" Students will indicate they would buy product Y.

2 Distribute the Teaching Master, "Your Nose Knows Not The Difference."

3 Explain that the labels on the Teaching Master are the actual labels from products. Explain that Product X is a brand name product. Explain that Product Y is a generic nasal spray sold in a large grocery store chain in the midwest. According to sales figures as of March, 1991, Product X sold for $6.79 and Product Y sold for $1.99 in the same supermarket.

4 Students can conclude that both products have the identical ingredients.

5 Have students discuss why people would pay more for one of the products. Discuss how each package may say the same thing, but in different ways. For example, Product X says "12 Hour Nasal Spray," and Product Y says, "Long Lasting Nasal Spray." But, a statement on the back of the label on Product Y states that "relief is offered up to 12 hours." Thus, both products do the same job.

Have students locate a brand name product and a supermarket or large chain store product. They are to compare the ingredients, advertising, and price for each of the two products.

Your Nose Knows Not The Difference

12 HOUR
NASAL SPRAY

INDICATIONS: For prompt temporary relief for up to 12 hours of nasal congestion due to colds, sinusitis hay fever and other upper respiratory allergies. ███ used in the morning allows free breathing all day without drowsiness. ███ used at bedtime helps restore freer breathing through the night. Also available for adults and children 6 years and over as ███ Nose Drops 0.05% and ███ Nasal Spray Pump 0.05%.

DIRECTIONS: For adults and children 6 years of age or over: With head upright, spray 2 or 3 times into each nostril twice daily-morning and evening. To spray, squeeze bottle quickly and firmly. Do not tilt head backward while spraying. Wipe nozzle clean after use. Not recommended for children under six.

WARNINGS: Do not exceed recommended dosage because burning stinging sneezing or increase of nasal discharge may occur. Do not use this product for more than 3 days. If nasal congestion persists consult a physician. The use of this dispenser by more than one person may spread infection. In case of accidental ingestion seek professional assistance or contact a Poison Control Center immediately. Keep this and all medicines out of the reach of children.

NOTE. This bottle is filled to correct level for proper spray action.

Contains phenylmercuric acetate 0.02 mg/mL as preservative.

Store between 2° and 3°C (36° and 86°F).

ACTIVE INGREDIENT: Oxymetazdine Hydrochloride.

ALSO CONTAINS: Benzalkonium Chloride, Glycine, Phenylmercuric Acetate, Sorbital, and Water.

X

LONG LASTING
Nasal Spray

INDICATIONS: FOR PROMPT, TEMPORARY RELIEF OF NASAL CONGESTION ASSOCIATED WITH COLDS, HAY FEVER, AND SINUSITIS THAT LASTS UP TO TWELVE HOURS. WHEN USED AT BEDTIME, THIS PRODUCT HELPS TO RESTORE FREER NASAL BREATHING THROUGH THE NIGHT. THIS PRODUCT CONTAINS THE LONGEST ACTING TOPICAL NASAL DECONGESTANT AVAILABLE.

DIRECTIONS: FOR ADULTS AND CHILDREN 6 YEARS OF AGE AND OVER: WITH HEAD UPRIGHT, SPRAY TWO OR THREE TIMES INTO EACH NOSTRIL TWICE DAILY-MORNING AND EVENING. TO SPRAY, SQUEEZE BOTTLE QUICKLY AND FIRMLY. NOT RECOMMENDED FOR CHILDREN UNDER 6.

WARNINGS: DO NOT EXCEED RECOMMENDED DOSAGE BECAUSE BURNING DISCHARGE MAY OCCUR. DO NOT USE THIS PRODUCT FOR MORE THAN 3 DAYS. IF SYMPTOMS PERSIST, CONSULT A PHYSICIAN. THE USE OF THIS CONTAINER BY MORE THAN ONE PERSON MAY SPREAD INFECTION. DO NOT USE THIS PRODUCT IF YOU HAVE HEART DISEASE, HIGH BLOOD PRESSURE, THYROID DISEASE, DIABETES, OR DIFFICULTY IN URINATION DUE TO ENLARGEMENT OF THE PROSTATE GLAND UNLESS DIRECTED BY A DOCTOR.

KEEP THIS AND ALL MEDICINES OUT OF THE REACH OF CHILDREN. IN CASE OF ACCIDENTAL INGESTION, SEEK PROFESSIONAL ASSISTANCE, OR CONTACT A POISON CONTROL CENTER IMMEDIATELY.

ACTIVE INGREDIENT: OXYMETAZOLINE HYDRO-CHLORIDE, 0.05%

ALSO CONTAINS: BENZALKONIUM CHLORIDE, GLYCINE, PHENYLMERCURIC ACETATE (0.02 MG/ML AS A PRESERVATIVE), SORBITAL AND WATER. STORE BETWEEN 2° and 30°C (36° AND 86°F).

Y

Stop Tooth Decay

Objective

Students will identify foods that are healthful for the teeth and foods that may cause tooth decay.

Life Skill

I will keep my teeth and gums healthy by including foods and drinks with calcium and vitamin C in my diet and limiting foods and drinks with sugar.

Materials

Apple, marshmallow, knife, construction paper, scissors, markers or crayons

Motivation

1 Explain to students that permanent teeth need to last a lifetime. It is important to brush and floss teeth daily, to have dental checkups every six months, to wear a safetybelt in an automobile to prevent mouth injuries, and to wear a mouthguard for playing sports. A fluoride toothpaste can also be used. These are ways to protect teeth.

2 Explain that diet is also important in helping teeth to last a lifetime. Whenever you eat, small pieces of food stick to the teeth. They combine with germs to form plaque. Keeping the teeth clean helps to prevent plaque.

3 Some kinds of foods help make plaque more than other kinds of foods. These foods are sticky and are high in sugar. Use the knife to slice the apple. Think of the knife as an incisor tooth. Explain that there is some natural sugar in an apple, but this is not the kind of sugar that sticks to teeth. Use the knife to slice the marshmallow. Some of the marshmallow will stick to the knife. Ask students to explain what happens when they eat foods like marshmallows, jelly beans, and licorice. These foods stick to the teeth. Children who eat large amounts of these foods are more likely to have cavities.

4 Discuss foods that are healthful for teeth. Foods with calcium make teeth strong. Milk and foods made from milk such as cottage cheese, yogurt, and cheese contain calcium. Foods with vitamin C keep the gums healthy. Fruits such as grapefruit, lemons, limes, and oranges contain vitamin C.

Identify snacks that do not contain sticky sugar in them. Encourage students to choose these snacks.

Have students make a Happy Tooth and a Sad Tooth from construction paper. Show students pictures of foods. When foods that are healthful are shown, students can hold up a Happy Tooth. When foods that contain sugar are shown, students can hold up a Sad Tooth.

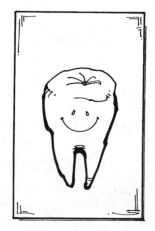

Collage of Ads

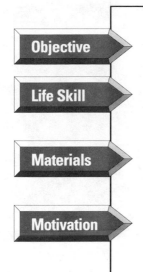

Objective
Students will identify common advertising techniques that are used to make advertisements appealing.

Life Skill
I will buy products and services that are needed rather than buying them because I am swayed by advertising.

Materials
Poster board, scissors, glue, magazines, newspapers

Motivation

1 Explain to students that advertisements are paid announcements that are designed to make a product appealing enough to buy. Sellers pay money so that they can convince you that you need their product or service. They hire advertising companies to help them. The advertising companies are aware of ways to appeal to you.

2 Some common appeals that are found in advertisements are:

Bandwagon appeal that tries to convince you that everyone wants this product and you should too.

Brand loyalty appeal that tells you that a specific brand is better than the rest.

False image appeal that tells you that you will be a certain way if you use the product even though you really won't.

Glittering generality that makes statements which greatly exaggerate the benefits of a product.

Humor appeal that is the use of a slogan, jingle, or cartoon to catch and keep your attention.

Progress appeal that tells you that a product is a new and better product than one you used to see advertised.

Reward appeal that tells you that you will receive a special prize or gift if you buy the product.

Scientific evidence appeal that provides the results of survey or laboratory tests to give you confidence in the product.

Snob appeal that tells you that you are worthy of this product because it is the best.

Testimony appeal that uses an endorsement by a well-known person who says a product is the best one for you.

3 Have students browse through magazines to find advertisements that appeal to them. They can cut out these advertisements and glue them to posterboard to make a collage.

4 Have students share their collages with the class explaining why they chose each of the advertisements they used. Have them tell what appeal was used in each advertisement.

Evaluation

Place all of the students collages around your classroom. Review the list of the eleven appeals. As each appeal is discussed, have students point out advertisements on the collages that are representative.

Medical Specialists Charades

Objective

Students will identify different medical specialists and will tell what each does.

Life Skill

I will seek prompt medical attention when needed.

Materials

None

Motivation

1 Discuss medical specialists. Explain that medical specialists have extra training in a specific area of medicine. Persons needing a specific kind of medical care might make an appointment with a medical specialist or they might be referred by a medical doctor.

2 Assign each student the name of a medical specialist about whom they must gather information. They are not to tell anyone in class which medical specialty they were assigned. A possible list of medical specialists to which you might add names:

    allergist
    anaesthesiologist
    cardiologist
    dermatologist
    general practitioner
    gynecologist
    hematologist
    internist
    neurologist
    nephrologist
    obstetrician
    oncologist
    opthalmologist
    orthopedic surgeon
    otorhinolaryngologist
    pediatrician
    plastic surgeon
    podiatrist
    proctologist
    psychiatrist
    radiologist
    urologist

After students have researched the medical specialty they were assigned, have students play Medical Specialists Charades. Divide the class into two teams. Students must act out the medical specialty they were assigned while their team tries to guess what it is. Each person has three minutes for his/her team to name the correct medical specialty. If the team answers correctly within the given time period, the team is awarded two points. If the team cannot name the correct medical specialty, the other team is given the opportunity. If the other team gives the correct medical specialty, they are awarded one point. Keep track of the points on the chalkboard to determine the winning team.

Evaluation

Have students list ten medical specialists and tell what they do.

Yellow Pages of Health Facilities

Objective ▶ Students will name health care facilities and describe the kinds of care provided by each.

Life Skill ▶ I will visit health care facilities in my community to learn what is available.

Materials ▶ Telephone book, Guide to Health Facilities for Your Community-if available, yellow paper, markers

Motivation ▶ **1** Introduce the topic of health care facilities. Explain that health care facilities are places where health care services are provided by health care providers. The following are examples of kinds of health care facilities:

Convalescent Home-a facility in which people can recover from illness or surgery; similar to a hospital but does not provide intensive care, surgical, and emergency treatment facilities.

Emergency Room-a facility within a hospital in which emergency care is provided without having a prior appointment; the facility is usually open at night, on weekends, and holidays to provide quick care.

Extended Care Facility-a facility that provides, nursing, personal, and residential care to persons who need assistance in daily living.

Government Hospital-a hospital facility run by the Federal government to provide health services for a specific population such as veterans.

Health Center-a facility that provides routine health services to a specific population such as low income families or college students.

Health Department Clinic-a clinic facility in most state and local health departments that keeps records and provides health services such as testing for sexually transmitted diseases and AIDS.

Mental Health Clinics-a facility that provides psychological services for persons having difficulty coping; usually open 24 hours a day in order to provide services for persons having a crisis.

*Private Hospital-*a hospital facility owned by private individuals operating for profit.

*Voluntary Hospital-*a hospital facility owned by the community which is non-profit.

*Urgent Care Center-*a facility that is separate from a hospital that provides health services for emergencies.

*Walk-in Surgery Center-*a facility in which surgery is performed on an outpatient basis.

2 Have students examine the telephone book and Guide to Health Care Facilities in Your Community (if there is one). They are to learn about all the health care facilities. They will want to know the hours the facilities are open, the services provided, the health care providers who work there, and the fees that are charged.

3 Using the yellow paper and markers, have students create a Yellow Pages of Health Facilities. They can work in groups to lay out a design for these pages. Different students can design different ads for the specific health facilities in your community.

Evaluation

Have students name five health care facilities in your community and the kinds of health care provided by each.

Grooming Products Auction

Objective

Students will identify grooming products and discuss how they are used to promote health.

Life Skill

I will have a neat and clean appearance.

Materials

Play money, grooming products or pictures such as Q-tips, tissues, dental floss, toothbrush, powder, toothpaste, mouthwash, anti-perspirant, lipstick, cotton balls, razor, soap, shampoo, nail file, nail polish, comb, brush, deodorant, perfume, after shave, conditioner, nail polish remover, eyeliner, skin makeup, tweezers, toe clippers, cuticle scissors

Motivation

1 Discuss grooming. Grooming is attention that is paid to having a neat and clean appearance. Have students discuss the importance of grooming.

2 Discuss health products that are used for grooming. These are listed in the materials above. Explain how and why each health product might be used.

3 Have students select one of the grooming products for the Grooming Products Auction. They will be asked to auction off this product when the auction begins. Give each student play money. Explain that they are to make the best buys possible. They need to decide which health products for grooming are most needed and to bid on those health products.

4 Select a student to begin the Grooming Products Auction. This student is to auction off his or her product to the highest bidder. The student should try to get the highest price possible by convincing the bidders that the product is necessary and will help the person to be appealing.

5 Have students discuss the grooming products upon which they bid. Which products demanded the highest price? Why? Which products were not in demand? Why? What were some of the ways the auctioneers tried to persuade the bidders to raise their bids? Which appeals were most convincing?

Have students explain why it is important to have a neat and clean appearance. Have them select five grooming products from the list that are most important and explain the reasons for their choices.

Sell That Cereal

Objective

Students will describe different appeals used to sell cereal and explain how to learn what ingredients are found in cereal.

Life Skill

I will eat cereal that is high in fiber and low in sugar.

Materials

Very large box, variety of empty cereal boxes some of which are high in sugar and some of which are high in fiber

Motivation

1 Show students two empty cereal boxes. One of the cereal boxes contained cereal that was flavored with sugar. The other cereal box contained cereal that was high in fiber. Explain that they can learn information by looking at the box and reading the food label. Show them the following:

- Name of each of the cereals.
- The amount of cereal in each box.
- The list of ingredients in each cereal.
- The name, address, and zip code of the company that makes the cereal.
- Any special claims that are made about the cereal. Are there prizes inside? Are there rewards for which you can send away?

2 Explain that it is important to eat cereal that is healthful. Emphasize the importance of really knowing what makes up the cereal. Show the box of cereal that contains high sugar. Point to where it says sugar on the list of ingredients. Explain that sugar may cause tooth decay. There are no vitamins or minerals in sugar. Then show the box of cereal that is high in fiber. Explain that fiber helps you have a bowel movement each day. Eating cereal with fiber is a healthful choice.

3 Make a television screen from the large box. Cut an opening in the box so that students might stand behind the box and pretend that they are on television.

Talk about cereal commercials that appear on television. Explain that there are many ways that companies try to get children to ask their parents to buy a certain cereal. These are some of the ways:

- Someone on TV or a sports person you like very much might tell you he or she eats this cereal.
- There might be a prize inside the cereal.
- They might tell you that the cereal will help you in some way like growing bigger and stronger.
- They might tell you that most children eat this cereal.
- They might show cute animals or something else you like on the box.

Ask students to volunteer to sell one of the boxes of empty cereal on television. The student is to stand behind the opening in the large box as if he or she is on television. Then the student is to talk about the cereal telling the class why they should ask their parents to buy it. Ask other students to volunteer to sell the other cereals for which you have empty boxes.

Evaluation

Ask students what they can learn from looking carefully at a cereal box. Have them tell you how they know if the cereal has sugar or fiber in it. Ask them ways that the commercials on television try to get them to ask parents to buy a specific kind of cereal.

Entertainment Coupon Book

| **Objective** | Students will differentiate between entertainment that promotes health and family values and entertainment that depicts risk behaviors and a lack of family values. |

| **Life Skill** | I will choose entertainment that promotes health and encourages family values. |

| **Materials** | Newspaper section depicting entertainment, *TV guide*, construction paper, markers, stapler |

Motivation

1 Explain to students that they are consumers. Consumers are persons who spend time and money on products and services. They are consumers when they spend time and money on entertainment.

2 Discuss the importance of choosing entertainment wisely. Explain that there is evidence that what you watch and what you read influence how you think and how you feel. Therefore, it is important to watch shows and read materials that promote health and healthful behaviors as well as family values.

3 Have students examine the newspaper section depicting entertainment and a *TV guide*. Discuss the programs that are listed that promote health and family values and those that encourage risk behaviors and suggest behaviors counter to family values. Which programs would be best to watch and why?

4 Divide students into groups. Give the students construction paper and markers. They are to discuss the entertainment available for teenagers in your community. For example, they might name restaurants in which teens enjoy eating, movie theatres, and sports facilities such as putt putt courses as well as amusement parks. Each group is to make an entertainment coupon book similar to the ones that are sold in most communities. Each coupon can state some type of entertainment, have a statement as to how it benefits health, and offer a bargain such as one free admittance with one paid admittance. Encourage students to be as creative as possible.

5 Have students share their Entertainment Coupon Books with classmates. Select the best ideas for coupons from each of the groups. Have students give reasons for their selections.

6 As an optional strategy, you might want to ask a select number of students to contact the owners of the places that were selected by students as the best ideas for coupons. The owners might agree to making the coupons a reality for students at your school.

Evaluation

Provide students with a list of televisions shows and movies that can be viewed in the upcoming week. Students are to pretend that they are writing critics and rating programs. They are to rate the programs with four stars being programs that promote health and family values and no stars as being those that do not. They can choose to rate programs with one, two, or three stars also. They are to rate each program on your list and give their reasons.

Quack, Quack, Quack!!

Objective

Students will identify ways that quacks try to sell them products.

Life Skill

I will not ask my parents to buy useless products.

Materials

Construction paper, markers, scissors, variety of empty cans and bottles, children's clothes

Motivation

1 Have students make ducks using construction paper, markers, and scissors.

2 Explain to students that they are going to learn about quackery. Quackery is the selling of products or services using false information. Here are some tips to recognize quackery:

- Someone tells you a product is a miracle cure for something.
- Someone tells you that there is a secret ingredient in a food or product.
- Someone comes to your door to sell you a product that should be sold at a grocery store or drug store.
- Someone tells you a product will help more than one kind of illness.
- Someone tells you that you can be just like someone else if you have a product.

3 Explain to the class you are going to sell them products. If they think you are using ways that a quack would use to sell products, they are to hold up their ducks and say "quack, quack, quack."

4 The following are examples of products and ways to sell them:

- Hold up an empty bottle. "This miracle drug will make you grow up to be very tall." (quack, quack, quack)
- "This cereal is low in sugar." (no quack)
- "I am coming to your door because this food is so new that no one has the secret recipe yet to make it. You can be the first to try it." (quack, quack, quack)

• "If you wear this clothing, you will
be just like...name someone your students
admire" (quack, quack, quack)

 **Evaluation**   Have each student pretend to be a quack and sell
one of the products to the class. Have the class tell
the way in which the person behaved as a quack.

Acid Power

Objective

Students will identify beverages that are healthful for the teeth.

Life Skill

I will drink low-fat or skim milk, fruit juices, and water rather than soda pop.

Materials

Two eggs, white vinegar, cola beverage containing sugar, two bowls, stannous fluoride, optional: two teeth

Motivation

1 Review the parts of a tooth. The crown is the part of the tooth above the gum. The root is the part of the tooth that holds it in the jawbone. The enamel is the hard tissue that covers the crown and keeps the tooth hard. The dentin is the hard tissue that forms the body of the tooth. The pulp is the soft tissue containing nerves and blood vessels. The pulp is in the center of the tooth. The cementum is the hard tissue that covers the root portion of the tooth.

2 Discuss the importance of the enamel in protecting the teeth and preventing decay. Perform the following experiment for students to show that acid will weaken substances containing calcium such as enamel and an eggshell. Place a whole egg in a bowl of white vinegar for twenty-four hours. Place another egg in a bowl of stannous fluoride for twenty-four hours. The eggshell soaked in vinegar will soften while the eggshell soaked in stannous fluoride will harden.

3 (Optional) Place a tooth in stannous fluoride for a week. Place another tooth in a cola beverage. In one week, there will be a hardening of the enamel of the tooth in the stannous fluoride while the enamel of the tooth in the cola beverage will soften.

4 Emphasize the importance of drinking beverages and eating foods that contain calcium. Discuss the benefits of avoiding cola beverages that contain sugar. The sugar and acid work together to soften enamel.

Have students make and follow a health behavior contract for one week in which they drink beverages that do not contain acid and sugar.

Owner's Manual

Objective

Students will discuss what is included in personal health management.

Life Skill

I will assume personal responsibility for managing my health.

Materials

Three ring notebooks, dividers, paper, pens, car owner's manual

Motivation

1 Show students a copy of a car owner's manual. Inside the manual, it will most likely say, "Important operating, maintainence, and service information." Explain that persons who buy a car need to read the owner's manual carefully to understand how to care for their new car and how to maintain it. They need to know when it needs service. Most new cars come with a warranty that indicates certain parts will work for a specified amount of time if the car is serviced properly or the parts will be repaired for free. This analogy can be applied to the body. Explain that with proper care, maintenance, and service that there is a specified life expectancy for males and females living in the United States.

2 Explain to students that they are going to create a Personal Health Management notebook. This notebook will be an owner's guide for taking personal responsibility for health. Students are to have the following dividers in their notebooks: Personal Health History, Family Health History, Medical Care, Dental Care, Health Facilities Used, Health Insurance Policies.

3 Have students gather information to include in their Personal Health Management Notebooks. Explain that a Personal Health History is similar to a diary of physical, mental-emotional, and family-social health. They should record facts about their health status. They should write a description of their habits. They can record observations about their health such as their body temperature, rate of respiration, pulse, and blood pressure. They should write dates next to each entry. Explain that the Personal Health History should be shared with their physician when they have a checkup.

4 Students should interview their families to get a Family Health History. If possible, they should have information on blood relatives including grandparents on both sides, parents, and siblings. They can include information about age of deceased family members and cause of death. For living family members, they can include habits as well as diseases and disorders.

5 For the Medical Care and Dental Care sections, students should record the names, addresses, and telephone numbers of their physicians and dentists. In this section, they can keep record of their visits to the physician and dentist. They can record the date and reason for the visit as well as the services received.

6 The students can record the names and addresses of health facilities where they have received services in the Health Facilities Used section. They can record the insurance provider of their parent or guardian in the Health Insurance Policies section.

7 Encourage students to share their notebooks with their parents or guardian and to keep their notebooks current.

Evaluation

Ask students to share what they have learned about themselves from assembling their Personal Health Management Notebooks. Remember to respect individual student's rights to privacy. Have students provide three reasons why keeping a Personal Health Management Notebook is beneficial.

The Message in Music

Objective

Students will explain the importance of choosing entertainment that promotes healthful living and positive moral values.

Life Skill

I will listen to music whose words promote healthful living and positive moral values.

Materials

Compact disc player, popular compact discs to which students listen, construction paper, aluminum foil, scissors, markers, tape

Motivation

1 Ask students to bring in compact discs to which they enjoy listening. Make a list of their favorite songs that appear on these discs. Play some of the songs. Ask students to summarize the message in each of the songs in one sentence.

2 Discuss the importance of choosing healthful entertainment. Healthful entertainment promotes physical, mental-emotional, and family-social health. It encourages the development of positive moral values.

3 Have students examine their list of favorite songs and the messages conveyed in each. Which of these songs promote health and positive moral values? Which songs encourage risk behaviors and immorality?

4 Make a bulletin board of "Healthful Messages in Music." Have students cut cardboard in the shape of a compact disc. Then have them cover their discs with aluminum foil. Now have them cut a strip of construction paper upon which they are to write a current song title and one sentence which summarizes the message conveyed in this song. The message must be healthful and moral. Place all the discs on the bulletin board.

Evaluation

Have students identify five current songs which promote health and positive moral values and five which do not. Have them discuss why it is better to listen to music which has a healthful and moral message.

THAT'S WHAT
FRIENDS ARE FOR
This song says friends
support you in good times
and bad times.

Teenage Magazine

Objective

Students will explain the importance of reading material that promotes healthful living and positive moral values.

Life Skill

I will read material that promotes healthful living.

Materials

Construction paper, markers, paper, pens, optional: computer, typewriter

Motivation

1 Explain to students that a Senate subcommittee report verified that persons who read materials replete with pornography and violence have changes in their attitudes regarding healthful sexuality and respect for the rights of others. Most likely students have heard the saying, "You are what you eat" relative to their nutritional health status. Another saying might also be very true, "You are what you read."

2 Have students provide examples of articles or books they have read that promote physical, mental-emotional, and family-social health.

3 Divide students into groups to create a Teenage Magazine that promotes healthful living and positive moral values. The construction paper and markers can be used to create a magazine cover. Each group should give its magazine a clever name related to health. Then each group should design ads for personal health products, write articles about physical, mental-emotional, and family-social health, and produce an advice column with letters and responses. Have students staple their magazines together.

Evaluation Have each group introduce its magazine to the class and give reasons why teenagers might want to subscribe. As they attempt to sell a subscription to classmates, they should mention the benefits of reading material that promotes healthful living and positive moral values.

What's My Line?

Objective
Students will identify consumer protectors and describe the services provided by each.

Life Skill
I will make a consumer complaint to the appropriate professional association, state and local association, or governmental agency when I feel my rights as a consumer have been violated.

Materials
Index cards

Motivation

1 Review the names and services provided by consumer protectors:

Professional Associations
- The American Medical Association (AMA) is an association that sets standards for the education and conduct of medical physicians. The AMA has a Department of Investigation and a Department of Health Education to assist the consumer and to investigate complaints.
- The American Dental Association is an association that sets standards for the education and conduct of dentists and educates the public about dental health.
- The Better Business Bureau is a nonprofit, voluntary, self-regulating organization that monitors unfair competition and misleading advertisements for private firms. Although this organization has no legal power, businesses want to have a favorable reputation and usually comply with recommendations from the BBB.
- The Consumers' Research and Consumers' Union are private groups that test products and provide ratings for consumers to make comparisons with regard to price, performance, and safety. Both groups are supported by private donations and by the sale of their publications.

State and Local Agencies and Associations
- The State health department usually has a consumer affairs office that investigates complaints and takes action when harmful products or services are sold in the state.
- The local or city health department may also

have a consumer affairs office that investigates complaints and takes action when harmful products or services are sold at the city or local level.

Governmental Agencies
- The Food and Drug Administration is a federal agency within the Department of Health and Human Services that tests the safety and effectiveness of medical devices and new drugs and the safety and purity of cosmetics and foods.
- The Federal Trade Commission is an independent agency that monitors the advertising of foods, drugs, cosmetics, and devices and advertising that appears on television.
- The United States Postal Service protects the public when products, devices, and services are sold through the mail.
- The Office of Consumer Affairs serves as the liason between the President and all consumers. This office coordinates investigations into consumer problems, coordinates research, and conducts seminars to inform the public.

2 Have students write examples of consumer problems on index cards. Their examples should highlight consumer problems that they believe persons their age might encounter.

3 Play "What's My Line?" Select three students to be the panel. One should be an imposter and one should be one of the consumer protectors about which the class has just learned. Students interview the three panelists and try to identify the consumer protector and the specific organization or agency with whom this person is affiliated.

Review the consumer problems about which students have written. Discuss the appropriate consumer protector who can help with each of the problems.

Evaluation

Make a matching quiz in which students must match each of the consumer protectors with the services they provide.

Warning Labels

Objective

Student will discuss ways that reading food labels can help them follow the seven dietary guidelines.

Life Skill

I will read food labels to gain information to help me follow the seven dietary guidelines.

Materials

Empty containers of foods, markers, construction paper, tape, cigarette package

Motivation

1 Show students the warnings that are on cigarette packages. Explain that in 1985, a new federal law came into effect that requires cigarette companies to print new, stronger health warnings in advertisements and on packages. There are four warnings that are rotated every three months. The warnings are based on the medical information contained in the *Reports of the Surgeon General on the Health Consequences of Smoking*.

2 Explain that The United States Department of Agriculture and The Department of Health and Human Services have developed seven dietary guidelines to promote health through proper diet. These are:

- Eat a variety of foods. The diet should be 30% fat, 12% protein, and 48% complex carbohydrates.
- Maintain a healthful weight. Being over-weight is linked with increased risk of heart diseases, high blood pressure, cancer, diabetes, and accidents.
- Choose a diet low in fat, saturated fat, and cholesterol. High fat diets particularly those high in saturated fats are linked to increased risk of cancers of the breast, colon, and prostate. There is also a link to heart disease.
- Choose a diet with plenty of vegetables, fruits, and grain products. Vitamin A helps reduce the risk of cancers of the larnyx, esophagus, and lungs. Vitamin C promotes the effectiveness of the immune system. Fruits, vegetables, and grain products that are sources of fiber reduce the risk of cancers of the colon and rectum.

- Use sugar only in moderation. High sugar intake is related to heart disease, obesity, and tooth decay.
- Use salt and sodium only in moderation. A diet higher than 6 grams of sodium is linked to high blood pressure.
- Do not drink alcohol or drink alcohol only in moderation as an adult. Do not drink at all as a minor. Alcohol consumption of more than one ounce per day is linked to cancers of the mouth, larynx, throat, liver, esophagus, and stomach.

3 Have students use construction paper and markers to create warning labels for foods. These warning labels can be taped on the containers. They might also make labels to show benefits. For example, they might label a cereal that has fiber in it, "This food product contains fiber which is known to reduce the risk of cancers of the colon and rectum."

Evaluation

Show students five different food containers. After reading the food labels, they are to determine whether or not they would be following dietary guidelines if they ate each food.

Each Minute Counts

Objective

Students will discuss the importance of having a time management plan that promotes physical, mental-emotional, and family-social health.

Life Skill

I will make and follow a time management plan that helps me to balance activities that promote physical, mental-emotional, and social health.

Materials

Copies of Teaching Master, "Time Management Plan," on page 443, paper, pencil

Motivation

1 Introduce the topic of time management. Explain to students that it is important to examine how they spend their time to learn if they are engaging in activities that promote balanced healthful living.

2 Have students list on paper the activities in which they participated yesterday. They should attempt to recall everything from when they got out of bed until when they went to bed at night. Next to each activity, they should write: (1) An M if the activity promoted mental health. (2) A P if the activity promoted physical health. (3) An F if the activity promoted family health. (4) An S if the activity promoted social health.

3 Have students draw three conclusions that show how they spend their time based on an analysis of their ratings beside each activity.

4 Give each student a copy of the "Time Management Plan." Have students make a time management plan for the next three days.

Evaluation

After completing their time management plans, ask students to describe the benefits they derived from physical activities (P), mental-emotional activities (M), family activities (F), and social activities (S).

Time Management Plan

TIME	Date _____	Date _____	Date _____
A.M.	Activity___Area of Health	Activity___Area of Health	Activity___Area of Health
7:00- 8:00 A.M.			
8:00- 9:00 A.M.			
9:00- 10:00 A.M.			
10:00- 11:00 A.M.			
11:00- 12:00 Noon			
12:00- 1:00 P.M.			
1:00- 2:00 P.M.			
2:00- 3:00 P.M.			
3:00- 4:00 P.M.			
4:00- 5:00 P.M.			
5:00- 6:00 P.M.			
6:00- 7:00 P.M.			
7:00- 8:00 P.M.			
8:00- 9:00 P.M.			
9:00- 10:00 P.M.			

Make Mine Lean

Objective

Students will discuss the importance of knowing the fat content of food when making diet choices.

Life Skill

I will be a wise consumer and check the fat content of food before making choices for what I will eat.

Materials

Shortening, teaspoon, eight test tubes, chalkboard, chalk

Motivation

1 Discuss the importance of following a low-fat diet. A high fat diet particularly one high in saturated fats and cholesterol is linked to both heart disease and cancer.

2 On the chalkboard, write the names of the fast food chains with the names of the foods listed below. Do not write the number of grams of fat. Have students rank the foods giving a one to the food they believe contains the least amount of fat. The source for the foods and the fat content of each was a chart that appeared in "Feeding Frenzy," *Newsweek,* May 27, 1991, pg. 51.

Fast Food Chain	Kind of Sandwich	Grams of Fat	tsp.
McDonald's	McLean Deluxe	10 grams	2
McDonald's	Filet-O-Fish	26 grams	5+
Burger King	BK Broiler Chicken	18 grams	3 1/2
Burger King	Double Whopper w/Cheese	61 grams	12+
Wendy's	Grilled Chicken	13 grams	2 1/2
Wendy's	Wendy's Big Classic	33 grams	6 1/2
Kentucky Fried Chicken	Lite'n Crispy drumsticks	14 grams	4 1/2
Kentucky Fried Chicken	Chicken sandwich	27 grams	5 1/2

3 After the students have completed their rankings, write the number of grams of fat next to each sandwich. Explain to students that one teaspoon is the equivalent of five grams.

4 Show the students how much fat enters the bloodstream when each of these foods is eaten. Use one test tube for each food. Look at the chart to learn approximately how many teaspoons of fat are in each food. Use the shortening to represent the fat. Place the approximate number of teaspoons of shortening in the test tube.

Explain that this is how much fat enters the bloodstream when each food is consumed.

Have students explain why it is important to know how many grams of fat are in a food before it is eaten. Have them tell reasons why it is healthful to cut down on fat in the diet.

Safety and Injury Prevention is the area of health that deals with ways to keep safe from injury, accidents, and personal assault as well as what to do to prevent and treat injuries.

Accidents

Each year, over 90,000 people die from accidents in the United States. Only heart disease, cancer, and stroke rank ahead of accidents as a leading cause of death. For school-age children as well as college-age youth, accidents are the leading cause of death.

According to the National Safety Council, accidents are categorized into four main groups. These groups are:

Motor Vehicles - Accidents in this group include automobiles, motorcycles, bicycles, and pedestrian accidents.
Workplace - These include job-related accidents, falls, electric shocks, and burns.
Home - Accidents in the home include falls, burns, poisoning, suffocation, and firearms.
Public Places - These include accidents related to recreation, motor vehicles other than on highways such as farm equipment, and accidents in parks and schools.

Motor Vehicle

Accidents in motor vehicles account for about half of all fatal accidents and about 20 percent of all injuries leading to disability. Usually, these accidents involve collisions between motor vehicles or fixed objects such as walls or guard rails. There are often deaths and injuries due to rollovers and automobile-train collisions.

Motorcycles prove to be dangerous vehicles as getting into accidents in these vehicles offers little protection when compared to an automobile. About 4,000 people die from motorcycle accidents each year.

About 10,000 people die each year from acci-

dents due to collisions between automobiles and bicycles and between automobiles and pedestrians. Most of the people killed in bicycle accidents each year are between the ages of five and twenty-four. Interestingly, most cases of fatalities involving bicycles were the fault of the bicycle rider. In spite of the fact that bicycle riders have been encouraged to wear helmets, only five percent of the riders in fatal bicycle accidents were wearing helmets at the time of the accident.

According to the National Highway and Traffic Safety Administration, alcohol is a factor in about half of all fatal accidents involving automobiles. Alcohol impairs the ability to coordinate muscular activities so that improper driving procedures become more numerous. About 75 percent of motor vehicle accidents involve improper driving procedures. Of course, alcohol need not be a factor in the implementation of improper driving procedures.

How can motor vehicle accidents be prevented? There are several basic ways motor vehicle accidents can be prevented. First, avoid drinking and driving. Second, avoid excessive speed. The faster one drives, the greater the chances of an accident. Third, heed warning signs. This means that one must drive defensively. To drive defensively means to anticipate what others might do. And fourth, do not drive if you are not at your physical best. For example, if taking a medication that may produce drowsiness, avoid operating a motor vehicle since you may fall asleep or not have the ability to react quickly.

Work Accidents

In the United States, there has been a shift away from hazardous jobs to less physically demanding jobs. This has resulted in a reduction of job-related accidents. However, there continues to be a large number of workers who become injured each year. Many of these injuries result from lifting, pushing, or pulling objects. They may also result from being hit with objects.

The best way to avoid work-related injuries is for employers to provide safe environments for their em-

SAFETY AND INJURY PREVENTION

13

ployees. There are on-job safety requirements that must be followed. These may be set by governmental decrees or employers may set their own rules for safety on the job. Many companies present educational classes for their employees. For example, there may be classes that teach people how to lift heavy objects so as to avoid injury to the muscles in the back.

Home Accidents

There is great concern about the number of accidents that occur in the home. Although these accidents have been on the decline, home accidents strike three million people annually with one-fourth of these injuries resulting in permanent disability. The major kind of accident in the home is falls. These falls usually result from a drop from a higher level to a lower level, such as falling off a ladder or falling from a roof. Falls on steps and stairwells account for nearly one million emergency room visits in a year. In a study released by the Consumer Product Safety Commission in 1991, it was found that the causes of the accidents on steps and stairwells ranged from women tripping due to wearing high-heeled shoes that became caught in carpet to problems of depth perception by elderly individuals.

Fires and burns are another cause of injuries in the home. More than half of all fire fatalities are to people under the age of four. The most common cause of fires are faulty heating equipment followed by improper cooking procedures, defective electrical wiring, and poor appliances.

Each year, more than 4,000 people die from accidental poisoning. Small children are the prime victims of poisoning. They gain access to medicines and other products that are harmful when ingested. Overdoses of prescription drugs as well as mixing medications also account for a large number of poison-related accidents. The older age group is often susceptible to poisoning due to mixing medications or taking the wrong medication. Exposure to gases and vapors in the home is another way people become poisoned accidentally. This can occur from gas leaks and expo-

sure to carbon monoxide. Faulty gas heaters and cooking stoves can emit poisonous vapors in the air that can be fatal.

There are many different ways home accidents can be prevented. Electrical problems should be identified and corrected immediately. Poisonous substances should be kept out of the reach of children. Home smoke detectors should be placed in strategic locations so they can serve as warnings should a fire begin. In many homes, smoke detectors are not operational so they are deemed useless. In most localities, representatives from fire departments will come to a home to offer advice on where smoke detectors should be located.

Public Places

Most of the accidents that occur in public places result from falls, drowning, firearms, and burns. Drowning is the second most common cause of accidental death in the one to twenty-four age group. Most cases of drowning result from a lack of knowing how to swim. Many people who drown become fatigued and cannot get back to shore safely.

Diving accidents are a major cause of spinal cord injuries. Diving accidents typically occur when people dive into water that is too shallow. Water depth should always be known before diving into it.

Other water related accidents occur while boating. Close to 1,000 people are killed each year in boating accidents. Many of the boating accidents result from collisions. In many of these accidents, alcohol is involved.

Many injuries occur each year from participation in sports activities. There are any number of reasons why injuries may occur while participating in sports. They may be caused by a lack of knowledge of the rules of the sport. They may result from improper use of equipment or lack of the appropriate equipment. Sports that may appear to be safe can, in fact, be dangerous. The statistics released by the Consumer Product Safety Commission in 1991 show that basketball injuries alone accounted for 640,000 hospital visits in the 1990 year. This number is higher than the number for football injuries which were at 400,000. Another 400,000 people were injured playing baseball.

Sexual Assault

A large number of injuries result each year from sexual assault. There are different types of sexual assaults. One type is rape. **Rape** is sexual penetration of a female or male by force, intimidation, fraud, or aggression. Rape can occur to very young children as well as older persons. Rape usually involves a male raping a female or a male raping a male. In most cases, it is committed by males, but rape can be committed by females.

Of great concern is acquaintance rape, also known as date rape. Since the rape need not occur on a date, the most appropriate term is acquaintance rape. Studies now show that about one in five women have experienced acquaintance rape. An even larger number of women report that they have been touched against their will.

Women who have been victims of acquaintance rape may often feel troubled about reporting it since they may feel confused or they believe no one will believe their story. They often feel emotionally depressed and may suffer nightmares and anxiety attacks.

There are steps a woman can take to avoid acquaintance rape.

1. Be leery of men who appear to be particularly dominant and demanding as these men may also be very demanding in their sexual expectations.
2. Do not get in risk situations that may be conducive to acquaintance rape. For example, it may be wise to go on a group date with a man about whom little is known. Avoid isolated places. Avoid meeting and leaving a place with someone who is not known.
3. Verbalize any feelings specifically and forcefully. A man should know where a woman stands and she need not be intimidated by him.
4. A date should know at the beginning of a relationship where a woman stands with regard to physical intimacy.
5. Learn to resist and respond to unwanted sexual advances. This may include screaming, fighting, scratching, or kicking. Many women enroll in self-defense classes to learn how to protect themselves.

While the focus of this section has been on the importance of a female protecting herself from a male, it should be noted that a male can rape another male. For the purposes of this section, the most common type of rape, a male raping a female is emphasized. It is also important to understand that acquaintance rape is not only a male phenomenon. Although in much lower numbers, women can also be the aggressor in a rape situation. A man should be able to send the same messages to a woman that a woman sends to a man. Men should also have standards by which they abide and they have every right to make sure their standards are followed.

Not all rapes are committed by persons known by the victim. There are several steps that can be taken to reduce the risk of rape.

1. You can vary the route that you take home from work or other places you frequent regularly.
2. Try to walk with other people at night. For example, certain university campuses have escort services to accompany students to their places of residence.
3. Always stay on well-lighted streets.
4. Always have keys prepared in advance. For example, when going to an automobile, have the keys out ready to insert into the door. When entering a home, have the keys prepared so that the door can be opened quickly.
5. Do not go near an approaching vehicle. Remain at least an arm's length away. If you are suspicious of the person in the automobile, run in the opposite direction in which the car is travelling.
6. Be careful about how you provide information over the telephone. Many people will not answer telephone surveys even if it sounds as if it is computer generated. The slightest information provided can serve as a clue about your lifestyle and when you are at home or not at home. Do not leave personal information on an answering machine.
7. If you fear danger, yell "Fire" or call police.

Sexual Harassment

Sexual harassment is unwanted sexual attention. This attention may consist of comments related to sex, pressure for a date, threats of harm if sexual activity is not undertaken, or unwanted attention.

Sexual harassment can occur in many different settings. It may occur in the workplace, on college campuses, and in schools. A person who is sexually harassed should keep a record of exactly what happened. The date and any witnesses should be recorded. The appropriate authorities should be notified. For example, a student in a university may consult an affirmative action officer or an academic dean. If no action is taken, someone else should be notified. There are policies and procedures that different organizations follow.

A Strange(r) Phone Call

Objective

Students will demonstrate how to respond safely to a telephone call from a stranger.

Life Skill

I will not give personal information to a stranger over the phone.

Materials

Telephone (Toy or real)

Motivation

1 Show students the telephone and have them pretend they are home alone. Then select one volunteer to come to the front of the classroom to help you demonstrate how to respond to a stranger who is calling.

2 Pretend you are the stranger and you are calling. What you will say is going to be followed by how a typical student will respond in a similar situation. Begin by having the student answer the telephone while you say "ting-a-ling."

> Student: Hello.
> Stranger: Hi! Who is this?
> Student: This is Fran:
> Stranger: Hi Fran. This is Mr. Smith. Is your mother home?
> Student: No.
> Stranger: Do you know when she will be home?
> Student: No.
> Stranger: Is anyone else home?
> Student: No.
> Stranger: Fran, I have a package your mom wanted me to deliver to your house and I lost your address. Could you give me your address and I'll stop by in a little while to deliver her package.
> Student: Sure. I live at 1234 5th Street.
> Stranger: Thanks. When I come over, just open the door and I'll drop the package in your house. Goodbye.

3 Review with the class that you were given information you should not have been given. You were given the child's name, the fact that mother was not home, and the address. Then review with another student the correct responses to follow.

4 The scenario should go as follows.

> Student: Hello
> Stranger: Hello. Who is this?
> Student: With whom do you wish to speak?
> Stranger: Is your mother home?
> Student: She's busy and cannot come to the telephone right now. Could I take a message?
> Stranger: I need to deliver a package to your home and I lost your address. Could I have it?
> Student: Why don't you leave me your name and telephone number and my mother will call you back?
> Stranger: Goodbye.

Evaluation

Review with students the information that was not given this time. The student did not give a name, address, and did not say mother was not home.

Avoiding Automobiles with Strangers

Objective

Students will describe what to do when approached by a stranger in an automobile.

Life Skill

I will run in the opposite direction in which the car is travelling when approached by a stranger in an automobile.

Materials

A cardboard box cut out as an automobile, a chair behind the cardboard box

Motivation

1 Line up a chair behind a cardboard box that is shaped like an automobile and pretend you are driving a car. Ask a student to play the role of a young child walking home from school. As the child is walking, pretend you are yelling toward that child to get his/her attention.

2 Say, "Excuse me. I have a picture of my puppy that ran away and I need to find her. Could you come here and tell me if you have seen her." (As the child approaches the car, reach out and grab the child by the arm.)

3 Explain to the class that once the child came to within an arm's length distance of the car, you were able to grab him/her into the car. Emphasize that a child should never approach a car having a stranger inside.

4 Explain that when approached by a stranger, a child should run in the OPPOSITE direction in which the car is travelling. The reason why a child should run in the opposite direction is that it is more difficult for a driver to back up a street than to drive forward on a street. Explain that a child can run into a neighborhood home that has a "Safe Home" sign in the window.

Evaluation ▷ Have students demonstrate what to do as you are driving the automobile. Using several students, have them demonstrate what they would do if they were asked by a stranger to approach the car. Make sure students run in the appropriate direction.

Staying Below the Smoke Line

Objective

Students will describe how they would escape from a fire.

Life Skill

I will crawl low to the ground with my head below the smoke line when I need to escape from a fire.

Materials

If possible, use several mats from the gymnasium in your classroom.

Motivation

1 Explain to students that when there is a fire, the smoke that results will always rise to the top. If you wish, you can demonstrate this by lighting a cigarette and having the class observe which way the smoke travels. They will observe that the smoke is rising to the ceiling.

2 Explain that when a house is on fire and a person must escape, that person should crawl low to the ground so that his/her head is below the level of the smoke.

3 Have a student practice escaping from a fire by crawling on hands and knees. If you use mats, it will make the crawl easier. It is also important to have the student crawl toward the door.

4 Once the student gets to the door, ask the class what he or she should do. The answer should center around the fact that before opening the door, feel it. If the fire is right outside the door, the door will feel hot to the touch. In this event, the door should not be opened.

Evaluation

Have the rest of the class take turns practicing how to crawl away from a fire. Review the technique to use as each child escapes. The children in the class should stay low to the ground and feel the door for heat as they leave.

Escape Plan Map

Objective

Students will draw a fire escape plan using their place of residence as the building from which they will leave.

Life Skill

I will make a fire escape plan for my place of residence.

Materials

Student Master, "Fire Escape Graph," on page 457

Motivation

1 Have students close their eyes and imagine that they are in their homes. (For the purpose of this activity, the word "home" also refers to apartment.) Have them describe to themselves what they would do if their home caught on fire. What would they do if the main exit from the home were not able to be used? What if they lived in a home in which they were on the upstairs level and they needed to escape via the stairs which were not usable?

2 Distribute the Student Master, "Fire Escape Graph" on page 457. Have students draw the inside of their homes. If they live in a home that has an upper level, they are to use the upper half of the page for the upper level and the lower half of the page for the lower level. Students should draw every room, hallway, and window.

3 Have students draw arrows to indicate the route they would take in leaving their homes. Then, ask students to block off the route and have them identify an alternative to use in escaping from the fire.

4 Have students share their escape routes with the class. Students should look at options for leaving their homes such as the use of windows, fire escapes, and special equipment. Emphasize the importance of having students have a meeting place outside the home so that all family members know they have escaped and that no one is trapped inside the home.

Have students offer suggestions to their peers about other ways they might leave their homes. This would also be a good opportunity for students to share the locations of smoke detectors inside their homes. You can invite a firefighter into the class to speak to students about fire safety and the correct locations for positioning smoke detectors in the home.

Fire Escape Graph

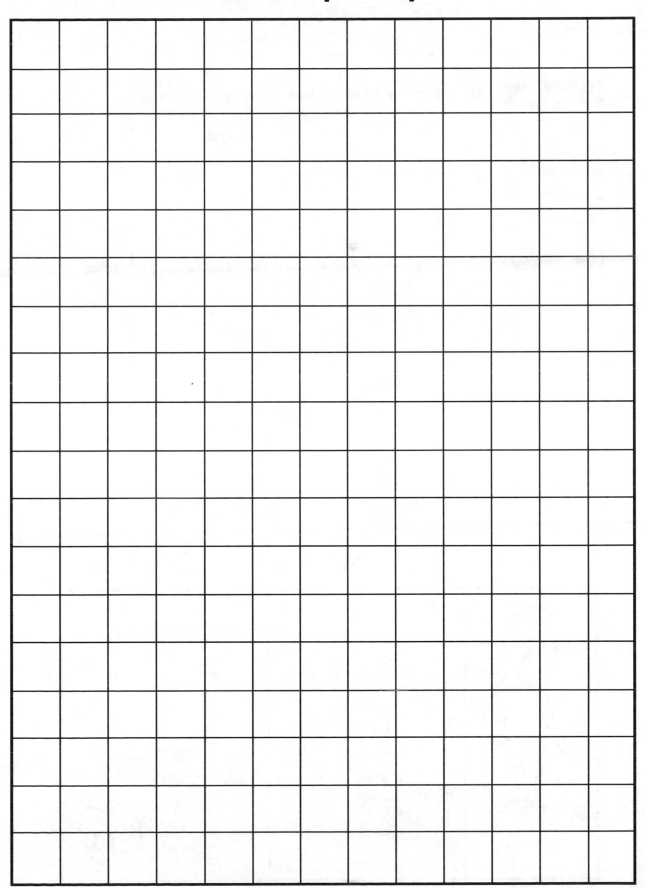

Fire Bug

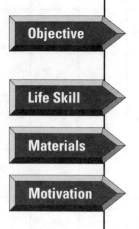

Objective

Students will demonstrate the stop, drop, and roll method to extinguish a fire on clothing.

Life Skill

I will use the stop, drop, and roll technique if my clothing were to catch on fire.

Materials

A mat from the gymnasium, colored paper cut in the form of flames, tape

Motivation

1 Teach the stop, drop and roll method of extinguishing a fire on clothing by first demonstrating this method. Take a mat and have students line up on each side. Be sure the students are not too close to each other. You do it first. Then break down each part by demonstrating stop, then drop, then roll.

2 Have the class try it in groups. The students are to say each segment out loud as they perform it. For example, each student will say STOP. They stand still. Then they say DROP and they fall to the floor. Finally, they say ROLL and they roll over.

3 Using a pattern, have each student cut out five "flames" from colored construction paper. The flames are then attached to their bodies in different areas. The flames can be applied to their bodies using tape. You can have students place flames on their chests, legs, arms, backs and any other body parts you deem appropriate.

4 As an option, you may choose to use balloons attached to the body instead of paper flames when practicing the stop, drop, and roll technique.

Evaluation

Have students use the stop, drop, and roll method with their flames attached. Have other students observe how the students use stop, drop, and roll to extinguish the "flames." Explain that the rolling causes the flames to become smothered, thereby denying the fire air. Without air, fires cannot burn.

Hazard Search

Objective

Students will describe ways to prevent accidents by eliminating hazards in the home.

Life Skill

I will check my home for the presence of safety hazards.

Materials

Common items found in the home such as an electrical cord, small rug, glass of water, and can of grease or cooking oil

Motivation

1 On your desk, lay out the following items - electrical cord, small rug, glass of water, and a can of grease or cooking oil. Tell the students they are going to be playing detective. Explain that the items on your desk are responsible for thousands of needless injuries in the home each year.

2 Have the students describe how each of the items can cause injuries in the home. The responses will be similar to the following: Electrical cord - people can trip over electrical cords that are spread across walkways. Electrical cords that are underneath carpeting can become frayed and the wires can become exposed to the carpet causing fires. A small rug can be hazardous in that one side can become tangled on a person's foot as he or she is walking. A person can trip over the rug and suffer an injury. The glass of water symbolizes how a spill on the floor can make it slippery and a person can slip and fall. Oil from a can can spill on the floor causing slippery conditions that can lead to injury.

3 Have students identify other common items in the home that can be hazardous. List the items on the chalkboard and for each item, have students describe what they would do to reduce the risk of injury from that item.

Have students draw a scene in a home in which they are to intersperse five dangerous situations in the picture that can cause injury. The students are to select only one room in the home. For example, students might select a kitchen and show water spilled on the floor, electrical cords stretched in walkways, food cooking on a stove that is next to curtains, pot handles sticking out in walking paths, and cabinet drawers open in walkways. Students are to show their pictures to the class and the class has to identify five safety hazards.

The World's Safest Car

Objective

Students will describe safety features that might be required for all cars.

Life Skill

I will follow safety rules when a passenger in a car.

Materials

Pictures from magazines of cars showing the inside and outside or brochures of new cars from new car dealers

Motivation

1 Explain to students that they are going to be playing the role of engineers who have been selected to design the world's safest automobiles. Tell students that there is no limit to their imagination and that money is no factor. Explain that around 45-50 thousand people in the United States lose their lives in automobile accidents each year and that almost all of these deaths could have been avoided.

2 Distribute brochures from a new car dealer that show the inside of new cars. You may choose to have students bring in pictures of the inside and outside of new cars to class for this activity. Explain to students that they can draw gadgets on their cars or they can label the places where they will show their safety gadgets.

3 Provide the class with insights of creative items they can place on their cars. Examples may be airbags on the sides of doors, solid metal bars that run through the sides and roof of a car, gadgets that require a driver to have his/her breath analyzed to be sure no alcohol is present inside the body, cushion bumpers so that a pedestrial who is hit would suffer minimal harm, and radar that warns the driver that the car is too near another automobile.

Evaluation

Have the students share their ideas with the others in the class. Explain that sometimes what people fantasize can become reality. Explain that the safest way to be injury free inside a car is to practice driving skills that focus on preventing accidents. Students will one day be consumers of automobiles and they will want to look at the safety features present in an automobile.

Red Light, Green Light

Objective

Students will identify what the different traffic signals indicate.

Life Skill

I will observe traffic signals and follow safety rules for crossing the street.

Materials

Quart milk containers with circles cut out to represent traffic lights. You will need green, red, and yellow signals

Motivation

1 Set up a safety street. Tape crosswalks on the floor. Tape street corners. Tell the students they are going to pretend they are pedestrians. Explain that a pedestrian is a person who walks on the street.

2 Have a milk container that represents a traffic signal. Set up your lights so that the red is on top, yellow in the middle, and green on the bottom. Explain that when the students see a red light, they are to stop. On a yellow signal, they are to slow down and proceed with caution, and on green, they are to go.

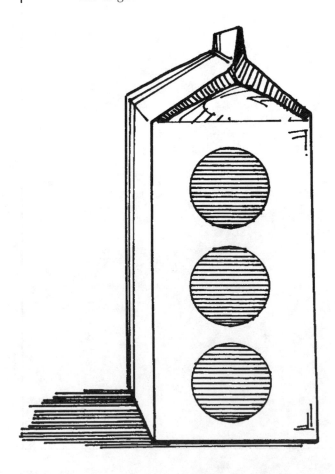

3 Have the students pretend they are walking on city streets. However, they will be walking in the "city" that is indicated by the markings on the floor. Explain that they are to walk by responding to the color to which you point. For example, when you point to the red, they are to stop and stand still. When you point to the yellow, they are to walk very slow. When pointing to the green, they are to walk at normal pace.

Evaluation

You can modify this activity by playing Simon Says to traffic signals. For example, you may say, "Simon Says green light." This means students are to walk in a normal pace. By observing their response, you will be able to tell if students are aware of the meaning of traffic signals.

Look Left-Right-Left

Objective

Students will identify safety rules to follow when crossing the street.

Life Skill

I will follow safety rules for crossing the street.

Materials

Tape

Motivation

1 Explain to students that they are going to learn the proper way to cross the street. Explain certain rules. One rule is to cross between crosswalks when one is present. Using masking tape, outline a crosswalk on the floor.

2 Explain that crossing the street at a crosswalk does not necessarily mean that it is safe to cross. Sometimes, people cross the street in the middle of that street as opposed to crossing at a corner. Regardless of where one crosses, it is important to follow certain rules for crossing safely.

3 Introduce the left-right-left procedure for crossing the street. Facing your students with your back to them, explain that they are going to be crossing the street at the marking of the crosswalk you have laid. Tell and demonstrate looking left-right-left before crossing. As you do this procedure, say out loud, "Look left-right-left, then cross."

4 Have students practice the same thing by doing and saying. You begin by saying it with them. Say, "Look left-right-left, then cross." Of course, students must know that they should not cross if they see any cars approaching.

Evaluation

Have students perform this task individually. They are each to say the same phrase before crossing. Have everyone observe to be sure students are looking left when saying "look left" etc.

Safety Town

Objective

Students will identify safety rules for riding their bicycles.

Life Skill

I will follow safety rules for riding my bicycle.

Materials

Masking tape, cardboard cartons to represent buildings, milk containers representing traffic signals, and wire hangers to represent handlebars on bicycles

Motivation

1 Explain to students that they will pretend they are going to be riding their bicycles through streets in the city. The first thing students will need to learn is the use of hand signals.

2 Explain and demonstrate the use of hand signals by having a volunteer come up to the front of the class and stand with the front of the body facing the chalkboard. Have the student demonstrate a hand signal for a right turn. (The left hand is held up at a right angle, bent at the elbow.) Trace the student's hand on the chalkboard. Now have the student give the signal for a left turn by having this student hold the left hand straight out on the side. Trace the left signal. Now have the student signal stop by having the left hand at a right angle bent down. Trace this signal. NOTE: By having the student standing facing the chalkboard, the class will be able to see the correct hand signal instead of the teacher facing students and causing confusion because of the opposite hands being used.

3 Set up a safety town. Use big, cardboard boxes to represent buildings, milk containers with colored circles to represent lights, and wire hangers that students can decorate to represent handlebars on a bicycle. With the teacher as a guide, tell the students you want them to take a trip through the safety town. You want them to stop when you point to a red circle on a light. When you say, "Right turn." the students at a corner are to use hand signals to make a right turn. Use the different signals to which the class must respond.

Evaluation

You can break the class into small groups and give them instructions to ride their bikes through the safety town. As you give signals, have the students respond. Have the rest of the class indicate when someone does not use the correct signal.

Belt Up

Objective

Students will describe how wearing safety belts in a car can help prevent serious injury and loss of life.

Life Skill

I will wear a safety belt when riding in a car.

Materials

Toy car, clay, tape, wood plank

Motivation

1 Ask students if they wear a safety belt while a passenger in an automobile. Find out if they wear a safety belt some, most, or all of the time. Explain that most accidents occur within a few miles of a person's home and that it is therefore important to wear a safety belt at all times when in an automobile.

2 Demonstrate to students that you will show them how safety belts work to keep people safe from injury. Use a toy automobile and a plank that leans against your desk and is slanted to the floor. At the end of the plank you would place something solid such as a pile of books. This will act as a wall into which the car would crash. Using clay, form the shape of a person and have this person seated in the car. Roll the car down the plank and have the students observe what happens. The person will fall forward or perhaps, fall out of the car. You might see dents on the clay. This would indicate parts of the body that would suffer injury if the person were real.

3 You will repeat this experiment, only this time, use any kind of tape to hold the person inside the car. After the car is left to roll down the plank and crash, the person will remain inside the car. The tape used to hold the person inside the car represents a safety belt. Students will notice that the person did not fall forward or out of the car.

Have students describe how they can can become injured in an automobile if they are involved in a crash and are not wearing a safety belt. You might choose to show pictures from magazines that show dashboards in cars and have students point out how the design of some of these dashboards can cause injury on impact. You might alo wish to have students make pledge cards that promise they will wear safety belts at all times when in a car.

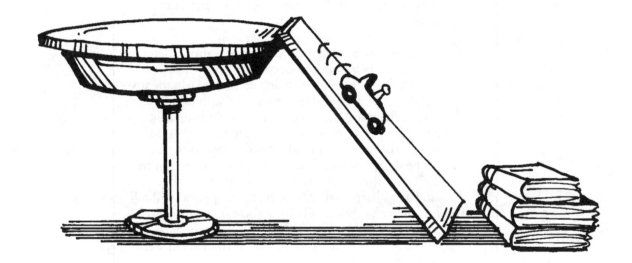

Being Tossed at the Speed Limit

Objective

Students will describe why a person in a moving vehicle can become seriously injured during sudden impact.

Life Skill

I will try to ride in cars with drivers who are responsible.

Materials

A ball of clay, a rubber ball, and markers

Motivation

1 Take a rubber ball and throw it hard against a wall in your classroom. If you do not wish to throw it directly into the wall, you can set up a pile of books or use a cardboard box. After students have observed what you have done, explain that you threw the ball at about 55 miles per hour.

2 Ask students if they can tell you the significance of 55 miles per hour. Explain that this number is the speed limit on many roads in the United States. On some kinds of roads, the speed limit is higher - 65 miles per hour.

3 Ask students to imagine that they are travelling in a car that is going 55 miles per hour. This means that every passenger inside the car is moving at 55 miles per hour. Take a piece of clay and roll it into a ball. Have a student take the ball of clay and use markers to draw a face on it. After the student has completed this task, ask him/her to throw the clay as hard as possible against the wall.

4 Next, have the students observe the shape of the ball. It is misshaped. Explain that this ball represented a person who was in an automobile that was travelling at 55 miles per hour. Since the automobile was travelling at 55 miles per hour, so were the people who were inside the automobile. The impact of the clay ball on the wall was analogous to the automobile crashing into a wall.

5 Students will begin to observe that a body travelling at 55 miles per hour is at great danger for injury when tossed into a fixed object such as a wall. This would be a good opportunity to suggest that airbags can play a significant role in the prevention of injuries. As an optional activity, you can take a balloon and blow it up. Show the class that if frontal impact occurs between the car and another object, the airbag will deflate. You can push the clay ball into the balloon and the class would notice that the impact is softened. Explain that even at frontal impact occurring at 55 miles per hour, an airbag can shield a person from serious injury.

Evaluation

Have students give examples of movements that may represent impact at high speeds such as those at 55 miles per hour. Examples may be a book dropping from a high level, a tennis ball being hit on a serve, and an apple falling from a tree. Have students share what they think might happen to them if instead it were the objects named, it were their bodies. Reinforce the concepts that wearing a safety belt at all times reduces the risk of injury in an automobile and that airbags in an automobile can help protect a driver.

Calling 9-1-1

Objective

Students will be able to demonstrate how to make an emergency telephone call.

Life Skill

I will call 9-1-1 or the operator if I need help in an emergency.

Materials

Telephone

Motivation

1 Ask students to pretend that they are home with a parent and that parent suddenly became ill. Explain that no one else is home and help is needed. Ask students for suggestions that describe how they would get help. Most students will indicate they may use the telephone to call for help. But do students know what to say when they make a telephone call requesting emergency medical help?

2 Introduce the term 9-1-1. Explain to students that most likely, they can dial that telephone number to get help for emergency medical conditions or if the police are needed. It is important to understand that in most areas that have 9-1-1, the location of the caller will be identified to the 9-1-1 operator automatically on computer so that help can be dispatched immediately. This is known as enhanced 9-1-1. But in other parts of the country, one needs to give specific information.

3 Give instructions about how to use 9-1-1. The first thing to tell students is that they are to dial or push the buttons that say "Nine, one,one." It is important to use this term rather than "Nine-eleven." If you say the latter, students may look for the number eleven and not be able to find it because it does not exist.

4 Instruct students to say the following after they have reached the 9-1-1 operator: provide the location, tell what has happened, and ask what should be done. Emphasize that the caller should not hang up until he/she has been told to hang up or told that help is on the way.

5 Tell students that if they live in an area that does not have 9-1-1, they can dial the NUMBER 0 for the operator. It is important that you stress the NUMBER 0 is to be dialed and NOT the LETTER O. The caller should provide the operator with the necessary information. The operator should be given the caller's name, telephone number, location, and what has occurred.

Evaluation

Using the telephone, give a student a scenario and ask him/her to call for help. One scenario may be: You are home with your father when he falls down a flight of stairs. He is unconscious. Call for help. Have the students simulate a telephone call saying the emergency telephone number they are dialing and have the rest of the class evaluate the information that is being given.

I'm Here to Take You Home

Objective

Students will describe procedures to follow when someone other than a person they are expecting comes to pick them up from school.

Life Skill

I will have a secret codeword that my parents can give to someone who might pick me up at school unexpectedly.

Materials

None

Motivation

1 Ask students if they had ever had someone pick them up from school to take them somewhere. Almost every student will raise his or her hand. Then ask students how they knew they were to leave with that person. Most students will say that they were told by their parent they will be picked up. They may say that they made a last-minute decision to go with that person because they knew that person.

2 Indicate that at almost all times, it is safe to accept an unexpected ride home from school from an acquaintance. But many parents now implement rules that say their sons or daughters should not leave the school building with anyone else other than who had planned to pick up that boy or girl.

3 The question that can be raised is, "How does one know when it is O.K. to be picked up from school by someone other than the expected person?" One way to do this is to use codewords. Students can make a secret codeword with their parents. Only the student and his or her parent would know this codeword. If the parent gives someone permission to pick up the child from school, that person must provide the child with the codeword. This will indicate that it is safe to leave school with that person.

Have a simulation in which you tell a child a secret codeword. That child is leaving school and another child in the class, acting as the adult approaches the child leaving school and says, "Could I give you a ride home?" The child leaving school can say, "No, thank you." If the child feels threatened, he or she should go back into the school and tell a teacher what has happened. Replay the scenario and this time, provide the child playing the adult with the secret codeword. Then have the class observe what has taken place. Review with students when someone goes or does not go with another person when leaving school.

Control That Bleeding

Objective — Students will describe proper first aid for bleeding.

Life Skill — I will apply direct pressure over a cut using a clean cloth.

Materials — Tomato, knife, and rag to act as a dressing

Motivation

1 Ask students if they have ever cut themselves or have come across another person who has suffered a cut and was bleeding. Have students share what they have seen done or what they would do.

2 After students have shared their experiences, tell them you are going to show them the proper first aid procedure to follow when a person suffers a cut. Take a tomato and tell students that this tomato will represent a person. Using a knife, place one very slight slice into the skin of the tomato but not entirely through the skin. Explain that the cut was only on the surface of the skin. It did not go through all the skin layers. Explain that often, students suffer cuts that do not go through the entire skin. No bleeding occurs. (No juice flowed through the cut in the skin of the tomato.) Paper cuts are typical kinds of injuries in which the skin is cut but there is no bleeding.

3 Now place a deep cut through the tomato. Squeeze the tomato slightly and the juice inside will flow. Explain that when a person suffers a cut, blood will flow. Explain that it is important to stop the flow of blood. The best way is through direct pressure. Explain that the best way to stop bleeding from a cut is to apply direct pressure over the wound. Explain that your rag or cloth represents something clean that is placed over the wound. Pressure is placed over the wound on the cloth. Squeeze the tomato slightly and more "blood" will flow. The "blood" will flow through the cloth. Tell students that if this happens, they are not to remove the cloth, but rather, place another cloth over the blood-soaked one. Then they are to apply direct pressure. Of course, they are to seek medical help in any case of bleeding.

Select a student to come up to the front of the room and tell the class the student has a cut below the elbow. Have a student volunteer to apply first aid to the cut. It is also important to tell students that the part of the body wounded should be raised above the level of the heart to reduce blood flow to the injured area.

Unclog the Block

Objective	Students will explain why applying chest pressure can help alleviate a blocked airway.
Life Skill	I will use an abdominal thrust as a way to force a lodged object from an airway.
Materials	A one-gallon plastic milk container, cork
Motivation	

1 Ask students if they have ever had a piece of food they were eating become lodged inside their windpipe. Have students describe what that experience felt like. Explain that they were not able to breathe because the airway was blocked.

2 Ask students how they would know if a person has a blocked airway. Provide them with the signals of a blocked airway. These include coughing or attempted coughing, clutching the throat, and the possibility that the lips and extremities are turning blue. If they notice a person with these signals, they should apply the abdominal thrust. Explain that the abdominal thrust is a way to force a lodged object from the airway.

3 Use a one-gallon milk container and outline the chest area on it. Use markers to make the lungs and the rib cage. Then place a cork that could fit over the opening of the bottle. Explain the technique of administering abdominal thrust to a choking person. Have students stand behind the person and make a fist placing it thumb side up in the abdomen over the navel and below the rib cage. The other hand is to be placed over the fist. To complete the abdominal thrust, the hands are squeezed into the abdomen in quick, upward thrusts. This will often force the dislodged object out of the airway. However, do not have the students practice this on each other. Students are to demonstrate this on the milk jug. They will notice the cork pop from the opening so that the airway can be reopened.

Evaluation

Have students practice giving the abdominal thrust using the milk container. Check for their positioning of the hands on the abdomen as well as how they position their fist and use the thrusting action.

Wind-Chill

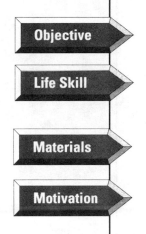

Objective

Students will describe how hypothermia can result from exposure to cold, moisture, and wind.

Life Skill

I will wear appropriate clothing in cool or cold, moist, windy weather to reduce my risks of hypothermia.

Materials

A bowl of cold water

Motivation

1 Provide students with the following scenarios.

Scenario #1. It is a 75 degree day and there is no wind. You have gone swimming and just gotton out of the pool. You do not even need a towel to wrap around you. You feel comfortable.

Scenario #2. It is a 75 degree day and there is a 15 mile per hour breeze. You have gone swimming and just gotten out of the pool. You get chilled quickly and are shivering. Your lips are turning blue. You desperately need a towel wrapped around you to help keep you warm.

2 Ask students to describe why the person in Scenario #2 reacted differently from the person in Scenario #1 when the outside temperature was exactly the same. Another assumption one could make is that the water temperature in the pool was the same in both scenarios. (In Scenario #2, there was a breeze. The breeze accounted for the difference in how the body reacted.)

3 Introduce the word hypothermia. Hypothermia is a reduced body temperature due to exposure to cold, moisture, and wind. You can demonstrate the effects in the scenarios by having a student place his/her hand in a bowl of water. Then have the student expose his/her hand to the air. Have the student do the same thing but this time, have the student blow in his/her hand to simulate exposure to the wind. In the latter, the student's hand will become chilled due to the simulation of the wind blowing on the cold. Explain that a person can be in relatively warm temperatures (i.e. 50 degrees F.) but because of exposure to moisture and wind, can be susceptible to hypothermia.

Ask students to describe which scenario would more easily result in hypotherima.

Scenario #1. It is 50 degrees and sunny. A runner in a marathon reaches the 20 mile mark and is slightly chilled and sweating. The shirt she is wearing is changed into a dry one.

Scenario #2. It is 50 degrees and sunny. A runner in a marathon reaches the 20 mile mark and is slightly chilled and sweating. This person does not want to change his shirt for fear of losing time to stopping and changing.

Have students describe which runner is more susceptible to experiencing hypothermia. (The runner in Scenario #2 would be more likely to experience hypothermia. This runner did not change a wet shirt so that his body would become chilled more easily due to the combination of the moisture in the shirt and the breeze created as he was running.)

The Cold Is Numbing

Objective

Students will describe how numbness caused by frostbite can impair the ability to perform simple tasks.

Life Skill

I will dress appropriately to prevent frostbite.

Materials

One thick glove, one coin

Motivation

1 Introduce the term frostbite. Explain that frostbite is the overexposure to cold so that the parts of the body that are affected become numb due to freezing. Most cases of frostbite occur to the extremities. Included in these body parts are the fingers, toes, nose, and ears. Explain to students that signals of frostbite are numbness in the affected areas, waxy appearance of the skin, and discolored skin.

2 Ask students if they have ever tried to use their fingers if they were exposed to cold air for a long period of time or if they had felt a numbness due to the initial signs of frostbite. Explain that one of the first signals of frostbite is an inability to feel, assuming the frostbitten area is the fingers. There would be an inability to manipulate objects such as trying to place a key inside a lock and turning the key. There would be an inability to pick up objects. This can be annoying as well as frustrating.

3 Tell students they will simulate what it might feel like to try to do something if their fingers were frostbitten. Have a volunteer come to the front of the room and place a glove over his/her hand. Then place a coin on your desk and ask the student to pick up the coin using the hand with a glove. The student will have great difficulty trying to lift the coin from the desk.

Evaluation

Have students describe how frostbite can be a limiting factor on performing tasks. Explain that if frostbite is not treated, it can lead to further destruction of the affected area. You can indicate to students that treatment for frostbite consists of handling the affected area gently and warming the affected area in water that has a temperature between 100-105 degrees Fahrenheit.

A Commercial for Bicycle Safety

Objective

Students will describe how to promote bicycle safety by developing a commercial focusing on specific rules for bicycle safety.

Life Skill

I will follow bicycle safety rules.

Materials

None

Motivation

1 Ask students how television commercials try to influence people to buy products. Students can describe some of the techniques used such as statistics about how good a product is, the ingredients in a product, the cost of a product, important people who use that product, and the results produced by that product, to name a few.

2 Divide your class into groups of about five students. Explain to students that they will be television producers. As producers, they are to have as their first assignment, the production of an advertisement that promotes bicycle safety. As a part of their advertisement, students can use jingles, songs, posters, or any other appropriate means to provide information to the class about bicycle safety.

3 Allow students about a half-hour to prepare their messages. Then they are to present their messages to the class. In presenting their messages, they are to identify at least five facts about bicycle safety. Students may use rap songs, make up original songs or jingles, or stage a skit.

Evaluation

For each group presentation, have the students write five facts that were presented. Summarize the facts presented by developing a master list of bicycle safety facts students should know.

I'M SINGING MY RAP TO LET YOU KNOW, NOT WEARING A HELMET IS DANGEROUS, YO!

Those Broken Bones

Objective

Students will identify procedures to follow if a person has a fracture.

Life Skill

I will recognize the signs of fracture and get appropriate help.

Materials

Pencil, tape

Motivation

1 Survey your class to determine how many students have suffered a broken bone. A large number of students in the class will have experienced a fracture. Have students share how they were treated for a fracture. Have them share how they knew they had suffered a fracture.

2 Review the signs and symptoms of a fracture. Indicate that a fracture may be evident when there is pain, discoloration to the affected area, or swelling and deformity.

3 Show students the pencil you have in front of you. Explain that the pencil represents a bone. Explain that there are different kinds of fractures. One kind of fracture may be in the form of a hairline fracture. To demonstrate this, break the pencil ever so slightly. After bending it to break slightly, try to straighten it. Explain that a hairline fracture may be evident only by a small crack in the bone. The crack may be so small that it may not be evident even by x-ray.

4 Next, break the pencil sharply. Have the class observe the break. Explain that sometimes a break can splinter such as the pencil has done. Tell the class that if they were to care for this fractured bone, they would need to keep it from moving. Take the tape and wrap it around the pencil. This is analogous to a bandage that is put over a suspected fracture.

5 Explain that you may wish to use the pencil again. But the way it is broken, it cannot be used. It must be straightened. After it is straightened, it must be fastened in place so that it will not break. A broken bone in the body may first need to be set in place. The broken parts of the bone may need to be connected. In some cases, a screw or plate would be used to keep the two ends of the broken bone in place and connected, so that the bone can grow together again.

Evaluation

Pretend you have broken your arm. Ask the class what they would do to treat your fracture. They should emphasize that your arm should not be moved, it should be held in place by perhaps a bandage so that it does not move around, and that medical help should be summoned.

Community and Environment is the area of health that focuses on environmental issues such as indoor and outdoor air pollution, depletion of the ozone layer, temperature changes, water pollution, acid rain, noise, pesticides, radiation and the community.

Air Pollution

Air is needed for life. Unfortunately much of the air in many parts of the world is replete with pollutants. There are certain major air pollutants that are dangerous to health.

Carbon monoxide is an odorless, tasteless, and colorless gas that is poisonous. It results from the incomplete combustion of organic materials. The automobile is the principle source of carbon monoxide in the environment.

When carbon monoxide enters the body, it attaches to the red blood cells. Oxygen is displaced in the blood so that the supply of this gas is reduced to various body cells including the lungs. There is some indication that long-term exposure to carbon monoxide can lead to a decrease in physical and emotional health. In fact, there is some concern that drivers in large cities who are exposed to high levels of carbon monoxide may have a decrease in the ability to react in avoiding an accident. The carbon monoxide slows reaction time.

Sulfur oxides are pollutants that result from the combustion of fuels containing sulfur. The sulfur combines with oxygen in the air to form sulfur oxides. In addition, the burning of other products such as coal adds sulfur dioxide to the atmosphere. When people are exposed to sulfur oxides, their respiratory systems become irritated. The airway can become constricted. Other studies are looking at the effects of sulfur oxides on other lung diseases.

The high-temperature combustion of energy sources such as coal and oil leads to the development of **nitrogen oxides.** The most significant contributor of nitrogen oxides in the air is the automobile. The health effects of nitrogen oxides are several. It causes irritation of the eyes and respiratory passages. Prolonged exposure results in increased damage to the respiratory tract and the development of lung disease. Cigarette smoke contains large amounts of nitrogen dioxide. When combined with nitrogen oxides, the harm to the body becomes more significant.

Hydrocarbons are compounds that contain carbon and hydrogen that are a source of air pollution. The most abundant hydrocarbons in air pollution are propane, benzene, and ethylene. Hydrocarbons are a major factor in the development of smog.

The natural rays of the sun result in chemical reactions in the atmosphere known as **photochemical oxidants.** One compound initiated by the rays of the sun is **ozone.** Ozone is a compound that is dangerous to a person's health. It causes irritation to the eyes, lungs, and throat. It produces headaches, coughing, and shortness of breath. Ozone also damages plants and harms animals. It is a major cause of damage to products in the environment such as the cracking of rubber.

Another form of air pollution is the development of particulates. Unlike the other products mentioned that are gases, **particulates** are particles in the air. Soot and dust are examples of particulates. Particulates are found in greater amounts in larger cities.

Not all particulates in the air are toxic to a person's health. However, some particulates such as asbestos are dangerous. Particulates can harm the surfaces of the respiratory system. The cilia can be harmed so that they cannot be as effective as they should in preventing foreign matter from entering the lungs.

Ozone Layer

The **ozone layer** is the layer of the atmosphere that acts as a filter from the ultraviolet rays of the sun. There have been a number of concerns about the wearing away of the ozone layer due to the emitting of chlorofluorocarbons and halogens into the air. **Chlorofluorocarbons** are odorless nonpoisonous chemicals that are used as aerosol propellants as well as in refrig-

COMMUNITY AND ENVIRONMENT

14

erators. They are also used to make plastic foam in disposable food containers. **Halogens** are chemicals that are used to extinguish fires. When these products are released into the air, they can remain there for twenty, thirty, or more years. When in the air, they destroy the ozone layer. As the ozone layer decreases or thins, more of the ultraviolet rays of the sun penetrate the lower part of the Earth. This has resulted in an increased risk of developing skin cancer and eye cataracts, as well as damage to forests and crops.

Greenhouse Effect

There has been a concern by scientists worldwide about the increased warming of the earth's temperature. This increased warming is known as the greenhouse effect. The **greenhouse effect** is defined as an increase in the concentration of carbon dioxide in the atmosphere that prevents normal heat loss from Earth. Generally, light rays from the sun strike the surface of the Earth. The radiations are reflected as heat energy that is absorbed into the atmosphere. The increase of carbon dioxide in the atmosphere causes an absorption of heat. As a result, the average temperature of the Earth may rise several degrees. This can create serious problems. The polar ice caps can melt with a change of only a few degrees of the Earth's atmosphere. Flooding in parts of the earth can result. Evidence indicates that there has been a decreased winter ice cover in parts of the Earth. Some projections indicate that by around the year 2050, the average temperature of the Earth will increase between three to nine degrees. This increase can result in the reduction of water levels in rivers and lakes. Droughts will become more common.

Another concern about the rise in temperatures is the possible rise in levels of oceans and seas due to melting of the polar caps. This can result in flooding along coastal areas. The results will not be known for sure for many years. But, it is becoming increasingly evident that major changes will occur.

Indoor Air Pollution

The indoor air can also become a health hazard. There are many different kinds of pollutants that can be found indoors.

Asbestos is a mineral that is found in building materials. It has been linked to lung and gastrointestinal cancer. But the development of these cancers may not be evident until after 20-30 years after exposure. If the asbestos becomes airborne, the fibers can be trapped inside the lungs causing lung cancer. Because of the dangers of asbestos, its use has been prohibited. There have been many expensive efforts undertaken to remove asbestos from buildings. **Lead** is an element that is found in many products used inside and outside the home. Lead is in the atmosphere as it is released from automobile exhaust. Lead poisoning is a problem for young children. Research indicates that about three million children in the United States suffer permanent neurological damage due to lead poisoning. Children may ingest lead by eating paint chips that contain this element. As a result, there is the risk of developing impaired concentration, loss of short-term memory, and learning disabilities. Government regulations have curtailed the use of lead in many products such as paints that are used inside the home.

Radon

Radon is a radioactive gas that is emitted from bricks and concrete materials. It is also emitted from rocks and other substances below the Earth. Radon is odorless and colorless so that people may not be aware if this gas is inside the home in significant amounts. There has been great concern about the amount of radon that enter homes from below the ground. As many as one in twelve homes may have radon levels that are above the danger level.

Radon enters a home through cracks in the floors or walls in basements. The gas moves through these small cracks as well as through drains and sump pumps.

Since newer homes are built with improved insulation over older homes, the radon that enters a home is more likely to remain inside.

There are many stores and agencies that sell radon testing kits. These kits will have specific directions for ways to measure radon levels. If radon levels are high, steps can be taken to lower them. These steps include sealing all cracks and installing fans in strategic locations so that radon can be vented from the home.

The major health problem related to radon is its ability to cause lung cancer. Some estimates indicate that 20,000 cases of lung cancer result from radon exposure. The radon gases enter the lungs when they stick to dust particles and are inhaled.

Water Pollution

On the average, each person in the United States consumes 125 gallons of water each day. Obviously, water is a most valuable resource. But the quality of water has been threatened by pollution. The main sources of water pollution are population growth, urbanization and suburbanization, industrial expansion, and increased use of technology.

From the standpoint of aesthetics, contaminated water is unsightly. But the unsightliness of water is not the only problem. Water pollution is also a health hazard. In many parts of the world, dysentery is a major problem. Almost any visitor to a foreign country such as Mexico is aware of this problem. Polluted water also results in an increase of the sodium content so that people with problems related to high blood pressure can be at risk of complications.

Sewage and wastes from animals as well as agricultural chemicals are also a concern as these products cause an increase in the amount of nitrates in water. There can be an increase in nitrates in ground water which supplies wells. Infants who drink water infiltrated with nitrates can suffer from blood diseases. Polluted ground water can also result in the development of other kinds of diseases and may be linked to development of cancer in adults.

Acid Rain.

Acid rain is the combination of sulfur oxides and nitrogen in the air that combine with moisture to form acids. When precipitation such as rain and snow fall, water in lakes, vegetation on land, and other objects such as buildings are damaged.

Coal is the major contributor to acid rain. The smokestacks from buildings whose industries use coal emit waste products that travel for hundreds of miles. This is one reason why acid rain can fall in communities that have no industry. When acid rain falls in water, algae growth increases. This causes a depletion of oxygen in water as well as causing a blockage of sunlight. The result is the killing of fish.

Noise

Noise is a major concern in the environment. Many people are not aware that noise has numerous detrimental effects on health. Exposure to loud noise can result in an increase in blood pressure, constriction of blood vessels in parts of the body, and possible increases in blood cholesterol levels. Obviously, increased exposure to loud sounds can cause permanent loss of hearing.

Since noise is considered to increase stress levels, headaches, tension, sleep disturbances, and increased anxiety are commonplace.

Radiation

There are many sources of radiation in the environment. Many of these sources are inside the home. Some people are concerned about video display terminals (VDTs) inside homes and businesses. VDTs have been accused of promoting increases in reproductive problems and formation of cataracts. However, most studies have shown that radiation measurements from VDTs are below dangerous levels. Microwaves are a form of radiation. But there is little evidence that microwaves in the environment pose a health risk to people.

You can begin to assume responsibility for keeping the environment healthful. Here are some steps you can take:
- Use public transportation such as buses when possible.
- Recycle products such as paper.
- Buy products that come in recycled packaging.
- Buy milk in paper rather than plastic cartons.
- Use both sides of scrap paper when writing notes.
- Request paper rather than plastic bags.
- Conserve energy at home by not using electricity unnecessarily.
- Use water efficient heads on faucets and shower heads to conserve water.
- Use flourescent lights instead of light bulbs.
- Try not to buy disposable items such as razors and flashlights.

If every person makes an effort, the environment can be made more healthful.

Community Health

There are many services in the community to assist people with information and other support services. Voluntary and public health agencies offer prevention and treatment services for a myriad of health problems ranging from communicable diseases to noncommunicable diseases and disorders. The local directory can serve as a valuable resource for identifying appropriate agencies.

Draft Check

Objective
Students will discuss how to detect drafts in the home that indicate loss of energy.

Life Skill
I will take steps to reduce energy loss in my home.

Materials
Pencil and cellophane paper

Motivation

1 Explain the importance of conserving energy in the home by identifying places where there may be leaks in the form of exchange of air between the inside and the outside of the home.

2 Explain to the students that they will discover how to detect places in the home where there is loss of energy through places such as around doors and windows. Take a pencil and wrap a sheet of cellophane around it. Allow the cellophane to hang a few inches from the pencil. Then go to places inside the classroom such as a window and hold the pencil with the cellophane in places where the window meets the frame. If the window is shut tightly, the cellophane will not move. But if there is a gap between the window and its frame, the cellophane will flutter.

3 As a continuation of this activity, have students try this experiment at home. Have them make a list of the different places in the home they checked for air leaks. Then have them record which places had leaks and which did not.

Have students share the findings of their experiments performed at home. This would also be a good time to discuss what to do when air leaks are discovered in the home. You can discuss ways to stop these leaks. For example, leaks around doors can be fixed by sealing around the door with weather stripping.

Environmental Mural

Objective

Students will describe how litter can change the beauty of the environment.

Life Skill

I will avoid littering in my home, school, and community.

Materials

Five foot sheet of butcher paper, tape, markers, plastic trash bag, products that are commonly found dumped on streets such as crumpled candy wrappers, tissues, and aluminum soda cans

Motivation

1 Take a five foot strip of butcher paper and lay it out on the floor. Tell students that they are going to make a mural of the environment. This mural should consist of scenery that shows the environment at its best. Students can draw pictures of mountains, lakes and streams, people swimming, trees, and any other scenes which are appealing to the eye. Have students use markers to draw the pictures on their murals.

2 Take the completed mural and tape it to the chalkboard. Have students observe the mural of the clean environment they prepared and have them provide you with feedback about how healthful this environment appears.

3 Now show the students a trash bag. Tell the students that they are going to have an opportunity to select items from your trash bag. Explain that the trash inside your bag consists of items that you placed inside and that are clean. Have each student select an item. They will select items such as crumpled tissue paper and candy wrappers, aluminum soda cans, and any other items used as litter. Have each student take a piece of tape and attach his/her item on the mural of the environment.

Have students observe their new environment. They will notice litter has interfered with the beauty of the environment they developed. Discuss what kind of impact litter has on the environment. You can also indicate that not only is litter something unappealing to the eye, but that litter serves as an attraction to insects and rodents.

Dirty Air

Objective

Students will describe how particulates pollute the air.

Life Skill

I will try to avoid being in environments that have polluted air.

Materials

One jar with a lid, one jar without a lid, cotton, a slide projector

Motivation

1 Begin by having students think about the air they breathe. Ask them if they think the air they breathe is clean and clear. Explain that people do not understand that the air in almost all environments has particulates. Particulates are specks of dust and dirt. Particulates may not be visible.

2 Show the class that there is always dust and dirt in the air. Obtain a slide projector and close the lights inside the classroom. Turn on the slide projector so that it is emitting light from the lens. However, do not show a slide. Have the class observe the space in the light that is projected. Students will notice dust. Explain that the air always has dust and that this dust is inhaled. Fortunately, the air passages have cilia that trap dust so that it does not travel into the lungs.

3 Tell students they will have the opportunity to observe particulates in the air. Take two jars and fill each with white cotton. Seal one jar with a lid while the other jar remains uncovered. Allow both jars to remain exposed to air outside your classroom window. The jars are to remain in place for three or four days. Try to keep the jars away from rain or snow.

Have the students observe the jars after they have been exposed to the environment outside the classroom. Have them describe their observations. Students will notice that the cotton in the jar that was uncovered had black specks on it. The black specks represent particulates in the air. These are the same particulates that are in the air that we breathe. The jar that had the lid contained cotton that had no specks of dirt on it. Have students conclude that the cotton in the jar with the lid was protected from the elements in the environment.

Murky Water

Objective

Students will discuss how water pollution is harmful to a person's health.

Life Skill

I will not swim in lakes or streams that are polluted.

Materials

A jar with clear water, a jar with mud and debris added

Motivation

1 Ask students if they have ever gone swimming in a stream or a lake. Most students have gone swimming in these environments. Explain to students that the water in which they went swimming most likely was clean. Then ask students if they have ever seen a sign that said, "No Swimming - Water Polluted." In many parts of the country, the water is so polluted that fishlife cannot exist due to contamination by runoff, garbage, and other substances considered toxic.

2 Show students two jars. In one jar, have water filled to the top that is clear. Have students describe how this water appears to them. Then have them describe how they would feel about swimming in this water.

3 Now show students another jar that is about three-quarters filled with clear water. Tell students you are going to change the environment of this water by adding substances that might be found in lakes. Take some mud and add it to the water. Explain that during heavy rains, runoff from the earth around lakes can carry mud into the water. Stir the mud around in the water. If possible, add a bit of dirty oil to the water. Stir it around. Take a few tissues or candy wrappers and add this to your mixture. Stir these substances around.

Ask students how they would feel about swimming in water that looks like the water in the jar with your mixtures added. Explain that in many lakes, streams, and rivers, substances such as these are dumped. These substances cause health-related problems to the fishlife as well as to people in surrounding areas. Polluted water will smell. It will cause fishlife to cease. It will cause recreational facilities to be shut down. People who swim in polluted water can become ill since polluted water breeds harmful microorganisms.

Acid Rain

Objective	Students will describe the effect of acid rain on structures in the environment.
Life Skill	I will take steps to keep my environment clean by not travelling in an automobile unnecessarily.
Materials	Cubes of sugar, bowl of water
Motivation	

1 Ask students if they have ever heard of the term "acid rain" and have them identify this term. (Acid rain is water that is formed in the atmosphere that has been combined with gases resulting from waste products. When it rains in certain parts of the environment, the composition of the rainwater is such that it can cause harm to the environment.)

2 Explain to students that acid rain is so strong that over a number of years, it can cause solid structures such as the brick on homes or the concrete on a statue to wear.

3 Tell students that you are going to build a house out of bricks. Tell students that the sugar cubes you are using are going to represent the bricks on a home. Begin to build the house out of the sugar cubes, but stop after you have begun to build. Then tell the class that you would like them to be aware of the liquid in the bowl that is on your desk. (The liquid is water.) Tell the class the water in the bowl is really acid rain. Tell the class you have accumulated this acid rain. Then show them a cube used to build the home. Show the class that the cube is strong. Tap it on the desk to show it is hard. Tell the class the cube is hard to break. But then tell the class you will put the cube inside the "acid rain." Have the class observe what took place.

4 Ask the class to tell you what they saw happen to the cube (brick). Students will indicate that the "brick" has dissolved. Explain to students that acid rain can do to real bricks what the water has done to the sugar. Explain that acid rain not only will dissolve hard structures. Acid rain can kill crops. When it falls on lakes and streams, it changes the composition of the water. Life in the water such as fish and plants can be killed.

Evaluation

Have students identify how their community has been affected by acid rain.

Odorless, Colorless, and Tasteless

Objective

Students will identify carbon monoxide in the environment as an odorless, colorless, and tasteless gas that can be harmful to the body and even cause death.

Life Skill

I will inform an adult when an automobile engine is running in a closed garage.

Materials

Material, balloon

Motivation

1 Bring a blown-up balloon into the class. Tell the students that there is something very dangerous inside this balloon. Explain that the substance inside the balloon is found in the environment. Certain products in the environment give off this substance as a waste product.

2 Tell the class that they are going to have the opportunity to discover what is inside the balloon. Tell them you are going to go next to someone and burst the balloon. What is inside the balloon will be released in the air next to where the ballon bursts.

3 As you walk up to a person, take something pointed such as a pin and burst the balloon. Ask the person or other persons around the balloon what they smell. Students will say that they do not smell anything. Then ask if they see anything. Students will not be able to observe anything. Tell the class that there is a poisonous gas that is odorless, colorless, and tasteless. This gas is called carbon monoxide. When significant amounts of this gas get into the bloodstream, it can cause the body organs to not function as they should. The body organs can shut down to the point that death can result. Explain to students that carbon monoxide is found in cigarette smoke. Automobile exhaust is a key contributor to carbon monoxide in the atmosphere.

4 Have students describe why a person should never run an automobile engine in a garage when the garage door is closed. (A buildup of carbon monoxide can result. The person inside the automobile may not know there is carbon monoxide present because it is odorless and colorless. The person can become ill and possibly die due to the overexposure to the carbon monoxide.)

Evaluation

Have students describe why carbon monoxide is harmful to a person's body.

Experiencing the Greenhouse Effect

Objective

Students will describe how the greenhouse effect occurs.

Life Skill

I will encourage others to plant trees that help use the carbon dioxide in the air.

Materials

None

Motivation

1 Introduce the term "greenhouse effect." Explain that the greenhouse effect is the warming of the Earth's surface that results when solar heat becomes trapped by layers of carbon dioxide and other gases. Many scientists believe that the greenhouse effect is the result of the buildup of carbon dioxide. Carbon dioxide is a byproduct of combustion. It is produced when fuels are burned.

2 To have students become aware of how the warming effect occurs on the Earth, have them imagine what it feels like to get into a car on a hot, summer day. What happens inside a car as it lies in the sun can help students understand what happens on Earth due to the warming effect.

3 When a car lies in the sun, heat is absorbed in many parts of the car. It is absorbed in parts such as the dashboard, seats, steering wheel, and roof. If the windows in the car are closed, there is no place for the heat to escape. Thus, the inside of the car becomes very warm. The same idea results on Earth. The sun's energy becomes absorbed. As heat rises, it is trapped within the layers of the Earth's atmosphere. The trapped heat increases the temperature of the Earth, thus causing what is known as the greenhouse effect.

Students can make their own experiments to show the development of the greenhouse effect. For example, a thermometer can be placed inside a covered glass that is receiving the sun's rays. Another glass with a thermometer inside may be placed in the the sun, but remain uncovered. After being in the sun for about an hour, students can compare the temperature inside the glasses. The glass with the cover that is trapping heat inside of it will have a higher temperature than the uncovered glass. Have students describe how their experiments demonstrate the greenhouse effect.

Music Concentration

Objective

Students will describe why exposure to noise can interfere with the ability to think clearly.

Life Skill

I will avoid loud noises when studying.

Materials

A casette player that can play loudly, a tape of a popular song that students like

Motivation

1 Have students pull out a sheet of paper from their notebooks. Tell them you are going to provide them with a list of objects. You will read this list and ask them to write down as many items from this list as they can remember. Students are not to begin to write until you have completed saying the last word on the list. Students do not necessarily need to write this list in the order in which you say the words. The words they need to know are as follows.

typewriter	automobile
basketball	crayon
pencil	chair
dictionary	shingle
telescope	giraffe

2 After students have written this list, repeat the words and have students write the number they were able to remember. They are then to place their papers away and you can continue with a lesson you were teaching.

3 Toward the end of class, have students take out another sheet of paper and tell them you are going to give them another list of words. But this time, you are going to play a song that they like. However, you will play this song loudly. As the music is playing, give students the following words. They are to remember the words and write them down after you have completed saying the last word. The following are the words they are to know:

telephone	refrigerator
picture	envelope
glasses	pen
window	computer
automobile	flower

After students have completed writing the second list, review the words and have them write the number they remembered. Have students compare the number correct on the first list versus the second list. Most likely students will have remembered more correctly from the first list than from the second. Ask students why this is so. (During the reading of the second list, there was loud music playing and this made it more difficult to concentrate.) Explain that loud noise is a form of pollution and that noise pollution can interfere with a person's ability to concentrate.

Gone Fishing

Objective

Students will review facts about the environment through participation in a game.

Life Skill

I will use the facts I learned to help keep the environment healthful.

Materials

Colored construction paper, paper clips, a stick that is between one and three feet long, a piece of string that is about two to three feet in length, a small magnet

Motivation

1 This activity can be used as a review for a unit on the environment. It uses an environmental theme in which to have a review.

2 Use different colored construction paper. Outline a picture of a fish. The number of questions you want to have in this review will determine the number of fish you will cut out. You will need one fish per question.

3 Write a question about the environment on one side of the fish. Also on this side, assign a point value of from one to three points. The higher the value of the points, the more difficult the question would be. To each fish, you are to attach a paper clip in the place where the fish's mouth would be. On the back of the fish, you are to write the answer to this question.

4 Divide the class into one or more teams. Each team will select one person to be the person fishing. A stick will serve as the pole and an string as the line. At the end of the string is a magnet. The person will "fish" for a question. The fish can be inside a box. The fish will attach to the magnet by the paper clip. When a person gets a fish attached to the line, another person on the team who is assigned the helper will pull the fish from the line. The helper will indicate the point value of the question and read it. The person gone fishing will try to answer the question. If the person answers the question correctly, that person's team will receive the point total allotted. If the question is not answered correctly, the team that would go next would have a choice at answering the question. The question would have to be answered by the person on that team who would go next. A team does not lose points for an incorrect answer. It just will not be awarded the points.

Evaluation

This review will enable the teacher to identify how well students know the information.

A Get Well Card for the Environment

Objective

Students will identify an environmental concern and identify facts about this concern to promote environmental health.

Life Skill

I will become involved in activities such as recycling to help improve the environment.

Materials

A large sheet of paper, color markers

Motivation

1 Ask students in the class to describe occasions in which they had to send cards to another person. Responses will center on occasions for birthdays, anniversaries, Mother's or Father's Day, Valentine's Day, and sympathy.

2 Ask the class to describe the different aspects of a card for a special occasion. For example, they may say that the card has a cover, there might be pictures on the cover, the inside of the card may have a poem, funny saying, or short story. Sometimes there will be information on the back of the card. Some cards may have a serious tone, others may by animated but serious, yet others may be humorous.

3 Explain to students that they are going to get a sheet of poster paper and markers that they can share. Tell students that they have been studying about the environment and that they have discussed many different kinds of environmental concerns. Some of these concerns may center around acid rain, the greenhouse effect, noise pollution, air pollution, water pollution, nuclear waste, hazardous waste disposal, depletion of the ozone layer, and many other issues.

4 Students are to use the paper and markers to develop a Get Well Card for the environment. This card should have a cover with a saying and a poem or message on the inside that promotes a healthful environment. Encourage students to be creative in their cards.

Evaluation

Have students share their cards with the class and then you can display them in the class. Have the class identify important facts they have discovered.

Environmental Pictionary

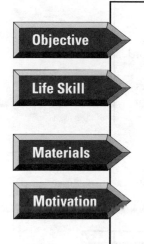

Objective

Students will identify names and terms related to environmental issues.

Life Skill

I will help keep my environment clean and conserve energy.

Materials

Chalkboard and chalk

Motivation

1 This game is an adaptation of the well-known game, Pictionary. Students will be required to identify a word or term based upon another person's drawing that relates to that word or term.

2 Divide the class into two equal groups. Begin by asking one member from each team to come to the front of the room. Use a coin toss to indicate which person goes first. Show that person a word or term that is related to an environmental issue or term. Some of the words you can use include litter, air pollution, radon, nuclear power, ozone layer, and greenhouse effect.

3 After a student sees the word, he or she is to draw a picture that will help his or her team identify the word. The team will have one minute to identify the term or word. If it is not identified in the time allotted, the next team will have the opportunity to guess the word or term. The team that guesses the word or term will get one point. Each team will alternate chances to go. Each person will only have one turn to draw. The team will rotate members to draw.

Environmental Smash Album

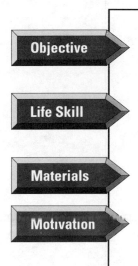

Objective

Students will identify five significant facts that describe ways they can help improve the environment.

Life Skill

I will select behaviors that promote a healthful environment such as not littering.

Materials

Poster paper, markers

Motivation

1 Explain to students that they will use their creative talents to identify ways they can help make the environment a more healthful place in which to live. Give the students enough poster paper so that they can glue two pieces together, the size of a record album. Explain that they are going to pretend they are music publishers and that they are going to have the opportunity to produce records. However, the records they produce will be related to making the environment a more healthful place in which to live.

2 Tell students to use their markers to come up with a title of their album. They should come up with a title that will focus on making the environment a healthful one for them. For example, they may come up with a title such as, Sweet Surroundings. They are to come up with a name of a group that has recorded the songs. One example of a fictitious group would be Ozzie and the Ozones. Students are then to design a cover for their album, focusing on a picture of the environment.

3 Tell students they are to take a sheet of paper and use it as sheet music. They are to write a ten-line song that identifies five facts that show the environment is important. They should give their song a title. If students wish, they can cut their paper in the form of a record and write their song on it.

Evaluation

Each student is to read (or sing) the words to his/her song. As each student does this, ask the class to identify five facts about the environment that were stated.

Filling Up With Pollution

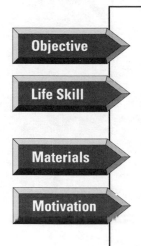

Objective

Students will identify steps they can take to contribute to the wellness of the environment.

Life Skill

Students will contribute to helping keep the environment healthful by identifying one behavior they can follow each day for a week.

Materials

Balloons

Motivation

1 Provide each student in the class with a balloon. The balloon should be large enough so that the student can draw a small picture of the planet. When students get their balloons, they can use a pen to draw a picture of the Earth. Emphasize that because the balloon is small, students need not draw anything extremely detailed.

2 Explain that you are going to identify ways the environment is being harmed. Each time you identify a way, students must blow a small puff of air inside their balloons. Emphasize that each puff of air should be small.

3 Begin identifying ways the environment is being destroyed. Use the following as a guide or you can add or substitute your own.

> *Environmental Concerns*
> 1. Automobiles are polluting the air.
> 2. Propellents in some household sprays are causing the ozone layer of the atmosphere to deplete.
> 3. Smoking indoors is a major cause of indoor air pollution.
> 4. Garbage is being dumped in rivers and streams.
> 5. Radon is leaking in high levels inside many homes.
> 6. People are having balloon releases into the air and the balloons are falling in rivers and streams where they have burst and now are being eaten by sea life and killing it.

4 For each statement, have students come up with ways they can reduce the risk of harm to the environment. For example, riding bikes instead of automobiles is one way to reduce air pollution as stated in Concern #1. As each student gives a way to reduce the risk of harm to the environment, tell the students to let air out of their balloons. Let air out until the balloons are deflated. Explain that the "Earth" did not burst, or become destroyed because people thought of ways of saving it.

Evaluation

Have students identify specific actions they can take as individuals to help keep the Earth's environment healthful.

Looks Can Be Deceiving

Objective

Students will describe the causes and dangers of acid rain.

Life Skill

I will try to help reduce the use of fossil fuels that get into the air via automobiles by using alternative means of travel such as riding a bicycle.

Materials

Two glasses of clear water

Motivation

1 Explain to students that acid rain has become a major health problem for the environment. More than 95 percent of acid rain is related to human sources. The greatest contributors to the formation of acid rain are coal-fired power plants, ore smelters, steel mills, and other industries.

2 Explain that acid rain is formed when fossil fuels are burned. The sulfur and nitrogen in the air combine with oxygen and sunlight in the atmosphere to become sulfur dioxide and nitrogen oxides which, in turn, are precursors of sulfuric acid and nitric acids. The acid particles are then carried by the wind and combine with moisture to produce acidic rain or snow.

3 Take two clear glasses and fill each with water from the tap. Show the class each glass. Tell the class that one of the glasses contains water that is acidic. Explain that the acidic water in one glass is strong enough to kill fish life and to destroy objects that are made of marble and copper. Tell students that the water in one glass is a collection of acid rain. Have the class vote on which glass contains the acid rain.

4 Of course, neither glass contained acid rain. But make the point that acid rain is crystal clear just like the water in both glasses. Yet acid rain is extremely dangerous. It can damage crops, destroy forests, and kill fish in lakes. The adverse effects on human health are not known clearly at this time.

Evaluation

Have students brainstorm a list of different contributors to acid rain in the environment. They can think of different products and industries that use fossil fuels. Then have students describe how their particular community can possibly be affected by acid rain.

Decibel Match

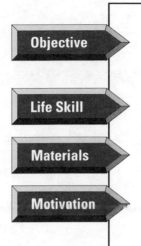

Objective

Students will identify the decibel level of different sounds and what they can do to lower their exposure to loud sounds.

Life Skill

I will take steps to avoid overexposure to loud sounds.

Materials

None

Motivation

1 Explain to students that overexposure to loud sounds is dangerous to health. Sound is measured in decibels (dB). A whisper is 20 dB. A conversation is 50 dB. Any dB that is under 60 is considered comfortable, and therefore safe for hearing.

2 Explain that high-intensity noise will damage the delicate hair cells inside the inner ear. These hair cells serve as sound receptors. High-intensity noise is considered as that being higher than 85dB.

3 Provide students with the following tips they can use to protect their hearing:

- If using headsets, keep the volume below the level at which there are vibrations.
- Limit exposure to loud noise as shorter exposures are better than constant, longer exposures.
- Wear hearing protectors if working in areas in which there are loud noises.
- Do not stuff ears with cotton to reduce exposure to noise. Use earplugs instead.

So that students can become aware of the dB of different sounds, play Sound Match. Write the names of the different sounds that follow on the chalkboard in a straight column down. Write the sound levels next to each sound in another column, but do not write these in order. Have the class match what they think are the correct dB to the corresponding sound source: garbage disposal (80), vacuum cleaner (70), normal

4 breathing (10), chainsaw (110), lawnmower (85), rock concert (125), washing machine (78), dishwasher (75), refrigerator humming (40), jet engine nearby (140).

After the students have determined the correct answers, have them identify sounds to which they are exposed daily and approximate the dB of each sound. For each sound over 60 dB, ask students what they can do to reduce their exposure.

Pollution Can Become a Sticky Problem

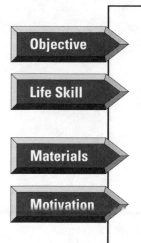

Objective

Students will describe why pollution has long-lasting effects on the environment.

Life Skill

I will practice behaviors such as riding a bike instead of a motor vehicle that help protect the environment.

Materials

Masking tape

Motivation

1 Explain that once a particular aspect of the environment becomes polluted, the effects that result can last up to thousands of years. For example, the ozone layer is located about 25 miles above the earth's surface. The ozone layer helps absorb the ultraviolet rays of the sun. The ultraviolet rays cause skin cancer. Explain that the use of products that contain chlorofluorcarbons has been depleting the Earth's ozone layer. Some products that contain chlorofluorocarbons include certain hairsprays, deodorants, cleaning solvents and halons that are used in fire extinguishers. Once the ozone layer becomes depleted, it may take hundreds or thousands of years to fill in again or perhaps it may never fill in.

2 Ask a volunteer to come to the front of the class. Take masking tape and attach it firmly to his/her fingers of one hand. Do not wrap it around the fingers. Ask the student to remove the masking tape without pulling it with his/her other hand. The student cannot use anything to assist in the removal of the tape. Basically, the student must shake it off. The student will have great difficulty shaking the tape from the hand. Explain that the tape represents a form of pollution. Have the class describe the relationship between the tape and different kinds of pollution in the environment. (Once something becomes polluted, it remains polluted for a long time.)

3 Identify other forms of pollution that have long-lasting effects. For example, air pollutants, asbestos, solid wastes, water pollution, and acid rain all remain in the environment to harm it.

Have students select a particular pollutant such as styrofoam and describe how it harms the environment.

Evaluation

It's Getting Kinda Crowded

Objective

Students will describe how overpopulation can affect the supply of natural resources.

Life Skill

I will take steps to conserve natural resources such as water and gas.

Materials

Masking tape, sheets of paper

Motivation

1 Explain that overpopulation on Earth affects people in all countries. By the year 2025, it is estimated that there will be more than 8 billion people on Earth. Even though the birth rate is decreasing, it is believed that the number of people in the world will continue to increase for many years.

2 Tell students that if current populations continue, we may reach zero population growth in the United States by the year 2025. Zero population growth is the point at which the number of births equals the number of deaths.

3 Explain that overpopulation results in starvation. There are too many people and not enough food in many parts of the world. About 50 million people around the world go hungry. With an increased population worldwide, there will be declines in fresh air, water, forest land, and agricultural land. Food prices will soar and energy costs will skyrocket.

4 Using masking tape, draw a box on the floor measuring three square feet. Select a volunteer to stand in this box. Ask for three volunteers. Give each volunteer a sheet of paper with a statement. Statement #1 says, "Your air will become more polluted." Statement #2 says, "Your supply of natural resources such as water will be reduced." Statement #3 says, "The amount of food available to you will be decreased." Each student who is outside the box will step inside, one at a time. As each student steps inside the box, that student will hand the student inside the box a statement on the sheet of paper. Each student who enters the box stays inside.

Evaluation

Have the class observe what happens as the box becomes overpopulated. Share the statements on the paper with the class and ask the students how what has happened in the small box relates to overpopulation. Have students share how they believe overpopulation in different parts of the world can affect the supply of natural resources. Have them tell ways they can conserve natural resources.

Environmental Match Game

Objective

Students will identify facts and life skills in the area of environmental health.

Life Skill

I will conserve gas, electricity, and water, and I will not litter or pollute.

Materials

Paper and pencil

Motivation

1 Explain to students that there are many facts they have learned about the environment. The following activity will enable them to review these important facts.

2 Divide the class into groups of five. Have each person in each group take out a sheet of paper. Tell students that they will each work independently within their groups but their objective will be to come up with as many matching answers as possible within groups to the questions you give. Each correct match will earn the team one point. For example, three members of the team who have the same answer will earn the team three points. Explain to students that you will give a question about the environment. Students will have fifteen seconds to write their answers on their sheets of paper. Then you will ask the students to place their pencils down. The students will then hold up their answer sheets, one team at a time. You will review their answers out loud for the class.

3 Below is a list of questions you can use in Environmental Match Game.

- Name a source of air pollution.
- What is the decibel number of a conversation?
- Name a type of waste disposal.
- Name a part of the Earth that is polluted.
- Name a city in the United States that is affected by air pollution.
- Name a way to conserve water.
- Name a way to prevent littering.
- Name a way you can reduce noise pollution.
- Name a way to conserve electricity.
- Name a kind of product you can recycle.

You can choose to add or substitute any questions you desire.

Evaluation

Review the answers students gave and clarify answers that may be incorrect as well as the many different answers that were correct.

Environmental Barometer

Objective

Students will identify environmental issues and describe actions they can take with regard to each.

Life Skill

I will encourage others to protect the environment.

Materials

Twenty-one sheets of standard notebook paper, a marker

Motivation

1 Explain to students that there are many different kinds of environmental issues that have been debated for many years. Many of these issues are not easily clarified. There are people who support some issues while others support contrary issues.

2 Explain to students that they will play Environmental Barometer. Take twenty-one sheets of paper and place a large number on each using a marker. The numbers will be in increments of ten. Beginning with plus ten, plus twenty, etc., number to one-hundred. Lay each down in the front of the room. The plus side will be laying on your left as you face the class. Do the same numbering scheme using negative ten, twenty, etc. These papers will lay side-by-side on your right as you face the class. In the middle, place the number 0.

3 Select ten volunteers to come to the front of the room. Explain that you or the class will identify controversial issues related to the environment. People will stand behind the number that best represents their feelings about the issue. For example, you might make the statement, "Cigarette smoking should be banned in all indoor places to reduce air pollution." A person who stands behind a minus 80 might believe that smoking should be banned in only certain places.

As you or the class ask questions, you can ask students to share why they stood behind certain numbers. Among the kinds of issues that can be raised are:

- Certain effective pesticides used on lawns should be banned.
- Nuclear power plants should no longer be built.
- All automobiles should get at least 35 miles per gallon.

Evaluation

Identify different kinds of issues students may raise and the depth to which these issues were addressed.

Conservation Connection

Objective

Students will identify steps they and others can take to conserve resources in the environment.

Life Skill

I will conserve natural resources.

Materials

None

Motivation

1 Tell students they are going to play a game called Conservation Connection. Explain that the class is going to think about ways they and others can help conserve energy in the environment. The game will operate as follows. One person will begin by identifying something he, she, or someone else can do that will help protect the environment. For example, the first person may say, "I will shut all lights in my room after I exit from it so that I will not waste electricity." The second person may say, "I will use both sides of scrap paper before throwing it away so that I will help reduce the amount of trash I use." A third person may say, "I'm going to recycle cans so they are not thrown away easily and thus contribute to waste disposal.

2 Explain to students that they are to not only describe how they will conserve but also to tell what value their conservation behavior has on the environment. Use the examples above to clarify this idea for students.

3 Tell students that an item cannot be repeated. A student is out when an item is repeated or that student cannot identify a way to conserve that has not already been stated.

4 You can have a student keep a list of how many ways the class identified in conserving the Earth's resources. Make the class aware that there are even many more ways they can help conserve energy.

Evaluation

Have students rank order the list of ways to conserve the Earth's resources. Have them defend their rankings.

Section 3

Totally Awesome Teaching Masters and Student Masters

This Section contains a chapter focusing on *Creating Meaningful Learning Experiences Using Teaching Masters and Student Masters*. The first part of the chapter identifies each of the Teaching Masters and Student Masters for the ten areas of health that are included in this book, provides the appropriate grade level at which each can be used, specifies an objective and life skill for each, and describes a teaching strategy to use. The remaining part of the chapter includes Teaching Masters and Student Masters for the ten areas of health. The Teaching Masters can be made into overhead transparencies and handouts. The Student Masters can be duplicated and used as student worksheets.

As a classroom teacher, you will want to vary your approach to teaching the important life skills that are identified in the comprehensive school health education curriculum. Teaching Masters and Student Masters are two teaching tools that can be used to create meaningful learning experiences. **Teaching Masters** are illustrations and/or outlines of content that can be made into overlays and used to teach various concepts that assist in the development of life skills. In some cases, you may want to duplicate Teaching Masters and use them as Student Masters. Students might label the illustrations and/or use the illustrations for review. The Teaching Masters that outline the content for a specific health topic might be used by students as an outline for taking notes. The format used for the Teaching Masters, thus affords flexibility.

Student Masters are worksheets that can be duplicated and used to provide students the opportunity to use critical thinking and to reinforce life skill development. Many of the Student Masters provide the opportunity for integrating health into other subject areas. For example, students might be asked to make computations in which they use mathematics skills as they apply critical thinking skills to learn more about a health topic. They might be asked to write reactions or to analyze situations affording the opportunity to use writing skills and to strengthen vocabulary. Some of the Student Masters focus on Health Behavior Contracts in which students practice taking self-responsibility for health. The varied Student Masters provide meaningful learning experiences for students.

Mental and Emotional Well-Being

Teaching Master 5-1
Wellness Scale

Grade level: Middle/Junior High, High School

Objective: Students will draw and label the Wellness Scale

with the factors that influence health and well-being.

Life Skill: I will choose wellness behaviors, healthful situations, and healthful relationships, make responsible decisions, and use resistance skills.

Teaching Strategy: Review the definitions of the terms used. Wellness is the quality of life that includes physical, mental-emotional, family-social, and spiritual health. The Wellness Scale depicts the ranges in the quality of life from optimal well-being to high level wellness, average wellness, minor illness or injury, major illness or injury, and premature death. Health status is the sum total of the positive and negative influence of these behaviors, situations, relationships, decisions, and use of resistance skills. Healthful behaviors are actions that promote health, prevent illness, injury, and premature death, and improve the quality of the environment. Risk behaviors are voluntary actions that threaten health, increase the likelihood of illness, injury, and premature death, and destroy the quality of the environment. Healthful situations are involuntary circumstances that promote health, prevent illness, injury, and premature death, and improve the quality of the environment. Risk situations are involuntary circumstances that threaten health, increase the likelihood of illness, injury, and premature death, and destroy the quality of the environment. Healthful relationships are relationships that promote self-esteem and productivity, encourage health enhancing behavior, and are energizing. Destructive relationships destroy self-esteem, interfere with productivity and health, and are energy depleting. Responsible decisions are those that lead to actions which 1) promote health, 2) promote safety, 3) protect laws, 4) show respect for self and others, 5) follow guidelines set by responsible adults such as parents and guardians, and 6) demonstrate good character and moral values. Ask students to describe how they would rate their health status giving reasons for their ratings. Have students provide a list of personal ways to promote their health status.

CREATING MEANINGFUL LEARNING EXPERIENCES USING TEACHING MASTERS AND STUDENT MASTERS

15

Teaching Master 5-2
The Model of Health and Well-Being

Grade Level: Middle/Junior High, High School

Objective: Students will diagram the Model of Health and Well-Being showing the relationship between the four dimensions of health and the ten areas of health.

Life Skill: I will practice healthful behaviors and make responsible decisions for each of the ten areas of health.

Teaching Strategy: Show students the Teaching Master. Explain to students that health and well-being is dependent upon choosing healthful behaviors, participating in healthful situations, developing healthful relationships, making responsible decisions, and using resistance skills for each of the ten areas of health. This, in turn, affects mental-emotional health, physical health, family and social health, and spiritual health. Ask students to share one healthful behavior in which they might engage for each of the ten areas of health. Discuss ways in which each of these behaviors influences mental-emotional health, physical health, family and social health, and spiritual health.

Teaching Master 5-3
The Responsible Decision Making Model

Grade Level: Middle/Junior High, High School

Objective: Students will identify the steps in the responsible decision making model.

Life Skill: I will make decisions that result in actions which 1) promote health, 2) promote safety, 3) protect laws, 4) show respect for self and others, 5) follow guidelines set by responsible adults such as parents and guardians, and 6) demonstrate good character and morals.

Teaching Strategy: Review the steps in the Responsible Decision Making Model. Give each student an index card. Have students describe a difficult situation in which a decision must be made by a person their age. Collect the cards. Select some of the cards for classroom discussion. Ask students to examine each of the steps in the Responsible Decision Making Model and then decide what decision might be made.

Teaching Master 5-4
Model for Using Resistance Skills

Grade Level: Middle/Junior High, High School

Objective: Students will identify resistance skills they can use when pressured to participate in risk behaviors and/or risk situations.

Life Skill: I will use resistance skills when pressured to participate in risk behaviors and/or risk situations.

Teaching Strategy: Provide an example to use before reviewing the resistance skills on the Teaching Master. The example might be that a person is pressuring you to smoke cigarettes. Then discuss each of the resistance skills. How might you respond with assertive behavior? Aggressive behavior? Passive behavior? Why should you avoid saying, "No, thank you?" What is an example of nonverbal behavior that supports your decision not to smoke? What are ways you might influence the person who pressures you? How might you have avoided being in this situation? Do you know others who engage in this risk behavior? How might you avoid being in this same situation again? What responsible adult might help the person who is pressuring you with his/her risk behavior?

Student Master 5-5
Health Behavior Contract

Grade Level: Middle/Junior High, High School

Objective: Students will develop health behavior contracts for a life skill.

Life Skill: I will make and follow a health behavior contract for each life skill I want to develop.

Teaching Strategy: Review the components of a health behavior contract. The "life skill" is the action that a person wants to practice for a lifetime. The "effect on my well-being" is a description of how this life skill improves health. The "plan" is a step by step procedure for making a life skill a habit. "Evaluating my progress" is a way of recording progress toward the completion of the plan. The "results" are a summary of the effort that was made to follow the plan and the effects on physical, mental, emotional, family and social, and spiritual health. Have students select a life skill they want to make a habit and make a health behavior contract for this life skill.

Student Master 5-6
Health Behavior Contract

Grade Level: Elementary, Middle School

Objective: Students will develop health behavior contracts for a life skill.

Life Skill: I will make and follow a health behavior contract for each life skill I want to develop.

Teaching Strategy: Discuss the parts of a health behavior contract. The "life skill" is the action the student wants to make a lifelong habit. "How this life skill helps me" tells how this habit will help the student to be healthy. "My plan" tells what the student is going to do to begin this habit right now. "How I follow my plan" is a place to write down how the student is doing on this plan. "How I feel" is a place where the student can indicate ways in which following this new life skill helps him/her to feel good. Have students make a personal health behavior contract for a skill they wish to follow.

Teaching Master 5-7
General Adaptation Syndrome

Grade Level: Junior High, High School

Objective: Students will discuss the alarm, resistance, and exhaustion stages of the general adaptation syndrome.

Life Skill: I will use stress management skills to reduce the harmful effects of stress.

Teaching Strategy: Discuss the general adaptation syndrome, the three stages in which the body responds to stress. During the alarm stage, the sympathetic nervous system regulates the body and the body responds by preparing for quick action: pupils dilate, hearing sharpens, saliva decreases, heart rate increases, blood pressure increases, bronchioles dilate, digestion slows, blood flows to muscles, and muscles tighten. The body attempts to meet the demands of the stressor. As the demands are met, the resistance stage begins. During the resistance stage, the parasympathetic nervous system is activated by the hypothalmus. The body responds in the following ways: pupils constrict, hearing returns to normal, saliva increases, heart rate decreases, blood pressure decreases, bronchioles constrict, intestinal secretions increase, blood flow to muscles returns to normal, and the muscles relax. If the demands of the stressor are not met, the GAS continues, and the exhaustion stage of the GAS begins. During the exhaustion stage, the body becomes fatigued from overwork and a person becomes vulnerable to disease. Ask students to share situations that are particularly stressful for them. Identify appropriate stress management skills: exercise, get plenty of sleep, eat foods with vitamins B and C, talk to family members and significant others, have a time management plan, pray, and eat healthful foods.

Student Master 5-8
Stress and Your Body

Grade Level: Elementary

Objective: Students will identify ways to manage stress.

Life Skill: I will use stress management skills when I experience stress.

Teaching Strategy: Duplicate copies of this Master for each student. Discuss stress. Stress is a demand on your mind or body. Have students tell what causes stress. Fighting with friends, having family changes, moving, and speaking in front of the class may be stressful for students in elementary school. Explain that there are ways to deal with stress. One way is to talk about stress with a parent. A parent can reassure you and help you feel loved. Have students connect the dots to make a number 1. Another way to deal with stress is to eat healthful foods. Vitamin C is found in orange juice. Vitamin C helps protect the body from disease during stress. Have students connect the dots to make a number 2. Another way to deal with stress is to exercise. Exercise helps the body by moving muscles. Have students connect the dots to make a number 3.

Another way to deal with stress is to get plenty of rest and sleep. Being under stress can be tiring. Have students connect the dots to make a number 4. Remind students to do something when they feel stress.

Family and Relationship Skills

Student Master 6-1
Family Chores

Grade Level: Elementary

Objective: Students will identify family chores they can do for their families.

Life Skill: I will help my family with chores.

Teaching Strategy: Duplicate this Master for each student. Discuss the importance of family members helping each other. Identify the chores that must be done around the home. Have students share chores that they do. Ask them what chores older brothers and sisters do and what parents, stepparents, and/or guardians do to help at home. Review the steps in how to complete this health behavior contract. Ask why they think they are to color a heart each time they do a chore. Explain that helping at home shows they care.

Student Master 6-2
A Stepfamily

Grade Level: Elementary

Objective: Students will define stepfamily and discuss ways to have good relationships in a stepfamily.

Life Skill: I will be a loving and responsible family member.

Teaching Strategy: Explain that some children belong to stepfamilies. A stepfamily is formed when a parent marries someone new after a divorce from or death of the other parent. A stepfather is a man who marries a person's mother. A stepmother is a woman who marries a person's father. A stepbrother is boy who is the child of someone's stepparent. A stepsister is a girl who is the child of someone's stepparent. Have the children color the picture of the stepfamily. Discuss the stepfamily. Explain that the child might be that of the mother or the father. The other parent is the stepparent. A new baby of a parent and a stepparent is a half-brother or half-sister. Ask the children to make up a story about this stepfamily. The story might tell ways in which these family members show love for one another.

Teaching Master 6-3
Dysfunctional Family Relationships

Grade Level: Junior High/High School

Objective: The student will identify the contributing causes of family dysfunction, messages that are conveyed in dysfunctional families, and characteristics of persons with co-dependence.

Life Skill: I will seek help if I show signs of co-dependence or if I have a dysfunctional family life.

Teaching Strategy: Have students examine the Master. Use the analogy of a tree. The roots of a tree provide the nourishment that makes a tree grow and develop. Explain the concept of growth and development within the family unit. The family has an impact on how family members grow and develop. The most healthful opportunity for growth and development is to have family roots that are filled with love, trust, sharing, and hard work. Loving family roots are void of any kind of abuse or chemical dependence. This is contrasted with a family whose roots are dysfunctional. These roots might be filled with chemical dependence, violence, workaholism, neglect, sexual abuse, abandonment, mental disorders, eating disorders, and/or extreme pressures to succeed. The messages learned in these families include: 1) It is not alright to talk about family problems, 2) I must present a positive family image to others, 3) I cannot change what is happening, 4) It is safer to keep my feelings to myself, 5) Others need not treat me with respect, 6) I cannot let others know how I feel, and 7) It is better to be serious than playful. Young people who receive these messages often develop a condition called co-dependence. It is believed to be the leading mental health disorder. Characteristics of persons with co-dependence include: may abuse drugs, denies feelings, afraid, accepts abuse, not capable of intimacy, lacks problem solving skills, and desires instant gratification. Discuss places in the community where help is available.

Student Master 6-4
Genogram

Grade Level: Elementary, Middle/Junior, High School

Objective: Students will trace their family's medical history.

Life Skill: I will keep a record of my family's medical history.

Teaching Strategy: Give students a copy of the genogram. This Master can be modified for use by different grade levels. Explain that a genogram is a map showing the history of disease in a family. Explain that the doctor can use a person's genogram to help make a plan for health. The children in elementary and middle school can take this Master home to their parents for discussion. Have junior high and high school students interview family members and complete the genogram themselves. They are to write the name of the person in the space provided. The "b" is for the person's birth date and the "d" is for the date of death for those who are deceased. Explain to students that they should keep the genogram and share it with their family physician.

Teaching Master 6-5
Setting Limits on Sexual Behavior

Grade Level: Junior High, High School

Objective: Students will identify the body changes that accompany strong sexual feelings and will give reasons why it is important to set limits on sexual behavior.

Life Skill: I will not be sexually active.

Teaching Strategy: Discuss sexual behavior with the class using the Teaching Master. Begin at the top of the master. Explain that there are ways that persons express affection for others. It is important to understand that expressing affection in a physical way causes the body to respond. The more physical the expression of affection, the greater the response of the body. This is why it is important to set limits on sexual behavior. Begin with the column labelled sexual behavior. Explain that this couple might behave in different ways. Suppose the couple limits its expressions of affection to holding hands, hugging, and casual kissing. With these limits, both the male and the female are able to think clearly. Although they have feelings for each other, their minds remain in control. But, suppose they cross this limit and begin deep kissing and petting. Petting is sexual touching. These behaviors result in strong sexual feelings. Bodily changes begin to occur. In the male, blood flows to the genitals. The penis becomes erect and a slippery fluid may cover the tip of the penis. In the female, blood flows to the genitals creating a warm, moist feeling in the vagina. These responses prepare the male and female for sexual intercourse. These responses also strengthen sexual feelings. It becomes very difficult for the mind to remain in control. This is why adults recommend that expressions of affection be limited to holding hands, hugging, and casual kissing.

Growth and Develoment

Teaching Master 7-1
Male Development

Objective: Students will describe the process of growth and development in males.

Life Skill: I will follow rules for proper hygiene such as regular bathing and using deodorant as my body begins to change.

Grade Level: Middle/Junior High, High School

Teaching Strategy: Explain background information about puberty. Puberty occurs when testosterone is secreted in the body. Many physical changes begin. The voice of a male during puberty will deepen. Hair will grow on the face. The penis becomes larger and longer. Muscles grow stronger. Often, a male will experience frequent erections at different times during the day and night. Males will experience a growth spurt that may result in a growth of five or more inches in a one year period. This may result in the male feeling awkward and uncoordinated during this time. But, this phase of awkwardness disappears. Typically, males will begin the growth spurt at around age 13 or 14.

Teaching Master 7-2
Female Development

Objective: Students will describe the process of growth and development in females.

Life Skill: I will follow rules for proper feminine hygiene such as using menstrual products and disposing of them properly.

Grade Level: Middle/Junior High, High School

Teaching Strategy: As a girl enters puberty, a number of physical changes begin to take place. The secretion of hormones results in the thickening of the vaginal walls. The uterus becomes larger and more muscular. Menstruation eventually begins. The first menstrual period is called menarche. Initially, menstrual periods may be irregular and occur without ovulation. It may even be several years before menstrual periods become regular. The female will also experience development of the breasts and the growth of body hair around the genital areas. The hips widen and there is an overall appearance of a feminine body. Since girls generally reach puberty before males, they may feel awkward as they are usually taller than their male counterparts. It is important for girls to be aware of menstrual products that are available. There are many different companies that develop educational guides that focus on what the different kinds of feminine hygiene products are, how they are used, and how they are to be disposed. You can obtain further information by contacting one of these companies for free and/or inexpensive materials to facilitate your teaching.

Teaching Master 7-3
The Skeletal System

Objective: Students will identify the different bones in the body that make up the skeletal system.

Life Skill: I will practice safety rules in physical activities to prevent injury to the bones in my body.

Grade Level: Elementary School, Middle/Junior High School

Teaching Strategy: Provide students with background information about the bones in the skeletal system.
Structure of bones. The outside of a bone is covered with a membrane called the periosteum. Blood vessels that run through the periosteum nourish the bone cells. Under the periosteum is compact bone. Compact bone is hard and it gets thicker as a bone grows. The end of a bone is called spongy bone. Spongy bone acts as a cushion for the rest of a bone by absorbing shocks. Red bone marrow is found in spongy bone. Red bone marow makes red blood cells.
Joints. The place at which two bones meet is called a joint. Joints are crossed by ligaments and tendons. Ligaments bind bones to one another. Tendons connect muscles to bones. There are three kinds of joints. Freely movable joints comprise most of the joints in the body. These joints allow for a wide range of movements. Examples of freely movable joints include hinge joints that swing back-and-forth, pivot joints that allow one bone to rotate around another, and gliding joints that allow a bone to slide over another bone. Partially movable joints provide strong support to bones but allow some movements. Examples of partially movable joints include the ribs and vertebrae. Immovable joints allow very little movement. The skull is an example of an immovable joint.
How bones change. Bones change as a person grows. The bones of a baby are soft and are called cartilage. Cartilage is soft and easy to bend. As a baby grows, cartilage is replaced by bone cells and minerals in a process called ossification. Ossification continues through adult life. As adults age, they may lose minerals from their bones. The bones become weaker and brittle.

Teaching Master 7-4
The Muscular System

Objective: Students will describe the importance of muscles in the body.

Life Skill: I will follow rules to keep my muscles strong and healthy.

Grade Level: Elementary, Middle/Junior High School

Teaching Strategy: Review the following information about muscles.
Types of muscles. There are three different kinds of muscles in the body. Skeletal muscles are muscles that are connected to bones. They are also called voluntary muscles because they are controlled by a person's conscious decisions. Smooth muscle, also called involuntary muscle, covers many of the internal organs in the body. Smooth muscle lines the digestive tract. It helps move food through the digestive system. Cardiac muscle is an involuntary muscle that lines the heart. Cardiac muscle must work for a lifetime so that the heart can constantly beat.
Muscle contraction. Bones move when muscles contract. All movement results when a muscle pulls a bone. A muscle pulls to bend at a joint. For that joint to straighten again, another muscle must pull the bone back to its original position. Muscles that bend joints are called flexors. Muscles that straignten joints are called extensors.

Teaching Master 7-5
The Nervous System

Objective: Students will identify the different parts of the nervous system.

Life Skill: I will follow healthful habits to keep my nervous system healthy such as getting adequate amounts of sleep.

Grade Level: Elementary, Middle/Junior High School

Teaching Strategy: Review the basic parts of the nervous system beginning with the components of a nerve cell.
The structure of nerves. A nerve cell is called a neuron. The main parts of a neuron consist of an axon and dendrites. The axon is a long fiber that carries messages away from the cell body to the neuron. One nerve cell can have more than 1000 axons bound together. Dendrites are fibers that receive impulses and send them to the cell body. At the end of an axon of one neuron and the dendrite of another neuron is a synapse or space. The synapse acts as a place where chemicals called neurotransmitters can pass from an axon to a dendrite.

The central nervous system. The central nervous system consists of the brain and spinal cord. The largest part of the brain is called the cerebrum. The cerebrum regulates thoughts and actions. The cerebellum is the part of the brain that coordinates muscle movements. The brainstem connects the cerebrum to the spinal cord. The medulla is the part of the brainstem that controls the most important functions of life such as breathing and blood pressure. The spinal cord is composed of nerves that reach out to all parts of the body.

The peripheral nervous system. The peripheral nervous system carries messages between the body and the central nervous system. The autonomic nervous system is the part of the peripheral nervous system that controls involuntary responses such as breathing. The parasympathetic nervous system is the part of the peripheral nervous system that slows the body functions. For example, when sleeping, activities in the body are reduced. The sympathetic nervous system is the part of the peripheral nervous system that works when you are active.

Teaching Master 7-6
The Digestive System

Objective: Students will identify the structure and function of the digestive system.

Life Skill: I will eat foods that promote the health of my digestive system.

Grade Level: Elementary, Middle/Junior High School

Teaching Strategy: Discuss the process of digestion with your class. Explain that digestion begins in the mouth. Saliva in the mouth moistens food. After the food is softened, the tongue rolls it into a bolus or ball. The food is then swallowed. It moves down the esophagus to the stomach by the action of peristalsis or wavelike contractions of the digestive muscles. In the stomach, food is broken down even further by chemicals as well as muscle contractions. Digested food is turned into thick paste called chyme. From the stomach, food moves into the small intestine. Food is broken down in the intestine by chemicals secreted by the pancreas and the liver. The nutrients are then absorbed in the small intestine into villi, fingerlike projections in the small intestine walls. The digested food enters the bloodstream through blood vessels in the villi.

Teaching Master 7-7
The Circulatory System

Objective: Students will describe the function of the circulatory system.

Life Skill: I will follow behaviors to improve the health of my heart by engaging in activities such as aerobic exercises.

Grade Level: Elementary, Middle/Junior High School

Teaching Strategy: The circulatory system is composed of blood vessels and the heart. The heart is a muscle that is the size of a clenched fist. The right side of the heart receives oxygen-poor blood from the body and pumps it to the lungs. The left side of the heart receives oxygen-rich blood from the lungs and pumps it to the body. The upper chamber of the heart is known as the atrium. The lower chamber of the heart is known as the ventricle.

Blood vessels. The largest blood vessels are arteries and veins. Arteries are blood vessels that carry blood away from the heart. Veins are blood vessels that carry blood to the heart. Arteries branch into smaller blood vessels called arterioles. Arterioles expand and contract to control the flow of blood into capillaries. Capillaries are blood vessels through which gases and nutrients pass.

Blood pressure. Blood pressure is the force of blood on the blood vessel in which it is contained. There are two kinds of blood pressure. Systolic blood pressure is the force of blood during the active phase of the heartbeat. Diastolic blood pressure is the force of blood when the heart muscle relaxes or is between beats. Normal blood pressure is 120/80. The upper reading is the systolic while the lower reading is the diastolic.

Teaching Master 7-8
The Respiratory System

Objective: Students will describe the structure and function of the respiratory system.

Life Skill: I will not smoke cigarettes so as to keep my respiratory system healthy.

Grade Level: Elementary, Middle/Junior High School

Teaching Strategy: Explain the functions of the major parts of the respiratory system. The respiratory system is made up of the lungs and air passages. The upper respiratory tract extends from the nasal passage to the opening of the windpipe. The lower respiratory tract extends from the windpipe to the lungs. When air is inhaled, it becomes moistened and warmed by the mucous membranes. Mucus and cilia in the nose trap dirt in the air. At the opening of the windpipe is the larynx. The larynx is known as the voice box. The mucous membrane of the larynx helps remove dirt from the air that is inhaled. The trachea is the windpipe below the larynx. Rings of cartilage help keep the trachea open. At the lower end of the windpipe are large air tubes called bronchi. Bronchi enter the lungs. Inhaled air goes through the bronchi into the lungs. The linings of the lungs are filled with alveoli or air sacs. The alveoli are surrounded by capillaries. Capillaries separate air in the lungs from blood in the capillaries. Oxygen passes through thin walls and enters red blood cells. At the same time, carbon dioxide moves from capillaries into air sacs. About one-half quart of air is exchanged with each breath.

Teaching Master 7-9
The Urinary System

Objective: Students will describe the structure and function of the urinary system.

Life Skill: I will drink the equivalent of 6-8 glasses of water each day.

Grade Level: Elementary, Middle/Junior High School

Teaching Strategy: Review the main purposes of the urinary system. The kidneys are the main parts of the urinary system. The kidneys are located on each side of the spine behind the intestines. Kidneys filter wastes from the blood via nephrons. Water and waste products are drawn from the blood into nephrons forming urine. Urine is a solution of urea, salts, water, and other substances. Urine flows through ureters that are tubes connecting kidneys to the bladder. The bladder stores urine. When the bladder becomes full, it relaxes and urine is released from the body through the urethra.

Teaching Master 7-10
The Endocrine System

Objective: Students will identify the structures of the endocrine system.

Life Skill: I will have regular medical checkups to be sure that the organs of the endocrine system are working as they should.

Grade Level: Elementary, Middle/Junior High School

Teaching Strategy: Show students the Teaching Master and explain that males and females have many of the same parts of the endocrine system. Explain that the endocrine system is made up of endocrine glands that produce and release hormones. The hypothalamus is a gland that is a part of the brain that controls breathing, heartbeat, and appetite. The pituitary gland produces hormones that regulate growth and influence the actions of other glands. The thyroid gland is located near the windpipe. It releases hormones that control metabolism. The parathyroid glands are at-tached to the thyroid gland. They release a hormone that releases calcium into the bloodstream. The adrenal glands are located on the kidneys. The adrenal glands produce adrenaline which helps the body prepare for action. The pancreas is a gland that releases digestive juices into the small intestine. The pancreas also produces insulin which regulates the metabolism of sugar in the body. In women, ovaries produce estrogen which helps produce the changes in the body during puberty. The testes in men produce testosterone that causes the changes in men during puberty.

Student Master 7-11
Food For Growth

Objective: Students will identify foods that are healthful for growth.

Life Skill: I will eat fruits and vegetables each day.

Grade Level: Elementary

Teaching Strategy: Distribute the Student Master. Explain to students that there are illustrations of different kinds of foods. Some of the foods are healthful while others are not. Tell students to put an X through the foods that are not healthful. The students will place an X through the piece of cake and the chocolate bar. Explain that these foods may taste good, but they do not contain enough important substances to help the body grow healthfully. Have students share what other foods they can eat to help them grow healthfully. You can also cut out pictures from magazines to show examples of different kinds of healthful foods.

Student Master 7-12
Your Body Parts

Objective: Students will identify where different body parts are located.

Life Skill: I will take steps to protect different body parts such as wearing a helmet when I ride a bike.

Grade Level: Elementary.

Teaching Strategy: Distribute the Student Master and have students connect the body part on the side of the page to the appropriate part on the body. Students can also name the part out loud and tell what that part does. Students can also share how they can keep that body part protected and healthy.

Nutrition

Student Master 8-1
Food Groups

Grade Level: Elementary

Objective: Students will identify food groups to which different foods belong.

Life Skill: I will eat a balanced diet.

Teaching Strategy: Discuss the food groups with students. Identify foods and beverages that belong to the milk group. These include milk, ice cream, yogurt, and cheese. Identify foods that belong to the grain group. These include bread, muffins, rice, barley, pasta, noodles, and cereal. Identify foods that belong to the fruits and vegetables group. These include apples, pears, bananas, carrots, broccoli, etc. Identify foods that belong to the meat group. These include legumes, beans, nuts, fish, meat, turkey, and chicken. Have the students complete the master. There are three foods in the milk group: ice cream cone, piece of cheese, and milk. There are five foods in the grain group: box of rice, muffin, pasta, cereal, and bread. There are four foods in the fruits and vegetables group: carrot, broccoli, banana, apple. There are three foods in the meat group: chicken drumstick, nuts, and fish. Ask students to name other foods which belong to each food group.

Teaching Master 8-2
Seven Dietary Guidelines

Grade Level: Middle/Junior High, High School

Objective: Students will identify the seven dietary guidelines.

Life Skill: I will follow the seven dietary guidelines.

Teaching Strategy: Use the Teaching Master to discuss each of the seven dietary guidelines. (1) It is important to eat a variety of foods. The best way to do this is to eat foods from the food groups. Recently, the USDA has created some new guidelines for eating. They recommend eating 6-11 servings of bread, cereal, rice, and pastas, 3-5 servings of vegetables, 2-4 servings of fruits, 2-3 servings of milk, yogurt, and cheese, and 2-3 servings of meat, poultry, fish, dry beans, eggs, and nuts. (2) Maintaining desirable weight helps to prevent heart disease, cancer, and diabetes. Desirable weight is the weight and body composition that is recommended for a person's age, height, sex, and body build. (3) A low fat diet helps to prevent atherosclerosis and cancers of the breast, colon, and prostate. (4) Choosing a diet with plenty of fruits, vegetables, and grains helps to prevent heart disease and cancer of the colon. (5) Using sugar in moderation helps to prevent heart disease, obesity, and tooth decay. (6) Limiting salt helps to keep blood pressure within normal range. (7) Avoiding alcohol helps prevent many types of cancer. Have students identify ways they can follow each of these dietary guidelines.

Student Master 8-3
Find The Vitamin

Grade Level: Elementary, Middle School

Objective: Students will discuss the benefits of eating foods and drinking beverages that provide vitamins E, C, and A.

Life Skill: I will eat foods and drink beverages that contain vitamins E, C, and A.

Teaching Strategy: Discuss vitamins with the class. Vitamin E keeps harmful compounds from forming in the body. Vitamin E is found in fish, eggs, vegetable oils, and whole grain cereal. Vitamin C helps the body stay strong and protects against some diseases. Eating foods with vitamin C helps protect against some kinds of cancer. Foods with vitamin C include lemons, strawberries, limes, and oranges. Vitamin A helps protect against some kinds of cancer and also night blindness. Foods with vitamin A include carrots, yellow orange vegetables and fruits, spinach, and kale. Have students complete the Student Master. Vitamin E is found in fish and eggs. Vitamin C is found in strawberries and oranges. Vitamin A is found in carrots and cantaloupe. Ask student what foods containing vitamins E, C, and A that they will eat today.

Teaching Master 8-4
Diet and Heart Disease

Grade Level: Middle/Junior High, High School

Objective: Students will identify diet guidelines to follow to reduce the liklihood of heart disease.

Life Skill: I will limit the amounts of fat, sugar, and salt that I eat.

Teaching Strategy: Discuss diet and heart disease. The American Heart Association recommends the following: (1) Cut total fat to less than 30 percent of daily calories, (2) Keep saturated fat below 10 percent and polyunsaturated fat to less than 10 percent of daily calories, (3) Keep daily cholesterol intake to no more than 300 mg per day, (4) Have no more than 55ml of alcohol, the equivalent of two drinks a day if an adult, (5) Limit salt to no more than 1,000 mg per 1,000 Calories a day. Review each of the 11 recommendations that appear on the Teaching Master. Ask students to write a health behavior contract for one of the 11 recommendations.

Teaching Master 8-5
Diet and Cancer

Grade Level: Middle/Junior High, High School

Objective: Students will identify dietary guidelines that reduce the risk of cancer.

Life Skill: I will eat foods that contain high-fiber, vitamins A, C, and E, selenium, and folic acid.

Teaching Strategy: Explain that the risk of cancer might be reduced 35% if a careful diet is followed. The recommendations for this anti-cancer diet are listed on the Master. Provide students with the following information about the 15 recommendations. (1) Persons who are 40% overweight have an increased risk of colon, breast, and uterine cancers. (2) Fats should consist of no more than 30 percent of total caloric intake. High fat intake is related to breast, colon, and prostate cancers. (3) The National Cancer Institute recommends a diet containing 20 to 35 grams of fiber each day. This is the equivalent of five or six servings of high-fiber foods. (4) Vegetables that contain vitamin A, also called beta-carotene, include carrots, other yellow-orange vegetables, spinach, chicory, and kale. Vitamin A is believed to reduce the risk of developing cancers of the larynx, esophagus, and lung. (5) Vitamin C is believed to protect against cancers of the larynx, esophagus, and lung. It also is believed to block the formation of cancer-causing chemicals, such as the nitrosamines produced when preservatives like nitrite are broken down in the body. (6) Cruciferous vegetables reduce the risk of cancers of the digestive organs. (7) The risk of cancers of the stomach and esophagus is reduced when salt-cured, smoked, and nitrite-cured foods are not eaten. (8) Consumption of alcohol is linked to cancers of the mouth, larynx, throat, liver, esophagus, and stomach. (9) Persons who drink milk have lower rates of colon and rectal cancers than those who do not drink milk. (10) Eating fish has been shown to protect against certain kinds of cancer. (11) Vitamin E helps prevent the formation of harmful compounds. Vitamin E is found in vegetable oils, eggs, fish, and whole grain cereals. (12) Selenium is found in many kinds of seafood, liver, kidney, and grains. Selenium helps protect against cancer by promoting the action of vitamin E in the body. (13) Folic acid is a B vitamin that helps the body's repair system. It is found in foods such as liver, kidney, dark-green vegetables, fruits, wheat germ, and peas. (14) Well-done hamburger meat is found to have at least six chemicals known to cause changes in a cell's genetic blueprint. (15) Frying and grilling have produced agents known to cause cancer in animals. Have students make health behavior contracts for the life skill identified for this Teaching Master.

Personal Fitness

Student Master 9-1
I Love 2 Be Fit

Grade Level: Elementary

Objective: Students will identify exercises which promote cardiovascular fitness.

Life Skill: I will do exercises that make my heart muscle strong.

Teaching Strategy: Discuss exercise. Explain that exercise is moving the muscles. When muscles are moved with exercise, they become stronger. Explain that the heart is a muscle. When certain exercises are done, the heart muscle becomes stronger. Then the heart can pump blood to the body's cells more easily. Have students feel the carotid artery at the neck. This will help them to feel the heart at work pumping blood. Then have students run in place or do jumping jacks. Have them feel the carotid artery at the neck. Mention that the heart beats faster during exercises that make the heart muscle strong. These exercises should be done for at least 15 to 20 minutes three times a week. Some good heart exercises are running, jumping rope, riding bikes, swimming, and skating. Give each student a copy of the Student Master to color. They also are to count the number of children who exercise. Three jump rope, two ride bikes, and seven run.

Teaching Master 9-2
Flexibility

Grade Level: Elementary, Middle/Junior High, High School

Objective: Students will demonstrate the following exercises that improve flexibility: alternate knee-to-chest, leg cross overs, and seated toe touch.

Life Skill: I will do stretching exercises daily to maintain flexibility.

Teaching Strategy: Discuss flexibility. Flexibility is the ability to bend and move in different directions.

Show students the Teaching Master to review exercises which help maintain flexibility. The alternate knee-to-chest is for the abdominals, hip, and lower back. The leg cross overs are for the hips and back. The seated toe touch is for the hamstrings. Discuss the importance of daily stretching exercises. Have students make health behavior contracts for this important life skill.

Teaching Master 9-3
Benefits of Physical Fitness

Grade Level: Junior High/High School

Objective: Students will identify the benefits of physical fitness.

Life Skill: I will make and follow a plan for achieving and maintaining physical fitness.

Teaching Strategy: Discuss the ways in which being physically fit benefits health and well-being using the Teaching Master as an outline. (1) Cardiac output is the amount of blood pumped by the heart to the body each minute. Heart rate is the number of times that the heart beats each minute forcing blood into the arteries. Stroke volume is the amount of blood the heart pumps with each beat. Being physically fit increases stroke volume and lowers resting heart rate allowing the heart to rest more often between beats. Being physically fit also increases the ratio of HDLs to LDLs. High density lipoproteins or HDLs are fats that transport excess cholesterol to the liver for removal from the body. Low-density lipoproteins are fats that form deposits on the artery walls and contribute to the development of atherosclerosis. (2) A study at the Harvard School of Public Health revealed that females ages 10-24 who participated in team sports at least twice a week for two hours had a lower incidence of breast and colon cancer when they were older. Regular exercise has a positive effect on the menstrual cycle and on bowel movements. Regular exercise also helps a person to maintain weight; being overweight is a risk factor for several kinds of cancer. (3) During the alarm stage of stress, adrenaline is secreted to speed the body's responses. Sugar is secreted into the bloodstream to provide quick energy. During the resistance stage of stress, the body returns to homeostasis. However, when stress is prolonged this does not occur and the body stays in a ready state for quick response. If this continues, the exhaustion stage would be reached. Exercise helps in the resistance stage. Adrenaline and excess sugar in the blood are used. The return to homeostasis is helped. Participating in exercises for twenty minute periods three times a week for three weeks causes the body to release beta-endorphins. Beta-endorphins are sub-stances produced in the brain that help reduce pain and create a feeling of well-being. (4) The energy equation states that caloric intake needs to equal caloric expenditure for weight maintainence. With regard to children and adolescents, overweight is often linked to inactivity rather than overeating. Regular exercise stimulates the hypothalmus of the brain helping to keep appetite in balance. Regular exercise also helps reduce the percentage of body fat and increases the percentage of lean muscle mass giving a toned appearance. (5) Osteoporosis is a disease in which the bones become brittle and break easily. The weight bearing bones become more dense as a result of regular exercise. Regular exercise strengthens muscles and improves flexibility helping to prevent injury. Osteoarthritis is a condition in which there is erosion in the moveable parts of a joint. Regular exercise in which the joints are moved through the full range of motion reduces the effects of this condition in old age.

Teaching Master 9-4
Developing A Physical Fitness Plan

Grade Level: Middle/Junior High, High School

Objective: Students will identify the components of physical fitness.

Life Skill: I will make and follow a plan for physical fitness.

Teaching Strategy: Discuss the components of a physical fitness plan. These are listed on the Teaching Master. Review some additional specifics. (1) When warming up, begin by increasing body temperature by slowly running in place. This helps to prevent injury. A small amount of perspiration indicates that it is alright to begin stretching. Warm-up should last about three to five minutes. (2) Stretching exercises which promote flexibility should be done for ten to fifteen minutes each day. There are two kinds of stretching. Static stretching or passive stretching consists of a relaxed stretch that is held for six to sixty seconds. An example might be to gradually reach the arms down to the toes with the knees slightly bent and hold for several seconds before straightening up. Ballistic stretching involves rapid bouncing or jerking bobs. For example, bobbing down to touch the arms to the toes would be ballistic stretching. It is generally believed that static stretching is better because there is less chance of stretching muscle fibers too far causing injury. The muscles will tighten rather than stretch. (3) Aerobic exercises such as running, walking, swimming, and skating at a steady pace at target heart rate promote cardiovascular endurance and decrease the percentage of body fat. (4) Exercises for muscular strength and endurance involve overloading the muscles for extended lengths of time. (5) Exercises for cooling down are similar to those for warming up. By decreasing from heavier to lighter exercise, blood flow returns to the heart more easily. Heart beat rate and blood pressure begin to return to resting rates. Body temperature returns to normal. After students complete the Student Master, have them develop a health behavior contract for making and following a physical fitness plan.

Teaching Master 9-5
Tips for Running

Grade Level: Middle/Junior High, High School

Objective: Students will identify guidelines for running that promote fitness and insure safety.

Life Skill: I will have a safe and healthful plan for running to improve physical fitness.

Teaching Strategy: Discuss the importance of following guidelines for running that promote fitness and insure safety. Review the list of tips on the Teaching Master. Then have students pretend to work for one of the major companies that sells running shoes. They can find advertisements for these shoes in sports magazines. Have them show these advertisements to classmates and try to sell their specific brand of shoe telling why the shoe is adequate for cushion and support and at the same time providing other tips for running.

Substance Use and Abuse

Teaching Master 10-1
Alcohol and The Body

Objective: Students will describe the process by which alcohol is oxidized in the body.

Life Skill: I will use refusal skills to say NO to alcohol use.

Grade Level: Middle/Junior High, High School

Teaching Strategy: Indicate to students that the effects of alcohol on the body are related to the blood alcohol concentration (BAC). There are several factors that influence BAC:
- How much a person drinks. The more alcohol a person places in his/her body, the greater the effect.
- How quickly a person drinks. BAC will increase more quickly if a person gulps a drink fast rather than sipping a drink.
- The size of the body. A person who has more fat and muscle will be affected more slowly than a thin person. A person who has increased fat and muscle also has increased water volume. Increased water volume dilutes alcohol in the body.
- Genetics. Research seems to indicate that parents who have alcohol-related problems are more likely to have children who experience the same. There appears to be a genetic predisposition toward alcoholism.
- Food in the stomach. Alcohol is absorbed slower when there is food in the stomach as opposed to an empty stomach. Food in the stomach absorbs alcohol.

Explain that there are many physical effects of alcohol on the body. Alcohol causes cirrhosis or severe scarring of the liver. It initiates the secretion of acids in the stomach that irritate its lining. Alcohol also inhibits the production of white blood cells. Fewer white blood cells are available to fight pathogens so that a person is at increased risk of developing diseases and infections.

Teaching Master 10-2
Dealing with Sidestream Smoke

Objective: Students will describe ways to reduce their exposure to sidestream smoke.

Life Skill: I will use assertive behavior to avoid exposure to sidestream smoke.

Grade Level: Middle/Junior High, High School

Teaching Strategy: Differentiate between sidestream and mainstream smoke. Mainstream smoke is what a smoker inhales from a cigarette (s)he is smoking. Sidestream smoke is the smoke that accumulates in a room from a cigarette that is burning. Sidestream smoke is more dangerous than mainstream smoke since sidestream smoke is not filtered through the cigarette or through the smoker's lungs. Research shows that children who live in homes in which a parent smokes are at increased risk for respiratory infections. Sidestream smoke is clearly a hazard.

Explain to students that they have a right to be free of sidestream smoke. Students can use assertive skills to tell smokers not to smoke. This is a good time to brainstorm different statements a person can make when asking others not to smoke. Have students come up with statements they can use to politely ask a smoker not to smoke. Emphasize that students should be polite in making their statements. Their statements should not show aggressive behavior but yet, should show they are assertive. For example, students can say, "I believe there is a nonsmoking section on the other side of the restaurant." Sometimes how a person makes a statement is as important as what is said. Emphasize the importance of being polite, but firm.

Teaching Master 10-3
Effects of Anabolic Steroids

Objective: Students will describe the physical effects produced by anabolic steroids on the body.

Life Skill: I will not use anabolic steroids at any time in my life.

Grade Level: Middle/Junior High, High School

Teaching Strategy: Explain that anabolic steroids are synthetic derivatives of the male hormone testosterone. In years past, it was common for bodybuilders, football players, and others to use these drugs. While their use remains popular among certain individuals, research shows that anabolic steroids are dangerous. In addition to their use by athletes, young people are using these drugs so that they can increase their muscle mass, therefore improving their appearance.

Today, athletes are tested for steroid use at random. These tests may be conducted among college athletes, Olympic participants, and professional athletes. Persons found using steroids can be banned from participation in athletic events.

Show the Teaching Master and review the physical effects of steroids on the body. Explain that some of these effects can be life-threatening.

Student Master 10-4
Keep Medicines Away

Objective: Students will describe why it is important to keep medicine stored so that only an adult can reach it.

Life Skill: I will tell an adult when I find medicine or another substance that is in my reach so that it will be stored in a safe place.

Grade Level: Elementary

Teaching Strategy: Distribute the Teaching Master and have students place the medicines in the cabinet. Have students differentiate between products that are medicine and products that are not medicine. You might have students work with a parent to identify medicines found in the home. You can contact your local poison control center for labels that can be placed on medicines. Students can work with a parent to place labels on all medicines in the home, all the time emphasizing that only a responsible adult can give a boy or girl medicine.

Student Master 10-5
Which Are Medicines?

Objective: Students will differentiate between products that are medicines and products that are not medicines.

Life Skill: I will differentiate between products that are medicines and products that are not medicines and take steps to avoid touching any medicine products if not supervised by an adult.

Grade Level: Elementary

Teaching Strategy: Distribute the Student Master and have students color the appropriate circles. Check students' papers to make sure they are able to distinguish between medicines and foods. You can supplement the information in this Student Master by cutting pictures from magazines. Hold up different examples of food and medicines for the class to see. Have the students identify which are medicines and which are foods. Emphasize to students that they can accept medicines only from a responsible adult such as a parent or physician.

Diseases and Disorders

Teaching Master 11-1
Causes of Stroke

Objective: Students will identify the causes of stroke.

Life Skill: I will reduce my risk of developing a stroke by eating foods that are healthful for my blood vessels.

Grade Level: High School

Teaching Strategy: Explain that stroke is a leading cause of death. Stroke is an interruption of blood flow to a blood vessel in the brain. There are different causes of stroke. Show the Teaching Master and review the information. A thrombus is a blocked blood vessel. A thrombus is also known as a cerebrovascular occlusion. A thrombus will block blood flow in a blood vessel so that the body cells that need blood are deprived of it. When a thrombus occurs in the brain, brain cells can die due to a lack of blood. Sometimes a thrombus lodges in the brain after having travelled from another part of the body. A thrombus that travels from another part of the body that lodges in a blood vessel is called an embolism. Some strokes result from a hemorrhage. A hemorrhage is a break in a blood vessel. The break can result from damaged or brittle arteries. Sometimes an artery in the brain can balloon. Perhaps the artery was weak in a particular area. The ballooning can cause the artery to burst resulting in a stroke.

Teaching Master 11-2
Incidence and Death From Cancer

Objective: Students will identify the leading cancer sites and the death rates from them.

Life Skill: I will follow behaviors to reduce my risk of developing cancer such as avoiding exposure to the sun's rays.

Grade Level: High School

Teaching Strategy: Show the Teaching Master and have students observe the leading cancer sites and the death rates from each. Share the following information that shows the major types of cancer and their associated risk factors.

- Lung cancer. Cigarette smoking for 20 or more years; exposure to asbestos and passive smoking.
- Breast cancer. Personal or family history of breast cancer; dense breast tissue; obesity; high fat intake.
- Uterine and cervical cancer. For cervical cancer: early age at having sexual intercourse; many sex partners; genital herpes; genital warts. For uterine cancer: infertility; prolonged estrogen therapy; obesity.
- Colon and rectum cancer. Personal or family history of polyps; inflammatory bowel disease; high-fat, low-fiber diet.
- Melanoma. Excessive exposure to sun; fair complexion.
- Oral cancer. Heavy cigarette or pipe/cigar smoking; use of smokeless tobacco; excessive drinking.
- Leukemia. Excessive exposure to radiation or certain chemicals.
- Testicular cancer. Males under age 35.
- Prostate cancer. Increase in age.

Teaching Master 11-3
How HIV Attacks T Cells

Objective: Students will describe how HIV attacks the T cells.

Life Skill: I will avoid any risks of becoming infected with HIV.

Grade Level: Middle/Junior High, High School

Teaching Strategy: Show Teaching Master 11-3 and describe what happens when the body becomes infected by a pathogen. Explain that when a virus such as the one that causes chicken pox enters the body, T

cells signal the B cells. B cells stimulate the production of antibodies. The antibodies remain in the body to fight the chicken pox virus. This is why a person gets chicken pox once. But when HIV enters the body, the same cycle begins. T cells sense a foreign body and signal B cells. Antibodies are produced. But now things change. HIV enters the T cell and begins to multiply. The T cells are destroyed. B cells cannot be signaled. The person's body is now susceptible to opportunistic infections. The immune system is broken down.

Student Master 11-4
Do Not Share Germs

Objective: Students will tell why it is important to not practice behaviors that increase the risk of getting germs from another person.

Life Skill: I will not share certain objects such as a drinking glass.

Grade Level: Elementary

Teaching Strategy: Show the Student Master and have students identify ways germs are being spread. Have students tell ways they can reduce spreading germs. Write student suggestions on the chalkboard. Then have students draw a picture that shows how others are taking steps to reduce the spread of germs.

Student Master 11-5
Count The Germs

Objective: Students will identify ways germs are spread.

Life Skill: I will not share eating and drinking utensils.

Grade Level: Elementary

Teaching Strategy: Distribute the Student Master and have students complete the task of writing the numbers. Have students share their answers. Use this information to talk about germs. Tell students that germs are so small they cannot see them. Explain that not all germs are harmful. People who keep healthy can fight germs easier than people who do not keep healthy. Explain that they can get germs when they share eating and drinking utensils such as forks and drinking glasses. Discuss the fact that the common cold is caused by germs. Germs from a person's body can be spread to another person, most often by touch.

Consumer Health

Teaching Master 12-1
Flossing The Teeth

Grade Level: Elementary, Middle/Junior High, High School

Objective: Students will demonstrate the correct procedure for flossing the teeth.

Life Skill: I will floss my teeth daily.

Teaching Strategy: This Teaching Master can be used for all levels by modifying information provided. Discuss the formation of cavities. Explain that plaque is a sticky substance on teeth that contains bacteria. When plaque combines with sugar, acid is formed. This acid can make holes or cavities in the teeth. Daily toothbrushing helps remove plaque from teeth. Daily flossing helps remove plaque and calculus from teeth. Calculus is hardened plaque. Calculus is often formed near the gumline making gums sore and causing them to bleed easily. Daily flossing stimulates the gums and removes the plaque keeping teeth clean and gums healthy. Lack of daily toothbrushing and flossing may lead to gingivitis or periodontal disease. Gingivitis is a condition in which the gums are very sore and bleed easily. Periodontal disease is a disease in which the gums pull back, the bones which support teeth are destroyed, and teeth loosen. A dentist can help with gingivitis and periodontal disease although prevention is better. A preventive dental health plan includes daily toothbrushing and flossing, using a fluoride toothpaste to keep the enamel of the teeth hard, eating healthful foods, avoiding sugary and sticky foods, and having regular dental checkups. The teeth need to be cleaned and polished every six months. X-rays may be taken to look at how the teeth are forming beneath the gums and to find early signs of decay.

Teaching Master 12-2
Product Label

Grade Level: Middle/Junior High, High School

Objective: Students will identify information found on a product label.

Life Skill: I will read product labels before purchasing and using products.

Teaching Strategy: Have students bring product labels to class from home. Review the information found on the product label on the Teaching Master. Explain that product labels contain the following information: (1) name of the product, (2) care for which the product is used, (3) net quantity, (4) directions for use, (5) warnings, (6) ingredients, (7) name, address, zip code of manufacturer. The net quantity of the product is the amount or weight of the product without the container. Have students analyze the product labels they have brought from home. They should find the seven kinds of information that were reviewed from the Master. As an alternate activity, have students make their own product labels for make believe products.

Student Master 12-3
Advertising Appeals

Grade Level: Middle/Junior High, High School

Objective: Students will identify appeals that are used to sell products and services.

Life Skill: Explain that advertising companies pay large sums of money to influence consumers to buy their products and services. There are ten different kinds of appeals they use to be convincing. Ads using bandwagon appeal try to convince you that everyone wants a particular product or service and you should too. Ads with brand loyalty appeal tell you that a specific brand is better than the rest. You would be cheating yourself to use anything but this brand. Ads with false image appeal convince you that you will be a certain way if you use the product even though you really won't. Persons who want a specific image might buy a product or service hoping that it will help them create that image. Ads with glittering generalities contain statements that greatly exaggerate the benefits of the product. Ads with humor appeal use a slogan, jingle, or cartoon to catch and keep attention. Ads with progress appeal tell you that a product is a new and better product than ones you used to see advertised. Ads with reward appeal tell you that you will receive a special prize or gift if you buy a product. Ads using scientific evidence appeal give you the results of survey or laboratory tests to provide confidence in a product. Ads with snob appeal convince you that you are worthy of a product or service because it is the best. Ads with testimony appeal include a promotion by a well-known person who says a product or service is the best one for you. Divide students into groups to complete the Student Master. Then have them sing their songs for their classmates. Discuss the appeals included in each of the songs.

Student Master 12-4
Consumer Complaint

Grade Level: Middle/Junior High, High School

Objective: Students will synthesize a sample consumer complaint.

Life Skill: I will write a consumer complaint when I am not satisfied with a product or service.

Teaching Strategy: Explain that a consumer is a person who spends time and money on products and services. More than fifty cents of every dollar is spent on health products and services. For this reason there are a variety of federal, state, and local agencies as well as professional associations who serve as consumer protectors. The American Medical Association is an association that sets standards for the education and conduct of medical physicians. The AMA has a Department of Investigation and a Department of Health Education to assist the consumer and to investigate complaints. The American Dental Association is an association that sets standards for the education and conduct of dentists. The Better Business Bureau is a nonprofit, voluntary, self-regulating organization that monitors unfair competition and misleading advertisements for private firms. The Consumers' Research and Consumers' Union are private groups that test products and provide ratings for consumers to make comparisons with regard to price, performance, and safety. State health departments usually have a consumer affairs office that investigates complaints and takes action when harmful products or services are sold in the state. Local or city health departments also have a consumer affairs office that investigates complaints and takes action when harmful products or services are sold at the city or local level. The Food and Drug Administration is a federal agency within the Department of Health and Human Services that tests the safety and effectiveness of medical devices and new drugs and the safety and purity of cosmetics and foods. The Federal Trade Commission is an independent agency that monitors the advertising of foods, drugs, cosmetics, devices, and advertising that appears on television. The United States Postal Service protects the public when products, devices, and services are sold through the mail. The Office of Consumer Affairs serves as the liason between the President and all consumers. This Office coordinates investigations into consumer problems, coordinates research, and conducts seminars to inform the public. After reviewing the information about consumer protectors, discuss the importance of making a consumer complaint. A consumer complaint is a way of reporting that you are not satisfied with a product or service. When making purchases, a consumer should be aware of the information that is needed should there need to be a complaint. The sales receipt is needed. This should show the price and date of sale. Many receipts indicate the sales number of the person making the sale. If not, keep a record of this especially when larger purchases are made. Keep copies of any warranties

or guaranties and directions for use of products. A consumer complaint can be made in person, by telephone, or in writing. Usually, it is most effective to write a letter. The letter needs to include: (1) a description of the product or service including any numbers used for identification, (2) the complete address of the place of purchase and the name and/or number of the sales person, (3) a copy of the sales receipt (always keep the original) showing the date of purchase and price, (4) a statement indicating the way that payment was made, (5) a specific reason(s) you are not satisfied with your purchase, (6) a specific desired result that will satisfy you (Do you want your money back? A credit given? An exchange?) Have students complete the Student Master. They should include all six items listed previously in their letters of consumer complaint. They can make sample receipts since they do not have them. Discuss the letters they write. Read several of them. Have the class analyze them and comment on their thoroughness.

Student Master 12-5
Grocery Shopping

Objective: Students will compare prices and ingredients in foods to determine the best buy.

Grade Level: Elementary/Middle School

Life Skill: I will comparison shop by analyzing foods in similar amounts for their price and ingredients.

Teaching Strategy: In addition to using the Student Master, you may want to have two labels for the same food. Show students these two different food labels, comparing the price for similar amounts and the ingredients. Discuss the concept of comparison shopping. Comparison shopping involves analyzing prices for similar amounts and ingredients to determine the best buy. There are two ways to use the Student Master. You might have students actually go to the grocery store and select ten pairs of food items to compare. You might also have ten pairs of food items in your classroom for students to compare. You might even have students volunteer to bring in different pairs of food items or ask a local grocery store to donate damaged food cans in pairs. This Teaching Strategy might be integrated into a math lesson.

Safety and Injury Prevention

Teaching Master 13-1
Abdominal Thrust

Objective: Students will identify the steps for using the abdominal thrust.

Life Skill: I will use the abdominal thrust when a person has an obstructed airway.

Grade Level: Elemenatry, Middle/Junior High, High School

Teaching Strategy: After showing the Teaching Master, review the information. Have students demonstrate how to do the abdominal thrust. Have every student pair off and review the steps of the abdominal thrust. Have students practice the positioning of the fist and the hands in the abdominal area. Do not have them perform the squeezing into the stomach. Observe how the students carry out the tasks. Tell students that if they are alone and they choke on a piece of food, they can forcefully place their abdomen over the top edge of a chair to hopefully force out the lodged object.

Teaching Master 13-2
How Poisons Enter the Body

Objective: Students will identify how poisons enter the body.

Life Skill: I will avoid contact with any poisonous substances.

Grade Level: Elementary, Middle/Junior High, High School

Teaching Strategy: Show the Teaching Master so that students can observe the different ways poisons enter the body. One of the more common poisons affecting school-age children is poison ivy. Emphasize to students that they should avoid being in areas where there is poison ivy. As a precaution, they should wear long-sleeve shirts and trousers when in the area of poison ivy. If they come in contact with poison ivy, they should wash the affected area with soap and water as soon as possible.

Teaching Master 13-3
Self-Protection Against Assault

Objective: Students will identify ways they can protect themselves from sexual assault.

Life Skills: I will avoid situations in which I will be at risk for sexual assault.

Grade Level: High School

Teaching Strategy: Review the Teaching Master with students. For many students, they may have just begun to date or they have been dating for a while. Indicate the importance of keeping safe on a date. For example, students can be encouraged to group date. Being with a group helps reduce the risk of being sexually assaulted. It is also important for students to understand the relationship between drinking alcohol and being sexually assaulted. Alcohol is often used when sexual assault occurs. Encourage students to avoid the use of alcohol. People who drink will have an increased risk of engaging in inappropriate behavior.

Student Master 13-4
Traffic Signals

Objective: Students will identify the meaning of the different traffic lights.

Life Skill: I will cross the street only when the light is green; I will cross in a crosswalk when appropriate.

Grade level: Elementary

Teaching Strategy: Distribute the Student Master and have students color the appropriate traffic signals. You can take a milk container and make it into a traffic signal. Use colored construction paper for the lights. Have the class form a line. When you point to a light, have the students do what they should. For example, when you point to a green light, the students are to walk. They slow down when you point to the yellow light. They stop when you point to the red light.

Student Master 13-5
Wear A Safety Belt

Objective: Students will describe the importance of wearing a safety belt when in a motor vehicle.

Life Skill: I will wear a safety belt in a car at all times.

Grade Level: Elementary

Teaching Strategy: Have students color the picture in the Student Master. Discuss with students the importance of wearing a safety belt when they are in a car. Explain that the safety belt keeps them from being thrown in a car during an accident. You can take strips of paper and have students pretend that the strips represent a shoulder harness and a lap belt. The students can use their crayons to color their belts. They can then take their belts and tack them on the bulletin board so that the shoulder harness and lap belt are in the position they would use as a passenger.

Community and Environment

Teaching Master 14-1
Depleting the Ozone Layer

Objective: Students will describe how the ozone layer becomes depleted.

Life Skill: I will not use spray products that are made with chlorofluorcarbons.

Grade Level: High School

Teaching Strategy: Use the Teaching Master to show how the ozone layer is depleted by the use of chlorofluoro-carbons (CFCs). Explain that the ozone layer is the upper layer of the atmosphere. Scientists believe that at least 7 percent of the ozone layer has been destroyed. Explain that the depletion of the ozone layer can lead to major health problems. As the ozone layer is depleted, exposure to ultraviolet radiation increases. This leads to an increased risk of skin cancer, eye cataracts, damage to forests, and possible changes in climate. Describe to students that CFCs break ozone molecules apart. This leads to changes in the chemical structures in the atmosphere. The ozone layer then becomes depleted.

Teaching Master 14-2
Indoor Air Pollution

Objective: Students will identify ways to reduce their risks of exposure to indoor air pollution.

Life Skill: I will take steps to keep the air in my home clean.

Grade Level: Middle/Junior High, High School

Teaching Strategy: Review the list on the Teaching Master. Have students add more items to the list. Emphasize the importance of checking the home for radon. Explain that radon is a colorless and odorless gas that is produced by the decay of bricks, stones, and other materials. Radon attaches to particles that can be inhaled. Some estimates indicate that as many as 20,000 cases of lung cancer are caused each year by radon. Radon levels are usually highest in areas that have a great deal of granite and black shale. Most hardware stores sell radon detectors that can help determine the radon levels in a home. It is also important for students to know that cigarette smoke is a major cause of indoor air pollution. If possible, students should live in a smoke-free home. Parents who smoke place their children at increased risk of respiratory illness.

Teaching Master 14-3
Ways to Save the Planet

Objective: Students will describe what they can do to improve the quality of the environment.
Life Skill: I will take steps to improve the quality of the environment.

Grade Level: Middle/Junior High School

Teaching Strategy: Share the information on the Teaching Master with students. Then have students divide into groups of five. Have them identify additional ways they can help make the environment a safer place in which to live. Have students share their ideas with the rest of the class. You can make a class book with suggestions on how to make the environment more healthful. Students can also share what they presently do to make the environment better.

Student Master 14-4
Keep Your Room Neat

Objective: Students will describe how they can keep their rooms neat.

Life Skill: I will place all toys in my room in a safe place.

Grade Level: Elementary

Teaching Strategy: Distribute the Student Master and have students color the picture. As students show their pictures to the class, have them describe what they do to keep their rooms neat. They may share that they place their toys in a toy box. They pick up all scrap from the floor and throw it in a waste basket, or they wipe all spills. Students can also draw a picture of their rooms showing how they keep them neat.

Student Master 14-5
Air Pollution

Objective: Students will identify pollutants entering the air.

Life Skill: I will avoid being around polluted air.

Grade Level: Elementary

Teaching Strategy: Show students the Student Master and have them identify the sources of air pollution. You can take a tour of your community with students and have them identify sources of pollution. For each source identified, have students share what they think can be done to reduce the causes of air pollution. You can introduce several ways students can act to reduce air pollution by mentioning car pooling, riding bikes instead of cars, and not using products that contain CFCs.

Teaching Masters
and
Student Masters

Wellness Scale

Factors that influence Health and Well-Being

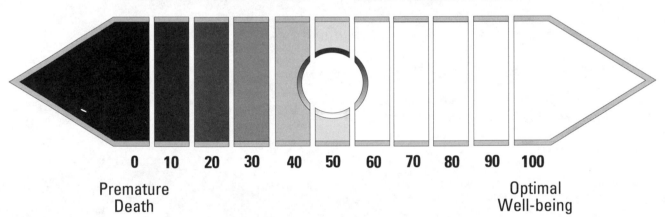

Risk behaviors	Wellness behaviors
Risk situations	Healthful situations
Destructive relationships	Healthful relationships
Irresponsible Decision-making	Responsible Decision making
Lack of Resistance skills	Use of Resistance skills

0   10   20   30   40   50   60   70   80   90   100

Premature
Death

Optimal
Well-being

Health status is the sum total of the positive and negative
influences of behaviors, situations, relationships,
decisions and use of resistance skills.

Model of Health and Well-Being

Physical Health

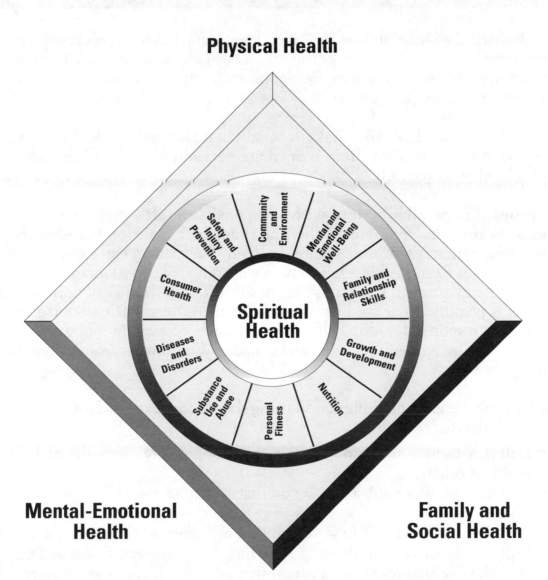

Spiritual Health

Community and Environment

Mental and Emotional Well-Being

Safety and Injury Prevention

Family and Relationship Skills

Consumer Health

Growth and Development

Diseases and Disorders

Nutrition

Substance Use and Abuse

Personal Fitness

Mental-Emotional Health

Family and Social Health

Health and Well-Being is dependent upon:

1 choosing healthful behaviors.
2 participating in healthful situations.
3 developing healthful relationships.
4 making responsible decisions.
5 using resistance skills.

Responsible Decision Making Model

1.**Clearly describe the situation you face.** If no immediate decision is necessary, describe the situation in writing. If an immediate decision must be made, describe the situation out loud or to yourself in a few short sentences. Being able to describe a situation in your own words is the first step in developing clarity.

2.**List possible actions that can be taken.** Again, if no immediate decision is necessary, make a list of possible actions. If an immediate decision must be made, state possible actions out loud or to yourself.

3.**Share your list of possible actions with a responsible adult who protects community laws and demonstrates character.** When no immediate decision is necessary, sharing possible actions with a responsible adult is helpful. This person can examine your list to see if it is inclusive. Responsible adults have a wide range of experiences that allow them to see situations maturely. They may add possibilities to the list of actions. In some situations, it is possible to delay decision making until there is the opportunity to seek counsel with a responsible adult. If an immediate decision must be made, explore possibilities. Perhaps a telephone call can be made. Whenever possible, avoid skipping this step.

4.**Carefully evaluate each possible action using six criteria.** Ask each of the six questions to learn which decision is best.
  - Will this decision result in an action that will promote my health and the health of others?
  - Will this decision result in an action that will protect my safety and the safety of others?
  - Will this decision result in an action that will protect the laws of the community?
  - Will this decision result in an action which shows respect for self and others?
  - Will this decision result in an action that follows guidelines set by responsible adults such as my parents or guardian?
  - Will this decision result in an action that will demonstrate that I have good character and moral values?

5.**Decide which action is responsible and most appropriate.** After applying the six criteria, compare the results. Which decision best meets the six criteria?

6.**Act in a responsible way and evaluate the results.** Follow through with this decision with confidence. The confidence comes from paying attention to the six criteria.

Model for Using Resistance Skills

1. **Use assertive behavior.** There is a saying, "You get treated the way you 'train' others to treat you." Assertive behavior is the honest expression of thoughts and feelings without experiencing anxiety or threatening others. When you use assertive behavior, you show that you are in control of yourself and the situation. You say NO clearly and firmly. You look directly at the person(s) pressuring you. Aggressive behavior is the use of words and/or actions that tend to communicate disrespect. This behavior only antagonizes others. Passive behavior is the holding back of ideas, opinions, and feelings. Holding back may result in harm to you, others, or the environment.

2. **Avoid saying "NO thank you."** There is never a need to thank a person who pressures you into doing something that might be harmful, unsafe, illegal, or disrespectful or which may result in disobeying parents or displaying a lack of character and moral values.

3. **Use nonverbal behavior that matches verbal behavior.** Nonverbal behavior is the use of body language rather than words to express feelings, ideas, and opinions. Your verbal NO should not be confused by misleading actions. For example, if you say No to cigarette smoking, do not pretend to take a puff.

4. **Influence others to choose responsible behavior.** When a situation poses immediate danger, remove yourself. If no immediate danger is present, try to turn the situation into a positive one. Suggest to others alternative ways to behave that are responsible. Being a positive role model helps you feel good about yourself and helps gain the respect of others.

5. **Avoid being in situations in which there will be pressure to make harmful decisions.** There is no reason to put yourself into situations in which you will be pressured or tempted to make unwise decisions. Think ahead.

6. **Avoid being with persons who choose harmful actions.** Your reputation is the impression that others have of you, your decisions, and your actions. Associate with persons known for their good qualities and character so you will not be misjudged.

7. **Report pressure to engage in illegal behavior to appropriate authorities.** You have a responsibility to protect others and to protect the laws of your community. Demonstrate good character and moral values.

Health Behavior Contract

Life Skill: I will engage in aerobic exercise for at least 30 minutes three times a week.

Effect on My Well-being: Aerobic exercise will strengthen my heart muscle and result in a lower resting heartbeat rate. Beta-endorphins are released after several weeks of regular aerobic exercise. They will help me to have a feeling of well-being. Aerobic exercise will reduce my percentage of body fat and help me to maintain my desirable weight.

My Plan: I will select one of the following aerobic exercises: walking, running, roller skating, swimming, bicycling, snow skiing.

Evaluating My Progress: I will complete the following chart to indicate the aerobic exercise selected and the amount of time in which I participated in the exercise.

Results: _____

_____

_____

Monday	Tuesday	Wednesday	Thursday

Friday	Saturday	Sunday

Health Behavior Contract

Life Skill: I will do exercises for my heart for thirty minutes three times a week.

How This Life Skill Helps Me: Exercise for my heart makes my heart muscle very strong. My heart will work better. I will not get out of breath when I work and play. These exercises help me look and feel good.

My Plan: I will draw a picture of an exercise I can do for my heart.

How I Follow My Plan: I will color one piece of the heart each day I do my heart exercise.

How I Feel: I will circle the way I feel when I do exercise for my heart.

General Adaptation Syndrome

During the ALARM STAGE, the SYMPATHETIC NERVOUS SYSTEM prepares to meet the demand of the stressor.

During the RESISTANCE STAGE, the PARASYMPATHETIC NERVOUS SYSTEM attempts to return the body to a state of homeostasis.

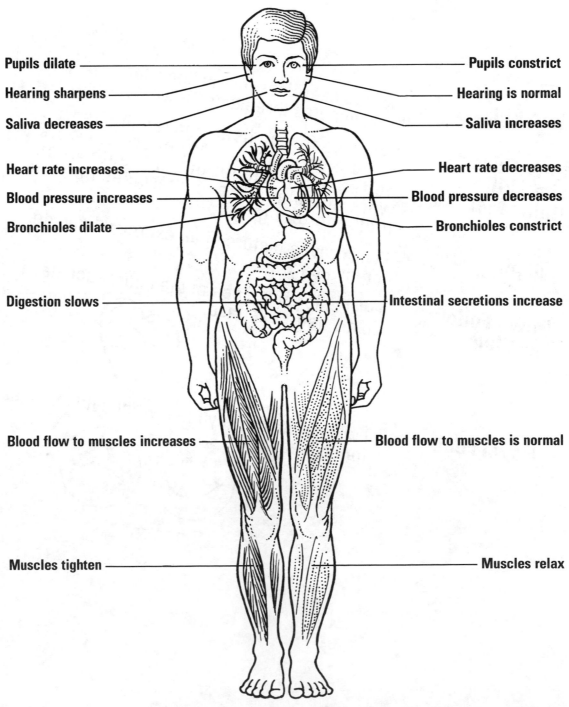

Pupils dilate

Hearing sharpens

Saliva decreases

Heart rate increases

Blood pressure increases

Bronchioles dilate

Digestion slows

Blood flow to muscles increases

Muscles tighten

Pupils constrict

Hearing is normal

Saliva increases

Heart rate decreases

Blood pressure decreases

Bronchioles constrict

Intestinal secretions increase

Blood flow to muscles is normal

Muscles relax

Stress and Your Body

Family Chores

Life Skill: I will help my family with chores.

How this Life Skill Helps Me: I can show love for my family by helping. My family will feel close to me. I will feel good about myself.

My Plan: I will talk to my family about chores I can do. Three chores I can do:

1.
2.
3.

How I Follow My Plan: I will color a heart for each time I do a chore.

Results: When I help, I feel

A Stepfamily

Dysfunctional Family Relationships

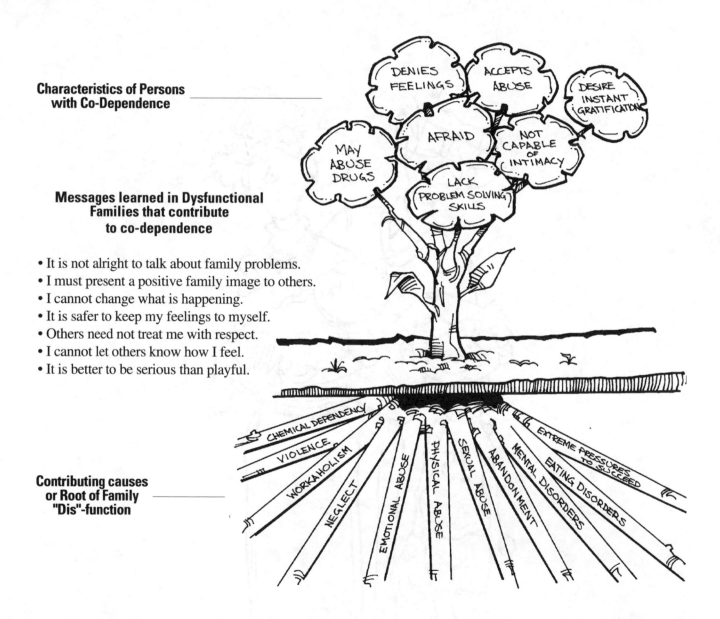

Characteristics of Persons with Co-Dependence

- DENIES FEELINGS
- ACCEPTS ABUSE
- DESIRE INSTANT GRATIFICATION
- MAY ABUSE DRUGS
- AFRAID
- NOT CAPABLE OF INTIMACY
- LACK PROBLEM SOLVING SKILLS

Messages learned in Dysfunctional Families that contribute to co-dependence

- It is not alright to talk about family problems.
- I must present a positive family image to others.
- I cannot change what is happening.
- It is safer to keep my feelings to myself.
- Others need not treat me with respect.
- I cannot let others know how I feel.
- It is better to be serious than playful.

Contributing causes or Root of Family "Dis"-function

- CHEMICAL DEPENDENCY
- VIOLENCE
- WORKAHOLISM
- NEGLECT
- EMOTIONAL ABUSE
- PHYSICAL ABUSE
- SEXUAL ABUSE
- ABANDONMENT
- MENTAL DISORDERS
- EATING DISORDERS
- EXTREME PRESSURES TO SUCCEED

Genogram

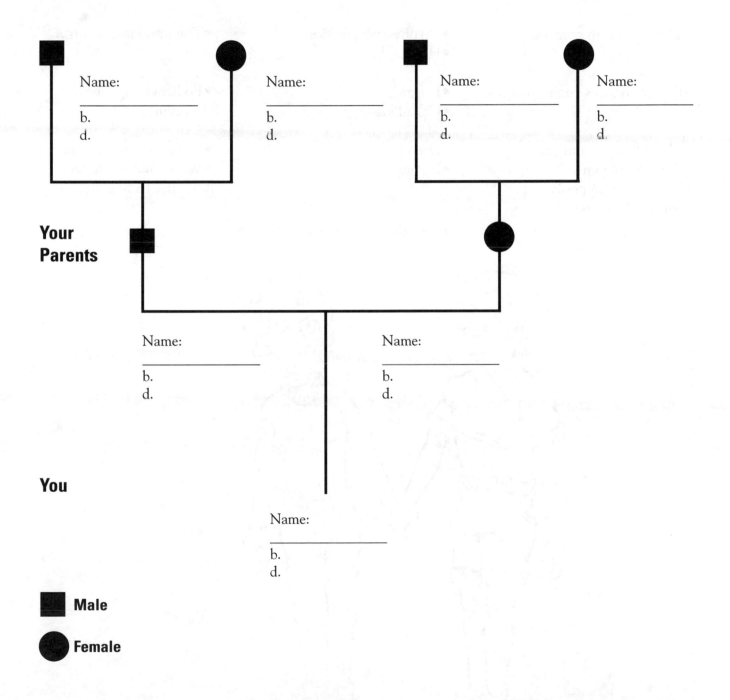

Your Grandparents

Name: _____
b.
d.

Name: _____
b.
d.

Name: _____
b.
d.

Name: _____
b.
d.

Your Parents

Name: _____
b.
d.

Name: _____
b.
d.

You

Name: _____
b.
d.

■ **Male**

● **Female**

Setting Limits on Sexual Behavior

Male Response	Sexual Behavior	Female Response
• The mind is in control	• No physical affection • Holding hands	• The mind is in control
• Bodily changes begin to occur	• Hugging • Casual kissing	• Bodily changes begin to occur
• Blood flow to genitals • Erection of penis • Fluid on tip of penis • Intense feelings	• Deep kissing • Petting	• Blood flow to genitals • Warm, moist vagina • Intense feelings
	• Sexual intercourse	

Male Development

1. Sex desire
2. Deepening of voice
3. Growth of body hair
4. Masculine body features
5. Development of sex organs
6. Muscle and tissue building

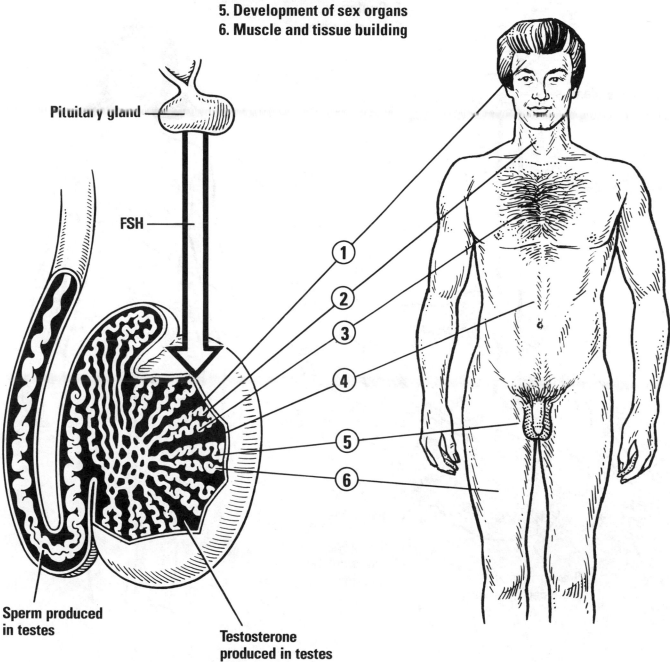

Pituitary gland

FSH

Sperm produced
in testes

Testosterone
produced in testes

Female Development

1. Sex desire
2. Body hair growth
3. Breast development
4. Feminine body
5. Ovulation
6. Menstruation

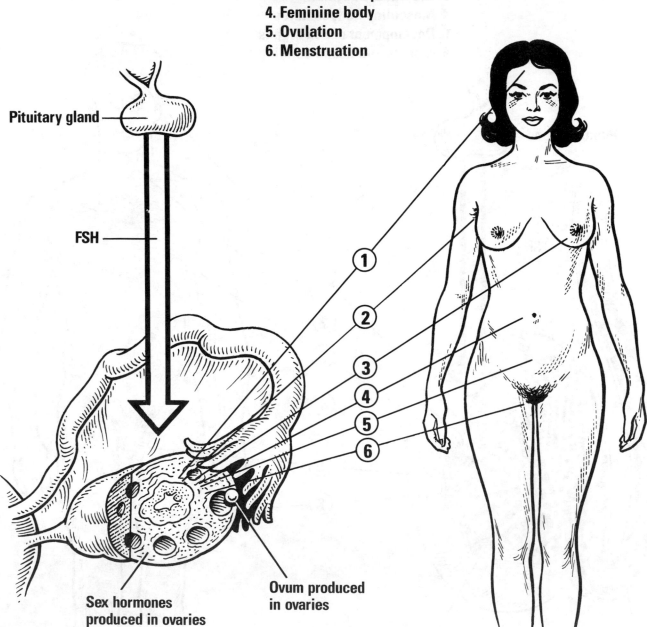

Pituitary gland

FSH

Sex hormones
produced in ovaries

Ovum produced
in ovaries

The Skeletal System

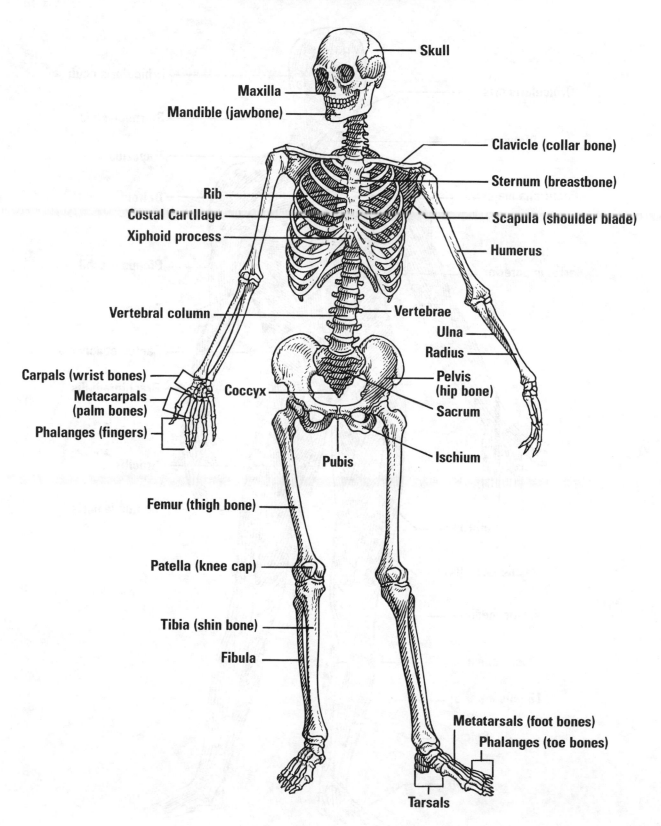

Skull

Maxilla

Mandible (jawbone)

Clavicle (collar bone)

Sternum (breastbone)

Rib

Costal Cartilage

Scapula (shoulder blade)

Xiphoid process

Humerus

Vertebral column

Vertebrae

Ulna

Radius

Carpals (wrist bones)

Coccyx

Pelvis (hip bone)

Metacarpals (palm bones)

Sacrum

Phalanges (fingers)

Pubis

Ischium

Femur (thigh bone)

Patella (knee cap)

Tibia (shin bone)

Fibula

Metatarsals (foot bones)

Phalanges (toe bones)

Tarsals

The Muscular System

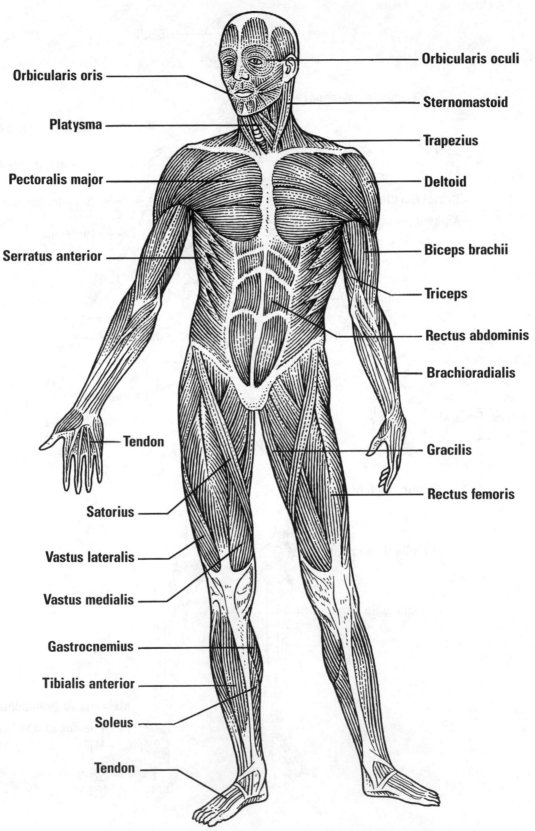

Orbicularis oris

Platysma

Pectoralis major

Serratus anterior

Tendon

Satorius

Vastus lateralis

Vastus medialis

Gastrocnemius

Tibialis anterior

Soleus

Tendon

Orbicularis oculi

Sternomastoid

Trapezius

Deltoid

Biceps brachii

Triceps

Rectus abdominis

Brachioradialis

Gracilis

Rectus femoris

The Nervous System

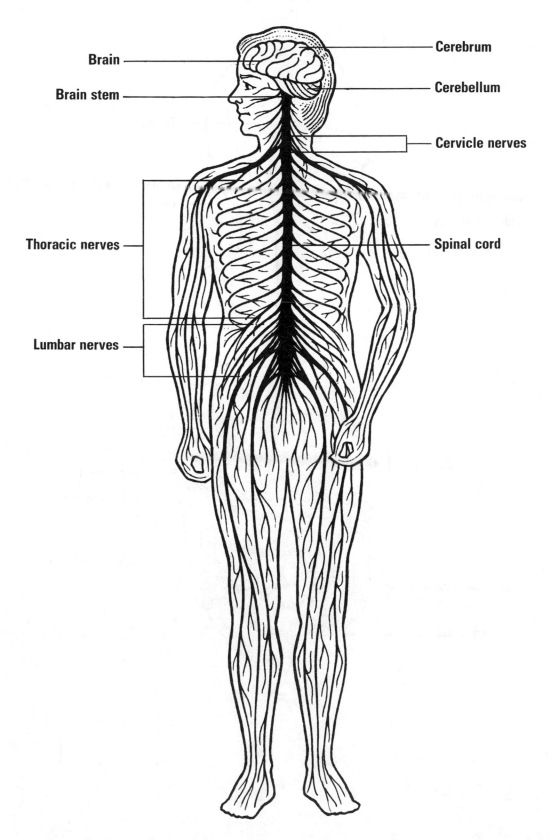

Brain

Brain stem

Thoracic nerves

Lumbar nerves

Cerebrum

Cerebellum

Cervicle nerves

Spinal cord

The Digestive System

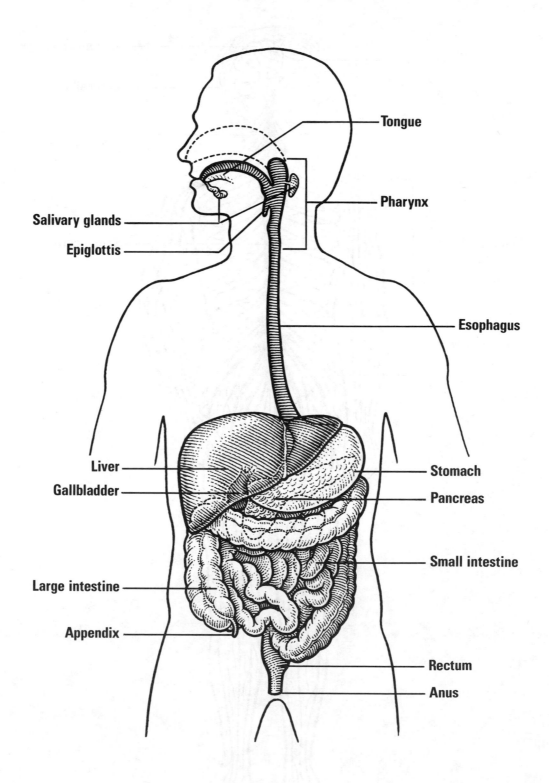

Tongue

Pharynx

Salivary glands

Epiglottis

Esophagus

Liver

Stomach

Gallbladder

Pancreas

Small intestine

Large intestine

Appendix

Rectum

Anus

The Circulatory System

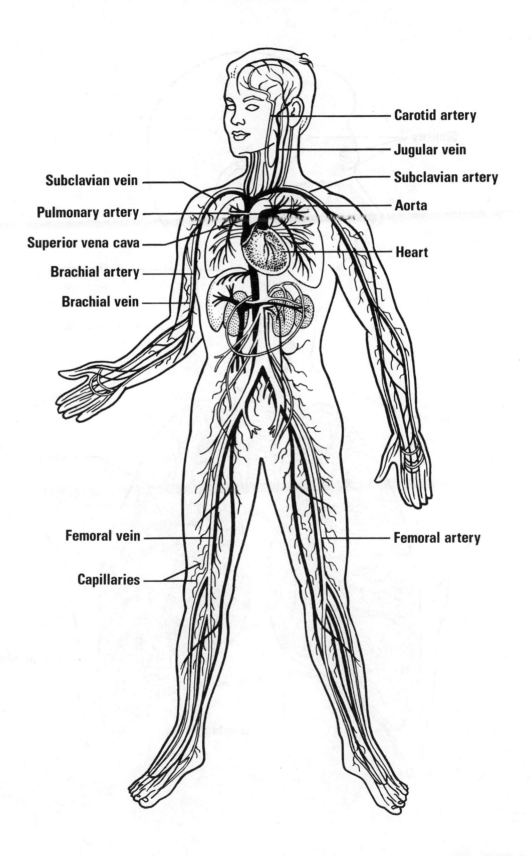

Carotid artery

Jugular vein

Subclavian artery

Aorta

Subclavian vein

Pulmonary artery

Heart

Superior vena cava

Brachial artery

Brachial vein

Femoral vein

Femoral artery

Capillaries

The Respiratory System

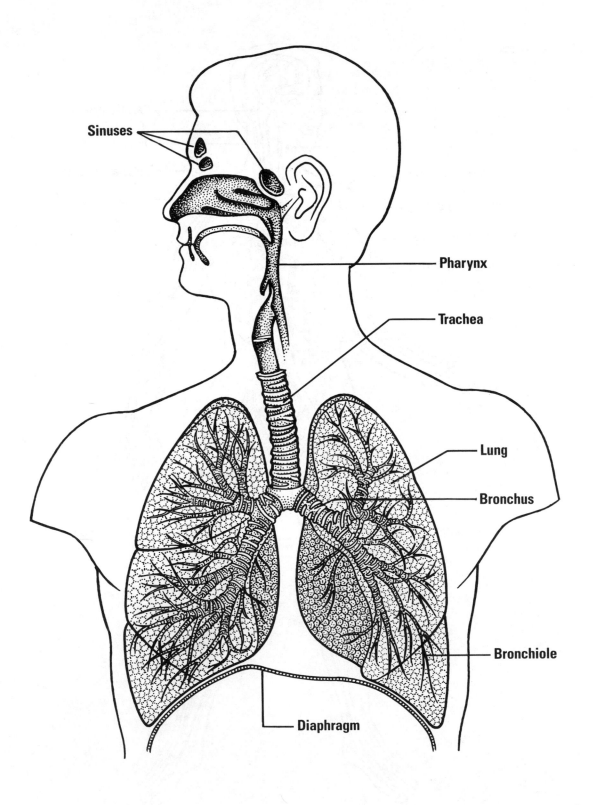

Sinuses

Pharynx

Trachea

Lung

Bronchus

Bronchiole

Diaphragm

The Urinary System

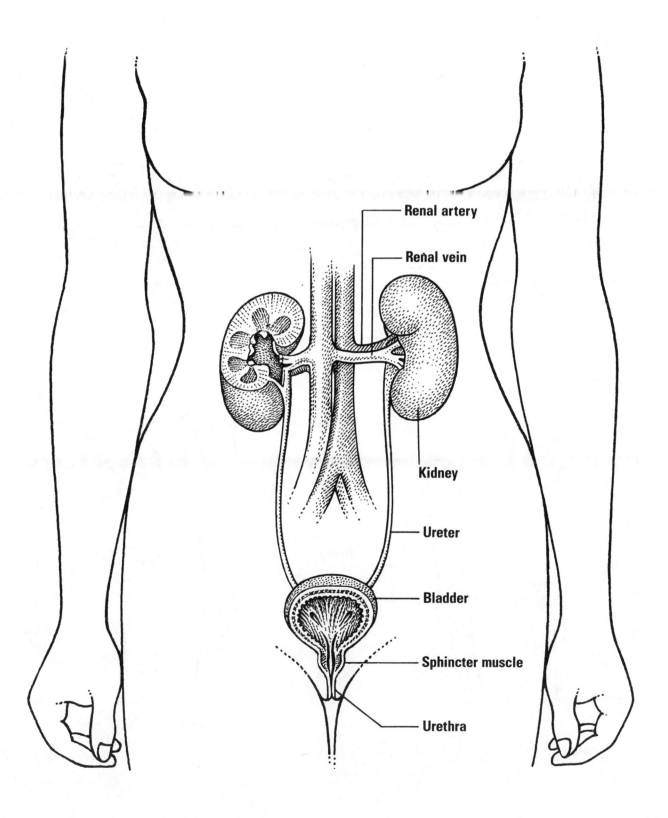

Renal artery

Renal vein

Kidney

Ureter

Bladder

Sphincter muscle

Urethra

The Endocrine System

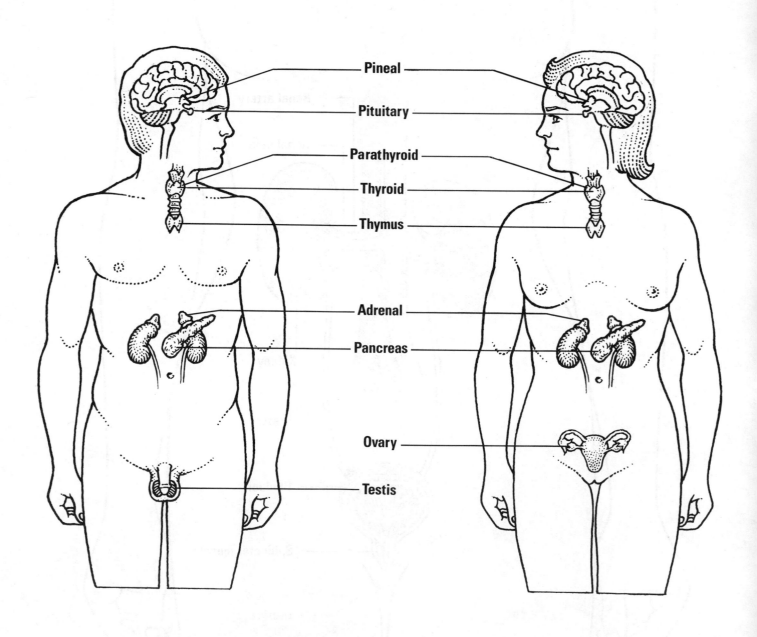

Pineal

Pituitary

Parathyroid

Thyroid

Thymus

Adrenal

Pancreas

Ovary

Testis

Foods for Growth

Color the foods that help you grow.
Put an X through the foods that are not healthful.

Your Body Parts

Draw a line from the body part to the body

1

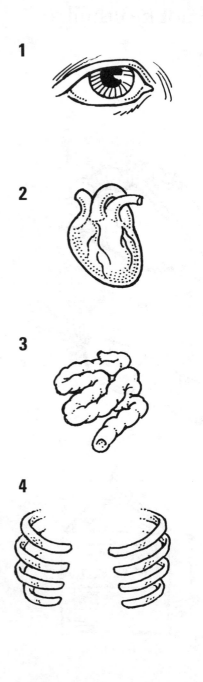

2

3

4

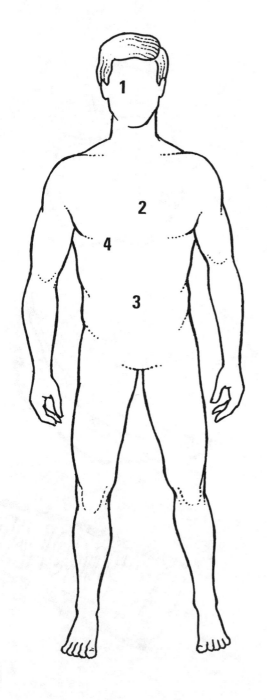

Food Groups

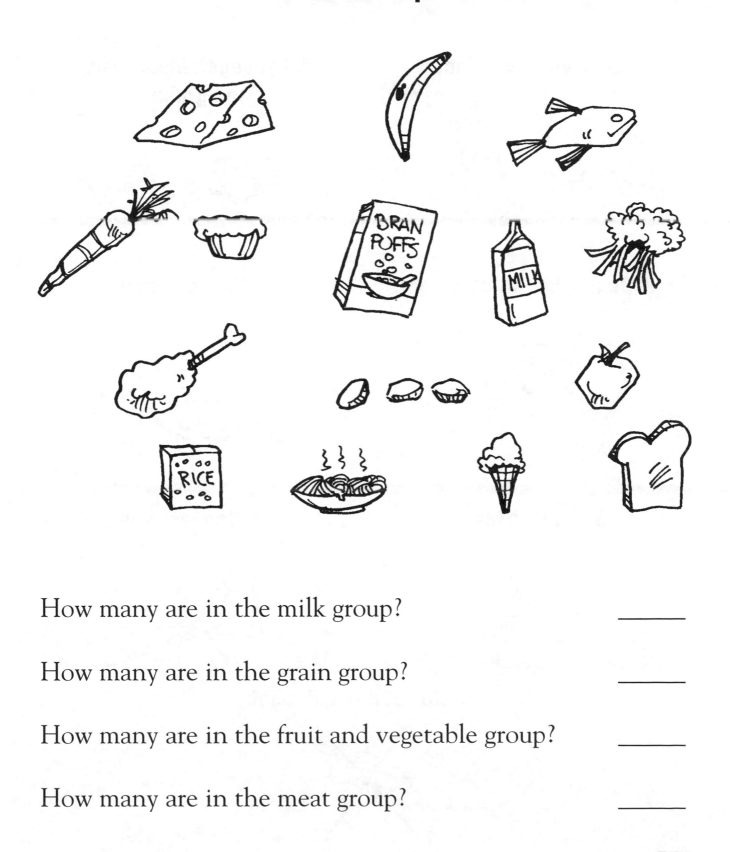

How many are in the milk group? _____

How many are in the grain group? _____

How many are in the fruit and vegetable group? _____

How many are in the meat group? _____

Seven Dietary Guidelines

1. Eat a variety of foods.

2. Be at a healthful weight.

3. Eat less fat

4. Eat vegetables, fruits, and grains.

5. Use less sugar.

6. Use less salt.

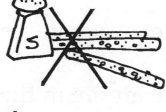

7. Do not drink alcohol.

Find the Vitamin

Make a ◯ around foods with Vitamin E.

Make a △ around foods with Vitamin C.

Make a ▢ around foods with Vitamin A.

Diet and Heart Disease

1. Use margarine instead of butter.

2. Drink skim or low-fat milk.

3. Trim visible fat from meat and remove skin from poultry.

4. Broil, bake, steam, or poach meat, fish and poultry.

5. Limit portion size of meat (two to three ounces).

6. Leave butter, gravy, and sauce off main dish and side dishes.

7. Eat fresh fruit or fruit in light syrup.

8. Avoid adding salt to food.

9. Eat low fat cheeses.

10. Eat fewer than three egg yolks a week.

11. Use unsalted vegetable oils such as corn, olive, canola, safflower, and peanut oil rather than butter, lard, bacon fat, chicken fat, coconut oil, and palm oil.

Diet and Cancer

1. Avoid obesity.

2. Reduce total fat intake.

3. Eat high-fiber foods.

4. Eat foods rich in vitamin A.

5. Eat foods and drink beverages that contain vitamin C.

6. Eat cruciferous vegetables.

7. Eat limited amounts of salt-cured and smoked foods.

8. Drink two to three glasses of low-fat or skim milk a day.

9. Include fish in the diet three times a week.

10. Eat foods that are a source of vitamin E.

11. Eat foods that are a source of the trace metal selenium.

12. Eat foods that are a source of folic acid.

13. Eat hamburger rare or medium rare instead of well-done.

14. Eat meat, poultry, and fish that is baked, broiled, steamed, microwaved, poached, or roasted rather than grilled or fried.

I  2 Be Fit

How many jump rope? _____

How many ride bikes? _____

How many children run? _____

Flexibility

Alternate knee to chest: (abdominals, hips, lower back)
Bend one knee up to your chest; raise your head and try
to touch your knee with your chin. Hold the bent leg
with both hands at the knee. Alternate first one leg
then the other.

Leg cross-overs: (hips, back)
Raise one leg and cross it over your
body. Keep your upper back flat and
your arms extended to the sides.
Alternate first one leg and then the
other. Turn only your hips.

Seated toe touch: (hamstrings)
Sit with your legs straight. Fold
one leg in front and gradually reach
for the toes of your other leg.
Eventually you will be able to grasp
your feet at the instep. Keep your
head down. Alternate legs.

Benefits of Physical Fitness

1. Promotes Cardiovascular Health
- Increases stroke volume
- Lowers resting heart rate
- Increases ratio of HDLs toLDLs

2. Reduces Cancer Risk
- Lowers breast and colon cancer risk in females who participated in team sports when they were 10-12
- Helps with weight management; overweight is a cancer risk

3. Reduces Harmful Effects of Stress
- Exercise uses up excess adrenaline and blood sugar
- Exercise helps the body return to homeostasis after alarm stage of GAS
- Exercise helps the body release beta-endorphins

4. Helps with Weight Management
- Exercise increases metabolic rate for up to six hours
- Influences the hypothalamus which affects appetite
- Decreases the percentage of body fat and increases lean tissue

5. Improves Strength and Condition of Bones, Muscles and Joints
- Weight bearing bones become more dense preventing osteoporosis
- Strengthens muscles reducing likelihood of injury
- Helps move joints through range of motion preventing osteoarthritis

Developing a Physical Fitness Plan

Directions: There are many health benefits that result from making and following a plan for physical fitness. In the space below, write those exercises that you might choose as a part of a complete physical fitness plan.

1. Exercises for warming up

2. Exercises for flexibility

3. Exercises for cardiovascular endurance and body composition

4. Exercises for muscular strength and endurance

5. Exercises for cooling down

Tips for Running

1. Wear appropriate clothing.

2. Wear running shoes with adequate support and cushioning.

3. Drink plenty of fluids.

4. Select a safe route.

5. Check weather conditions before running.

6. Let others know where and when you will be running.

7. Know your capabilities.

8. Prepare a training schedule.

9. Warm up before you begin.

10. Cool down when you finish.

Alcohol and The Body

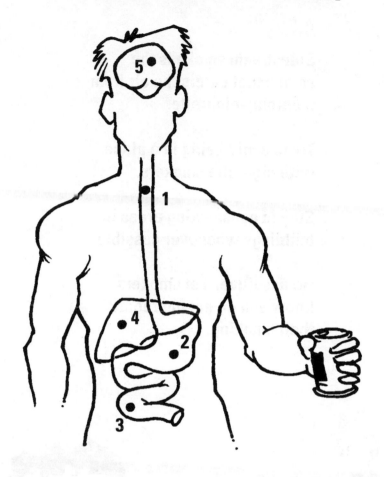

1. When it is swallowed, alcohol travels through the esophagus to the stomach.

2. Absorption of alcohol in the stomach. Food in the stomach wall will delay passage of the remaining alcohol into the small intestine.

3. The majority of alcohol (80%) is absorbed into the small intestine. Once in the small intestine, alcohol is transported to the liver for oxidation.

4. In the liver, alcohol undergoes oxidation. The liver is capable of oxidizing approximately 2/3 oz of alcohol per hour. Surplus alcohol is circulated throughout the body and BAC rises.

5. As BAC rises in the blood and reaches the brain, bodily activities are affected.

Dealing With Sidestream Smoke

Sidestream smoke is the smoke that enters the air from a burning cigarette.

Try to avoid being in a place with cigarette smokers.

Stay in nonsmoking areas in buildings whenever possible.

Be assertive. Let smokers know you do not appreciate their smoking.

Effects of Anabolic Steroids

Brain
- Psychological dependence
- Aggression
- Depression

Head and Face
- Facial hair growth
- Body hair growth
- Baldness in women
- Acne in men and women

Throat
- Deepening of voice in women

Chest and Heart
- Breast growth in men
- Breast cancer in women
- High blood pressure
- Clogged arteries

Liver and Prostate
- Liver cancer in men and women

Reproductive Organs
- Sterility in men and women
- Enlarged genitals in women
- Menstrual irregularities in women

Keep Medicines Away

- Medicines should be kept away from children.
- Cut out the medicines.
- Paste the medicines in the cabinet.
- Color your picture.

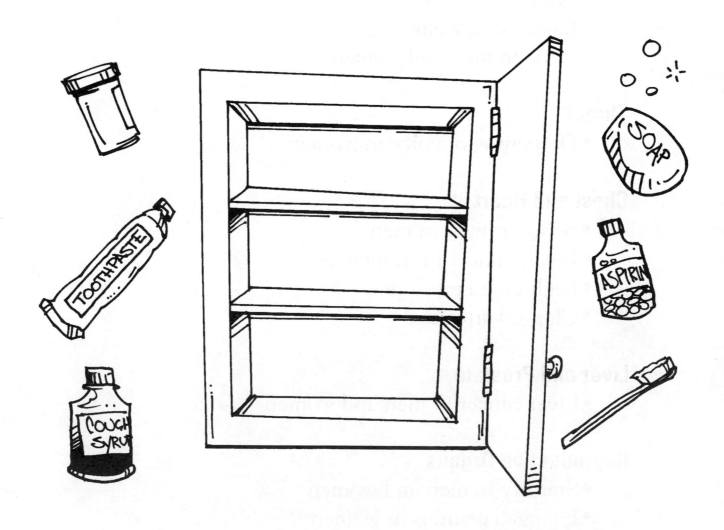

Which are Medicines?

- Color each medicine red.
- Color each food blue.

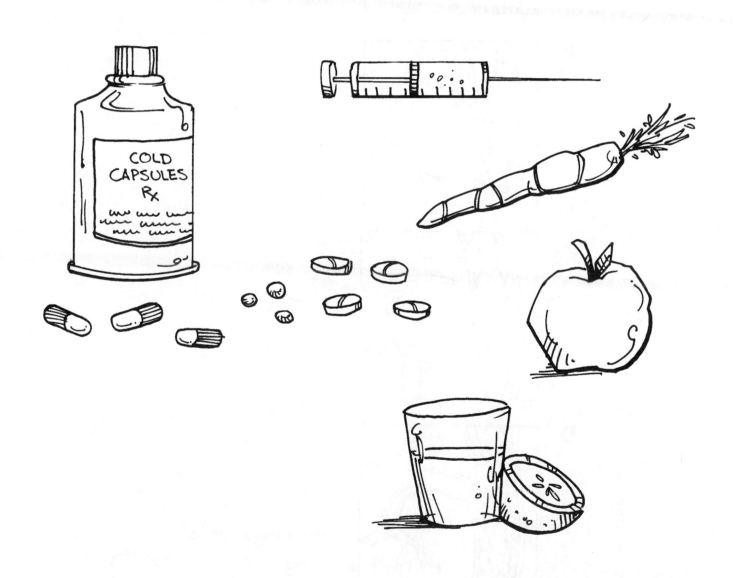

Causes of Stroke

A 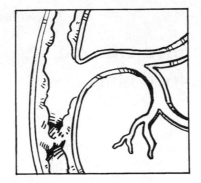 Thrombus

B 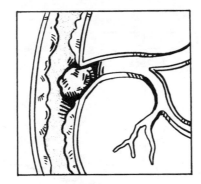 Embolism

C 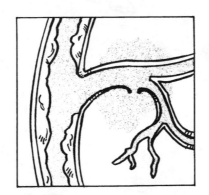 Hemorrhage

D 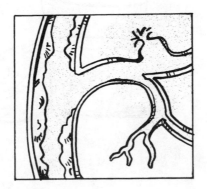 Aneurysm (ruptured)

Incidence and Death From Cancer

Type	Incidence	Death
1. Skin	2%	2%
2. Oral	4%	3%
3. Lung	22%	35%
4. Pancreas	3%	5%
5. Colon-Rectum	14%	12%
6. Prostate	18%	10%
7. Urinary	9%	5%
8. Leukemia-Lymphomas	8%	8%
9. All others	20%	20%

Type	Incidence	Death
1. Skin	2%	1%
2. Oral	2%	1%
3. Breast	26%	18%
4. Lung	10%	18%
5. Pancreas	3%	5%
6. Colon-Rectum	15%	15%
7. Ovary	4%	6%
8. Uterus		
9. Urinary	12%	5%
10. Leukemia-Lymphomas	7%	9%
11. All others	15%	15%

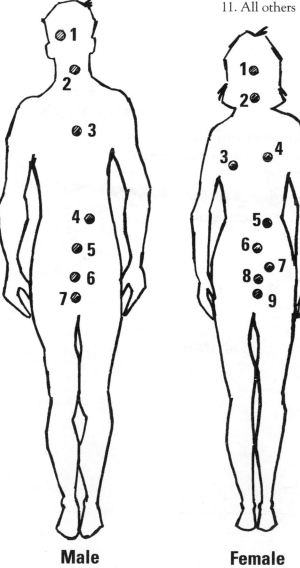

Male   **Female**

How HIV Attacks T Cells

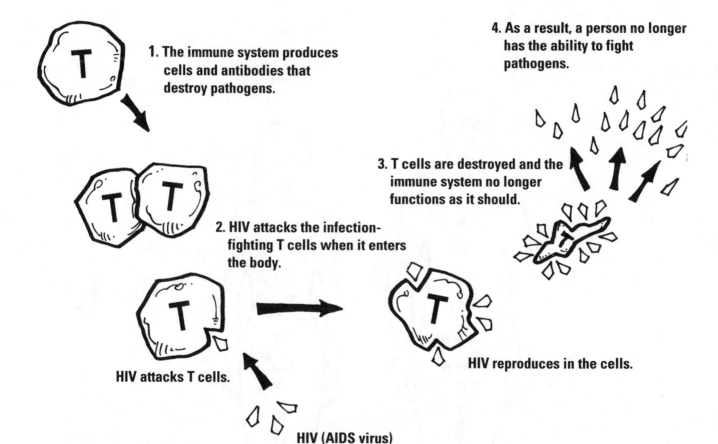

1. The immune system produces cells and antibodies that destroy pathogens.

4. As a result, a person no longer has the ability to fight pathogens.

3. T cells are destroyed and the immune system no longer functions as it should.

2. HIV attacks the infection-fighting T cells when it enters the body.

HIV attacks T cells.

HIV reproduces in the cells.

HIV (AIDS virus)

Do Not Share Germs

Count the Germs

Count the germs.
Write the number.

Flossing the Teeth

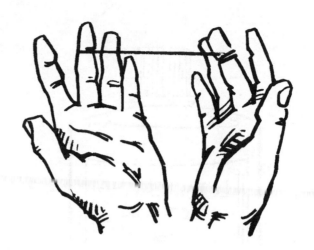

1. Use dental floss.

2. Gently move floss between teeth to gum line.

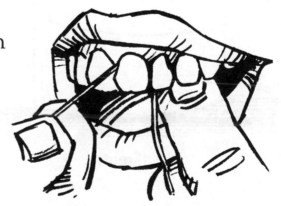

3. Wrap floss around tooth and slide up and down.

Product Label

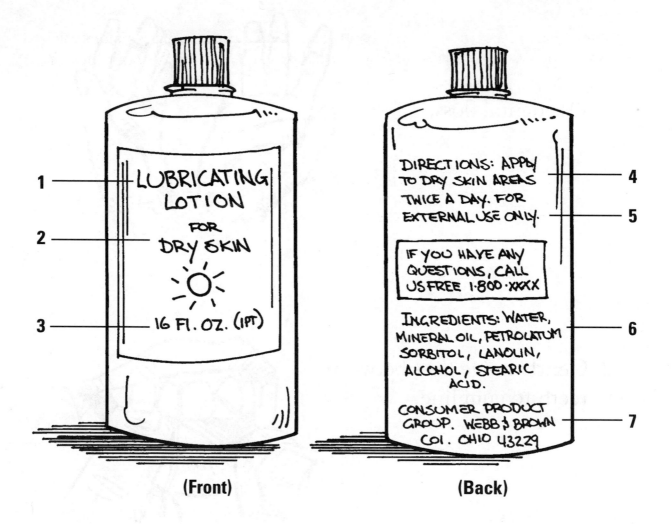

(Front)   (Back)

1. Name of the product
2. Care for which product is used
3. Net quantity
4. Directions for use
5. Warnings
6. Ingredients
7. Name, address, zip code of manufacturer

Advertising Appeals

Directions: You are a member of the band "Hard Sell." Think of a popular tune and write the words for your newest release entitled "You Can't Live Without Me." Your song should contain the advertising appeals we studied in class.

Identify the advertising appeals you used in your song.

_____

_____

_____

Consumer Complaint

Directions: You have saved money and purchased a compact disc player. You bought the compact disc player on sale. The sign at the store said, "final purchase on sale items, no returns." When you try to use the compact disc player at home, you discover that it is broken. You take the compact disc player and your receipt back to the store. The sales person who helped you refuses to exchange it for another compact disc player and she refuses to give you your money back. She reminds you of the sign that was displayed that said, "final purchase on sale items, no returns." You explain that you were not made aware that some of the compact disc players were not working as they should. She tells you to write a letter to the manager explaining why you should receive your money back or be able to exchange the broken compact disc player for a new one. In the space below, write a letter of consumer complaint that provides the information that is needed and states your position clearly.

Grocery Shopping

Directions: Make a list of ten foods your family enjoys eating. Visit a grocery store. Locate each of the foods. Find two brands of each food. One of the foods might be a food produced with the store's label. The other food might be a well-known brand that you have seen advertised on television or in magazines. Make a comparison of the two foods. Check the main ingredient in each. Write the main ingredient in the column, "Main Ingredient." Then make a price comparison. You must compare a similar amount. Write the amount you are comparing in the column, "Amount." Then write the lower price of the two brands of the same food in the column, "Price #1." Then write the higher price of the two brands of the same food in the column, "Price #2." When you have done this for all ten foods, total the amount in column, "Price #1 and column, "Price #2." How much of a difference in price would there be if you bought all the lower priced foods versus those which are higher priced?

	Food	Main Ingredient	Amount	Price #1	Price #2
1					
2					
3					
4					
5					
6					
7					
8					
9					
10					

Total _____ _____

What is the total price difference? _____

Abdominal Thrust

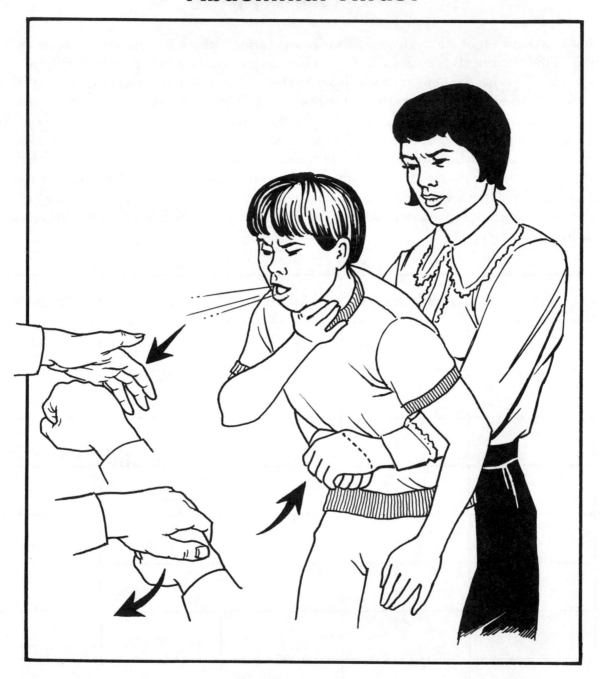

- Wrap your arms around child's waist.
- Make a fist.
- Place thumb side of fist on middle of child's abdomen just above navel and well below lower tip of breastbone.
- Grasp fist with your other hand.
- Press fist into child's abdomen with a quick upward thrust.

How Poisons Enter the Body

Ingestion

Inhalation

Absorption

Injection

Self Protection Against Assault

1. Yell "fire" if threatened by another person.
2. Walk with friends at night.
3. Know how to respond to telephone callers.
4. Wear clothing that allows easy movement.
5. Let others know where you are going.
6. Do not answer phone surveys.
7. Learn self defense.
8. Do not allow strangers in your home.
9. Notify responsible adults of abuse.
10. Be firm in saying "No" to unwanted behavior.
11. Walk on well-lighted streets.
12. If being followed, cross street and walk in opposite direction.

Traffic Safety

- •Color the top light red.
- •Color the middle light yellow.
- •Color the bottom light green.

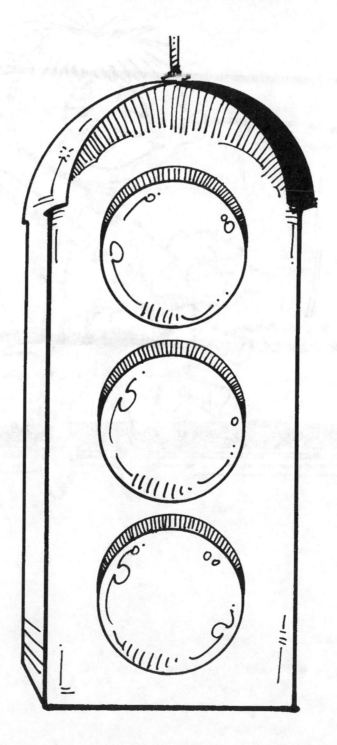

Wear a Safety Belt

Depleting The Ozone Layer

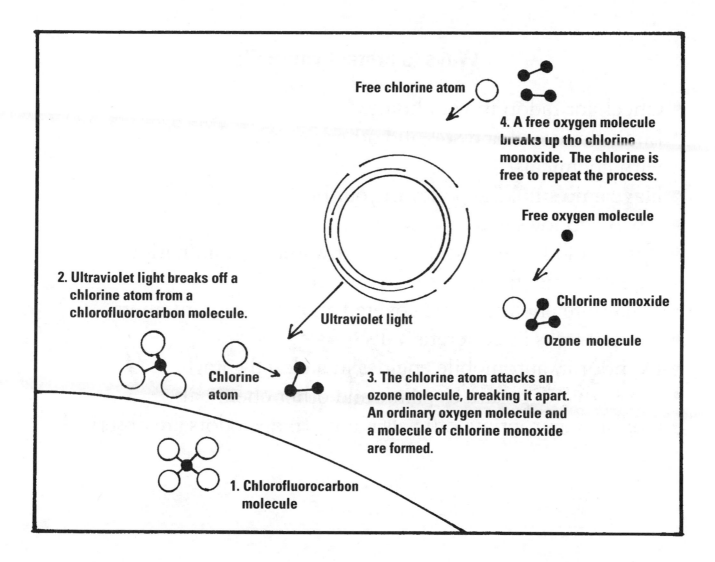

Free chlorine atom

4. A free oxygen molecule breaks up the chlorine monoxide. The chlorine is free to repeat the process.

Free oxygen molecule

2. Ultraviolet light breaks off a chlorine atom from a chlorofluorocarbon molecule.

Ultraviolet light

Chlorine monoxide

Ozone molecule

Chlorine atom

3. The chlorine atom attacks an ozone molecule, breaking it apart. An ordinary oxygen molecule and a molecule of chlorine monoxide are formed.

1. Chlorofluorocarbon molecule

Indoor Air Pollution

Ways to protect yourself:

• Check for radon in your home.
• Limit the use of aerosols and other products that fill your home with chemicals.
• Have a no smoking policy in your home.
• Open windows when possible.
• If in an old house, check pipes for water contamination.
• Do not come in contact with asbestos.
• Make sure chemicals are covered and in their containers.
• Cover cracks in concrete walls.
• Do not run automobile engines in a closed garage.
• Avoid overexposure to paints and other chemicals.
• Contact appropriate officials if any strange odors are observed.

Ways To Save The Planet

- Recycle products.
- Ride a bike instead of using a car.
- Don't litter.
- Fix leaks from faucets.
- Use paper rather than plastic bags.
- Use both sides of scrap paper.
- Use fluorescent instead of incandescent bulbs.
- Do not use aerosol sprays.
- Use water-efficient heads.
- Carry a cloth bag when shopping.
- Use products in glass jars.
- Use sponges rather than paper towels.
- Shut off faucet when brushing teeth.
- Look for logo on product to indicate it is recycled.
- Turn out lights when you leave a room.

Keep Your Room Neat

Color the room.

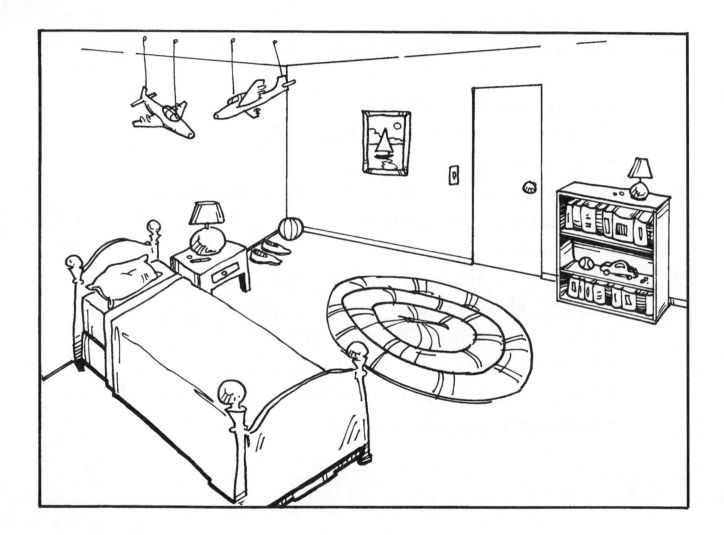

Air Pollution

Circle the causes of air pollution.

Section 4

Resources That Enhance The Teaching of Health

This Section contains a chapter that serves as a guide of resources available to enhance the teaching of health. *The Health Resource Guide* contains names, addresses, and telephone numbers of agencies and organizations involved in promoting health. The guide is structured so that each of the ten areas of health education serves as a major heading. Within each major heading are subheadings that contain the names of agencies and organizations specific to that subhead topic. Whenever possible, toll-free telephone numbers are listed to reduce costs. Many of the agencies and organizations listed will provide free and/or inexpensive materials that can be used with specific health education lessons. Many of these organizations and agencies have chapters in local communities. These chapters provide speakers free of charge to give presentations to classes on specific health topics. A local directory can be used to identify local chapters of health agencies and organizations. When it is difficult to locate a local chapter, the national office might be called to provide the listing for the local chapter.

This part of the text serves as a guide of resources available to enhance your teaching of health. The *Health Resource Guide* contains names, addresses, and telephone numbers of agencies and organizations involved in promoting health. The guide is structured so that each of the ten areas of health education serves as a major heading. Within each major heading is a subheading that contains the names of agencies and organizations specific to that subhead topic.

Where possible, toll-free telephone numbers were listed to reduce any costs you may encounter. Many of the organizations and agencies listed will provide you with free and/or inexpensive materials that you can use in specific health education lessons. You may find that many of these organizations and agencies have chapters in your local community. These chapters may provide speakers free of charge to give presentations to your classes about particular health topics. You can look in your local directory to determine if there are chapters in your community. You can also call the national offices of some of the agencies and organizations listed to find the address and telephone number of the chapter nearest to you.

Mental and Emotional Well-Being

General Information

American Mental Health Counselors Association
800-345-2008

American Psychiatric Association
1400 K Street, N.W.
Washington, DC 20005
202-682-6000

American Psychological Association
1200 17th Street, N.W.
Washington, DC 20036
202-965-7600

National Alliance for the Mentally Ill
2101 Wilson Boulevard
Suite 302
Arlington, VA 22201
703-524-7600

National Clearinghouse for Mental Health Information
Public Inquiries Section
5600 Fishers Lane
Room 11A-21
Rockville, MD 20857
301-442-4513

National Institute of Mental Health
Science Communication Branch
Public Inquiries Section
5600 Fishers Lane
Room 15C-17
Rockville, MD 20857
301-443-4513

National Mental Health Association
1021 Prince Street
Alexandria, VA 22314
703-684-7722

National Self-Help Clearinghouse
25 West 43rd Street, Room 620
New York, N.Y. 10036
212-642-2944

Family and Relationship Skills

Family Information

Displaced Homemakers Network
1411 K Street, N.W.
Suite 930
Washington, DC 20005
202-628-6767

16

Family Service America
11700 West Lake Park Drive
Milwaukee, WI 53224
414-359-2111

Parents Anonymous
22330 Hawthorne Boulevard
Suite 208
Torrance, CA 90505
213-371-3501

Parents of Murdered Children
100 East 8th Street
Cincinnati, OH 45202
513-721-5683

Parents Without Partners
8807 Colesville Road.
Silver Spring, MD. 20910
301-588-9354

Toughlove
P.O. Box 1069
Doylestown, PA 18901
215-348-7090

Growth and Development

Child Development

Acne Helpline
888 West 16th Street
Newport Beach, CA 92663
800-222-SKIN

National Center for Education in Maternal and Child Health
3520 Prospect Street, N.W.
Suite 1
Washington, DC 20057
202-625-8400

National Council on the Aging, Inc.
640 Washington Street
Washington, DC 21502
301-724-5626

National Institute of Child Health and Development
9000 Rockville Pike
Bethesda, MD 20014

Nutrition

Eating Disorders

American Anorexia Nervosa/Bulimia Association, Inc.
133 Cedar Lane
Teaneck, NJ 07666
201-836-1800

Bulimia and Anorexia Self-Help Hotline
Deaconess Hospital
6150 Oakland Ave.
St. Louis, MO 63135
800-762-3334

Overeaters Anonymous
213-542-8363

Nutrition Information

American Institute of Nutrition
9650 Rockville Pike
Bethesda MD 20814
301-530-7050

Food and Drug Administration
Office of Consumer Affairs
Public Inquiries
5600 Fishers Lane
Rockville, MD 20857
301-443-3170

Food and Nutrition Board
Institute of Medicine
2101 Constitution Avenue, N.W.
Washington, DC 20418
202-334-2238

Food and Nutrition Information Center
National Agricultural Library Building
Room 304
Beltsville, MD 20705
301-344-3719

United States Department of Agriculture
6505 Belcrest Road
Hyattsville, MD 20782
202-436-8470

Nutrition Education

National Dairy Council
Nutrition Education Division
6300 North River Road
Rosemont, Ill. 60019
312-696-1020

North America Vegetarian Association
P.O. Box 72
Dolgeville, NY 13329
518-568-7970

Nutrition Education Association
P.O. Box 20301
3647 Glen Haven
Houston, Texas 77025
713-665-2946

National Nutrition Education Clearinghouse
Society for Nutrition Education
1700 Broadway, Suite 300
Oakland, CA 94612
415-444-7133

Pennsylvania State Nutrition Center
Benedict House
University Park, PA 16802
814-865-6323

Personal Fitness

Physical Fitness

Aerobics International Research Society
1200 Preston Road
Dallas, Texas 75430
214-661-3374

American Running and Fitness Association
2420 K Street N.W.
Washington, DC 20027
202-667-4150

Office of Health Information, Health Promotion, Physical Fitness, and Sports Medicine
Department of Health and Human Services
200 Independence Avenue, S.W.
Washington, DC 20201

President's Council on Physical Fitness and Sports
450 5th Street, N.W.
Suite 7103
Washington, D.C. 20001
202-272-3430

Women's Sports Foundation
342 Madison Avenue
Suite 728
New York, NY 10017
800-227-3988

Substance Use and Abuse

Alcohol

Al-Anon Family Groups
1372 Broadway
New York, N.Y. 10018
212-302-7420

Alcoholics Anonymous
P.O. Box 459
Grand Central Station
New York, N.Y. 10163
212-686-1100

Alcohol, Drug Abuse, and Mental Health Administration
5600 Fishers Lane
Rockville, MD 20857
301-443-2403

Mothers Against Drunk Driving
669 Airport Freeway
Suite 310
Houston, Texas 76053
817-268-6233

National Clearinghouse for Alcohol Information
P.O. Box 2345
Rockville, MD 20852
301-468-2600

Specific Types of Drugs

Food and Drug Administration
Office of Consumer Affairs, Public Inquiries
5600 Fishers Lane (HFE-88)
Rockville, MD 20857
301-344-3719

Narcotics Anonymous
P.O. Box 9999
Van Nuys, CA 91409
818-780-3951

National Cocaine Hotline
800-COCAINE

National Clearinghouse for Drug Abuse Information
P.O. Box 416
Department DQ
Kensington, MD 20795
301-443-6500
800-729-6686

National Coordinating Council on Drug Education, Inc.
1830 Connecticut Ave., N.W.
Washington, DC 20009

National Institute on Drug Abuse Helpline
800-662-4357

National Institute on Drug Abuse
11400 Rockville Pike
Room 110
Rockville, MD 20852
800-638-2045

PRIDE - Parents Resource Institute for Drug Education
50 Hurt Plaza
Suite 210
Atlanta, GA. 30303
404-577-4500
800-67-PRIDE

Diseases and Disorders

AIDS

National AIDS Hotline
800-342-AIDS
800-344-SIDA (Spanish)

National AIDS Information Clearinghouse
800-458-5321

Allergy

American Allergy Association
P.O. Box 7273
Menlo Park, CA 94026
415-322-1663

Asthma and Allergy Foundation of America
1717 Massachusetts Ave., N.W.
Suite 305
Washington, DC 20036

Alzheimer's Disease

Alzheimer's Disease and Related Disorders Association
70 East Lake St.
Chicago, Ill. 60601
800-621-0379

Arthritis

Arthritis Foundation
1314 Spring St. N.W.
Atlanta, GA. 30309
404-872-7100

National Institute of Arthritis and Musculoskeletal and Skin Disease Clearinghouse
P.O. Box 9782
Arlington, VA 22209
703-558-8250

Blindness

American Foundation for The Blind
15 West 16th St.
New York, NY 10011
800 232-5463
212-620-2000

National Federation for the Blind
1800 Johnson Street
Baltimore, MD 21230
301-659-9312

National Library Service for the Blind and Physically Handicapped
1291 Taylor Street, N.W.
Washington, DC 20542
800-424-8567
202-707-5100

Cancer

American Cancer Society
1599 Clifton Road
Atlanta, GA 30329
404-320-3333

Cancer Connection
H & R Block Bldg.
4410 Main
Kansas City, MO. 64111
816-932-8453

Cancer Information Service
National Cancer Institute
9000 Rockville Pike
Bethesda, MD 20205
301-496-4000
800-4-CANCER

Cancer Research
800-227-2345

Leukemia Society of America, Inc.
733 Third Ave.
New York, NY 10017
212-573-8484

National Cancer Institute
9000 Rockville Pike
Bethesda, MD 20205
800-638-6694

Dental Health

American Dental Association
211 East Chicago Ave.
Chicago, Ill. 60611
312-440-2510

National Institute of Dental Research
Office of Communications
9000 Rockville Pike
Building 31, Room 2C35
Bethesda, Md. 20892
301-496-4261

Diabetes

American Diabetes Association
1660 Duke Street
Alexandria, VA 22314
703-549-1500
800-232-3472

Juvenile Diabetes Foundation International Hotline
800-223-1138

National Diabetes Clearinghouse
Box NDIC
Bethesda, MD 20892
301-468-2162

Digestive Disorders

National Digestive Diseases and Education and Information Clearinghouse
Box NDDIC
Bethesda, MD 20892
301-468-6344

National Down Syndrome Congress
1800 Dempster
Park Ridge, Ill. 60068
800-232-6372

National Down Syndrome Society Hotline
666 Broadway
New York, NY 10012
800-221-4602

Epilepsy Foundation of America
4351 Garden City Drive
Landover, MD 20785
301-459-3700
800-332-1000

Handicapped and Disabled

National Rehabilitation Information Center
8455 Colesville Road
Suite 935
Silver Springs, MD 20910
800-34-NARIC

Special Olympics
1359 New York Avenue, N.W.
Suite 500
Washington, DC 20005
202-628-3630

Headache

National Headache Foundation
800-843-2256

Hearing Impairment

American Society for Children
814 Thayer Ave.
Silver Springs, MD 20910
301-585-5400

Better Hearing Institute
Box 1840
Washington, DC 20013
800-EAR-WELL

National Hearing Aid Hotline
800-521-5247

Heart Disease and Hypertension

American Heart Association
7320 Greenville Avenue
Dallas, Texas 75231
214-373-6300

NHLBI Educational Program Information Center
4733 Bethesda Ave.
Suite 530
Bethesda, MD 20814
301-951-3260

National Heart, Lung, and Blood Institute
9000 Rockville Pike
Building 31, Room 4A21
Bethesda, MD 20892
301-496-4236

Infectious Diseases

Centers for Disease Control
1600 Clifton Road, N.E.
Atlanta, GA 30333
404-639-3534

Kidney

American Kidney Fund
6110 Executive Blvd.
Suite 1010
Bethesda, MD 20852
800-638-8299

National Kidney Foundation
30 East 33rd Street
New York, NY 10016
212-889-2210

Lung Disease

American Lung Association
1740 Broadway
New York, NY 10019
212-315-8700

Lupus

Lupus Foundation of America
1717 Massachusetts Ave., N.W.
Suite 203
Washington, DC 20036
800-558-0121

Reye Syndrome

National Reye's Syndrome Foundation
426 North Lewis
Bryan, Ohio 43506
800-233-7393

Sexually Transmitted Diseases

Center for Prevention Services
Centers for Disease Control
1600 Clifton Road, N.E.
Atlanta, GA 30333
404-329-1819

National STD Hotline
800-227-8922

Sickle-Cell Anemia

Center for Sickle Cell Disease
2121 Georgia Ave., N.W.
Washington, DC 20059
202-806-7930

Skin Disease

National Psoriasis Foundation
6443 S.W. Beaverton Highway
Suite 210
Portland, OR 97221
503-297-1545

Stroke

National Institute of Neurological and Communicative Disorders and Stroke
National Institutes of Health
9000 Rockville Pike
Bethesda, MD 20505
301-496-4000

Consumer Health

Consumer Information

Consumer Information Center
General Services Administration
Washington, DC 20405
202-566-1794

Consumer Education Research Center
439 Clark Street
South Orange, NJ 07079
201-762-6714

Consumer Products

Consumer Product Safety Commission
Washington, DC 20207
800-638-CPSC

Food and Drug Administration
Office of Consumer Affairs
Public Inquiries
5600 Fishers Lane (HFE-88)
Rockville, MD 20857
301-443-3170

Safety and Injury Prevention

Accidents

National Safety Council
444 North Michigan Avenue
Chicago, Ill. 60611
312-527-4800

Burn Injuries

National Burn Victim Foundation
308 Main Street
Orange, NJ 07050
201-731-3112

Injury Prevention

National Injury Information Clearinghouse
5401 Westbard Avenue
Room 625
Washington, DC 20207
301-492-6424

Sexual Assault

National Assault Prevention Center
P.O. Box 02015
Columbus, Ohio 43202
614-291-2540

National Center for the Prevention and Control of Rape
5600 Fishers Lane
Room 6C-12
Rockville, MD 20857
301-443-1410

National Committee for the Prevention of Child Abuse
332 S. Michigan Avenue
Suite 1600
Chicago, Ill. 60604
312-663-3520

Suicide

National Adolescent Suicide Hotline
800-621-4000

Community and Environment

Information

Environmental Protection Agency
Public Information Center
PM 211-B
401 M Street S.W.
Washington, DC 20460
202-382-2080

Sierra Club
730 Polk Street
San Francisco, CA 94109
415-776-2211

Hazardous Wastes

Hazardous Waste Hotline
800-424-9346

Nuclear Energy

Council for a Livable World
100 Maryland Ave. N.E.
Washington, DC 20002
202-543-4100

Pesticides

National Pesticide Telecommunications Network
Texas Tech University
School of Medicine
4th and Indiana
Lubbock, Texas 79430
800-858-7378

Other Significant Agencies and Organizations

Government

National Center for Health Services Research
Publications Branch
5600 Fishers lane
Room 18-12
Rockville, MD 20857
301-443-2403

National Center for Health Statistics
Scientific and Technical Information Branch
Department of HHS
6525 Belcrest Rd.
Room 1064
Hyattsville, MD 20782
301-565-4167

National Institutes of Health
9000 Rockville Pike
Bethesda, MD 20892
301-496-4000

Public Health Service
200 Independence Ave., S.W.
Washington, DC 20201
202-245-6867

Health Education

American Alliance for Health, Physical Education, Recreation, and Dance
1900 Association Drive
Reston, VA 22091
703-476-3400

American School Health Association
Kent, Ohio 44240
216-678-1601

Index

A

AAHPERD Physical Best, 280
Abandonment, 150, 535
Abdominal thrusts, 47, 62, 87, 479-480, 548, 602
Abstinence, 27, 61, 151
Abuse
    emotional, 9, 36, 62, 150
      neglect, 3, 36, 62, 150, 535
      physical, 9, 36, 62, 150
      sexual, 9, 36-37, 62, 150, 190-191
Accidents, 62, 332, 446
Acid rain, 488, 490, 499-500, 517-518, 522
Acquaintance rape, 448
Active listening, 150
Addison, Joseph, 130
Adolescent nutrition and diet choices, 7
Adolescents, 148
Adrenal glands, 132, 539
Adrenaline, 132, 542
Adult teeth, 196
Adulthood, 194
Advertisements, 402
Advertising appeals, 546, 599
Advertising techniques, 417-418
Aerobic exercise, 60, 282, 289, 297-299, 307,
      312, 322, 367, 542
Agility, 306
Aging, 165
AIDS. (*see also* HIV infection)
    blood transfusions, 37
    children and adolescents, 4
    communicable diseases, 37
    education programs, 38
    guidelines for school districts, 37
    infection, 232, 303, 366, 368, 371-372
    opportunistic infection, 37, 368
    signs and symptoms, 37
Air pollution, 510, 525, 549-550, 611
Airbags, 472
Airway obstruction, 47
Alcohol, 3-5, 17-19, 27, 40, 60, 235, 326-328,
      332-333, 337, 346, 350, 541, 543,
      548, 587
Alcoholism, 150, 160-161, 352-353, 543
Allergies, 50, 61
Alveoli, 193, 330, 539
American Cancer Society, 60, 80, 236, 275,
      383
American College of Sports Medicine (ACSM),
      312

American Dental Association (ADA), 403,
      438, 547
American Heart Association, 60, 80, 236, 540
American Heart Association's Guidelines for
      Eating Out, 273-274
American Institute for Cancer Research, 262
American Medical Association (AMA), 14,
      403, 438, 547
American Red Cross, 47, 49, 113
American School Health Association (ASHA), 3
Amino acids, 234
Amotivational syndrome, 40, 327
Amphetamines, 326, 337
Amyl nitrate, 328
Anabolic steroids, 40, 42, 302, 328, 544, 589
Anaerobic exercise, 60, 282, 307, 322
Analogies, 87
Angina pectoris, 366
Anorexia nervosa, 42, 236, 271
Anorexia Nervosa and Related Eating
Disorders Organization (ANRED), 236
Antibody, 232-233, 368, 375
Appearance, 348
Areola, 194
Arrhythmia, 366
Arteries, 193, 228, 293-296, 379-380, 538
Arterioles, 538
Arteriosclerosis, 366
Arthritis, 166, 398-399
Asbestos, 489, 522
Ascorbic acid, 264
Assertive behavior, 55, 533
Atrium, 538
Association for the Advancement of Health
      Education (AAHE), 3
Asthma, 39
Astigmatism, 395
Atherosclerosis, 235, 289
Athlete's foot, 283, 322
Audio-visual material
    cassettes, 95
    filmstrips, 95
    instructional guides, 95
    slides, 95
    transparencies, 95
    video, 95
Authors, 95
Automobile accidents, 462-463
Automobiles, 515
Autonomic nervous system, 538
Axon, 537
AZT, 368

B

B cells, 232-233, 368
Baby teeth, 196
Balance, 306
Balanced diet, 239, 241, 243, 255, 267
Ball-and-socket joints, 192
Ballistic stretching, 542
Balloon angioplasty, 367
Balloon releases, 515
Bandwagon appeal, 402, 417
Barbiturates, 326, 337, 346
Basal cell carcinoma, 367
Basketball injuries, 447
Battered spouse, 150
Behavioral objectives
    affective domain, 57
    analysis objectives, 57
    application objectives, 57
    characterizing objectives, 58
    classification, 57
    cognitive domain, 57
    comprehension objectives, 57
    comprehensive school health
      education, 52
    construction, 57
    evaluation objectives, 57
    finely coordinated movement
      objectives, 58
    gross bodily movement objectives, 58
    knowledge objectives, 57
    nonverbal communication objectives, 58
    organizing objectives, 57
    psychomotor domain, 57-58
    receiving objectives, 57
    responding objectives, 57
    strategy selection, 86
    speech objectives, 58
    synthesis objectives, 57
    valuing objectives, 57
Behavioral toxicity, 327
Benefits, 404
Benefits of physical fitness, 542, 584
Benign tumor, 367
Benzene, 488
Beta-blockers, 367
Beta-carotene, 541
Beta-endorphins, 101, 282, 292, 542
Better Business Bureau, 403, 438, 547
Biceps muscle, 192
Bicycle safety rules, 62, 467, 484

Heart disease, 61, 86, 195, 257, 366, 381, 540
Heart rate, 216, 281, 285, 297-299, 542
Heat emergencies
    heat cramps, 50
    heat exhaustion, 50
    heat stroke, 50
Heimlich maneuver. (*see* Abdominal thrusts)
Hemorrhage, 544
Heredity, 367
Heroin, 41, 326-327, 337
Herpes simplex type I, 44
Herpes simplex type II, 45
High blood pressure, 7, 193
High-density lipoproteins (HDL),
    281, 289-290, 366-367, 542
Higher order thinking skills (HOTS), 79, 86,
    89, 91
Hinge joints, 192
HIV
    education, 32, 37-38
    infected mother, 368
    infection, 2, 61, 232, 303, 327, 368,
    371-372
Holistic health, 55
Home accidents, 447
Homeostasis, 137, 542
Homicide
    firearms, 4
    knifes, 5
    objectives, 22
    socioeconomic status, 4
Human papillomavirus, 45
Humerus, 224
Humor appeal, 402, 417
Hunter, Madeline, 79
Hydrocarbons, 488
Hydrochloride, 42
Hyperactivity, 326
Hypertension, 366-367
Hypoglycemia, 40
Hypothalamus, 534, 539
Hypothermia, 51, 481-482

I

"I" messages, 59, 150, 168
Ideal weight, 277-278
Illegal drugs, 61, 86, 338
Immune system, 327, 368
Immunization, 2, 28
Impaired vision, 395
Impotence, 328
Incest, 37, 190-191
Incidence and death from cancer, 545, 593
Incomplete proteins, 234
Indoor air pollution, 488-489, 515, 549, 608
Infectious diseases, 2
Infertility, 328
Influenza, 2, 4
Inhalants
    aerosols, 42
    anesthetics, 42
    chloroform, 42
    description, 328
    ether, 42
    glue, 43
    solvents, 42
    volatile substances, 42
Injuries,
    abrasions, 48

avulsions, 48
children and adolescents, 2
dislocation, 49
eye, 49
fractures, 48
lacerations, 48
punctures, 48
prevention, 4
signs of infection, 48
soft tissues, 48
sprain, 49
strain, 49
Insect poisoning
    allergic reactions, 50
    black widow spider, 50
    brown recluse spider, 50
    lyme disease, 50
    Rocky mountain spotted fever, 50
    ticks, 50
Inservice programs, 34, 94
Instant gratification, 9
Institute of Medicine of the National Academy
    of Sciences, 14
Instructional aids
    audio-visual material, 95
    computers, 96
    printed material, 94
Insulin, 39, 539
Integrating skills, 80
Integumentary system, 206
Intimacy
    creative, 8
    philosophical, 8
    physical, 8
    psychological, 8
Intravenous drug abuse, 28
Involuntary action, 202
Involuntary muscles, 192
Iodine, 267
Iron, 267
Isokinetic exercise, 282, 307, 322
Isometric exercise, 282, 307, 322
Isotonic exercise, 282, 307, 322

J

Joint, 192, 398, 537, 542
Joint injuries, 283, 322
Jourard, Sidney, 54

K

Kidney, 208, 539
Kubler Ross, Elizabeth, 8, 49

L

Large group discussion, 88
Large intestine, 194, 214
Larynx, 538
Laxatives, 7
Lead, 489
Leading cause of death, 446
Lead poisoning, 3
Learning activities, 86
Learning environment, 10
Lecture
    fascinating facts, 87
    humor, 87
    nervousness, 87

personal anecdotes, 87
Lecture-discussion, 88
Leukemia, 42, 328
Leukoplakia, 329
Life events, 155
Life skills, 13, 52, 55, 58, 75, 77-79, 534
Ligaments, 49, 192, 537
Lipids, 366
Lipoproteins, 281
Litter, 62, 493-494, 525
Liver, 208, 538, 543
Local health department, 403, 438
Loving functional families, 148
Low birthweight, 6, 26
Low-density lipoproteins (LDL), 281, 289-290,
    366-367
LSD, 61, 327
Lung cancer, 330, 545
Lungs, 193, 200, 330-331, 341, 360, 489, 538
Lyme disease, 50

M

Macrominerals, 234
Macrophages, 368
Magnesium, 267
Mainstream smoke, 543
Male development, 536, 565
Male reproductive system, 210-211
Malignant melanoma, 367
Malignant tumor, 367
Mammogram, 194, 368
Marijuana, 3, 40, 327, 345
Marriage, 184-185
Maslow's hierarchy of needs, 103
Maternal and infant health, 26
Maximum heart rate, 282
MDMA. (*see also* Designer drugs), 40, 328
Meat group, 255
Medical examinations, 61
Medical health specialists, 405-406, 419-420
Medicare, 404
Medicine, 340, 544, 590-591
Medulla, 194, 538
Memories, 59
Menarche, 536
Meningitis, 2
Menstrual health, 60
Menstrual period, 49
Menstrual products, 536
Menstruation, 194, 328, 536
Mental and emotional well-being, 53, 59, 75,
    100-145, 532-535
Mental disorders, 535
Mental-emotional health, 13, 19-20, 52, 55,143
Mental health clinics, 421
Mental retardation, 3
Mescaline, 327
Metabolism, 539
Methods of instruction, 86
Microwaves, 490
Milk group, 255
Minerals, 234, 262-263, 267-269
Minibikes, 4
Model of health and well-being, 55, 533, 553
Monogamous relationship, 368
Mononucleosis, 391
Moral values, 54, 435-436
Morphine, 327
Motor vehicle accidents, 2, 446